THE SHEPHERD OF HERMAS

THE SHEPHERD OF HERMAS

A Literary, Historical, and Theological Handbook

Jonathon Lookadoo

LONDON • NEW YORK • OXFORD • NEW DELHI • SYDNEY

T&T CLARK

Bloomsbury Publishing Plc

50 Bedford Square, London, WC1B 3DP, UK
1385 Broadway, New York, NY 10018, USA
29 Earlsfort Terrace, Dublin 2, Ireland

BLOOMSBURY, T&T CLARK and the T&T Clark logo are trademarks
of Bloomsbury Publishing Plc

First published in Great Britain 2021
This paperback edition published 2023

Copyright © Jonathon Lookadoo, 2021

Jonathon Lookadoo has asserted his right under the Copyright, Designs and
Patents Act, 1988, to be identified as Author of this work.

For legal purposes the Acknowledgments on p. ix constitute an extension
of this copyright page.

Cover design: Charlotte James
Cover image © United Archives GmbH / Alamy Stock Photo

All rights reserved. No part of this publication may be reproduced or
transmitted in any form or by any means, electronic or mechanical, including
photocopying, recording, or any information storage or retrieval system,
without prior permission in writing from the publishers.

Bloomsbury Publishing Plc does not have any control over, or responsibility for, any
third-party websites referred to or in this book. All internet addresses given in this
book were correct at the time of going to press. The author and publisher regret any
inconvenience caused if addresses have changed or sites have ceased to exist, but can
accept no responsibility for any such changes.

A catalogue record for this book is available from the British Library.

Library of Congress Cataloging-in-Publication Data
Names: Lookadoo, Jonathon, 1987– author.
Title: The Shepherd of Hermas : a literary, historical and theological
handbook / Jonathan Lookadoo.
Description: London ; New York : T&T Clark, 2021. |
Includes bibliographical references and index. | Summary: "Jonathon Lookadoo
guides researchers through the early Christian apocalypse known as the
Shepherd of Hermas, providing a clear overview of the numerous literary,
historical, and theological insights the text has for those researching
early Christianity"– Provided by publisher. Identifiers: LCCN 2020051478 (print) |
LCCN 2020051479 (ebook) | ISBN 9780567697912 (hardback) |
ISBN 9780567697929 (pdf) | ISBN 9780567697943 (epub)
Subjects: LCSH: Hermas, active 2nd century. Shepherd–Criticism, interpretation, etc.
Classification: LCC BS2900.H5 L66 2021 (print) | LCC BS2900.H5
(ebook) | DDC 229/.94–dc23
LC record available at https://lccn.loc.gov/2020051478
LC ebook record available at https://lccn.loc.gov/2020051479

ISBN: HB: 978-0-5676-9791-2
PB: 978-0-5676-9994-7
ePDF: 978-0-5676-9792-9
ePUB: 978-0-5676-9794-3

Typeset by Newgen KnowledgeWorks Pvt. Ltd., Chennai, India

To find out more about our authors and books visit www.bloomsbury.com
and sign up for our newsletters.

To Jieun
별을 노래하는 마음으로
(윤동주, "서시")

CONTENTS

Acknowledgments ix
List of Abbreviations xi

INTRODUCTION 1

Part I
INTRODUCING THE *SHEPHERD OF HERMAS* 3

Chapter 1
AN OVERVIEW OF THE *SHEPHERD* 5

Chapter 2
HOW WAS THE *SHEPHERD* PRESERVED? 19

Chapter 3
WHO READ THE *SHEPHERD*? 35

Chapter 4
CRITICAL QUESTIONS FOR THE *SHEPHERD*: WHAT, TO WHOM,
WHERE, WHEN, AND WHO? 55

Part II
STUDYING THE *SHEPHERD OF HERMAS* 71

Chapter 5
FASTING AND THE VINEYARD: EXEGETING SIMILITUDE 5 73

Chapter 6
THE CHARACTERS IN THE *SHEPHERD* 91

Chapter 7
THE *SHEPHERD* IN ITS GRECO-ROMAN AND EARLY JEWISH SETTINGS 111

Chapter 8
THE *SHEPHERD* AND EARLY CHRISTIAN LITERATURE IN THE FIRST
TWO CENTURIES 129

Chapter 9
GOD IN THE *SHEPHERD* — 147

Chapter 10
SIN AND REPENTANCE — 167

Chapter 11
METAPHORS AND IMAGERY IN THE *SHEPHERD*: THE TOWER AND THE HOUSE — 187

Chapter 12
SPIRIT LANGUAGE IN MANDATES 5–11: FROM ANCIENT PHILOSOPHY TO CONTEMPORARY THEOLOGY — 205

Bibliography — 225
Index of Authors — 265
Index of References — 271
Index of Subjects — 293

ACKNOWLEDGMENTS

The completion of a book allows one to acknowledge the many people who have contributed throughout the writing process. I have received aid from others in a host of different forms. Although many scholarly debts can be acknowledged in footnotes, others are incurred in forms that are better expressed in prose at the beginning of the book.

I would like to begin by thanking Dominic Mattos, Sarah Blake, and everyone at Bloomsbury T&T Clark. I am grateful to the anonymous reviewers, whose perceptive comments enabled me to improve the manuscript. It has been an honor to work with everyone to bring this manuscript through the publication process.

University relationships have also played a vital role in bringing this book into being at every stage in the process. I am especially grateful to Allen Ross for his willingness to assume the time-consuming task of supervising a masters-level thesis while I was studying at Beeson Divinity School. His guidance, encouragement, criticism, and willingness to give up hours of his mornings to meet with me provided the seed from which this book grew. In the middle of the research for this project, I had the pleasure of presenting some of the results at the University of Otago as part of a conference entitled "Trajectories in the Interpretation of Scripture: Models, Issues, and Prospects." I am grateful to Jonathan Robinson for his work in organizing the sessions and to the other presenters and participants for their stimulating reflections. Traces of the conference paper and the forthcoming article in *Revue Biblique* are scattered across Chapters 6, 7, and 8.

The Presbyterian University and Theological Seminary has provided a stimulating and supportive environment in which to teach and research. I am grateful to the library staff for maintaining a strong collection in the stacks and their quick turnaround time in obtaining hard-to-find sources through Interlibrary Loans. Shalom Cho generously gave of her time to help with bibliographic formatting prior to submitting publication proposals. Finally, I am especially grateful to members of the Herd, who joined with me during the summer of 2020 in seeking to understand Hermas's apocalyptic revelations. My thanks are due to Sung Hoon Choung, Taemine Jang, Lu Yao Jeon, Changdae Jung, Yeeun Jung, Hohyun Kim, Jintae Kim, Jieun Lee, Dojun Park, Sungmin Woo, and Lifeng Yang for their enthusiastic interest and probing questions that significantly improved the manuscript prior to publication. Any remaining faults in the book are, of course, my own.

The continued support of family and friends has been vital not only in allowing this book to be completed but also in offering consistent happy reminders that there is more to life than second-century Christian history. Weekly video calls with my parents, Fred and Charlene Lookadoo, and my brother, Joel, have provided central points in the calendar around which to reorient myself to truly important matters. Chantelle, Chloe, and Harper never cease to bring love, encouragement, and joyful surprises to life, wherever we may be. Most importantly throughout this project, my wife, Jieun, has never failed in her support, never faltered in her interest, and never faded in her willingness to see this book improve. Conversations with her spurred the choice to begin writing this book in earnest, while her fingerprints can be found in methodological reflections within Part II of the text. Few husbands can say that their wife read the *Shepherd of Hermas* with them (and perhaps even fewer should), but I gladly dedicate this book to my wife with gratitude and love.

ABBREVIATIONS

The abbreviations in this work are found in Billie Jean Collins, Bob Buller, and John F. Klutsko, eds. *The SBL Handbook of Style: For Biblical Studies and Related Disciplines*. 2nd ed. Atlanta: Society of Biblical Literature, 2014. Abbreviations that are not listed in *The SBL Handbook* are listed below:

ABG	Arbeiten zur Bibel und ihrer Geschichte
Adol.	Galen, *De adolore* (*On the Avoidance of Grief*)
AFCS	Apostolic Fathers Commentary Series
Aleat.	Pseudo-Cyprian, *De aleatoribus* (*On Dice Players*)
Art.	Galen, *Artium studere exhortatio* (*An Exhortation to Study the Arts*)
ASE	*Annali di Storia dell'Esegesi*
Bib Aug	Bibliotheca Augustana
BICS	Bulletin for the Institute of Classical Studies
BMSSEC	Baylor-Mohr Siebeck Studies in Early Christianity
BSAW	Berlin Studies of the Ancient World
BTH	Bibliothèque de théologie historique
BTS	Biblical Tools and Studies
Carm. Marc.	Pseudo-Tertullian, *Carmen adversus Marcionitas*
CL	Collection Latomus
Cog Clas	Cognitive Classics
COMSB	*Comparative Oriental Manuscript Studies Bulletin*
Conf.	John Cassian, *Collationes patrum in scetica eremo* (*Conferences of the Desert Fathers*)
CurBibRes	*Currents in Biblical Research*
EC	*Early Christianity*
ESEC	Emory Studies in Early Christianity
GCP	Graecitas Christianorum Primaeva
GSCC	Groningen Studies in Cultural Change
GSECP	Gorgias Studies in Early Christianity and Patristics (Gorgias Dissertations)
Hom.	Pseudo-Clement, *Homilia* (*Homilies*)
HSR	*Historical Social Research*
IASRF	*Investigación Agraria: Sistemas y Recursos Forestales*
Instr.	Commodian, *Instructiones* (*Instructions*)
JECH	*Journal of Early Christian History*
JFSR	*Journal of Feminist Studies in Religion*
JP	*Journal of Philology*
KAV	Kommentar zu den apostolischen Väter
Ker. Petr.	*Kerygma Petri*

KTTVÜ	Kleine Texte für theologische Vorlesungen und Übungen
LCA	Letteratura cristiana antica
LDAB	Leuven Database of Ancient Books
MBPS	Mellen Biblical Press Series
MVS	Menighedsfakultetets Videnskabelige Serie
NHMS	Nag Hammadi and Manichaean Studies
NTM	New Testament Monographs
Opt. Med.	Galen, *Si quis optimus medicus est, eundum esse philosophum* (*A Good Physician Must Also Be a Good Philosopher*)
PPS	Popular Patristics Series
PPSD	Pauline and Patristic Scholars in Debate
Puls.	Galen, *De pulsibus libellus ad Tyrones* (*On the Pulse for Beginners*)
RHT	*Revue d'Histoire des Textes*
SAPERE	Scripta Antiquitatis Posterioris ad Ethicam REligionemque pertinentia
SAR	Studies in the Abrahamic Religions
Sciv.	Hildegard of Bingen, *Scivias*
SMT	Galen, *De simplicium medicamentorum facultatibus* (*On the Powers of Simple Remedies*)
Tab. Ceb.	*Tabula Cebetis*
TB	Theologischer Bücherei
TSEC	Texts and Studies in Eastern Christianity
VetChr	*Vetera Christianorum*
YPR	Yale Publications in Religion

INTRODUCTION

My awareness that a book like this could be useful began to grow during the autumn of 2012. Then an M.Div. student, I had the opportunity to write a masters-level thesis that explored interpreting angels in Second Temple apocalyptic literature. Due to the kindness of my supervisor, Allen Ross, I was allowed to indulge my interest in second-century texts by incorporating the *Shepherd of Hermas* into the discussion. The seeds for this book were thus planted in no small part because of Dr. Ross's encouragement to study deeply and his model of *fides quaerens intellectum*. I was enchanted by the *Shepherd's* simple narrative style, the various ways in which the *Shepherd* could be studied, and the light that it could shed on apocalyptic literature, early Christian history, and life as a second-century Roman Jesus-follower.

However, the length of the text along with its repetition proved to be intimidating. When searching for outside help to get my head around the *Shepherd*, my rough and limited masters-level schema found that there were brief overviews such as those found in Ehrman (2003) and Holmes (2007), single-chapter introductions like those by Verheyden (2007) and Hellholm (2009; 2010), as well as academic commentaries and monographs (e.g., Brox 1991; Henne 1992b; 1992d; Humphrey 1995; Osiek 1999). Yet it was difficult to find a study that fell somewhere between introductory chapters and technical treatises. Given the meandering nature of the *Shepherd's* narration, I wished for such a book when I was starting to study the text. The situation has continued to evolve since 2012 and my awareness of the scholarly literature has expanded. Yet I would argue that there is still a place for a handbook to the *Shepherd* that welcomes those in the scholarly guild to the study of the *Shepherd* while aiming to contribute insights about the *Shepherd* that are simultaneously useful to veterans. In so doing, this book hopes to fill a lacuna in studies of this fascinating but challenging text.

The aims of the book are therefore twofold. First, it endeavors to guide advanced postgraduates and researchers in neighboring fields of study through the early Christian apocalypse known as the *Shepherd*. The immense size and unwieldy structure of the *Shepherd* can make the text difficult to appreciate. Yet I hope to show that the *Shepherd* offers numerous literary, historical, and theological insights for readers who have a guide along the way. The book is simultaneously intended to be a contribution to research on the *Shepherd*. To fulfill this aim, it maintains a textual focus throughout the book, offers a prosopographical study of the *Shepherd* to illustrate the social dynamics at work in the text, and engages with knotty interpretive, historical, literary, and theological issues. The book is divided into two parts in order to accomplish these goals, although the bipartite division does not correspond strictly to the goals. Both parts seek to keep the focus on the text by beginning with chapters that emphasize the importance of reading the *Shepherd* well instead of starting with traditional scholarly questions. Further glimpses into the material within each part can be found in the introductions to Parts I and II.

Lastly, the introduction should point out a few orthographical choices in the book that follows. References to "the *Shepherd*" are a reference to the literary work known as the *Shepherd of Hermas*. On the other hand, "the shepherd" is used to designate the title character of the work. The abbreviations for the portions of the *Shepherd* in this book are as follows: Visions (Vis.), Mandates (Mand.), and Similitudes (Sim.). In light of the volume of repetition for these abbreviations, they are not italicized to improve readability. Similarly, due to the large volume of references to the *Shepherd*, the abbreviation "Herm." that often precedes these references in modern style guides will be dropped. In addition, two referencing styles are simultaneously employed to locate texts in the *Shepherd*. The first style is the traditional citation of a text within the Visions, Mandates, or Similitudes. For example, I may refer to Sim. 2.1 or parenthetically to (Sim. 2.1). A second reference style will immediately follow either in parentheses or in brackets within a parentheses. A text may thus be cited as coming from Sim. 2.1 (51.1) or (Sim. 2.1 [51.1]). The hope is that the dual way of referring to the text will make it easier for readers to locate the citation. A final choice regarding capitalization should be observed that is minor but may be annoying if left unstated. Throughout the work, I follow the traditional practice of capitalizing several English references to the divine (e.g., Father, God, Christ, Son). As Chapter 9 will illustrate in more detail, however, the *Shepherd* employs the term *holy spirit* or *holy spirits* in a surprising number of ways. Rather than attempt to arbitrate between references to the divine hypostasis (*Holy Spirit*) or a form of the spirit related to human beings (*holy spirit*), I follow the example of other recent translators and lowercase all instances of *spirit* or *holy spirit* in the *Shepherd*. Holmes (2007, 444) explains that "distinctions of the sort implied by the modern conventions of capitalization (or noncapitalization) would have been quite foreign to the author and his readers, as Greek documents typically were written in a single case." Although this choice does not result in any substantive change to the content of the book, the discrepancy in capitalization practice is highlighted from the outset in order to explain its existence.

Part I

INTRODUCING THE *SHEPHERD OF HERMAS*

The chapters contained in Part I introduce the story and critical issues associated with the study of the *Shepherd*. These chapters maintain a thoroughly text-based focus on the *Shepherd* and only come to matters such as authorship and date after the narrative, manuscripts, and reception of the *Shepherd* have been discussed. The rationale for this organization stems from a belief that scholarship on ancient documents must begin with a thorough knowledge of the document itself. With that in mind, Chapter 1 opens the volume by introducing the narrative shape of the *Shepherd*. This brief introduction may be useful given the winding narrative form and lengthy interpretations that can distract from the main narrative thread. By summarizing and necessarily simplifying the narrative, Chapter 1 begins with a focus on the events narrated in the text.

Chapters 2 and 3 turn to the questions of how the *Shepherd* may be known. Most readers gain access to the *Shepherd* through printed editions of the Greek text and translations into modern languages. Given that the text originated in the Roman Empire, though, it is important to consider the ways in which the text was transmitted from its earliest readers to readers in the present day. Chapter 2 explores the manuscripts and translations of the *Shepherd* that are extant. Greek manuscripts of the *Shepherd* have been preserved in numbers that are analogous to some books of the New Testament. It was also translated into other ancient languages. Knowledge of these textual witnesses will enable readers of this book to understand and evaluate variants that are listed in the textual apparatuses of modern critical editions. Further understanding of how the text was viewed, cited, and interpreted may also aid current readers of the *Shepherd* in making judgments about how best to understand certain passages. Of particular interest is the question of how much authority was granted to the *Shepherd* by readers in antiquity. Chapter 3 introduces the reception history of the *Shepherd* with a particular focus on what was said about the text during the second through fifth centuries and on the authority attributed to the text by these readers.

Finally, Chapter 4 turns to the questions that are perhaps most commonly associated with critical introductions of ancient texts. These are matters such as the genre, audience, authorship, and composition of a document. Chapter 4 is structured with a view to questions that may be asked of the *Shepherd*. For example, "what is the *Shepherd*" examines the issue of genre, while "for whom was the *Shepherd* written" leads to the matter of audience. By answering critical questions, considering the ways in which the *Shepherd* was transmitted, and exploring the narrative arc of the text, Part I aims to offer a thorough introduction to critical matters related to the study of the *Shepherd* in a way that privileges a direct examination of the text by all who wish to engage it.

Chapter 1

AN OVERVIEW OF THE *SHEPHERD*

This chapter summarizes the lengthy text known as the *Shepherd of Hermas*. The reasons for doing this are twofold. First, this overview may enable those who have never read the *Shepherd* to grasp the contours of a text that is no longer particularly well-known and whose length and episodic style can make for difficult reading. Although this summary is no substitute for reading the text directly, it may serve as a rope by which to begin to climb aboard the ship with those who study this fascinating early Christian text. Second, for those who have read the *Shepherd* and may even be familiar with some of the critical introductory issues, this chapter is a reminder that the historical study of an ancient text should begin with a focus on the text itself. Since this book is intended to assist a broad range of readers in coming to a better understanding of the *Shepherd*, continued reflection on how the *Shepherd* unfolds is vital to fulfilling the aim of this volume. The *Shepherd* should ideally be read alongside and in conversation with this book, and the summary that follows aims to place the text at the center of the discussion.

Visions (1.1–25.7)

The opening section of the *Shepherd* is referred to as the Visions. This section comprises four primary visions in which Hermas interacts with a woman who shows him his failings and offers an opportunity for him and his family to repent. The fifth vision is shorter and opens the Mandates and Similitudes by recording the first appearance of the shepherd to Hermas. Collectively, the Visions introduce Hermas and his two revelatory agents as the three main characters in the *Shepherd*. The Visions also familiarize readers with the primary reasons why Hermas is visited, while also elaborating visionary and pedagogical themes that are key to the entire work.

Vision 1 (1.1–4.3)

The story begins by introducing Hermas, the recipient of the visions and the implied author of the text.[1] When he was still a slave, he saw his owner, Rhoda,

---

1. The implied author may or may not be the real author. See the discussion of authorship in Chapter 4.

bathing in Rome's Tiber River and wished for a wife of similar beauty and conduct (Vis. 1.1.2 [1.2]). While walking later, he is taken away in a vision where he meets Rhoda. Rhoda recalls Hermas's earlier thought and says that she will accuse him of his sins soon. Shaken by these words, Hermas looks up to find an enormous white chair with an elderly woman holding a book sitting there (Vis. 1.2.2 [2.2]). The woman asks Hermas why he is weeping. When he tells her about Rhoda, the elderly woman confirms that such thoughts are not befitting of God's servant. However, the more serious reason for God's anger toward Hermas is so that he might turn his family from their current ways (Vis. 1.3.1 [3.1]). Because he loves his children, Hermas has not corrected them and has allowed them to become corrupt. God will heal these deeds, but Hermas must instruct his children. The elderly lady then begins to read from her book, but Hermas can only remember the last words, which describe God's creation of heaven, earth, and the church as well as how God is making all things level for his chosen people if they keep his commandments (Vis. 1.3.3-4 [3.3-4]). When she finishes reading, she tells Hermas that the incomprehensible words are for Gentiles and defectors, while the last words are for the righteous (Vis. 1.4.2 [4.2]). She then tells Hermas to be courageous as she is taken away by two men.

Vision 2 (5.1–8.3)

As Hermas walks along the same route one year later, he recalls his earlier vision. He thanks the Lord for revealing his sins to him. When he rises from his prayer, he sees the elderly woman from the previous year. She asks him to send a message to God's elect. Due to Hermas's limited memory, he takes a book from her so that he can copy the message. When he finishes copying it, the book is snatched away from him (Vis. 2.1.3-4 [5.3-4]). After another fifteen days during which he fasts to know what the writing means, Hermas reveals what was written to his readers (Vis. 2.2.1-2.3.4 [6.1-7.4]). The message describes the sin of Hermas's wife and children. God will forgive their previous sins if they repent, but God's tolerance for their sin has reached its limit and they cannot sin again. Hermas has neglected his family by allowing these things to occur, but he has been rescued because he has not fallen away from the living God. He must remain steadfast in his single-mindedness and inform a certain Maximus that suffering is coming. After Hermas falls asleep, a young man shows him that the elderly woman to whom he has been speaking is the church (Vis. 2.4.1 [8.1]). She soon returns and instructs Hermas to write to Clement and Grapte, who will send the messages abroad and to widows and orphans, respectively.

Vision 3 (9.1–21.4)

Hermas continues to request revelation and is told that night to return to the field where the elderly lady will come to him the next morning. After she listens to his prayers, the woman invites Hermas to sit next to her. She shows him a large tower that is being built by six young men (Vis. 3.2.4–9 [10.4–9]). Other men are bringing stones from the land and from deep under the water. These fit neatly into the tower. Unsuitable stones from other places are thrown away, broken, or left near the tower with cracks. Hermas wants to know what his vision means and begs the woman to explain it to him. She tells him that the construction of the tower represents the construction of the church. The tower is built upon water because salvation comes through water, while it has been set on its foundation by the word of the glorious name (Vis. 3.3.5 [11.5]). The men who are building symbolize angels who work in the church. The stones, in turn, are people who are brought into the church. Hermas records an explanation of the types of people represented by stones that fit well and those that are not incorporated into the building (Vis. 3.5–7 [13–15]).

The woman next offers to show Hermas something else about the tower. Seven women support the tower. They are qualities such as faith, self-control, and single-mindedness (Vis. 3.8.1–8 [16.1–8]). In light of this, Hermas's audience should cease from their sins (Vis. 3.9 [17]). The woman emphasizes sins that stem from overconsumption, greed, and wealth. The elderly woman is then taken into the tower by the six young men. Following this, Hermas explains that the elderly woman's appearance has changed during the three visions. She was very old in the first, had a younger face with an old body in the second, and appeared younger except for her hair in the third. A young man comes at night to clarify the significance. The woman mirrors Hermas's spirit (Vis. 3.11–13 [19–21]). His spirit was old and weak in the first vision, so the woman appeared similarly. Hermas next recognized God's compassion and received some strength. Finally, Hermas was relieved of his sorrow in the third vision and received good news that made his spirit and the woman's appearance more youthful.

Vision 4 (22.1–24.7)

Twenty days later, Hermas has a vision along the Campanian Way that foreshadows an impending persecution. He hears a voice that tells him not to be double-minded (Vis. 4.1.4 [22.4]). A cloud of dust then becomes visible in front of him, and a huge beast comes out from the cloud. Hermas is afraid but remembers what he has heard. He faces the beast, and the beast stretches itself along the ground, merely sticking its tongue out while Hermas passes. Hermas notices that its back is multicolored. As he continues, he is met by a young woman who is dressed like a bride. He recognizes her as the church and she tells Hermas that he acted rightly by putting his trust in the Lord. The Lord sent an angel, Thegri, who has authority over the beasts and enabled Hermas to come through the tribulation (Vis. 4.2.4 [23.4]). The woman also explains the colors before urging him to remain faithful in persecution and to teach the saints. She then leaves, and Hermas does not see where she goes.

Vision 5 (25.1–7)

In addition to introducing the title character of the *Shepherd*, the fifth vision also plays a transitional role. After an unspecified length of time, Hermas is at home praying when he is met by a man who looks like a shepherd. The shepherd has been sent by the most holy angel, and Hermas has been entrusted to him. The shepherd will show Hermas again the things he has seen before. Hermas should write down the commandments and parables that follow. Hermas explains to the audience that he has followed this instruction and urges the audience to follow what he has written.

Mandates (26.1–49.5)

The shepherd begins his lengthy interactions with Hermas by giving Hermas twelve mandates. These are generally, though not always, shorter than the visions that Hermas has already received, and they often include a rationale for why a specific command should be obeyed. Hermas occasionally asks questions so that the Mandates, like the Visions and Similitudes, contain dialogues between Hermas and the one who reveals things to him. The title Mandates is thus traditional and useful in setting this section of the *Shepherd* apart. However, the title is not given on purely generic grounds.

Mandate 1 (26.1–2)

Hermas is instructed to believe in the one God who created all things. By believing and fearing God, Hermas will be able to put aside evil works and live in self-control.

Mandate 2 (27.1–7)

The shepherd tells Hermas to be single-minded and innocent, neither speaking evil against others nor listening to such accusations. Hermas should stay away from slander and work instead at what is good so that he can give to others who are in need.

Mandate 3 (28.1–5)

The third command is to love and speak truth because those who lie defraud the Lord. Hermas cries upon hearing this because he has never told the truth. The shepherd urges him to live and speak truthfully from this point on.

Mandate 4 (29.1–32.4)

The shepherd teaches Hermas to be pure and to keep away from thoughts about sexual sins. Such desires are inappropriate in God's servants. Hermas asks for clarification in specific cases, such as adultery and repentance after adultery. The shepherd answers his questions. The purpose of the answers is for sin to cease. When Hermas declares that he is struggling to comprehend, the shepherd states that repentance is a way for him to understand. Hermas then asks about the opportunity for repentance after baptism. The shepherd claims that this is possible but that God has only allowed one opportunity for post-baptismal mercy. After this, Hermas resumes his inquiries about marriage and is curious about what to do when a spouse dies. Remarriage is permitted, but it is more honorable to remain single.

Mandate 5 (33.1–34.8)

The shepherd instructs Hermas to be patient and understanding so that he can overcome evil deeds. He contrasts patience with angry irritability. Patience characterizes the holy spirit that lives within a person, but anger is a characteristic of the evil spirit. When both spirits dwell in the same person, the evil spirit chokes the holy spirit, just as the sweetness of honey becomes bitter when only a little wormwood is added. Irascibility makes a person bitter when they see others who prosper, while patience is joyful, free, and glorifies the Lord.

Mandate 6 (35.1–36.10)

Mandates 6–8 develop the first mandate's comments about faith, fear, and self-control.[2] Faith should be placed in what is righteous, while unrighteousness should not be trusted. Righteousness and unrighteousness are two different paths, and Hermas is urged to walk along the path of righteousness. Likewise, there are two angels—one of righteousness and one of unrighteousness. Both angels dwell within a person. The angel of righteousness is gentle and discusses holiness, contentment, and virtue. The angel of unrighteousness is irritable, bitter, and foolish. Hermas is to understand and trust the angel of righteousness.

Mandate 7 (37.1–5)

Hermas should fear the Lord and keep his commandments so that he will do good. The devil should not be feared because he is powerless, but the devil's works ought to be feared because they are evil. When Hermas wants to do something evil, he should fear the Lord and not do evil. If Hermas wants to do good, he should fear the Lord so he does what is good.

Mandate 8 (38.1–12)

Self-control is necessary in the face of evil but not needed when it comes to good. Mandate 8 then contains a dialogue between the shepherd and Hermas in

---

2. The three virtues in Mand. 6.1.1 (35.1) parallel the imperatives in Mand. 1.2 (26.2).

which evil and good are defined primarily in terms of vice and virtue lists. Evil includes adultery, the extravagance of wealth, lying, hypocrisy, and greed. Good is comprised of such things as love, harmony, patience, being hospitable, and caring for widows and orphans.

Mandate 9 (39.1–12)

The ninth mandate contrasts faith and double-mindedness with a particular interest in prayer. God has compassion toward what he has made. If someone asks God for something in faith, God is inclined to grant that person's requests. If someone hesitates, however, or wonders how they can receive something from God despite their sin, such a person is double-minded and will not receive what they ask.

Mandate 10 (40.1–42.4)

Hermas should get rid of distress because it is a sister to double-mindedness and irascibility. Hermas wants to know more about the relationship between these three. The shepherd begins by explaining that those who are interested in business affairs become corrupted so that they cannot understand divine truth. They are distracted. When such double-minded people try to act rightly and fail, they grieve, become embittered, and grow angry. Such distress may lead to salvation. However, both double-mindedness and anger grieve the holy spirit. Instead, Hermas should be cheerful and delight in cheerfulness because such people do good things.

Mandate 11 (43.1–21)

The shepherd shows Hermas people who are sitting on a bench and another person who is sitting on a chair. The one on the chair is identified as a false prophet. The false prophet is empty on their own but filled by the devil's spirit when prophesying. Such prophets attract the double-minded and those who change their minds by practicing fortune-telling. A false prophet can be discerned by the activities of their life. They avoid the righteous, want the honored seats, and require money in return for their prophecy. The true prophet has the divine spirit, is gentle, avoids the futile cravings of their time, and considers themselves poorer than others. The power of true prophecy is like that of a hail pellet or water falling from the roof when contrasted with a stone or stream of water thrown upward with the aim of penetrating the sky.

Mandate 12 (44.1–49.3)

Finally, Hermas is instructed to strip off evil desire and replace it with good and holy desire, since good desire has the capacity to control evil. Evil longings are wild and include the desire for someone else's husband or wife, for extravagant riches, and for an overabundance of food and drink. Healthy aspirations involve the fear of God and conquer such covetousness. Good desire also deals in righteousness, excellence truth, faith, and gentleness.

The shepherd finishes his commands in Mand. 12.3.2 (46.2). He encourages Hermas to walk in the commandments but grows angry when Hermas expresses doubt about whether he can keep them all. Upon seeing Hermas's fear and agitation, he returns to speaking gently and acknowledges Hermas's double-mindedness as well as his lack of understanding. Since God has made human beings lord over all created things, the shepherd reasons that those with the Lord in their hearts are able to master everything. The devil is powerless because the shepherd, who calls himself the angel of repentance, rules over the devil. Hermas responds that everyone desires to keep God's commandments, but they are challenged by the devil. The shepherd employs a wrestling metaphor in response. The devil can wrestle with God's servants but cannot defeat them. The angel of repentance has come to be with all those who repent. He will make them strong in faith, so they should fear God rather than the devil. Hermas is empowered by these words, and the Mandates conclude with a final exhortation to purity.

Similitudes (50.1–114.5)

The Similitudes, or Parables,[3] combine elements of the Visions and Mandates that precede them. They can thus be seen as a continuation of the shepherd's purpose to show Hermas the most important points of what he has seen (Vis. 5.5 [25.5]). There are ten similitudes of varying length. The longest of these is the ninth, which reprises the tower construction in Vis. 3. The shortest parable is the third, which takes up only three verses (52.1–3). Throughout the Similitudes, Hermas asks further questions and exhibits a desire to know more about the things that he has seen. Along with visions and allegorical explanations, the shepherd offers instructions, commandments, encouragement, and correction.

Similitude 1 (50.1–11)

The first similitude compares the Christian life to one lived in a foreign territory. Since their hometown is far away, the shepherd asks why some of the audience

---

3. The terms are used interchangeably throughout this book. Both are English transliterations of non-English words. *Similitudes* comes from the Latin title *Similitudines*, which is in the plural and denotes likeness, resemblance, and, by extension, analogy. *Parables* comes from the Greek title Παραβολαί, which is again in the plural and refers to a type or figure, on the one hand, or an illustration or proverb, on the other. For a concise discussion of how parable should be defined, see Snodgrass (2018, 7–9). For a list of where the word *parable* occurs in the Greek Bible and Apostolic Fathers, see Snodgrass (2018, 603–5, 609–11).

prepares fields and buildings in the foreign city. Such activities do not allow arrangements to be made for a return journey to one's hometown. These people are foolish and double-minded. The lord of the foreign city in which the audience now dwells can demand that they either conform to the rules of their city or leave. The shepherd urges readers to serve the Lord and to use their wealth to redeem the oppressed and visit widows and orphans. Such extravagant practices do not bring shame before God.

Similitude 2 (51.1–10)

The shepherd finds Hermas walking and contemplating an elm tree and vine. Hermas notes that they are well-suited to each other. The shepherd employs the vine and the elm as a model for God's servants. When Hermas asks to know more, the shepherd observes that the vine bears fruit but can only do so by climbing the elm. It does not bear fruit properly when spread along the ground. On the other hand, the elm is fruitless on its own, but the vine bears fruit for both itself and the elm when it grows along the tree. The parable applies to the rich and poor among those who serve God. The rich have money but are poor in confession and prayer because they are distracted by their wealth. By supplying the poor, however, they can bear fruit because the poor intercede richly with God. This reciprocity continues to grow because the poor require their needs to be provided and the rich desire the prayers of the poor. They thus complement one another and become partners in doing right.

Similitude 3 (52.1–3)

The shepherd then shows Hermas trees with no leaves that appear to be withered. Hermas notes that the trees all appear the same as in winter. The shepherd explains that the trees represent people living in this age, because the righteous and the sinners look the same in this age.

Similitude 4 (53.1–8)

Similitudes 3–4 should be read together. The shepherd again shows trees to Hermas. Some trees are budding while others are withered. The budding trees represent righteous people who will soon inhabit the coming age. The age to come will be like summer for the righteous but winter for sinners. The fruit of the righteous will then be known just as fruit is obvious on the trees in summer. However, the sinners will be shown to be dry and withered, good for little else than firewood. The shepherd instructs Hermas to bear fruit now so that his fruit may become evident in summer. In particular, he should avoid excessive engagement in business because such practices are distracting. These people do not receive what they ask for because they do not serve the Lord and their minds have been corrupted.

Similitude 5 (54.1–60.4)

The next parable opens with the shepherd's appearance to Hermas while he is fasting on a mountain. Sitting next to Hermas, the shepherd asks him why he has come to the mountain so early. Hermas explains that he has a station—a duty to fast. The shepherd informs Hermas that he is not keeping this fast properly. A true fast involves not committing evil, serving the Lord with a pure heart, keeping God's commands, and not allowing evil desires to enter into the heart (Sim. 5.1.5 [54.5]). The shepherd then tells a parable about a landowner who planted a vineyard in his field. Before going on a journey, he chooses a slave to put a fence around the vineyard while the landowner is away. The slave dutifully fences in the vineyard and goes on to cultivate the vineyard and remove the weeds. When the slave's master returns to find his cultivated vineyard with a fence around it, he is overjoyed. He calls his son and his friends to tell them the good news. He not only grants the slave his freedom, he also makes him a coheir with his son (Sim. 5.2.7 [55.7]). The landowner puts on a celebratory feast and sends food to the slave from the feast. While the slave eats a small portion, he gives the rest to the other slaves. The result is that the slaves pray for the favored slave to receive more. When the master hears this, he reports the news to his friends and his son, and they collectively approve of the slave's status as coheir.

Hermas does not understand the parable and asks for clarification. The shepherd interprets the parable in multiple ways. He first instructs Hermas to keep the Lord's commandments and reflects on the nature of fasting. Going beyond the Lord's commandments brings greater glory to God's servants (Sim. 5.3.3 [56.3]). Thus fasting is good if Hermas keeps what God has mandated. When Hermas does this, he should have nothing but bread and water on the day that he fasts. The money that he would have spent on food should be donated to a widow or orphan. After these instructions, Hermas again begs the shepherd to explain the parable. The shepherd next explains that the landowner is God, and the vines are the people that God has planted himself. The son depicts the Holy Spirit, while the slave represents the Son of God. The parable thus becomes a Christological story narrating how the Son labored for believers. Hermas inquires further as to why God's Son is depicted as a slave. The shepherd shows him that the slave is powerful because he is entrusted with the vineyard and cleanses the people of their sins. Finally, the shepherd uses the similitude to discuss the relationship between flesh and spirit (Sim. 5.6.4–5.6.8 [59.4–8]). Hermas is glad upon hearing this explanation (Sim. 5.7.1 [60.1]). The shepherd concludes by urging Hermas to keep the Lord's commands and by promising that the Lord will heal his previous sins.

Similitude 6 (61.1–65.7)

The sixth parable contains a different episode. This time the shepherd appears to Hermas at home while he is glorifying the Lord and pondering the commandments. The shepherd asks Hermas why he is double-minded about the commandments that the shepherd has given. Since the mandates are good, Hermas should walk in them, repent, and rid himself of evil things by clothing himself with righteous virtue. After the shepherd's speech (Sim. 6.1.1–4 [61.1–4]), Hermas and the shepherd walk to a field where they see a young shepherd wearing a saffron-colored robe. His flock is large, and both the shepherd and the sheep are happy. The shepherd who is with Hermas informs him that the happy shepherd is the angel of luxury and deception (Sim. 6.2.1 [62.1]). Since the sheep are allowed to follow their desires freely, they are destroyed by the angel in death and corruption. Hermas inquires further into death and corruption. The shepherd clarifies that those sheep that hand themselves over completely to worldly desires are unable to repent and thus enter death, while those who overindulge in pleasure but do not blaspheme the Lord are corrupt. For the latter, there is hope for repentance.

As they continue walking, Hermas sees another shepherd who is wild, dressed in white goatskin, and carrying a bag, a staff, and a long whip. This shepherd takes the sheep that are well-fed but not skipping from the happy shepherd and puts them into thorns and briars. The sheep are unable to eat as they want, not given rest, and unhappy. Hermas feels sorry for them (Sim. 6.3.1 [63.1]). The shepherd who is with Hermas explains that the wild shepherd is the angel of punishment and a righteous angel. The sufferings that the sheep experience are found in this life and include loss, illness, and deprivation. When the sheep repent, they glorify God and serve him with pure hearts. Hermas then asks about the duration that those who live in luxury must suffer. The shepherd declares that they are tormented for the same amount of time as they spent in luxury (Sim. 6.4.1 [64.1]). Hermas protests that they should suffer seven times as long. Hermas is sternly assured by the shepherd that this is not the case because the power of torment is greater than luxury. This has to do with the way in which luxury, deception, and torment stay in the memory. Things done in luxury are quickly forgotten, but tormenting punishment is remembered for long periods of time. Hermas then requests a better understanding of luxury. The shepherd reveals that anything that people enjoy is a luxury (Sim. 6.5.5–7 [65.5–7]). This includes the pleasure that angry people derive from indulging their tempers and the freedom that adulterers, slanderers, and liars grant to their sinful acts. The shepherd concludes, however, by noting that some luxuries save people, offering the example of one who is carried away by their desire to do good.

Similitude 7 (66.1–7)

Hermas sees the shepherd on the same plain a few days later and demands that the punishing angel leave his house. However, the shepherd informs Hermas that he is being tested because of the sins committed by members of his household. Hermas protests that he should not be afflicted on account of their sins, but the shepherd rebuts Hermas's claim. His family will only suffer if he suffers as their head. Even though the family has repented, they must still be tormented. Hermas will suffer for a short time, but the shepherd will be with him and promises to ask the punishing angel to work lightly. For his part, Hermas should walk in the Lord's commandments.

Similitude 8 (67.1–77.5)

The shepherd next points out a willow tree, and Hermas sees people who are called in the Lord's name enjoying its shade. An angel of the Lord also stands by the willow wielding a pruning hook. The angel cuts off branches from the willow and hands them out to each of the people gathered there. Hermas is amazed that, despite having had so many branches cut from it, the tree remains healthy. When he asks the shepherd about this, the shepherd tells him to wait until he has seen everything for an explanation. After giving the sticks to the people, the angel recalls them. He examines the sticks as they are brought to him, and the condition of each branch is recorded (Sim. 8.1.6–18 [67.6–18]). These include branches that are withered, moth-eaten, green, budding, fruit-bearing, and various combinations of these states. The angel orders crowns for those whose sticks are bearing fruit and sends them to the tower along with those who had branches that are green and budding but without fruit.[4] The angel informs the shepherd that he is leaving the other branches in the shepherd's charge because he must leave. The shepherd is to examine their branches carefully. He suggests to Hermas that they should plant the branches to see if any can live. After receiving the branches in their respective groups, they plant them and flood them so that the branches are no longer visible. They then leave for a few days and plan to return to inspect the growth.

At this point, Hermas queries the meaning of the parable (Sim. 8.3.1 [69.1]). The tree that has been cut and is healthy is God's law and God's Son, while the people represent those who believe in him. The angel of the Lord is Michael. The branches illustrate how well the people have kept God's law. Those for whom the shepherd must now care ought to repent, but the people who are already in the tower delighted in the law.

Hermas and the shepherd return to inspect the cuttings a few days after the shepherd's explanation (Sim. 8.4.1 [70.1]). The shepherd sits in the place of Michael, and Hermas aids the shepherd by ushering each group of people along with their branches. The branches are inspected, and the condition has changed under the water. In each group, some are healthier, while others have withered. Hermas records the conditions of each group, and the shepherd asks the people to stand with others whose branches are in the same condition (Sim. 8.4.4–8.5.6 [70.4–71.6]). After their work is finished, the shepherd recalls the health of the willow and explains that the parable shows the greatness of the Lord's compassion. The Lord grants repentance to those who serve him with a pure heart, but those who are deceitful are not given another chance to dishonor him (Sim. 8.6.1–2 [72.1–2]). Hermas asks to know more about what the condition of the branches represents. The shepherd catalogs the significance of each branch and the characteristics that underlie the appearances of the branches (Sim. 8.6.4–8.10.4 [72.4–76.4]). For example, half-withered branches with cracks in them represent people who are double-minded and slanderers. Such people cause dissension (Sim. 8.7.1–2 [73.1–2]). Those whose sticks are half-green and half-withered are

---

4. Hermas has already watched the construction of the tower in Vis. 3.

absorbed in business and do not join the saints. Many of these, though not all, repent and live in the tower (Sim. 8.4.1–2 [74.1–2]).

After the shepherd's interpretation, he instructs Hermas to tell the people to repent and live for God because God has been patient (Sim. 8.11.1 [77.1]). The shepherd promises to show more to Hermas in a few days.

Similitude 9 (78.1–110.3)

When the shepherd returns to Hermas, he explains that he wants to reveal again what the spirit told Hermas in the form of the church. Thus Sim. 9 reprises much of what Hermas saw in Vis. 3 (9–21). The rationale behind the shepherd's statement is that Hermas can see more clearly with the shepherd's aid (Sim. 9.1.3 [78.3]). The shepherd leads Hermas to a mountain in Arcadia and seats him on top. From there he can see a broad plain with twelve mountains around it. Each mountain appears distinct from the others; one is black, another is full of thorny plants, and yet another has fruit trees that are in season. In the middle of the plain, Hermas sees an enormous and ancient rock that has a brightly shining gate which has recently been chiseled into it. Twelve virgins wearing linen tunics stand around the gate, four of whom Hermas regards as particularly majestic. Hermas is perplexed by what he sees, but the shepherd assures him that later he will understand better (Sim. 9.2.6–7 [79.6–7]).

Six glorious men come next and summon a crowd of other men. The six men mandate that a tower should be built on top of the rock. They call up ten, twenty-five, thirty-five, and forty stones from the depths and order the virgins to carry the stones through the gate. Having done this, the six men begin to construct the tower, and the stones fit together so that they look like a single stone (Sim. 9.3.3–9.4.3 [80.3–81.3]). The six glorious men then order the other men to bring stones from the mountains. Stones of various appearances are brought, handed to the virgins, and carried through the gate. These turn white after entering the tower. Some of the men, however, bring stones into the tower without going through the gate. These stones do not change colors, and the six glorious men emphasize that all stones must be carried through the gate by the virgins if they are to be suitable for building.

Construction pauses at the end of the day, and only the virgins remain to guard the tower. Hermas asks about the pause and discovers that the lord of the tower must inspect the tower before building can continue. Hermas's other questions must wait for an answer. He and the shepherd return to the tower after a few days to find a procession with a man at its center whose height is greater than the tower (Sim. 9.6.1 [83.1]). This is the lord of the tower. He strikes every stone three times to check its suitability. Some stones crack or turn black. These stones are taken out of the tower and placed nearby. Other stones are brought in to replace them that have been excavated from the plain. The lord of the tower instructs the shepherd to clean the stones and place the usable ones back in the tower. The other stones will be flung far from the tower.

Hermas wonders how the unsuitable stones can be replaced in the tower (Sim. 9.7.4 [84.4]). The shepherd explains that he will cut most of the stones so that they fit properly. After two days, they examine the stones and hew or remove the stones depending on their state. Weak stones that can still be placed in the tower are put in the central section, while the larger stones support the exterior walls. After they finish, the shepherd inspects the tower and is pleased that it is well constructed. Hermas marvels that it appears to have been cut from a single stone. They fill in the holes in the plain left by the stones, while the virgins sweep around the tower. With everything clean, the shepherd leaves to address other business. Hermas stays with the virgins, who are cheerful and treat him well. They spend a night together in prayer before the shepherd returns to interpret what Hermas has seen (Sim. 9.11.7–9 [88.7–9]).

Hermas's first question when the shepherd returns concerns the identity of the rock and the gate. The shepherd explains that they are both depictions of the Son of God (Sim. 9.12.1 [89.1]). The shepherd shows him that the rock is old just as God's Son is older than creation. The newness of the gate represents the Son's revelation in recent times. The stones are required to enter the tower through the gate in the same way that people must enter God's kingdom by receiving the name of the Son. The crowd of men who build the tower stands for the angels, while the six men and the tall man who is lord of the tower represent six glorious angels and the Son of God. As in Vis. 3, the tower symbolizes the church. The virgins are described as holy spirits and God's powers who must clothe everyone who will enter the tower. The rejected stones bear Jesus's name but not the virgins' clothes. They will be able to reenter only if they accept the aid of the virgins.

Hermas next inquires about the reason that the tower is built on the rock and the gate rather than on the ground. The shepherd is mildly frustrated, but he shows Hermas that all creation is sustained by the Son of God. If the Son sustains all that is, he must also sustain those whom he calls. Hermas next asks the names of the virgins. They include figures like Faith, Self-Control, and Single-Mindedness (Sim. 9.15.1–2 [92.1–2]). The various stones from the depths stand for early generations of Christians, apostles, and prophets. By coming through the water, these are made alive.

Having explained these matters, Hermas and the shepherd turn their attention to the twelve mountains around the plain (Sim. 9.17.1–9.29.4 [94.1–106.4]). The twelve mountains represent twelve tribes of people, but the tribes are not characterized by shared ethnicity. They represent all people but are divided in terms of their activities and lifestyles. Two examples may offer a flavor of how this extended dialogue progresses. Thorns and briars are found on the third mountain. These represent believers who are rich and entangled in business. As it is difficult to walk through briars, so it is difficult for such people to enter God's kingdom. Yet there is a possibility if they repent quickly. Stones from the third mountain that do not repent will be handed over to the women dressed in black. Later in the discussion, Hermas sees springs of water on the eighth mountain. Rocks taken from the eighth mountain represent apostles and teachers. They teach well, do not give in to evil desires, and walk in truth. The shepherd explains that these stones will enter the tower with the angels.

Following the discourse about the mountains, the shepherd tells Hermas about the round stones that are excavated from the plain. These are innocent people who have been rounded by their wealth. Once their wealth is cut away, they will be able to enter the tower. Stones that remain too attached to their riches are flung away from the tower. Despite the varied appearances of the stones when they entered, the shepherd explains the uniform appearance of the tower with reference to the one thought, mind, faith, and body that characterize the tower. He concludes this lengthy parable by encouraging Hermas and his readers to live in such a way as to keep their stones in good condition.

Similitude 10 (111.1–114.5)

After Hermas finishes his book, he is visited in his house by the shepherd, the virgins from Sim. 9 (78.1–110.3), and the angel who handed Hermas over to the shepherd. The angel informs Hermas that the shepherd and the virgins will remain in Hermas's house. He should live rightly and obey the commandments that have been given to him. The purpose of the angel's exhortations is so that Hermas will persevere and tell others about what he has seen (Sim. 10.2.2 [112.2]). The shepherd will stay to instruct and encourage Hermas, while the virgins will help Hermas to keep the commandments as long as his house remains clean. After some final instructions, the *Shepherd* ends with the angel, virgins, and shepherd leaving Hermas's house with a promise that the shepherd and virgins will return.

Conclusion

This chapter has recapitulated the narrative flow of the *Shepherd* while utilizing the traditional headings of Visions, Mandates, and Similitudes. The summary is located at the start of this book to place the focus on the text of the *Shepherd*. Chapter 1 can be used as a supplement to reading the *Shepherd*, but this précis is no substitute for reading the text itself. Nevertheless, it may assist readers by keeping the entire story of Hermas's revelation in view. The summary may also be helpful in those places where the *Shepherd*'s discussions become lengthy and somewhat circuitous (e.g., Vis. 3; Sim. 8–9) because summary must necessarily be selective in its focus.

After reading this chapter, one may rightly wonder how scholars know the text of the *Shepherd*. Chapters 2 and 3 turn to this issue. Chapter 2 examines the Greek manuscripts and various translations of the *Shepherd*, while Chapter 3 takes up the early reception history of the *Shepherd* by its readers.

Chapter 2

HOW WAS THE *SHEPHERD* PRESERVED?

The best versions of the *Shepherd* printed today rely on older manuscripts to reconstruct the *Shepherd*. The *Shepherd* is attested by numerous ancient witnesses. Manuscripts of the *Shepherd* contain the text in Greek—the original language of composition—as well as in Latin, Ethiopic, Coptic, Middle Persian, and Georgian translations. However, early witnesses did not always preserve the text well because they existed largely in fragmentary forms. For example, there are only fragmentary Greek witnesses for Sim. 9.30.3–10.4.5 (107.3–114.5), so other translations become particularly important in this section of the *Shepherd*.

Although many readers study the *Shepherd* primarily from Greek texts in printed critical editions,[1] it remains important to know something about both the manuscripts and earlier editions for three reasons.[2] First, the eclectic editions that are printed today are compiled and edited with reference to earlier manuscripts and editions. When manuscripts do not contain the same wording, editors must make choices about which reading is most likely to be the earliest. In order to evaluate their decisions, which are often recorded in a textual apparatus at the bottom of the page, readers must know something about the manuscripts that editors cite. Second, reading manuscripts and translations can shed light on how the *Shepherd* was understood by some of its earliest readers. Since translation involves a certain amount of interpretation, this is particularly true when reading early translations of the *Shepherd*. Finally, it is important to remember that new manuscripts can result in changes to the text. The twentieth century saw a number of manuscript discoveries that involved the *Shepherd*. Thus, when consulting editions of the *Shepherd* from the nineteenth or early twentieth century, it is worth noting that there may now be additional textual evidence.

In view of these reasons, this chapter offers an overview of the most important manuscripts and translations. These include Greek, Latin, Ethiopic, Coptic, Middle Persian, and Georgian texts. It also introduces the abbreviations that are used to refer to these manuscripts and translations in other editions and in the rest of this book. In addition to ancient manuscripts, printed editions of the text can be

---

1. See the texts and English translations in Ehrman (2003, 2.162–473); Holmes (2007, 442–685).

2. See similarly Kirkland (1990, 134).

found dating back to 1513.[3] Thus, this chapter highlights select editions of the text in order to familiarize readers with how earlier scholars understood the *Shepherd*. The chapter concludes with an overview of two monks whose extensive quotations of the *Shepherd* provide a transition between Chapters 2 and 3.

Greek Witnesses

Since Greek was the language in which the *Shepherd* was first composed, Greek witnesses to the text take a special place in how readers encounter the *Shepherd*. These witnesses include two codices, a florilegium of patristic texts that include quotations from the *Shepherd*, and more than twenty fragmentary papyri. Although these witnesses do not comprise a complete Greek text even when combined, they provide the most important basis for textual criticism.

Codex Athos (A)

Found in a monastery library on Mt. Athos during the 1850s, A is the most complete extant Greek manuscript.[4] A dates to the fourteenth or fifteenth century and contains Vis. 1.1.1–Sim. 9.30.3 (1.1–107.3). Nine leaves were found, but the final leaf has been lost.[5] Six leaves are found in Codex Athous Grigoriou 96, while three leaves were taken to the University of Leipzig.[6] Lambros measures the length of the written portion of the codex as 18.5 cm by 12 cm. The handwriting on the manuscript is "extremely fine," allowing for an average of seventy-two lines per page with roughly ninety characters per line.[7] Lambros also offers a collation of A that can be checked against the text of the *Shepherd* in Gebhardt and Harnack's edition.[8]

Codex Sinaiticus (S)

In addition to the prominent place rightly given to S in Septuagint and New Testament studies, S also contains the *Epistle of Barnabas* and the *Shepherd*.[9]

---

3. The *editio princeps* is found in d'Etaples (1513).

4. For a recent account of Constantine Simonides's discovery and forgery of parts of Codex Athos, see Porter (2015, 38–9).

5. Lambros (1888, 5–6); Lake (1912–13, 2.4).

6. For the Athos portion of the manuscript, see http://hdl.handle.net/20.500.11957/96903 (accessed August 29, 2020). On the Leipzig portion, see Bandini and Lusini (1998, 628n.20).

7. Lambros (1888, 5–6).

8. Lambros (1888, 11–23). See Gebhardt and Harnack (1877). The Athos portions of the manuscript, that is, leaves 1–4, 7–8, can be viewed in Lake (1907).

9. The entire codex can be viewed at https://codexsinaiticus.org/en/ (accessed August 29, 2020). On Tischendorf's discovery of S, see Porter (2015, 24–9, 40–54).

Portions of the *Shepherd* (Vis. 1.1.1–Mand. 4.3.6 [1.1–31.6]; Sim. 6.5.5–8.2.5 [65.5–68.5]; Sim. 9.14.4–9.18.5 [91.4–95.5]) are found among the last remaining pages of the codex.[10] The *Shepherd* was transcribed in S by Scribe B and is found in the fragmentary quires Q93 and Q95.[11] The beginning of the work comes at the start of a new quire, and the title is listed simply as *Shepherd* (ΠΟΙΗΜΗΝ). As in the rest of the codex, the text of the *Shepherd* is placed in four columns and is written with an uncial script. The codex is paleographically dated to the mid-fourth century,[12] and the work of correctors may also be found in the *Shepherd* as recorded in S.[13]

The position of the *Shepherd* in a manuscript containing other canonical writings raises additional questions about how the *Shepherd* was perceived by those who commissioned S. Was the *Shepherd* viewed on par with other canonical books? If not, why was it included in S with no obvious way to set the text apart? These questions become particularly significant when the fourth-century codex is placed alongside other fourth-century discussions of canon, such as those by Eusebius and Athanasius.[14] While a definitive argument may not be possible, it seems on balance that the place of the *Shepherd* in the manuscript does not require the text to be classified as canonical. Although the *Shepherd* is treated very much like the other texts in S, unlike other texts, it is not grouped with a text of similar genre. In the case of the *Shepherd*, it is separated from Revelation, the other New Testament apocalypse, by the *Epistle of Barnabas*.[15] The *Shepherd* may have been viewed as worthy of inclusion in the codex as a recommended book that may also have some authority. However, the *Shepherd*'s authority is likely secondary and thus not canonical. Such an understanding of the *Shepherd*'s authority fits well with comments like those in the Muratorian Fragment (lines 77–80) in which the *Shepherd* can be read but not among the prophets or the apostles.[16]

Florilegium Patristicum (F)

F is contained in two manuscripts: Paris gr. 1143 and Athos Lavra K 96. The manuscripts date to the thirteenth century and likely originated from the

---

10. On the Similitudes in Sinaiticus, see Cecconi (2010–11); Carlini and Bandini (2011).

11. Batovici (2015a, 150; 2015c, 40–1). For a history of research on the scribes of S, see Jongkind (2007, 9–18).

12. Jongkind (2007, 18–21); Parker (2010, 27–42).

13. Batovici (2014); Cecconi (2018, 291). For further comparison of S with other Greek and Latin manuscripts as well as a reconstruction of the *Shepherd*'s textual transmission, see Cecconi (2018).

14. Eusebius, *Hist. eccl.* 3.24.1–3.25.7; Athanasius, *Ep. fest.* 39.

15. The *Epistle of Barnabas* is thereby also separated from the other letters. See further Batovici (2016a).

16. Markschies (2015, 214–16); Batovici (2016a, 589–90). These comments anticipate the further discussion of the *Shepherd*'s authority in early Christianity at the end of Chapter 3.

libraries on Mount Athos. The fragments from the *Shepherd* contained in the Paris manuscript were published in 1965.[17] These include: Sim. 2.8–10 (51.8–10); 5.3.4–9 (56.4–9); 7.4–5 (66.4–5); 9.23.3–5 (100.3–5); 9.33.1–3 (110.1–3). After the Athos portion of the manuscript was discovered, additional fragments of the *Shepherd* were published in 2000.[18] These include Greek witnesses to Sim. 6.1.1–6.5.7 (61.1–65.7); 7.1–7 (66.1–7); 9.31.4–9.33.3 (108.4–110.3).[19]

Michigan Papyrus 129 (M)

M comes from a collection of papyri jointly acquired by the British Library and the University of Michigan from an Egyptian dealer.[20] While an Egyptian provenance is likely for the manuscript, it is difficult to be more precise. The manuscript is missing leaves at the front and back. Some of the remaining leaves have also been damaged. The leaves measure roughly 25 cm by 22.5 cm and contain two columns of text. The width of the columns averages 8–9 cm with a 2–3 cm space between.[21] M provides an important witness to the *Shepherd* because of its date in the mid-third century.[22] M contains Sim. 2.8–9.5.1 (51.8–82.1),[23] and it is possible that the codex originally contained only Vis. 5.1–Sim. 10.4.5 (25.1–114.5) without the first four Visions.[24]

Bodmer Papyrus 38 (B)

B is named for the collection of manuscripts from whence it originated. These manuscripts were collected by Martin Bodmer and contain other early Christian texts.[25] Along with Bodmer Papyri 29–37, B comprises part of the Codex Visionum.[26] As the name suggests, these papyri contain a series of visionary texts that were contained in a single-quire papyrus codex. B contains portions of the *Shepherd* that have been transmitted under the title "Visions."

---

17. Lappa-Zizicas (1965).
18. Bandini (2000).
19. Unfortunately, the Athos portion is not included in the editions of Ehrman (2003), Holmes (2007), or Prinzivalli and Simonetti (2010–15).
20. Bonner (1934, 4).
21. Bonner (1925, 116–17; 1934, 16–17).
22. Bonner (1925, 121; 1934, 16).
23. Published in Bonner (1934, 37–124).
24. Bonner (1925, 117–19; 1934, 7–14); Lake (1925, 279–80).
25. For an introduction to Bodmer and his collection of documents, see Robinson (2011, 3–8).
26. These papyri have been published in Hurst, Reverdin, and Rudhardt (1984) (P.Bodmer 29) and Hurst and Rudhardt (1999) (P.Bodmer 30–37).

Specifically, B contains Vis. 1.1.1–3.13.4 (1.1–21.4) and dates to the fourth or fifth century.[27]

Other Greek Witnesses

In addition to the five Greek witnesses already listed, other fragmentary papyri and parchments contain smaller portions of the *Shepherd*. These date between the end of the second century and the sixth century.[28] Some of these witnesses are found in collections that contain multiple copies of the *Shepherd*, while others contain a solitary papyrus.

The most numerous collection of witnesses to the *Shepherd* has been discovered in the rubbish dumps at Oxyrhynchus. Eleven fragments have been found on papyrus or parchment dating from the second or third centuries to the fourth century.[29] P.Oxy. 69.4706 contains twenty-seven small fragments of the *Shepherd*, while P.Oxy. 50.3528 holds Sim. 9.20.3–4 (97.3–4); 9.22.1 (99.1).[30] Both date to the second or third centuries. Several papyri date from the third century. These include P.Oxy. 50.3527 (Sim. 8.4.1–8.5.2 [70.1–71.2]), P.Oxy. 69.4705 (Vis. 1.1.8–9 [1.8–9]), P.Oxy. 69.4707 (Sim. 6.3.1–7.1.2 [63.1–66.2]), and P.Oxy. 15.1828 (Sim. 6.5.3, 5 [65.3, 5]).[31] Others date from the late third or early fourth century, including P.Oxy. 3.404 (Sim. 10.3.2–5; 10.4.3–4 [113.2–5; 114.3–4]) and P.Oxy. 15.1783 (Mand. 9.2–5 [39.2–5]). The latest manuscripts discovered so far in this collection come from the fourth century. These consist of P.Oxy. 9.1172 (Sim. 2.4–10 [51.4–10]), P.Oxy. 13.1599 (Sim. 8.6.4–8.8.3 [72.4–74.3], and P.Oxy. 50.3526 (Mand. 5.2.3–6.1.2 [34.3–35.2]).[32]

Five fragments are housed in the Ägyptisches Museum und Papyrussammlung within the Staatliche Museen zu Berlin. Accordingly, these can be referred to as the Berlin Papyri. P.Berol 5513 dates from the third or fourth century and contains Sim. 2.7–10 (51.7–10); 4.2–5 (53.2–5).[33] P.Berol 13272 provides a fourth-century witness for Sim. 5.1.5–5.2.2 (54.5–55.2) and Sim. 5.2.4–6 (55.4–6).[34] Mand.

---

27. Published in Carlini and Giaccone (1991). Digital images are available in the Bodmer Lab at https://bodmerlab.unige.ch/fr/constellations/papyri/barcode/1072205367 (accessed August 29, 2020).

28. See further Horsley and Llewelyn (1982, 159–61); Tornau and Cecconi (2014, 1–2).

29. These fragments have been usefully collected along with other extracanonical texts in Blumell and Wayment (2015, 201–82).

30. The Oxyrhynchus papyri are cited in the form P.Oxy. vol.no.(.)pap.no. The papyri are published by the Egypt Exploration Society in its series Graeco-Roman Memoirs.

31. Mercati (1925).

32. Tornau and Cecconi (2014, 1–2) also mention P. London British Library 2067, P. Lond. Brit. Lib. 2467, P. Lit. Lond. 224, and P. Lit. Lond. 225 in conjunction with the Oxyrhynchus Papyri. On identifying fragments from the same codex, see Batovici (2016c, 390–4).

33. Diels and Harnack (1891, 427–31).

34. Stegmüller (1937, 456–9).

4.4.4–5.1.4 (32.4–33.4) is found in the fifth-century P.Berol 5104,[35] and Sim. 8.1.1–12 [67.1–12]) is attested in P.Berol 6789, which dates to the sixth century.[36] Finally, P.Berol 21259 dates to the sixth century and contains Vis. 3.6.4, 6 (14.4, 6).[37]

The Michigan Papyri have already been mentioned in relation to Michigan Papyrus 129 (M). An additional witness should be mentioned from this collection. Although not as extensive, Michigan Papyrus 130 contains a second-century copy of Mand. 2.6–3.1 (27.6–28.1).[38] It is written on papyrus and is significant for being the oldest extant manuscript of the *Shepherd*. Although there are quotations from texts that may predate P.Mich. 130, this manuscript makes clear that the *Shepherd* was composed by the second century at the latest.

Among the witnesses that are found in collections that contain only a single manuscript of the *Shepherd*, P.Iand 1.4 probably dates from the late third or early fourth century.[39] It measures 11.8 cm by 6 cm and was originally published in 1912.[40] However, it was not until 1979 and 1980 that P.Iand. 1.4 was identified as a fragment of the *Shepherd*.[41] It contains a fragmentary copy of Mand. 11.19–21 (43.19–21) and 12.1.2–3 (44.2–3).

Another witness is found in the Hamburg Papyri located in the Hamburger Stadtbibliothek. P.Hamb. 24 dates to the fourth or fifth century and contains a fragmentary copy of Sim. 4.6–5.1.5 (53.6–54.5).[42] The leaf is 15.6 cm at its highest point and 12.5 cm at its widest.

Portions of a late-fourth- or early-fifth-century papyrus are found in two collections. P.Prag. 1.1 contains three fragments with portions of the *Shepherd*.[43] The Prague Papyri were collected by Carl Wessely and were sold to the National Library of Prague in 1934. Dan Batovici has recently published a papyrus from the collection of Raymond-Charles Isaac Weill that is found in Paris.[44] P.Weill 1.96 provides the bottom portion of P.Prag. 1.1 frag. b. P.Prag. 1.1 frag. a contains Mand. 8.9–12 (38.9–12). Much of Sim. 5.7.3–6.1.5 (60.3–61.5) occurs in the combined P.Prag. 1.1 frag. b + P.Weill 1.96. Although P.Prag. 1.1 frag. c does not have enough remaining text to identify it with a portion of the *Shepherd*, it has been identified as a portion of the same manuscript as the other two fragments on paleographic grounds.

---

35. Treu (1970).
36. Schmidt and Schubart (1910).
37. Ioannidou (1996).
38. Bonner (1927; 1934, 129–36). Based on the handwriting on the verso side of the papyrus, Bonner suggests a date around 200 (1927, 106–7).
39. Choat and Yuen-Collingridge (2010, 206) note, however, that the dating of this papyrus is difficult. They suggest a date in the late-second or third century.
40. Schaefer (1912).
41. Lenaerts (1979); Gronewald (1980). See also Wayment (2013, 106–7).
42. Schmidt and Schubart (1909).
43. Pintaudi, Dostálová, and Vidman (1988, 17–25).
44. Batovici (2016b, 20–36).

Among the papyri collected by J. Rendel Harris,[45] G. D. Kilpatrick identified P.Harris 1.128 as a portion of Vis. 5.5, 7 (25.5, 7).[46] The fragment is small, and the average number of characters per line is just over nineteen. The papyrus has been dated to the fifth century.

The Amherst Papyri were collected by William Tyssen-Amherst, who collected ancient books and works of art in the late nineteenth and early twentieth centuries. P.Amh. Gr. 2.190 contains seven fragments from a sixth-century papyrus codex of the *Shepherd*.[47] The text is written in an uncial script, and the remaining fragments vary in size. The papyrus attests Vis. 1.2.2–1.3.1 (2.2–3.1); 3.12.3–3.13.4 (20.3–21.4); Mand. 12.1.1, 3 (44.1, 3); Sim. 9.2.1–5 (79.1–5); 9.12.2–5 (89.2–5); 9.17.1–4 (94.1–4); 9.30.1–4 (107.1–4).

Finally, the text of the *Shepherd* is attested in two quotations and in an additional list from other works that are also found in fragmentary papyri. They have been included here instead of in the following chapter because the works in which the *Shepherd* is quoted are unknown in all cases and because the citations appear in fragmentary papyri.

P.Oxy. 1.5 contains a citation of Mand. 11.9–10 (43.9–10) in an early Christian text on prophecy. The papyrus dates to the late third or early fourth century, and the quotation was identified roughly simultaneously by F. C. Coneybeare and Adolf von Harnack.[48] P.Mich. 6427 is a fourth-century papyrus that contains a prayer (frag. 1) and a portion of Dan 3:52–53, 58–68, 77–84 (frag. 2).[49] Fragment 1 measures 12 cm by 13.5 cm. It includes what appears to be a reference to Mand. 1.1 (26.1) in lines 7–8. Finally, the *Shepherd* is listed in P.Ash. 3, a fourth-century papyrus fragment that measures 13.9 by 8 cm. Along with the *Shepherd*, Leviticus, Job, the Acts of the Apostles, and some works of Origen are also listed. Although P.Ash 3 does not quote the *Shepherd*, it provides another reference to the *Shepherd* in a fourth-century papyrus.[50]

Translations

After examining the extant Greek witnesses to the *Shepherd*, one can now observe that the Greek text is widely, albeit incompletely, attested. Although the precise number of manuscripts may vary slightly depending on how different scholars decide that fragments should be combined, the *Shepherd* is one of the most widely attested early Christian texts. Indeed, its preservation in papyri manuscripts

---

45. Powell (1936).
46. Kilpatrick (1947).
47. The text is published in Grenfell and Hunt (1901, 195–200). Images are found in Grenfell and Hunt (1901, plate 24).
48. Coneybeare (1898); Harnack (1898). See also Chadwick (1957, 278–9).
49. Gronewald (1974).
50. See further Otranto (1997, 104–6).

approaches some New Testament books that are most often attested in papyri witnesses.[51] In light of the fragmentary nature of much of this evidence, however, students of the *Shepherd* should also be familiar with its early translation history. Of particular note are translations into Latin, Ethiopic, and Coptic. These three translations will be the focus of this section, but it is worth noting that Middle Persian and Georgian translations also exist.

Latin (L)

Two Latin translations of the *Shepherd* were made prior to the sixth century. The earlier translation is known as the Vulgate and probably dates around 200 CE.[52] The Vulgate is often referred to by the siglum L^1 and formed the basis of d'Etaples's *editio princeps*.[53] It is now known in twenty-eight manuscripts that date from the ninth to the sixteenth centuries.[54] Tornau and Cecconi have recently attempted to show the relationships between the manuscripts in a complex *stemma*.[55] Their edition replaces and improves upon the Vulgate text edited by Adolf Hilgenfeld,[56] which was quoted in the apparatus of all subsequent editions of the Greek *Shepherd*.[57] The relationship of the vulgate to the primary Greek witnesses is difficult to ascertain precisely. At times, the Vulgate agrees with A against the other witnesses. In other places it lines up with B. It may be that the translator had access to a different Greek text from any of the extant witnesses.[58] If so, this makes the Vulgate an important witness in establishing the earliest recoverable text of the *Shepherd*.[59] The Vulgate also provides the earliest text of the *Shepherd* where no Greek witnesses remain available and may allow insight into early translation practices and the communities that used them.

If the Vulgate belongs to the time of the earliest Latin translations of early Christian literature, the Palatine translation (L^2) may be analogous to Jerome's revision of the Vetus Latina.[60] The Palatine translation dates to the fourth or fifth century and was edited by Anna Vezzoni in 1994.[61] It is preserved in three

---

51. Choat and Yuen-Collingridge (2010, 196); Batovici (2016b, 21).

52. Turner (1920, 206); Tornau and Cecconi (2014, 10). Christine Mohrmann (1949, 74–8) similarly suggests a date around the end of the second century. Gleede (2016, 268–70, 277–80) argues that the Vulgate translation should be located in the first half of the third century.

53. d'Etaples (1513).

54. Tornau and Cecconi (2014, 12–19).

55. Tornau and Cecconi (2014, 19–27, 36).

56. Hilgenfeld (1873).

57. Cecconi (2012, 38).

58. Tornau and Cecconi (2014, 10).

59. Batovici (2018, 152–3).

60. Tornau and Cecconi (2014, 7).

61. Vezzoni (1994). Much of this paragraph is indebted to Vezzoni's introduction. On the date of the Palatine translation, see Gleede (2016, 268–70, 296–7).

manuscripts. Two manuscripts date from the fifteenth century and are found in the Vatican library (Vat.pal.lat. 150 [94r–180r]; Vat.Urb.lat. 486 [69v–129v]).[62] An earlier fragment dates to the eighth century and attests portions of Mand. 8–10.[63] Vis. 1–4 may have been freshly translated by the Palatine translator, and Tornau and Cecconi conclude that the differences throughout the Palatine *Shepherd* are sufficient to treat the Palatine translation as an additional witness to the Vulgate text.[64]

One passage can serve as an example of why L¹ and L² should be treated as separate witnesses. In Sim. 2.6–7 (51.6–7), the Vulgate reads:

⁶The poor gives thanks to God for the rich ⁷ because they do the work from the Lord.[65]

This is dramatically shorter from the Greek text used for modern translations.[66] Like the Vulgate, the Palatine translation likewise differs from the Greek text.

---

62. Vat.pal.lat. 150 can be viewed online at https://digi.vatlib.it/view/bav_pal_lat_150 (accessed August 29, 2020). Vat.Urb.lat. 486 can be viewed online at https://digi.vatlib.it/view/MSS_Urb.lat.486 (accessed August 29, 2020). Mazzini (1980) offers a helpful comparison of readings contained in these two manuscripts.

63. Vezzoni (1988).

64. Tornau and Cecconi (2014, 8–9).

65. "⁶ Pauper deo gratias agit pro diuite ⁷ quia opus faciunt a domino" (Tornau and Cecconi 2014, 77).

66. ⁶ Since the poor is supplied by the rich, he prays to God and gives thanks to him on behalf of the one who has given to him. That [rich] one hurries more and more for the poor in order that he may be constant in his life. For he knows that the prayer of the poor is pleasing and rich before the Lord. ⁷ Therefore, both complete the work. The poor works at prayer, in which he is rich, which he received from the Lord, and by which he repays the Lord who supplies him. Likewise, the rich offers without hesitation the wealth that he has received from the Lord to the poor. And this work is great and pleasing to the Lord, because he understands his riches and works for the poor out of the Lord's gifts and completes the service rightly.

(⁶ ὁ πένης οὖν ἐπιχορηγούμενος ὑπὸ τοῦ πλουσίου ἐντυγχάνει τῷ θεῷ εὐχαριστῶν αὐτῷ ὑπὲρ τοῦ διδόντος αὐτῷ κἀκεῖνος ἔτι καὶ ἔτι σπουδάζει περὶ τοῦ πένητος ἵνα ἀδιάλειπτος γένηται ἐν τῇ ζωῇ αὐτοῦ οἶδε γάρ ὅτι ἡ τοῦ πένητος ἔντευξις προσδεκτή ἐστιν καὶ πλουσία πρὸς κύριον. ⁷ ἀμφότεροι οὖν τὸ ἔργον τελοῦσιν ὁ μὲν πένης ἐργάζεται τῇ ἐντεύξει ἐν ᾗ πλουτεῖ ἣν ἔλαβεν παρὰ τοῦ κυρίου ταύτην ἀποδίδωσι τῷ κυρίῳ τῷ ἐπιχορηγοῦντι αὐτῷ καὶ ὁ πλούσιος ὡσαύτως τὸ πλοῦτος ὃ ἔλαβεν παρὰ τοῦ κυρίου ἀδιστάκτως παρέχεται τῷ πένητι καὶ τοῦτο ἔργον μέγα ἐστιν καὶ δεκτὸν παρὰ τῷ θεῷ ὅτι συνῆκεν ἐπὶ τῷ πλούτῳ αὐτοῦ καὶ ἠργάσατο εἰς τὸν πένητα ἐκ τῶν δωρημάτων τοῦ κυρίου καὶ ἐτέλεσεν τὴν διακονίαν ὀρθῶς; Sim. 2.6–7 [51.6–7].)

However, it is longer and closer to the Greek witnesses than the Vulgate in this instance:

> ⁶ The poor gives thanks to the Lord for the rich who gives to him. Therefore, as the rich person hurries for the poor, lacking nothing for him [the poor] in all his life, so also the poor prays for the rich. ⁷ Therefore, both are at work. For one works in prayer in which he is blessed, and the wage from the Lord is given back. Similarly, the rich too is without a doubt superior to the poor with regard to these things which he received from the Lord. This is also a great work and is acceptable to the Lord because the rich knew and did the Lord's work to the poor from the gifts of the Lord. He ministered and rightly completed his ministry.⁶⁷

Although both translations differ from the available Greek witnesses and provide evidence that readers of the *Shepherd* must weigh carefully when making decisions about which text is earliest, the most important point to make when discussing the Latin translations in themselves is that the Palatine translation cannot be reduced to a revision of the Vulgate. Instead, the Vulgate and Palatine are better conceived of as separate Latin translations of the *Shepherd*.

Ethiopic (E)

The Ethiopic translation was made from a Greek text during the Aksumite era, perhaps during the fifth century.⁶⁸ The translation into Ethiopic, or Geʿez, is found primarily in three manuscripts. The *editio princeps* was published by Antoine d'Abbadie in Latin and based on a sixteenth-century copy of the Ethiopic *Shepherd*.⁶⁹ The manuscript was placed in the Bibliothèque Nationale de France and catalogued as BnF.Abd. 174. The choice to translate the Geʿez manuscript into Latin in the published version may have made it more accessible to scholars but unfortunately prevents the text from being consulted directly. A second witness

---

67. ⁶Pauper deo gratias agit pro divite qui tribuit illi.Quomodo ergo ille diues festinat pro paupere, ne quid ei desit in omni uita sua, sic et pauper orat pro diuite. ⁷Uterque ergo sunt in opera. Alter enim operatur oratione, in qua beatus est, et reddi facit mercedem a domino. Similiter et diues de his, quae accepit a domino, sine dubitatione praestat pauperi. Hoc quoque opus magnum est acceptumque domino, quia diues intellexit et domini opus fecit in pauperem ex donis domini, et ministrauit et recte compleuit ministerium suum.

In addition to being found in the appropriate place in Vezzoni (1994), this text is also printed in the apparatus of Tornau and Cecconi (2014, 77). On this passage, see also Gleede (2016, 282–3).

68. Erho (2015, 99); Villa (2015, 115).

69. d'Abbadie (1860).

was found during the Second World War and dates to the late fifteenth century.[70] Since it is now preserved in the Biblioteca Palatina in Parma, it has come to be known as Parm. 3842. Ted Erho has published notices about two additional Ethiopic manuscripts of the *Shepherd*. The third Ethiopic witness to mention is the fourteenth-century EMML 8508, which provides a third witness to the Ethiopic *Shepherd*.[71] Unlike the first two witnesses, both of which were found in the library at Gunda Gundē, EMML 8508 was found in a monastery at Tarā Qirqos and seems to represent a different textual family. Yet another witness was found at Dabra Aśa Abbā Yoḥanni that likewise dates to the fourteenth century. This fourth witness to the Ethiopic text contains portions of the Visions, Mandates, and Similitudes, but the presence of both the opening and closing leaves may be the most surprising discovery of all.[72] In addition to these witnesses, references to copies of the *Shepherd* have been found in monastery inventory lists, and there may also be fragments of another manuscript that has been mentioned in a Russian catalogue.[73] A complete publication of the Geʿez translation with all available manuscript evidence is still needed, although Villa's critical edition of the Visions and Mandates may go some way toward filling this lacuna.[74]

Coptic (C)

Two different Coptic translations bear witness to the *Shepherd*.[75] The most complete translation is in the Sahidic dialect (C^2) and is currently available in two manuscripts. BnF.Copte 130 dates to the sixth or seventh century and was published piecemeal between 1903 and 1909.[76] It provides a witness for Mand. 8.7–12 (38.7–12); 12.3.4–12.4.5 (46.4–47.5); Sim. 2.3–3.3 (51.3–52.3); 4.8–5.2.2 (53.8–55.2); 5.3.7–5.4.1 (56.7–57.1); 6.1.4–6.2.7 (61.4–62.7); 8.10.3–8.11.5 (76.3–77.5); 9.2.7–9.6.1 (79.7–83.1); 9.11.7–9 (88.7–9); 9.12.2 (89.2); 9.13.5–9 (90.5–9). Bibliothèque de l'Université de Louvain no. 26 dates to the fifteenth century, and two leaves contain a Sahidic translation of Sim. 8.5.6–8.6.4 (71.6–72.4).[77]

The second Coptic translation is found in the Achmimic dialect (C^1) and seems to have been translated from Sahidic rather than Greek. The papyrus manuscript

---

70. van Lantschoot (1962).
71. Erho (2012).
72. Erho (2020). Erho transcribes the text of the available leaves in this chapter.
73. Erho (2015, 100–1, 107–16) (inventory lists), 105 (catalogue).
74. Villa (2016). Unfortunately, I have not seen this thesis and am following the summary published in Villa (2015).
75. These are published in Lefort (1952a) and Lucchesi (1981). Lefort made a French translation available in 1952b.
76. For publication details, see Lefort (1952a, v n.11). Batovici notes that Lefort's transcription of part of BnF.Copte 130 (2) f. 127 is flawed. For a fuller transcription, see Batovici (2017b) or refer to the original publication by Leipoldt (1909–10).
77. For a more detailed treatment of the Sahidic manuscripts, see Lefort (1952a, v–ix).

dates to the fourth century and contains Mand. 4.3.5–5.1.4 (31.5–33.4); Sim. 9.1.5–9.5.5 (78.5–82.5); 9.6.6–9.7.6 (83.6–84.6); 9.9.5–9.10.6 (86.5–87.6); 9.11.8–9.12.5 (88.8–89.5). When the fourth-century date of the Achmimic papyrus is combined with Lefort's arguments that the translation follows the Sahidic, the Coptic translations must predate the fourth century. They thus provide an early but incomplete witness to the *Shepherd*. It may also be worth noting that, as in the case of M, these manuscripts may never have contained Vis. 1–4 (1.1–24.7).[78] However, given the fragmentary state of the manuscripts, caution should be exercised before placing too much weight on this evidence.

Middle Persian

The Middle Persian and Georgian translations can be dealt with more quickly because they are rarely used when reconstructing the earliest text of the *Shepherd*. They are of more interest for studying how the *Shepherd* was received. The Middle Persian translation is found in a manuscript known as M 97.[79] One leaf has been preserved that contains text on both sides. Two partial columns of the text are preserved on each side. It preserves portions of the Shepherd's explanation of the tower. Among the fragments of Sim. 9 that remain are the interpretations of the mountains in Sim. 9.19.2–9.24.2 (96.2–101.2).

Georgian

The last early translation of the *Shepherd* to be mentioned here is the translation into Georgian. The Georgian translation should be dated after the fifth century and may have been made at Mar Saba.[80] The manuscript in which it is found dates to the ninth or tenth century. Bernard Outtier has argued that the Georgian translation does not record a translation of the *Shepherd* directly from Greek. Instead, he proposes that it is a translation of a lost Arabic translation.[81] If so, the Georgian translation is a translation of a translation.

Modern Editions and Translations

While present-day readers of the *Shepherd* should know about the way in which the text has been transmitted and check the various papyri and translations when possible, the way in which most readers encounter the *Shepherd* is in modern critical editions and translations. When an editor undertakes a critical edition of

---

78. Lefort (1952a, v–ix); Lucchesi (1989).
79. Müller (1905, 1077–83). In addition to a description and transcription, Müller's article also includes photographs of M 97.
80. Outtier (1990–1, 211–16; 2004–11, 2.1186–1189).
81. Outtier (1990–1).

the *Shepherd*, they check the various Greek texts and translations listed above and attempt to reconstruct the earliest text that can be recovered. New manuscript discoveries can shed new light on the text of the *Shepherd*. Yet as these discoveries have become available, editing the text has become an increasingly complicated task. When discrepancies appear between manuscripts, different editors may arrive at different conclusions about what reading is likely to be the earliest. It is best, then, for current readers of the *Shepherd* to refer to multiple editions of the text in their studies. This is also true of modern translations of the *Shepherd*, since translators often opt for alternative ways to render the Greek or Latin text. Having listed the various ancient manuscripts in which the *Shepherd* can be found, it will be useful to conclude this chapter with references to some printed editions and translations.

The first editions to note are the *editiones principes*. As noted earlier, the first edition of the *Shepherd* to be printed appeared in 1513. It was published in Paris and was edited by Jacques Le Fèvre d'Etaples.[82] The edition was made from the Vulgate translation of the text. The first printed edition of the Greek text was edited by Rudolf Anger and includes a preface written by Guilelmus (Wilhelm) Dindorf.[83] Both were professors at the University of Leipzig and construct their edition primarily on the basis of A. These editions are important because all future printed editions of the *Shepherd* respond to their predecessors. Viewed from this perspective, these early editions set the tone for all future printings of the text. Although it is important to be aware of these editions, the current textual state of the *Shepherd* renders these editions of limited usefulness for present-day studies of the text.

Recent editions are deeply indebted to Molly Whittaker's editorial work.[84] In addition to Whittaker's introduction and careful reconstruction of the text, this edition has had lasting effects for the citation of the *Shepherd*. It was Whittaker who developed the continuous citation system that more closely resembles the references made to biblical and other early Christian texts.[85] Around the same time, Robert Joly released his text of the *Shepherd* in *Sources Chrétiennes*.[86] Joly offers an extensive introduction, a useful text, as well as interpretive and textual notes. In addition, Joly's edition contains a French translation on the facing page of the Greek text. More recently, Martin Leutzsch has provided an extensive German introduction to the *Shepherd* along with a Greek text, text-critical apparatus, and German translation on facing pages.[87] Leutzsch also provides extensive

---

82. d'Etaples (1513).

83. Anger and Dindorf (1856).

84. Whittaker (1967).

85. E.g., Sim. 9.2.5 is referred to by Whittaker as 78.5. A simplified form of reference was called for prior to the publication of Whittaker's first edition (1956)-by Herbert Musurillo (1951, 383n.5). For an analysis of Whittaker's first edition, see Chadwick (1957).

86. Joly (1968). The first edition of Joly's *Pasteur* was published in 1958.

87. Körtner and Leutzsch (1998). This edition has been thoroughly reviewed in Lusini (2001).

commentary on cross-referencing to related texts in endnotes. There are two editions of the Apostolic Fathers for English readers by Bart Ehrman and Michael Holmes, respectively.[88] Both Ehrman and Holmes introduce important critical matters before offering clear translations that closely follow the Greek text, which is included on facing pages in both editions. Finally, Emanuela Prinzivalli and Manlio Simonetti have recently edited a new edition of the *Shepherd* with a critical text, apparatus, and Italian translation.[89] Prinzivalli and Simonetti also offer a brief commentary on the text using endnotes.

A final note should be made of two older editions that may still prove helpful for current readers of the *Shepherd*. The first of these is the Greek text in the collection of the Apostolic Fathers edited by Oscar de Gebhardt, Adolf von Harnack, and Theodor Zahn.[90] Although new manuscripts have been published since then, this edition remains valuable not only for the clarity of the Greek text contained within but also for the judicious choices of the editors based on the manuscripts that were before them. The second edition to note is the text and translation by Kirsopp Lake in his edition of the Apostolic Fathers.[91] Similar to the edition just mentioned, the textual state has moved on, and this should be taken into account by current readers. Nevertheless, for those interested in the text of the *Shepherd* or in a winsome English translation, Lake's volume remains a valuable option to consult.

Conclusion

This chapter has outlined the primary Greek manuscripts that are employed in order to reconstruct the text of the *Shepherd* and has offered a description of the various manuscripts that textual critics use. It has also explored the significance of early translations of the *Shepherd*. All of these are important for investigating early interpretations of the *Shepherd*, and the Latin translations are particularly significant for textual critics. Finally, this chapter has introduced a few key editions of the *Shepherd*. Such editions will be the primary way in which most researchers engage the text of the *Shepherd*. However, it is important to know something both about the manuscripts and translations upon which the text of an edition is based and about how the editors compiled the text.

The following chapter complements this chapter by exploring how the *Shepherd* was received by some of its earliest readers. By way of transition, this conclusion introduces two early Christian authors whose works contain extensive citations

---

88. Ehrman (2003, 2.162–473); Holmes (2007, 442–685).

89. Prinzivalli and Simonetti (2010–15, 2.177–489). Cecconi (2018, 285n.30) makes the exciting note that a new critical edition is already in the works.

90. Gebhardt, Harnack, and Zahn (1906, 129–215).

91. Lake (1912–13, 2.1–305).

from the *Shepherd*. These are Pseudo-Athanasius and Antiochus the Monk. The reason for including them at this point is that they could fit into either chapter. They are church fathers, so their works can be viewed in terms of reception. However, their works are often utilized in reconstructing the *Shepherd*'s text, which suggests that they should be included in this chapter.[92] They are included at this point to provide a transition from considering the manuscripts and translations of the *Shepherd* to reflecting on its early reception.

To begin with, Pseudo-Athanasius's *Praecepta ad Antiochum* (Ath) is found in two primary manuscripts. In the edition of this work edited by Dindorf, Codex Guelferbytanus Gudianus 51 is designated A.[93] The manuscript likely dates from the tenth century and includes excerpts from Mand. 1–10; 12. Dindorf's main contribution to the study of this text, however, was to add the evidence of a second manuscript. This manuscript is Codex Parisinus gr. 635, whose readings Dindorf marked as B.[94] The manuscript likely dates to the fourteenth century and contains portions of Mand. 1–10; 12; Sim. 5.3; 6. The extensive quotations of the *Shepherd* in Pseudo-Athanasius's fifth- or sixth-century work makes this text not only a valuable example of reception but also an indispensable witness for textual criticism of the Mandates.

The second text to mention comes from Antiochus the Monk (Ant), whose *Pandectes* contains portions of Mand. 2–3; 5–12; Sim. 1; 5.3; 9.31–32.[95] The *Pandectes* is a collection of sermons that Antiochus preached and that draw from the extensive library that was available in the seventh century at the monastic library in Mar Saba. Along with the *Shepherd*, Antiochus also quotes from pseudo-Clementine literature, Polycarp's *Philippians*, and the middle recension of Ignatius's letters.[96] Although some progress has been made in producing a critical edition of Antiochus's sermons,[97] a full edition is still needed. Nevertheless, the quotations from Antiochus's sermons cannot be ignored when studying either the reception or the text of the *Shepherd*.

With these two church fathers and their extensive excerpts from the *Shepherd* in view, this chapter on the text of the *Shepherd* can now give way to the chapter on the *Shepherd*'s reception.

---

92. E.g., see the listings of Pseudo-Athanasius and Antiochus the Monk in Körtner and Leutzsch (1998, 121); Holmes (2007, 449); Prinzivalli and Simonetti (2010–15, 218).

93. Dindorfius (1857, iv–vi).

94. Dindorfius (1857, iii–iv).

95. The text of Antiochus used here is PG 89.1421–1849. The citations from the *Shepherd* appear in *Pand.* 7; 15; 25; 29; 61; 66; 74; 77; 79; 85; 94; 98; 102; 110; 122; 127.

96. For an overview of extensive quotations from the Apostolic Fathers found in Antiochus's sermons, see Grant (1962, 427).

97. E.g., Gerardo Americano (2017a); Gerardo Americano (2017b).

Chapter 3

WHO READ THE *SHEPHERD*?

For those wanting to study the *Shepherd* directly, it may not be immediately obvious how this chapter can be useful. After all, the primary focus of this book is the *Shepherd* itself, not its reception. Although it is helpful to note that reception history has become a topic of interest in academic circles,[1] two further reasons can be given for why it is helpful to know something about who read the *Shepherd*. First, quotations of the *Shepherd* found in later writers can provide more evidence for what text of the *Shepherd* was available in the centuries after it was written. This chapter thus follows naturally from the previous one by giving an overview of early citations and references to the *Shepherd*. Second, studying early readers of the *Shepherd* can further illuminate how the *Shepherd* was interpreted by others and thereby inform modern-day interpretations.

This chapter will focus most of its attention on the reception of the *Shepherd* during the second through the fifth centuries.[2] Ecclesial writers from Irenaeus and Clement of Alexandria to Athanasius and John Cassian refer to the *Shepherd*. Some attention will then be given to how the *Shepherd* was received from the sixth century to the publication of the *editio princeps* in 1513. Along with the references to pseudo-Athanasius and Antiochus that were mentioned in Chapter 2, the citations in this chapter indicate continued knowledge of the *Shepherd*. In light of the popularity of the *Shepherd* and the authority that some early Christians attributed to the text, the chapter concludes by exploring a question that comes up often in studies of how the *Shepherd* was received, namely, what authority was attributed to the *Shepherd* by its readers?

---

1. See, for example, the *Journal of the Bible and Its Reception*, the *Encyclopedia of the Bible and Its Reception*, and the monograph series Studies of the Bible and Its Reception.

2. Due to limitations in my expertise and in the materials to which I have had access, the focus of this chapter is on textual reception. However, the *Shepherd* was also taken up in early Christian art, on which, see Brox (1991, 71–4); Osiek (1999, 7–8).

The Shepherd from the Second through the Fifth Centuries

Before taking up the complex question of authority, though, the chapter begins with the earliest extant references to the *Shepherd*. Writing at the end of the second century, Irenaeus provides the earliest quotations of the text. All of Irenaeus's quotations come from Mand. 1.1 (26.1) and identify God the Father as the creator of the world. For Irenaeus, this operates as both a fundamental truth that believers must confess and a polemical statement over and against those whom Irenaeus would label heretics and who believe that a demiurge of some sort created the physical world.

The clearest citations come from *Haer.* 4.20.2 and *Epid.* 4. As Irenaeus introduces the way in which God created the world through his hands, that is, through the Son and the Spirit, he insists, "First of all, believe that there is one God who created and ordered all things and made everything that exists from what does not exist and contains all things but alone is uncontained."[3] Irenaeus introduces this with a quotation formula: "Rightly, therefore, the writing that says" (καλῶς οὖν ἡ γραφὴ ἡ λέγουσα). It is thus clear that Irenaeus here employs a written text. Moreover, the quotation is virtually verbatim from Mand. 1.1 (26.1).[4] A similar quotation is found in *Epid.* 4: "And therefore it is proper, first of all, to believe that there is One God, the Father, who created and fashioned all things, who made that which was not to be, who contains all and is alone uncontainable."[5] No introductory formula is given in *Epid.* 4, but the similarities with Mand. 1.1 (26.1) along with the citation of the same passages in *Haer.* 4.20.2 make this citation almost certain. If so, Irenaeus quotes the *Shepherd* in both a polemical (*Haer.* 4.20.2) and a confessional (*Epid.* 4) writing.

Irenaeus also uses language that is similar to Mand. 1.1 (26.1) earlier in *Adversus Haereses*, but these references are shorter and less exact than the two that have already been examined. As in the clearer citations, so also these references to the *Shepherd* are used to emphasize God the Father's role as the one creator who cannot be contained. Thus Irenaeus argues against Marcus's depiction of Silence (Σιγή) as a revelatory agent by appealing to the Father's creation through the Word. Rather than dividing the Father, as Irenaeus accuses Marcus of doing, Irenaeus insists that the Father is "the one who contains all things but is uncontained by anything" (*Haer.* 1.15.5). In *Haer.* 2.30.9, Irenaeus again appeals to the Father's inability to be contained. Instead, God contains all things. Irenaeus cites the rule of truth (*regula*

---

3. Unless otherwise noted, all translations are my own. The text of Irenaeus, *Haer.* 4.20.2, is also quoted in Eusebius, *Hist. eccl.* 5.8.7.

4. Bertrand Hemmerdinger (1966, 308–9) proposes that Irenaeus also cites Mand. 26.1 in the preceding words of *Haer.* 4.20.1. While much of the vocabulary is similar, it is difficult to know whether or not to classify *Haer.* 4.20.1 as a reference to the *Shepherd*. It may be that Irenaeus simply employs similar vocabulary as he introduces the topic and quotation in *Haer.* 4.20.2. For further discussion, see Soyars (2019, 22–3).

5. Translation from Behr (1997, 42).

ueritatis) in *Haer.* 1.22.1 and speaks of the same Almighty God who creates and formed all things through the Word. He also made everything that exists from that which does not exist. Although similar language about God's creation can be found elsewhere in early Jewish and early Christian texts, the similarities with the *Shepherd* in order are striking.[6] If *Haer.* 1.22.1 is indebted in some way to Mand. 1.1 (26.1), then Irenaeus incorporates the language of the *Shepherd* into his rule of faith.[7] Given the use of the *Shepherd* elsewhere in Irenaeus's writings, this is not implausible.[8]

"The most enthusiastic early user" of the *Shepherd* was Clement of Alexandria.[9] A question from the *Shepherd* is found already in the opening words of what remains of Clement's *Strom.* 1.1.1 (1). The text begins in the middle of a sentence: "that you may read them at hand and may be able to keep them."[10] This phrase is also found in Vis. 5.5 (25.5). At this point in the *Shepherd*, the shepherd has just been introduced to Hermas and tells him that he should write what he sees and hears so that he can refer back to the shepherd's commands and keep them. Clement employs the *Shepherd* in his justification for writing his work. Just as Clement quotes the *Shepherd* at the start of Book 1, Clement places another quotation from the *Shepherd* in the final chapter of the book. Here Clement quotes from Vis. 3.4.3 (12.3): "'These visions,' she says, 'and the revelations are on account of the double-minded, who debate in their hearts whether or not these things are so'" (*Strom.* 1.181.1 [29]).[11] As Clement compares the relative youth of Greek philosophy to scripture, Clement's citation of the *Shepherd* portrays the Greeks as double-minded and indicates that revealed scripture is necessary for those who want to grow out of philosophy alone.

Clement discusses Greek philosophy at the beginning of Book 2 of the *Stromateis*. Early in the book, he urges those who want to know the truth to seek it out. He again quotes the *Shepherd* early in the book: "Whatever is allowed to be revealed to you will be revealed" (*Strom.* 2.3-5 [1]). The quotation is similar to Vis. 3.13.4 (21.4) and confirms Clement's exhortation to search diligently for truth. Later in Book 2, Clement quotes a series of passages from the *Shepherd* that include a summary of Vis. 3.8.3-6 (16.3-6; *Strom.* 2.55.3 [12]); a reference to Mand. 7.1-4 (37.1-4; *Strom.* 2.55.4-5 [12]); a loose quotation of Mand. 4.2.2 (30.2; *Strom.* 2.55.6 [12]); and what appears to be a summary of Mand. 4.2-3

---

6. See similarly, Batovici (2015b, 14-15). For similar wording to *Haer.* 1.22.1, note 2 Macc 7:28; Eph 3:6.

7. On the difference between Irenaeus's *regula* and his *hypothesis*, see Briggman (2015, 506-8; 2019, 14-16).

8. Other possible references may be found in Irenaeus, *Haer.* 2.2.2; 2.6.2; 2.10.2.

9. Osiek (1999, 5).

10. The beginning of Clement's *Stromateis* is no longer extant.

11. Reiling (1973, 179-80) notes this passage as one of several in which Clement describes Hermas as the recipient of revelation. The book's authority comes from the revealers rather than from Hermas. See also *Strom.* 2.3.5 (1); 6.131.2 (15).

(30–31; *Strom.* 2.55.6 [12]). Between the first two quotations in this series, there is a further citation that Clement attributes to the *Shepherd*: "Faith leads the way, fear builds up, and love perfects" (*Strom.* 2.55.4 [12]). Batovici notes that nothing in the *Shepherd* resembles Clement's quotation,[12] but it is worth noting that a similar role is given to faith and love at places in Ignatius's letters.[13]

Three points are particularly important to note regarding Clement's use of the *Shepherd*.[14] First, Clement refers to the text by name.[15] He thus provides another secure reference to the *Shepherd* at the turn from the second to the third century. Clement mentions Hermas in *Strom.* 1.181.1 (29); 2.3.5 (1); 6.131.2 (15), and he speaks of the shepherd in *Strom.* 2.43.5 (9); 2.55.3 (12); 4.74.4 (9); 6.46 (6). In addition to indicating knowledge of the text by name, Clement's citations are often close to the text that has been reconstructed in critical editions of the *Shepherd*.[16] For example, *Strom.* 1.1.1 (1) reproduces Vis. 5.5 (25.5) verbatim,[17] while *Strom.* 2.3.5 (1) cites a text that differs somewhat from Vis. 3.13.4 (21.4) but that is easily recognized as a quotation of the same text.[18] Although it is difficult to place Clement's reference to the *Shepherd* in *Strom.* 2.55.4 (12), there are enough citations to demonstrate Clement's knowledge of the Visions, Mandates, and Similitudes. Finally, Clement often employs an introductory formula that indicates his belief that the *Shepherd* was revealed.[19] This suggests that Clement understood Hermas to be a prophetic figure who received genuine visions.[20]

Not everyone was as enthusiastic about the *Shepherd* as Irenaeus and Clement, however. In his discussion of prayer, Tertullian takes up the *Shepherd* in a series of pragmatic reflections following his exegesis of the Lord's Prayer. Tertullian argues that it is not necessary for people to sit down when praying (*Or.* 16), an argument that it seems some people were making with reference to Vis. 5.1 (25.1). Following the four visions revealed by the woman, Hermas sits either while he prays or after

---

12. Batovici (2013, 46).

13. Ign. *Eph.* 9.1; 14.1; *Smyrn.* 6.1. See further Tarvainen (2016, 1–9; 1967, 16–23).

14. Other possible references to the *Shepherd* are found in *Strom.* 2.43.5–44.3 (9; Sim. 9.16.5–7 [93.5–7]); *Strom.* 2.56.1 (13; Mand. 4.3.2 [31.2]); *Strom.* 4.74.4 (9; Vis. 4.2.5 [23.5]); *Strom.* 6.46 (6; Sim. 9.16.6 [93.6]); *Strom.* 6.131.2 (15; Vis. 2.1.3–4 [5.3–4]).

15. Brooks (1992, 46).

16. On Clement's citation techniques more generally, see van den Hoek (1996).

17. Compare Clement's text in Stählin (1906, 3) to the *Shepherd* in Joly (1968, 142); Körtner and Leutzsch (1998, 190); Ehrman (2003, 2.236); Holmes (2007, 502); Prinzivalli and Simonetti (2010–15, 2.272–4).

18. Clement repeats the verb "reveal" (ἀποκαλύπτω) where the *Shepherd* only employs the verb once. Different expressions are used at the beginning of Clement's quotations as well. Clement uses "whatever" (ὃ ἐάν), while the *Shepherd* reads "if anything" (ἐάν τι). See further Stählin (1906, 114); Joly (1968, 132); Körtner and Leutzsch (1998, 182); Ehrman (2003, 2.226); Holmes (2007, 494); Prinzivalli and Simonetti (2010–15, 2.264).

19. E.g., *Strom.* 1.181.1 (29); 2.3.5 (1).

20. Batovici (2013, 50–1).

he prays. Tertullian argues that Hermas is describing what he did rather than prescribing a practice for all. He then shows that the argument employed by his opponents is absurd. If they are correct, Tertullian claims that they could only pray when there was a bed on which to sit.

Tertullian's adversarial stance toward the *Shepherd* only intensified as he aged.[21] When he writes about modesty in the early third century, Tertullian takes aim at the *Shepherd* for teaching that there is a second repentance. The *Shepherd* came to be remembered for allowing Hermas to repent after his lustful look at Rhoda (Vis. 1.1.2 [1.2]), and Tertullian refers to the *Shepherd* as a text that supports adulterers. Tertullian may have in mind the teaching that a woman who repents of adultery should be taken back by her husband (Mand. 4.1.7–8 [29.7–8]).[22] He insists that other church councils had declared the *Shepherd* apocryphal (*Pud.* 10.12), although the citations from Irenaeus and Clement along with Tertullian's own stringent counterarguments indicate that the text maintained a significant place in the church. Tertullian later refers to "the apocryphal *Shepherd* of the adulterers" (*illus apocryphus Pastor moechorum*; *Pud.* 20.2). In this brief statement, Tertullian dismisses the *Shepherd* as both apocryphal and too lenient in treating adultery.[23]

Tertullian's dismissal of the *Shepherd* can be contrasted somewhat with the cooler treatment of the Muratorian fragment, which lowers the authority of the *Shepherd* but allows it to have a place in the church. Discovered by Ludovico Antonius Muratori in Milan in the eighteenth century, the Muratorian fragment consists of eighty-five lines but is missing the beginning of the text. There has been considerable controversy regarding the date of this text since the middle of the twentieth century.[24] One reason for this discussion has to do with the claim in the Muratorian fragment that the *Shepherd* was written "very recently, in our times" (*nuperrim, e temporibus nostri*; 74). Although this phrase can be understood otherwise, it suggests a date in the second century.[25] The Muratorian fragment describes Hermas as the author of the *Shepherd* and as the brother of Pius, who was

---

21. See further D'Alès (1905, 229).

22. Brox (1991, 206); Osiek (1999, 111); Bandini (2001, 127).

23. The Coptic Apocalypse of Peter (NHC VII, 3) refers to a man named Hermas as "the firstborn of unrighteousness" (78.18–19). This appears to be a caustic and dismissive statement that is similar to Tertullian. See further Koschorke (1978, 54–60); Havelaar (1999, 96–7).

24. For summary and evaluation, see Verheyden (2003); Schnabel (2014). The controversy can be traced in many ways to Albert C. Sundberg, who argued that the Muratorian fragment should be dated to the fourth century (1968; 1973). Sundberg's arguments were developed by Hahneman (1992; 2002). Everett Ferguson provided a response to Sundberg in which he maintained that the Muratorian fragment can be dated to the second or third century (1982). For continued discussion of the date of this text, see also Henne (1993); Armstrong (2008); Rothschild (2018); Guignard (2019).

25. I am inclined to accept a date near the end of the second or in the early third century (see similarly Markschies 2015, 208). Although this decision has implications for the authority of the *Shepherd* discussed at the end of the chapter, it does not have significant

bishop of Rome in the middle of the second century.[26] This suggests that Hermas may have had an important place in the church, and this respect is extended to the text of the *Shepherd*, which "ought to be read, therefore. But it should not be read publicly in the church either among the Prophets, which are complete in number, nor among the Apostles, for it is after their time."[27] The Muratorian fragment thus distinguishes between the writings of the Prophets and Apostles and grants the *Shepherd* less authority. The *Shepherd* cannot be read publicly when believers gather together. Yet the Muratorian fragment indicates that the *Shepherd* should be read. Tertullian and the Muratorian fragments exemplify contrasting ways to lower the authority of the *Shepherd*. Tertullian castigates the text, while the Muratorian fragment relegates it to private reading.

The *Shepherd* continued to enjoy popularity in the third century among writers such as pseudo-Cyprian, Origen, and Commodian.[28] In a tractate written against gambling and playing dice, pseudo-Cyprian refers to Sim. 9.31.5–6 (108.5–6) as divine scripture (*scriptura divina*; *Aleat*. 2).[29] Quoting from this part of the *Shepherd*, he warns, "Woe to the shepherds!"[30] Although the parallels are not exact, pseudo-Cyprian's admonition is followed by a list of questions that is similar to Sim. 9.31.6 (108.6).[31] The series of questions may have been adapted to suit pseudo-Cyprian's context. A second passage is referred to in *Aleat*. 4. As pseudo-Cyprian urges his hearers to stay away from those who gamble if they want to pursue justice, he cites a series of passages that includes Mand. 4.1.9 (29.9). The citation again does not match the text of the *Shepherd* exactly, yet it is again reminiscent of the *Shepherd* and indicates that pseudo-Cyprian knew and respected the *Shepherd*.[32]

Origen lived in Alexandria and moved to Caesarea in the early 230s. Origen employs Mand. 1.1 (26.1) at multiple points in *De principiis*.[33] In his discussion of

bearing on how the *Shepherd*'s authority should be understood within the Muratorian fragment.

26. A similar connection between Hermas and Pius is made in Pseudo-Tertullian, *Carm. Marc.* 3.293–295.

27. *Ideo legi eum quide oportet se pu / plicare uero in ecclesia populo neque inter / profetas conpletum numero neqe inter / apostolos in fine temporum* (77–80; Lietzmann 1902, 8–10).

28. Another text worth mentioning from this time is Hippolytus's *Refutation of All Heresies*. The author describes Alcibiades, who describes the source of his revelation as an angelic man who was twenty-four reeds tall (about 5.8 kilometers). There is a female angel with him, who is identified as the Holy Spirit. However, the male is identified as the Son of God (*Ref.* 9.13.2–3). A similarly tall man is identified as the Son of God in Sim. 9.6.1 (83.1); 9.12.8 (89.8). See further Joly (1968) (SC 53), 300n.1; Litwa (2016, 661n.98).

29. For discussion of this phrase, see Brox (1991, 63).

30. Carroll (1991, 88n.23) notes similarities with Ezek 34:2, but the parallels with the *Shepherd* are closer.

31. See the helpful synopsis in Gleede (2016, 252).

32. On the use of the *Shepherd* in *de Aleatoribus*, see Harnack (1888, 126–8); Gleede (2016, 249–52).

33. *Princ.* 1. Praef. 4; 1.3.3; 2.1.5.

the Holy Spirit, Origen strengthens his argument that the Holy Spirit is not part of creation by appealing to the unity of God and to the *Shepherd*.

> For even in that little book, which is called *The Shepherd* or *The Angel of Repentance* and which Hermas wrote, it is thus recounted: "First of all, believe that God is one, who created and brought together all things, who made everything exist when nothing existed, who contains all things but is contained by no one." (*Princ.* 1.3.3)[34]

Like Irenaeus before him, Origen refers to the opening of the Mandates to demonstrate that God is one and the creator (Mand. 1.1 [26.1]). Origen employs the *Shepherd* when describing how scripture should be interpreted in Book 4. Just as Hermas was told to speak to the elders, Grapte was to teach the widows and orphans, and Clement to communicate with the cities (Vis. 2.4.3 [8.3]), so Origen argues that scripture must be interpreted in three ways. He provides a further analogy with human beings, who are said to be composed of bodies, souls, and spirits. Along with the body, the *Shepherd* provides an example that Origen uses to support his multiple ways of interpreting scripture (*Princ.* 4.2.4).[35]

Citations of the *Shepherd* are not restricted to Origen's systematic writings alone. They are also found in his sermons and commentaries. He employs the shepherd's description of different perceptions of time during sin and repentance in Sim. 6.4.4 (64.4) when he preaches on Num 14:33–34 (*Hom. Num.* 8). When discussing Ps 37:2 (*Hom. Ps.* 37.1.1), Origen refers to the angel of repentance (*angelus paenitentiae*) whom the shepherd describes to Hermas in Sim. 6.3.2–3 (63.2–3). The same passage also seems to be in view in Origen's commentary on Romans. Origen again refers to the suffering that comes at the hand of the angel of repentance when introducing Hermas in *Comm. Rom.* 10.31. In addition, Origen is the first to connect the Hermas mentioned in Rom 16:14 to the character who receives visions in the *Shepherd*.[36] Origen's freedom in citing the *Shepherd* indicates that he knew the text well.[37] It also suggests that he had access to the text. Moreover, he grants an authority to the *Shepherd* in his arguments that is enhanced by the

---

34. "Nam et in eo libello qui 'Pastoris' dicitur, 'angeli paenitentiae', quem Hermas conscripsit, ita refertur: 'Primo omnium crede quia unus est deus, qui omnia creauit atque conposuit; qui cum nihil esset prius, esse fecit omnia; qui est omnia capiens, ipse uero a nemeine capitur'" (Origen, *Princ.* 1.3.3).

35. Dorival (2013, 619). The *Shepherd* is also referenced at *Princ.* 3.4.2 (Mand. 6.2.1–10 [36.1–10]). Origen also refers to Mand. 6.2 in *Hom. Luc.* 35.3 with reference to Luke 12:58–59.

36. See the translation of *Comm. Rom.* 10.31 in Scheck (2002, 296–7).

37. See other references to the *Shepherd* in Origen, *Comm. Matt.* 59 (Mand. 12.5.3 [48.3]); *Hom. Jes. Nav.* 10.1 (Sim. 2.2–4.8 [51.2–53.8]); *Comm. Matt.* 53 (Sim. 3.1–4.8 [52.1–53.8]); *Hom. Ezech.* 13.3 (Sim. 9.13.1–9.14.5 [90.1–91.5]). On the use of the *Shepherd* by Origen, see Harnack (1919, 34–6).

book's connections to a man named in Paul's letter to the Romans. Origen thus grants the *Shepherd* a respected place among the books that he utilizes.

Likely writing in the middle of the third century,[38] Commodian's *Instructiones* contains a series of Latin poems that discuss how the Christian life should be lived. As Commodian discusses the relationship between rich and poor (*Instr.* 30),[39] he appeals to the imagery of elm and vine. The rich should not despise those around them. Rather, "As the elm loves the vine, so you [the rich] love those who are insignificant" (*Instr.* 30.16).[40] The imagery of the elm and vine can be found elsewhere,[41] but Gleede rightly points out that Commodian does not merely employ similar imagery. He applies the imagery to rich and poor, just as the shepherd does when speaking to Hermas (Sim. 2.1–10 [51.1–10]).[42] Later in the text, Commodian discusses false peace when he writes, "Either obey the law of the city or go out from it" (*Instr.* 65.4).[43] In Sim. 1.4 (50.4), the shepherd speaks for God and similarly tells Hermas, "Either use my laws or get out of my city."[44] It is possible that Commodian is not here indebted to the *Shepherd*, since Commodian speaks of historical cities rather than a metaphorical one as in the *Shepherd*.[45] In light of the similarities between *Instr.* 30 and Sim. 2 (51), however, it is more likely that Commodian makes reference to the *Shepherd* in *Instr.* 65.

While the authority of the *Shepherd* was mixed among some of its earliest readers, the canon lists of the fourth and fifth centuries categorize the *Shepherd* more definitively as a text that was useful to read but not scriptural. Although Eusebius reports that Irenaeus accepted the *Shepherd* as scripture (*Hist. eccl.* 5.8.7),[46] he is skeptical of proposals like the one put forth by Origen, namely, that the Hermas mentioned in the *Shepherd* is the same man greeted by Paul in Rom 16:14 (*Hist. eccl.* 3.3.6).[47] Accordingly, Eusebius does not place the *Shepherd* in his

---

38. For more on the date of Commodian, see Goodspeed (1946); Poinsotte (2009, xiii–xvi).

39. Numbering of Commodian's text follows ANF 4.

40. "Sicut ulmus amat uitem, sic ipsi pusillos."

41. Catullus 62.48–57; Ovid, *Am.* 2.16.41; *Metam.* 14.661–668. See further Chapter 7 of this volume.

42. Gleede (2016, 253–4). Writing after Commodian, Ambrose may also refer to the *Shepherd* when discussing a vine in the context of the third day of creation (*Hex.* 3.12.50). However, if he refers to the *Shepherd*, the citation comes from Sim. 5.5.3 (58.3). For Ambrose, the vine represents members of the church, and it is protected by a fence of heavenly precepts and a guard of angels.

43. "Aut facite legem ciuitatis aut exite de illa."

44. "Aut legibus meis utere aut recede de ciuitate mea." Although A reads "country" (χώρα), L¹ reads "city" (*ciuitas*). Since Commodian wrote in Latin, I follow the Vulgate translation.

45. So Gleede (2016, 253).

46. Eusebius quotes Irenaeus, *Haer.* 4.20.2.

47. See Origen, *Comm. Rom.* 10.31.

list of the New Testament scriptures (*Hist. eccl.* 3.25.1–7). Rather, the *Shepherd* is listed with the *Acts of Paul*, the *Apocalypse of Peter*, the *Epistle of Barnabas*, and the *Didache* among the books which are not confessed (ἀντιλεγούμενα; *Hist. eccl.* 3.25.4).[48] Rufinus, who translated Eusebius's *Ecclesiastical History* into Latin,[49] follows Eusebius in not placing the *Shepherd* among the canonical books (*Sym.* 37). Rather, Rufinus argues that the *Shepherd* belongs in a secondary group that he calls "ecclesiastical" (*ecclesiastica*). This list includes the *Shepherd*, Wisdom of Solomon, Ben Sira, Tobit, Judith, the books of the Maccabees, and the Two Ways (*Sym.* 38). Writing in 367 CE, Athanasius likewise separates the *Shepherd* from the Old and New Testaments. The Wisdom of Solomon, Ben Sira, Esther, Judith, Tobit, the *Didache*, and the *Shepherd* belong to another category. Athanasius clarifies that the Old and New Testaments are included in the canon, while the *Shepherd* and other books are books that should be read (*Ep. fest.* 39.7).

All of these claims distinguish the *Shepherd* and other books from those included in scripture. However, they grant a place for Christians to read these books. Nowhere is this clearer than in the writings of Athanasius. Although he would eventually place the *Shepherd* outside the canon, references to the *Shepherd* may be found at several points in his writings. In one of Athanasius's earliest writings, he contrasts his understanding of the biblical creation account ex nihilo with spontaneous creation and creation out of preexistent matter. In order to do this, Athanasius appeals to Gen 1:1, Mand. 1.1 (26.1), and Heb 11:3. Athanasius's quotation of the *Shepherd* closely follows the text printed in modern critical editions except that Athanasius does not repeat "all things" (τὰ πάντα).[50] Moreover, Athanasius introduces the citation as God speaking "through the particularly helpful book of the Shepherd" (*Inc.* 3.1). This sets the citation of the *Shepherd* apart from the way that God spoke through Moses and Paul.[51] Athanasius again juxtaposes Heb 11:3 and Mand. 1.1 (26.1) in his account of what happened at the Council of Nicaea, arguing that the *Shepherd* does not include the Son of God among the things that God creates (*Decr.* 18.3). He cites Mand. 1.1 (26.1) in his festal letter of 339 (*Ep. fest.* 11.4) and his letter to the bishops of Africa (*Ep. Afr.* 5). Like Irenaeus before him, Athanasius shows an affinity for this passage from the *Shepherd*. Yet it is not the only passage from the *Shepherd* that Athanasius knows. He refers to the *Shepherd* when discussing the actions of the Eusebians at Nicaea. Athanasius characterizes their initial commendation of the council's statement

---

48. Eusebius also is aware of the use of the *Shepherd* for catechetical purposes (*Hist. eccl.* 3.3.6).

49. Humphries (2008) offers a helpful analysis of the quality of Rufinus's translation.

50. Athanasius's quotation reads πρῶτον πάντων πίστευσον ὅτι εἷς ἐστὶν ὁ θεὸς, ὁ τὰ πάντα κτίσας καὶ καταρτίσας καὶ ποιήσας ἐκ τοῦ μὴ ὄντος εἰς τὸ εἶναι (*Inc.* 3.1), while the text of the *Shepherd* repeats the words τὰ πάντα at the end of this quotation. See Prinzivalli and Simonetti (2010–15, 2.274).

51. The attribution of Hebrews to Paul is in keeping with Athanasius's comments in *Ep. fest.* 11.2; 39.5.

and later complaints against the statement as double-minded (δίψυχος; *Decr.* 4.2). After referring to Jas 1:8, Athanasius reminds his readers that such double-mindedness is the child of the devil and uses a similar phrase to Mand. 9.9 (39.9) in order to make his claim.[52]

Athanasius's Alexandrian contemporary, Didymus the Blind, also made use of the *Shepherd* in his commentaries on Zechariah and Job. When Didymus comes to the woman of lawlessness who is mentioned in Zech 5:8, he points out that women signify both vices and virtues elsewhere in scripture. In this list, he also points out that many things are brought forth through women "in the book of catechesis which is called the Shepherd" (*Comm. Zach.* 86.24–27).[53] Likewise, Didymus refers to the *Shepherd* alongside references to the destruction of the Ethiopians in Zeph 2:12 (*Comm. Zach.* 234.19–22; see similarly 355.20–24).[54] Ehrman points out that both references to the *Shepherd* are likewise linked with references to the *Epistle of Barnabas*, and he is probably right to see Didymus as having a passage like Sim. 9.19.1 (96.1) in mind, in which the black mountain that Hermas sees represents the dwelling of apostates and blasphemers.[55] Didymus draws from Hermas's earlier vision of the tower when commenting on Job 8:17 as he notes that the ungodly person lives among stones that do not fit together "in the building of the tower, according to the Shepherd" (*Comm. Job*; see similarly Vis. 3.2.7 [10.7]). Finally, Didymus refers to the instruction not to slander in Mand. 2.2 (27.2) when commenting on Job 6:28 (*Comm. Job*).

Two of Didymus's younger Latinophone contemporaries also employed the *Shepherd* in their writings. Jerome closely follows Origen's interpretation of Paul's letters. He had read many of Origen's works, translated some of his commentaries on Paul's letters, and continued to employ Origen's exegesis even after the Origenist

---

52. "Now this, as the Shepherd has said, is a child of the devil" (τοῦτο δὲ, ὡς ὁ Ποιμὴν εἴρηκεν, ἔκγονόν ἐστι διαβόλου; *Decr.* 4.3). The shepherd tells Hermas, "This double-mindedness is a daughter of the devil" (αὕτη ἡ διψυχία θυγάτηρ ἐστὶ τοῦ διαβόλου; Mand. 9.9 [39.9]). Hans-Georg Opitz (1935, 4) does not view Athanasius's words as a reference to the *Shepherd*. However, the references to the *Shepherd* elsewhere in Athanasius's works, Athanasius's explicit reference to the *Shepherd*, and the similar concepts in his statement suggest that this passage should be included as a reference to the *Shepherd* within Athanasius's corpus.

53. Ehrman (1983, 12) points out that the reference to the *Shepherd* follows a list of references that is ordered canonically and argues, in part from this observation, that the *Shepherd* is part of Didymus's canon. However, the *Shepherd* is also the only book in the list to be referred to as a "book of catechesis," which may indicate that the *Shepherd* belongs in a different category.

54. Didymus connects the *Shepherd* to the *Epistle of Barnabas*, particularly *Barn.* 4.10; 20.1, where the devil is mentioned with reference to black color. See further Rothschild (2019, 236).

55. Ehrman (1983, 12–13).

controversy broke out in the late fourth century.⁵⁶ It should come as no surprise, then, that Jerome follows Origen in describing Hermas as both the author of the *Shepherd* and the man whom Paul greeted in Rom 16:14 (*Vir. ill.* 10). The *Shepherd* is said to be a useful book that is quoted as an authority by various ancient writers. Jerome notes that the *Shepherd* is read publically (*publice*) in some Greek churches, but he claims that the book is almost unknown among Latin speakers (*Vir. ill.* 10). Nevertheless, the presence of quotations in the writings not only of Tertullian and pseudo-Cyprian but also of Rufinus and John Cassian suggests that Jerome's statement should not be read flatly.⁵⁷

Writing at approximately the same time in southern Gaul, John Cassian refers to the *Shepherd* twice in his *Conferences*. In a wide-ranging conversation about principalities and power, Cassian reports that Abbot Serenus believed there were two angels that cling to each person. One angel is good, and examples are found in Matt 18:10, Ps 34:8 (33:8 LXX), and Acts 12:15. The other angel is evil, and the encounters of Job and Judas with the devil are cited as examples. However, the *Shepherd* is said to be a book that "teaches fully" about both sorts of angels (*Conf.* 8.17). Although no explicit citation is given, Cassian seems to have in mind passages like Mand. 6.2.1–10 (36.1–10) and Sim. 6.2.1–6.5.7 (62.1–65.7). The discussion in the Mandates immediately follows the discussion of the two ways in the *Shepherd* (Mand. 6.1–5 [35.1–5]).⁵⁸ Like the two ways, the two angels are characterized by righteousness and evil (Mand. 6.2.1 [36.1]).⁵⁹ In the Similitudes, one angel is referred to as the angel of luxury and deception (Sim. 6.2.1 [62.1]), while the other is called the angel of punishment, who is one of the just angels (Sim. 6.3.2 [63.2]). John Cassian refers to the same line of thought in the *Shepherd* in *Conf.* 13.12. He reports that there are two angels that surround a person. In a long list of scriptural passages that are intended to illustrate the role that freedom of the will plays for human beings, he refers to the *Shepherd* and declares that people are free to choose which of the angels that they will follow.

The Shepherd *from the Sixth through the Fifteenth Centuries*

For those who are interested in studying the *Shepherd* itself, it is most helpful to have an understanding of how widely the text was read from the second through the fifth centuries. The number of references to the book dwindled in the following centuries, especially in what was the eastern part of the Roman Empire. "Yet in the West, *Hermas* seems never to have completely disappeared."⁶⁰ As the face of

---

56. Schatkin (1970, 50). On the relationship between Jerome and Origen, see further Hammond Bammel (1981; 1996); Heine (2000).

57. See similarly Osiek (1999, 6–7). For more on Jerome's citation of the *Shepherd*, see Brox (1991, 68).

58. See the similar imagery of two ways in *Did.* 1.1–6.2; *Barn.* 18.1–20.2.

59. Hwang (2010, 98n.22).

60. Osiek (1999, 7).

Europe changed drastically over the next millennium, the various ways in which the *Shepherd* was referenced suggests that the text continued to be studied in monastic and episcopal settings.

A reference to the *Shepherd* is found in Codex Claromontanus, a codex that contains a Western text of the Pauline epistles. A catalogue of biblical books has been inserted into the codex between the letters of Philemon and Hebrews. Although Codex Claromontanus probably dates from the fifth to the seventh centuries,[61] it is unclear when the catalogue was composed. It has been included here because of its place in an early manuscript. The catalogue is unusual because it omits Philippians, 1–2 Thessalonians, and Hebrews, while it includes the *Epistle of Barnabas*,[62] the *Shepherd*, the *Acts of Paul*, and the *Apocalypse of Peter*.[63] Although the reason why this catalogue was composed is unclear, the inclusion of the *Shepherd* alongside other scriptural books suggests a high degree of respect for the *Shepherd*.

In the sixth century, Caesarius of Arles employed the imagery of the elm and vine as the guiding imagery of one of his sermons. In *Sermon 27*, he introduces the sermon by saying, "We read in a certain book" (*legimus in quodam libro*; *Serm*. 27.1). Marie-José Delage rightly observes that Caesarius here refers to Sim. 2.[64] The elm and the vine represent the rich and the poor in both Caesarius's sermon and in the *Shepherd* (*Serm*. 27.1; Sim. 2.4 [51.4]). Caesarius notes that the elm is unable to produce fruit on its own, while the vine's fruit will rot on the ground and must be lifted up. He urges the rich to alleviate the financial burdens placed on the poor so that the poor can read scripture, pray, and keep their vigils. Caesarius connects the imagery of the *Shepherd* to Paul's desire for some believers' abundance to supply others' needs (2 Cor 8:14) and to Jesus's description of what happens to trees that bear good fruit (Matt 7:17–20; *Serm*. 27.2). As the sermon continues, the imagery of elm and vine is further

---

61. Fifth century: Parker (2008, 259–60); Houghton (2016, 243); sixth century: Aland, Hannick, and Junack (1980, 123). The codex is listed as a seventh-century manuscript by the Bibliothèque Nationale de France, where the manuscript is described and preserved (https://archivesetmanuscrits.bnf.fr/ark:/12148/cc21107b; accessed August 29, 2020).

62. B. F. Westcott understands *Barnabae Epistula* as another name for *Epistula ad Hebraeos* (1875, 557n.1). Since Hebrews follows the catalogue in the codex, one point in favor of Westcott's argument would be if the catalogue listed the letters contained in the codex. However, since the catalogue was inserted into the codex later, it is not clear whether the catalogue is referring to Hebrews or to the *Epistle of Barnabas* that is now included in collections of the Apostolic Fathers. On balance, it seems better to understand Codex Claromontanus as referring to the *Epistle of Barnabas*.

63. For the text, see Tischendorff (1852, 468–9); Westcott (1875, 555–7). Codex Claromontanus (BnF gr. 107) can be viewed online at https://gallica.bnf.fr/ark:/12148/btv1b84683111 (accessed August 29, 2020). The catalogue is found on folios 467v, 468r, and 468v.

64. Delage (1978, 93n.2).

intertwined with Jesus's words in the Gospels and with Paul's letters before Caesarius concludes by urging his listeners to strive to be good servants who can enter into their Master's joy (*Serm.* 27.3; see Matt 25:21–23). Although it is not clear why the *Shepherd* is referred to as a "certain book," the elm and the vine are interpreted in line with the way in which the imagery is used in the *Shepherd* and is brought into alignment with the New Testament. The *Shepherd* is important in at least one of Caesarius's sermons and provides the structural image upon which the rest of the sermon is built.

Moving forward a few centuries, Hildegard of Bingen describes a vision that she had with imagery that is reminiscent of the most enduring image in the *Shepherd*: the tower of Vis. 3 (9.1–21.4) and Sim. 9 (78.1–110.3). Writing in the twelfth century, Hildegard describes a brilliantly splendid tower in *Scivias* 3.9. The tower is set in the south side of the wall of a building, and four women stand in the tower ready to resist the devil. These women are Wisdom, Justice, Fortitude, and Sanctity (*Sciv.* 3.9.1–6). Although the identities and the number of the women differ from the *Shepherd*, in which there are seven (Vis. 3.8.1–8 [16.1–8]) or twelve (Sim. 9.2.3–4 [79.3–4]; 9.15.1–2 [92.1–2]), the presence of women in a tower is suggestive of what is found in the *Shepherd*.[65] Yet the strongest resonances come when Hildegard describes the tower. She sees the construction of the tower beginning after the Son becomes incarnate. The tower is fortified against the enemy, and Hildegard proclaims that the tower represents the church (*Sciv.* 3.9.7). As Hildegard's vision continues, she notes that the splendor of the tower represents the light that is given to the church by the Son's humanity (*Sciv.* 3.9.8). Although mortal human beings cannot comprehend fully what God is doing in the church (*Sciv.* 3.9.10), the teachers in the church are enabled to call back into the tower those who are in error (*Sciv.* 3.9.14). Hildegard does not quote the *Shepherd* exactly.[66] The metaphor has been modified from what is found in either account of the tower in the *Shepherd*, and Hildegard mixes imagery in a way that is uniquely her own. Nevertheless, Hildegard identifies the church as a tower in one of her visions and sees women placed at various points in the tower. However Hildegard may have come by this experience, the literary form contains striking similarities to the *Shepherd* and suggests that the *Shepherd* was still known in medieval Europe.

Although this chapter stops its study of the reception of the *Shepherd* with the 1513 publication of the text by Jacques Le Fèvre d'Etaples, further comparisons with other authors might be carried out to show additional similarities between the *Shepherd* and medieval allegorical and visionary literature. Theodore Bogdanos finds that the Visions of the *Shepherd* provided a prototype which authors as diverse as Boethius (*Consolations of Philosophy*), Langland (*Piers Plowman*), and Dante (*Divine Comedy*) utilized to inform their writing.[67] Yet this is not a book

---

65. See similarly Newman (1990, 39).

66. For more on the *Shepherd* in Hildegard's writings, see Mews (2000, 48–9); Huber (2013, 96, 104).

67. Bogdanos (1977).

solely about the reception of the *Shepherd*, and an important question should yet be considered when discussing the *Shepherd*. This concerns the kind of authority the *Shepherd* had in the first few centuries after it was written.

The Authority of the Shepherd among Early Readers

After exploring some of the ways in which the *Shepherd* continued to exercise influence on texts that were written for centuries after the composition of the *Shepherd*, the question of the *Shepherd*'s authority can be asked with increased clarity. In some scholarship, questions regarding the *Shepherd*'s authority have been framed in terms of canonicity. Was the *Shepherd* part of a specific author's canon? How does an author's use of the *Shepherd* differ from how they employ other books that came to be in the New Testament? Are there additional categories or ways of framing this question that may better fit the *Shepherd*'s context within the early Christian world?

Some authors utilize the *Shepherd* in a way that is difficult to differentiate from how they refer to other scriptural texts. For example, Steenberg argues that Irenaeus's reference to Mand. 1.1 (26.1) as γραφή in *Haer.* 4.20.2 should be understood as a reference to *scripture* rather than a *writing*.[68] If this is so, one might reason further that the *Shepherd* should be included in a list of Irenaeus's authoritative books alongside other books now included in the Old and New Testaments. Ehrman argues that this is the case in the writings of Didymus the Blind, even as Eusebius and Athanasius, two of Didymus's fourth-century counterparts, excluded the *Shepherd* from their canonical lists. When looking at the use of the *Shepherd* to comment on lawlessness in Zech 5:8, Ehrman finds that Didymus refers to the *Shepherd* both to interpret scripture and to substantiate a figurative interpretation of a passage elsewhere in scripture. Such usage indicates to Ehrman that the *Shepherd* has the same level of authority as scripture.[69] Yet not all are convinced. Returning to Irenaeus, Hill contends that the use of γραφή in *Haer.* 4.20.2 with reference to the *Shepherd* varies from other uses of the word

---

68. "'The scripture rightly says' is an ascription thus made to the whole collection of texts, offered in authoritative witness to his cosmological points—texts drawn from *Hermas*, Malachias, Paul, and Christ. Irenaeus' whole intention in *Haer.* 4 is to add to his theological defense from the writings of scripture, and here he does precisely this" (Steenberg 2009, 64).

69. Quite instructive is the progression Didymus follows in his discussion—from the books of the OT to the Gospels, to the Pauline epistles, to Revelation, to Hermas. Here the Shepherd is paralleled to the other canonical books in order to validate a figurative interpretation of Zechariah. Hence, in its use and in its relation to other books of the canon the Shepherd is again construed as canonical (Ehrman 1983, 12).

which denote books now found in Christian scripture.⁷⁰ It is necessary, then, to reflect on the relationship between canon, scripture, and authority. This chapter will maintain its focus on issues of authority in historical writers rather than engaging in an ontological discussion of the canon.⁷¹

Before progressing further, it will be helpful to highlight the various issues that suggest to some that the *Shepherd* was given roughly equal authority to the books that eventually comprised the New Testament and to others that the *Shepherd* was placed in a separate category. In a recent review article on canonicity and the *Shepherd*, Batovici highlights four ways in which the *Shepherd* was received. These observations suggest that early readers attributed a high level of authority to the *Shepherd*, but the precise level of authority is difficult to determine.⁷² All four have been discussed over the course of the previous two chapters, and they can be briefly summarized here.

First, the *Shepherd* was quoted as an authoritative text by authors such as Irenaeus, Clement of Alexandria, Origen, and Didymus the Blind. Although it is difficult enough to determine if the *Shepherd* had precisely the same level of authority as, for example, the Pauline letters, in any individual author,⁷³ the difficulty of determining the level of authority that the *Shepherd* held across various segments of the church is enhanced by the clear demarcations drawn by Tertullian, Eusebius, and Athanasius. A second set of evidence is the number of papyri that have preserved the *Shepherd*. Choat and Yuen-Collingridge compare the preservation of the *Shepherd* to the four Gospels that came to be included in the New Testament in pre-Constantinian papyri. They find eleven papyrus copies of the *Shepherd* from that time. On the other hand, they find one papyrus of

---

70. Hill argues against Steenberg (2009) that Irenaeus's use of γραφή in *Haer.* 4.20.2 is qualified. If this is correct, Hill would move Irenaeus's use of the word in this passage into a different category from Steenberg. "But if he did not consider SH to be Scripture, why would Irenaeus use the term ἡ γραφή at all when referring to it? It seems to me that he did so precisely because he had no 'Scriptural' category for this writing" (Hill 2013, 131). On Irenaeus's view of the *Shepherd* vis-à-vis scripture, see also Brox (1991, 57–61); Batovici (2015b).

71. For a nuanced discussion of issues relating to canonicity, see Kruger (2012).

72. Batovici (2017a). On the issues and difficulty surrounding the *Shepherd* and canon, see also Schröter (2015, 168–9).

73. To mention two examples drawn from scholarship on Clement of Alexandria, Brooks cites the use of the *Apocalypse of Peter*, the *Preaching of Peter*, the *Shepherd*, and the *Epistle of Barnabas* and concludes that "it is possible—even probable" that Clement recognized certain texts as scriptural that are not contained in the later New Testament canon (1992, 47). Citing a slightly different list of books, Cosaert prefaces his remarks by noting that "it is impossible to say definitively what additional books Clement would include in his New Testament canon" (Cosaert 2008, 22n.8). In light of the difficulty of determining precisely which books were thought to be of the highest level of authority, such caution only seems to be appropriate.

Mark, six of Luke, fourteen of Matthew, and seventeen of John.[74] Third and closely related, the *Shepherd* is included at the end of S, a codex containing primarily texts that are now included in the Christian canon. The evidence is difficult to interpret in terms of canonicity, and scholars are divided on the issue. Christopher Tuckett understands the *Shepherd*'s place in S as evidence for canonicity,[75] while Norbert Brox does not think that the inclusion in Sinaiticus is intended to mark the *Shepherd* out as canonical.[76] Finally, the Muratorian fragment plays a role in discussions of the *Shepherd*'s authority because the fragment limits the purpose for which the *Shepherd* can be read. The *Shepherd* ought to be read, but it should not be read publically and is not included among the books of the prophets or apostles.[77] Yet ambiguities regarding the date, purpose, and authority of the Muratorian fragment allow for multiple interpretations of the text.

With these observations firmly in view, one may now notice that scholars who argue that the *Shepherd* held an authority among early Christians which was comparable to texts later included in the New Testament highlight different portions of the evidence from scholars who place the *Shepherd* in a lesser category.[78] For the former, references to the *Shepherd* by Irenaeus, Clement of Alexandria, Origen, and Didymus are adduced alongside the inclusion of the *Shepherd* in S to show that the *Shepherd* was used in an analogous way to texts that were placed in the New Testament. The number of papyri may also be brought in as evidence, while the testimonies of the Muratorian fragment and Tertullian are downplayed.[79] Conversely, scholars who find a clear differentiation between the *Shepherd* and texts that would come to be in the New Testament highlight the claims of the Muratorian fragment regarding the composition of the *Shepherd* "in our times" (74), emphasize the clear separations of the *Shepherd* from the New Testament in the writings of Eusebius and Athanasius, and argue that the *Shepherd* is placed at the end of S as an appendix. Citations of the *Shepherd* in Irenaeus and others tend to be viewed with less importance, and the amount of papyri can be explained in terms of piety and popularity rather than authority or canonicity.

This strict bifurcation oversimplifies the state of scholarship by focusing on ways in which the evidence can be interpreted to fit a definite division. Nevertheless, it captures something important when reviewing discussions of how the

---

74. Choat and Yuen-Collingridge (2010, 196). The publication of P134 (John), P137 (Mark), and P138 (Luke) would add more witnesses to Choat and Yuen-Collingridge's count for each of these Gospels.

75. Tuckett (2014, 172n.51). See also Elliott (1996, 111) and Ehrman (2003, 2.169).

76. Brox (1991, 71).

77. Turner (1913) interprets this statement as evidence, along with his observations about how S was compiled, that the *Shepherd* was in fact transmitted among the prophets.

78. I am indebted to Batovici (2017a, 104) for this observation.

79. Some have also dated the Muratorian fragment to the fourth century, which would further undercut its utility in discussions of how the *Shepherd*'s earliest readers viewed its authority. See, e.g., Sundberg (1973); Hahneman (1992).

Shepherd was understood by early writers with regard to canonicity. A sharp dichotomy that sees the *Shepherd* as either canonical or non-canonical is, if not false, at least unhelpful when considering the *Shepherd* in the second and third centuries. In order to more accurately define the term *canon*, Kruger has proposed a multifaceted definition in exclusive, functional, and ontological terms.[80] The historical questions about how authors in the second and third centuries understood the *Shepherd*'s role in the church might then be most appropriately considered as part of the functional canon. Sundberg follows a study by W. C. van Unnik when he distinguishes the term *scripture*, defined as "writings regarded as in some sense authoritative," from *canon*, defined as "a closed collection of scripture to which nothing can be added, nothing subtracted."[81] McDonald makes a similar distinction between two different meanings of canon. Although all language regarding canon has limitations, "canon 1" refers to "those texts or traditions that functioned authoritatively in their communities," while "canon 2" denotes "those texts that were eventually placed in a fixed tradition in the churches."[82]

The move to expand categories in order to avoid a false dichotomy is salient.[83] Nevertheless, each of the options surveyed so far keeps the discussion restricted to using terms like canon and scripture. The *Shepherd* has taken a prime place in such scholarly discussions precisely because of the difficulty in determining the bounds of the canon in its earliest readers and in determining how to deal with boundaries in the canon that do not always match exactly, as in the canons of Eusebius, Athanasius, or Rufinus. Rather than perpetuating this debate, it would be better to reframe it in terms of authority. A similar move has been made by François Bovon regarding the terminology that should be employed when discussing the New Testament Apocrypha. Bovon argued that a category like "books useful to the soul" best describes several early Christian texts that had some authority and that was recognized by many early Christians but less authority than early Christian texts that were ultimately deemed canonical in the way that the word is used today.[84] Adopting Bovon's terminology, then, the *Shepherd*'s reception in its earliest times may be best understood not in terms of whether or not the book is canonical but instead as a book that is useful for the soul. In other words, the *Shepherd* held a significant amount of authority for many of its earliest readers. Yet this authority should be differentiated from the type of authority that was granted to the words of Jesus, Peter, and Paul, on the one hand, or Plato, Aristotle, and Cicero, on the other.

---

80. Kruger (2012).

81. Sundberg (1973, 35). See further van Unnik (1949).

82. McDonald (2009, 25). In this, McDonald follows Sanders (1972, 91) and especially Sheppard (1987).

83. Ruwet likewise finds it necessary to describe "une classe de livres intermédiare" in Origen's use of scriptural and apocryphal books (1944, 325–32). In addition to the references to Origen's writings that Ruwet cites, see also Eusebius, *Eccl. hist.* 6.25.

84. Bovon (2009; 2012; 2015).

Although attempts to find more nuanced understandings of textual authority have been ongoing, the advantage of following a categorization like Bovon's is that it more closely approximates the categories used in early Christian texts and employed by early Christian authors when writing prefaces.[85] These works do not draw a distinction between canon 1 and canon 2 or between canon and scripture. Eusebius acknowledges that the books that he rejects in *Hist. eccl.* 3.25.4 are nevertheless known to most writers in the church (*Hist. eccl.* 3.25.6). Moreover, he separates the *Shepherd*, *Acts of Paul*, and *Epistle of Barnabas* from texts that he considers doctrinally problematic, such as the *Gospels of Peter, Thomas*, and *Matthias* (*Hist. eccl.* 3.25.4, 6). Likewise, Athanasius advises that the books that are useful should be read by catechumens (*Ep. fest.* 39.7).[86] A third category is thus appropriate when considering how much authority the *Shepherd* had, and Bovon's terminology provides a helpful way forward.

Indeed, it may be necessary to further differentiate understandings of how much authority was granted to early Christian texts. For example, the Protoevangelium of James does not seem to have been a serious contender for inclusion in the New Testament canon, nor does it have the same number of early citations and papyri that characterize the *Shepherd*'s preservation. It is not mentioned in the discussions of Eusebius, Athanasius, or Rufinus. Nevertheless, the Protoevangelium is well-attested in manuscripts from the Byzantine period, and it played an important role as a base text for later infancy gospels, such as the Gospel of Pseudo-Matthew and the Arundel form of the Latin infancy gospels.[87] The Protoevangelium was viewed by at least some Christians in late antiquity as useful, but its authority appears to have differed from the higher value that was placed on the *Shepherd* by its early readers and from the still higher authority given to texts that were included in the New Testament. Thus, a further distinction may be necessary within this intermediate category of authority.

This is not the place to outline a thoroughgoing schematic of textual authority in early Christianity. For this study, it is enough to say that the authority of the *Shepherd* was widely, although not universally, regarded in early Christianity. However, its authority was held to a lesser degree than texts like the Gospels and Pauline epistles when the scope of early Christian writings is considered collectively. The *Shepherd* is best placed in an intermediate category of authority that may, following Bovon, be termed "books that are useful for the soul."

---

85. Bovon (2012, 128–30).

86. Brakke (1994, 413–14). Didymus similarly refers to the *Shepherd* as a book of catechesis (*Comm. Zech.* 86).

87. On the textual traditions for the Protoevangelium of James, see Toepel (2014, 16–31). For introductions, texts, and translations of the gospel texts mentioned in this paragraph, see Ehrman and Pleše (2011, 31–155).

Conclusion

Beginning with the earliest references to the *Shepherd* in the second half of the second century, this chapter has explored those who read the *Shepherd* by outlining figures who demonstrate knowledge of the *Shepherd*. Because the interest of this book is to enable better readings of the *Shepherd* itself, the chapter focused on the earliest readers—those who wrote during the second through fifth centuries. Although the *Shepherd* was not valued equally by early Christian authors, it was generally held in high esteem. It continued to be read from the sixth through fifteenth centuries and is particularly evident in visionary literature from the time. The survey in this chapter stopped with the publication of the *editio princeps* in 1513. The chapter concluded by considering the authority that was given to the *Shepherd* in the first four centuries after it was written. Although the *Shepherd* was an authoritative text, its authority does not seem to have been employed in the same way as Paul's letters or the Synoptic Gospels. Rather, the *Shepherd* was most often regarded as a book that should be read because it was useful for the development of a proper life.

Chapter 4

CRITICAL QUESTIONS FOR THE *SHEPHERD*: WHAT, TO WHOM, WHERE, WHEN, AND WHO?

After summarizing the *Shepherd* and analyzing how the text has been preserved and understood prior to printed editions of the text, this chapter now turns to traditional critical questions that are asked, not only of the *Shepherd* but of most ancient Greco-Roman texts. These questions are sometimes handled at the very beginning of a book, but the discussion has waited for Chapter 4 in this volume so that the question may be approached with more background knowledge of the text. The questions that are addressed in this chapter include the following: What kind of text is the *Shepherd* (genre)? To whom as the *Shepherd* written (audience)? Where was the *Shepherd* composed (location)? When was the *Shepherd* created (date)? Finally, who wrote the *Shepherd* (authorship)? Chapter 4 will address these questions in order. However, the issues of date and authorship—along with composition history—are closely linked in the *Shepherd*, and these questions will be handled together in due course.

Genre: What Is the Shepherd?

The majority of scholarship regards the *Shepherd* as an apocalypse. However, the *Shepherd* may be a surprising apocalypse for readers who are accustomed to thinking of apocalyptic literature along the lines of Dan 7–12 or the New Testament book of Revelation. It may also be surprising for English speakers who are accustomed to the everyday meaning of *apocalyptic* as "describing or prophesying the end of the world."[1] Although the *Shepherd* refers to the destruction of the world (e.g., Vis. 4.1.10 [22.10]; 4.3.1–5 [24.1–5]; Sim. 4.4 [53.4]), the comparatively minimal focus on eschatology in the text along with the emphasis on repentance and ethics have provided reasons for some scholars to doubt the *Shepherd*'s apocalyptic credentials.[2] Indeed, there is a stream within scholarship on the *Shepherd* that refers to the generic shortcomings of the text.

---

1. This definition comes from Oxford Dictionaries online (https://en.oxforddictionaries.com/definition/apocalyptic). Last visited on January 21, 2019.

2. Bauckham (1974, 30) rightly observes that the *Shepherd* "is largely content to assume rather than describe the *eschaton*."

This academic tradition stretches back at least to the nineteenth century. In a review of Karl Jachmann's *Der Hirte des Hermas*,[3] Karl Josef von Hefele doubts whether the *Shepherd* should be called an apocalypse because the ethical character of the writing predominates.[4] J. Christian Wilson asserts, "It is as if the author is trying his best to write an apocalypse but fails."[5] Aimé Puech cites the *Shepherd* as an example of "transformation" in the apocalyptic genre. He mentions the discussions of prophecy,[6] Hermas's brother Bishop Pius (Muratorian Fragment, ll. 75–7), and the minimal references to persecution in his discussion of how the *Shepherd* differs from other examples of apocalyptic literature.[7] Kirsopp Lake likewise refers to the *Shepherd* as a "practical apocalypse," suggesting that changes in second-century Roman life drew Jesus-followers away from a focus on an imminent Parousia.[8] "Practical apocalypse" may be correct in one sense, but Lake's designation sets the *Shepherd* apart from other, "real" apocalypses.[9]

Although some scholars continue to exclude the *Shepherd* from the category "apocalypse" or to highlight generic failures in the text,[10] this way of speaking has declined as studies of apocalyptic literature have increased. This decline has occurred as the definition of the apocalyptic genre in early Judaism and early Christianity has become a key matter to consider alongside the genre of the *Shepherd*.[11] The definition of "apocalypse" has been a matter of significant debate over the past forty years. Christopher Rowland has rightly observed that a particular eschatological orientation cannot be the sole criterion by which to judge an apocalypse and has suggested that "the distinguishing feature is a belief in direct revelation of the things of God which was mediated through dream, vision or divine intermediary."[12] John Collins offered the now classic definition of the genre in *Semeia* 14.[13]

3. Jachmann (1838).
4. Hefele (1839, 179).
5. Wilson (1995, 41).
6. Puech (1928, 71).
7. Puech (1928, 72–7).
8. Lake (1911, 26). Elsewhere Lake (1920, 111) writes that the *Shepherd* "was written with the practical purpose of guiding Christians in Rome."
9. "Though the form of the book is apocalyptic and visionary, its object is practical and ethical" (Lake 1912–13, 2.2). See similarly Joly, who describes the *Shepherd* as an "apocalypse refroidie" (1993, 527).
10. E.g., Vielhauer (1975, 522); Müller (1989, 600). Schüssler Fiorenza (1989, 299) is also hesitant to designate the *Shepherd* an early Christian apocalypse. See further Brox (1991, 36n.10).
11. On the difficulty of defining genre in popular discussions outside of biblical studies, see Gavaler (2015).
12. Rowland (1982, 21). Yet Collins (1998, 26) has observed that there is little to separate an apocalypse from traditional Hebrew prophecy on Rowland's definition.
13. The *Semeia* volume arose alongside increased discussions about apocalyptic literature in the 1970s, such as Koch (1972); Hanson (1976a; 1976b); Stone ([1976] 1991).

"Apocalypse" is a genre of revelatory literature with a narrative framework, in which a revelation is mediated by an otherworldly being to a human recipient, disclosing a transcendent reality which is both temporal, insofar as it envisages eschatological salvation, and spatial insofar as it involves another, supernatural world.[14]

On this definition, "there is no good reason to exclude it [the *Shepherd*] from the genre 'apocalypse.'"[15] Yet the definition that Collins and his colleagues wrote has not ended the debate about what precisely an apocalypse is. Nor has the definition been found sufficient by all. David Hellholm argued that the discussion of the form of the genre was not enough. Rather, something should be said about the function of the genre, and Hellholm added the qualification that apocalypses were "intended for a group in crisis with a purpose of exhortation and/or consolation by means of divine authority."[16] Yarbro Collins emended the *Semeia* 14 definition to say something about the purpose of apocalypses in another *Semeia* volume devoted to early Christian apocalypticism. An apocalypse is "intended to interpret present, earthly circumstances in light of the supernatural world of the future, and to influence both the understanding and the behavior of the audience by means of divine authority."[17]

Still, the problem of drawing precise boundaries around a genre has continued to create issues. Researchers may differ about which criteria that one should employ when defining a genre. By grouping texts together around necessary criteria, one also risks obscuring the particularity of each text included in the genre.[18] Carol Newsom argues that genre classifications should be thought of as "a critical category devised by the critic for the purposes of the critic."[19] Collins's

---

On the history of apocalyptic scholarship, see Yarbro Collins (2011, 447–51); Collins (2014, 1–5; 2016, 21–3).

14. Collins (1979, 8). Jean Carmignac (1979, 20) independently developed a similar definition of an apocalypse as a "genre littéraire qui présente, à travers des symboles typiques, des révélations soit sur Dieu, soit sur les anges ou les demons, soit sur leurs partisans, soit sur les instruments de leur action." See further the helpful summary and analysis of both definitions in Sanders (1989, 451–5).

15. Yarbro Collins (1979, 75). She classifies the *Shepherd* as an apocalypse "of cosmic and/or political eschatology with neither historical review nor otherworldly journey" (Yarbro Collins 1979, 63–4). See similarly Osiek (1986, 118).

16. Hellholm (1986, 27).

17. Yarbro Collins (1986, 7).

18. Collins's definition has also been accused of circularity by Fletcher-Louis (2011, 1582). Although there is some circularity in defining an apocalypse in line with certain characteristics and then finding texts that fit those characteristics that can be defined as apocalyptic, it is not clear that this is an unhelpful circularity. The more significant question involves the characteristics that are selected as constitutive of the genre.

19. Newsom (2005, 439).

definition should thus not be considered a way of defining apocalypse that would be recognized by early Jewish readers. It is rather a useful way of grouping a series of ancient texts together based on similarities that the texts share. Collins has also returned to the issue of definition in recent years and has argued that prototype theory is a more useful way of defining the genre of apocalypse than the strict classifications that were employed in 1979.[20] On this understanding, certain texts embody the apocalypse genre better than others. These texts may be regarded as prototypes of the genre. However, prototype theory allows for blurry edges. Some texts may play with the boundaries of a genre, but this does not negate the usefulness of the genre categorization.

When using Collins's definition of the apocalypse genre, along with prototype theory and continued academic conversations about how to determine exactly what an apocalypse is, the *Shepherd* is best viewed as an apocalypse. The text may not fit the prototype of some apocalypses, but it remains the case that there is no good reason to exclude the *Shepherd* from the apocalyptic genre.[21] The *Shepherd* has a narrative framework or, perhaps better said, a series of narrative frameworks. These narrative frames revolve primarily around two revelatory figures—the woman and the shepherd—who do not come from Hermas's everyday world and can thus be described as otherworldly beings. Together they mediate a transcendent reality that derives from the words that God has given them for Hermas. Hermas then transmits their revelation to readers by writing what he sees and what they say so that the revelation can also be received by the audience. Although the *Shepherd* may not be one of the prototypes selected for early Christian apocalypses, the text remains comfortably within the formal boundaries of the apocalyptic genre.[22]

While the *Shepherd* should be classified as an apocalypse, more can be said about how exactly the *Shepherd* functions to communicate its apocalyptic message to readers. In light of the repeated conversations about repentance in the text, the revelation that Hermas receives legitimates his teaching about repentance by allowing both Hermas and his audience to confront directly what God is saying to them.[23] Repentance itself may be viewed as a direct encounter of the believer with God. Hermas undergoes a transformation throughout the visions, commandments, parables, and allegories that he is taught.[24] The teaching about repentance is thus part of an apocalyptic exchange between the Lord and Hermas that is mediated by an otherworldly figure for the purpose of Hermas's transformation.[25] Repentance,

---

20. Collins (2014, 5; 2016, 32–3). See similarly Yarbro Collins (2011, 455); Batovici (2015d, 155–6).

21. Yarbro Collins (1979, 74–5).

22. See further Rüpke (2016, 148–50).

23. Rowland (1982, 392). On the legitimation strategies that might be at work in the *Shepherd*, see further Rüpke (1999, 150; 2005, 291–6).

24. "Hermas's character becomes an ideal, undergoing in the course of the work the transformation which the audience must replicate" (Maier 1997, 142).

25. Hellholm (2009, 246–9; 2010, 235–7); Batovici (2015d, 163–9).

however, is not the only topic about which the *Shepherd* has something to say. The revelatory figures speak with Hermas about the roles of the rich and poor as well as the need to stay away from double-mindedness (διψυχία). This suggests an environment in which at least some Christians have been able to obtain money or in which comparatively wealthy people have become a part of the community. The author may have perceived this as a crisis, and the *Shepherd* may be a response to a growing problem in the church.[26] Although Hermas's economic status remains unclear, his lackadaisical approach to his wife and children (Vis. 1.3.1–2 [3.1–2]; Vis. 2.2.2 [6.2]) suggests a situation in which the author understands the Christian community to be degenerating due to its complacency. An apocalyptic text throws these understandings of the community into sharp relief with what the author understands to be God's revelation to the community. The revelation that Hermas receives in the *Shepherd* thus functions to direct the church's eyes toward the God who is revealed to the community through the woman and the shepherd.

In terms of both form and function, the *Shepherd* may be categorized within the apocalyptic genre. Although it may not serve as the prototype of either an early Christian apocalypse or an apocalypse more broadly defined in early Judaism and early Christianity, the *Shepherd* should be included comfortably within the genre of apocalypse. The *Shepherd* employs these generic conventions to bring Hermas, his community, and his readers into an encounter with God that is mediated through otherworldly figures. What, then, can be said of the community to which the *Shepherd* was addressed?

Audience: To Whom Was the Shepherd *Written?*

The *Shepherd* makes regular mention of double-mindedness and of wealth. In order for the emphasis in the *Shepherd* on the right handling of wealth to say something about how the apocalyptic genre of the *Shepherd* was utilized, the teaching must say something about the audience. Admittedly, this requires a certain amount of mirror-reading, but mirror-reading is required to say almost anything about the audience of the *Shepherd* because the text does not refer to the audience in descriptive terms.[27] Yet the text refers to disparities in wealth, and these references suggest real disparities in the community.[28] The woman tells

---

26. Osiek (1986, 117–19; 1999, 11–12). It is, of course, not the case that all Christians were destitute. Paul is able to ask for a collection to be taken up from the church in Corinth (2 Cor 8–9), while James refers to the need not to show favoritism to a man with a gold ring (Jas 2:1–4). Jesus himself was supported in part by wealthy women (Luke 8:3). Nevertheless, if the author perceived wealth as a crisis in Rome, this may be reflected in an apocalyptic document. On wealthy individuals in the New Testament letters, see Weiß (2015, 106–54).

27. On mirror-reading early Christian texts, see Barclay (1987); Gupta (2012); Dyer (2017, 61–74).

28. Verheyden (2007, 69) likewise refers to the social mix of the *Shepherd*'s audience that is evident in the text's emphasis on economic inequality.

Hermas that those who desire evil things "exult in their wealth" (Vis. 1.1.8 [1.8]), and Hermas perceives the woman's appearance as an elderly woman in the first vision because he was weakened from the matters of this life and had become indifferent (Vis. 3.11.3 [19.3]).[29] The first parable that the shepherd tells Hermas is about two cities, while the second parable describes an elm and a vine. The shepherd instructs Hermas to buy souls and visit widows and orphans rather than buying fields (Sim. 1.8 [50.8]), and he observes that rich should partner with the poor so that the poor can continue their ministry of prayer (Sim. 2.4–10 [51.4–10]). The description of Hermas as a freedman and the varied economic statuses of freedpersons in the Roman Empire may be taken as supporting evidence for issues of wealth in the community.[30] Statements about money may be linked to discussions of double-mindedness as a split focus in the community and outside of the community, especially with regard to business matters.[31] For example, the false prophets attract the double-minded and benefit from their money (Mand. 11.1–6, 11–15 [43.1–6, 11–15]), while the shepherd refers to those who prepare fields and houses in the wrong city as "foolish and double-minded" (Sim. 1.3–4 [50.3–4]). The audience that Hermas addresses has at least some intracommunal issues with economic inequities.

Because of the limited information about the community, another way to describe the audience is to note what the audience is not. Using a *via negativa*, one might observe, for example, that the audience of the *Shepherd* is not primarily the ecclesial leaders. Although leaders are named (Vis. 2.3.4 [7.4]; 2.4.3 [8.3]) and allusions are made to elders in the community (Vis. 2.4.2–3 [8.2–3]; 3.1.8 [9.8]), the *Shepherd* is addressed to a broader audience.[32] It does not outline ecclesial hierarchies in detail, nor is the text set out for academic theologians who may have been active in schools.[33] Although the text implicitly limits the power of state authorities by giving supreme authority to God alone, the *Shepherd* is not primarily interested in critiquing the Roman Empire as in the case of certain anti-imperial comments found in Revelation.[34]

Jörg Rüpke has pushed scholarly imaginations to consider whether anything more specific can be said about the audience than that there is an interest in

---

29. The young man addresses Hermas in the second-person plural in Vis. 3.11.2–3 (19.2–3), suggesting that this phrase is meant to describe Hermas's audience in the address.

30. On Hermas as a freedman and the circumstances of freedpersons in the Roman Empire, see Leutzsch (1989, 138–41); Weiß (2009); Beavis (2018).

31. Osiek (1986, 117–18).

32. For the different audiences that may be in view in the *Shepherd*, see Körtner and Leutzsch (1998, 129).

33. On the role of teachers and academies in early Christianity, see Markschies (2015, 31–91).

34. The clearest example is the use of Babylon as a cipher for Rome and the reference to Babylon's destruction in Rev 17:1–18:24. For discussion of Revelation and anti-imperialism, see Friesen (2014).

economic dynamics within the community. In particular, he proposes that the *Shepherd* may be viewed as a text that allows insight into a local history of religion.[35] Noting the centrality of the tower in Vis. 3 (9.1–21.4) and Sim. 9 (78.1–110.3), Rüpke observes that Hermas is charged to go to the field where he is working (Vis. 3.1.2 [9.2]). Although several interpreters understand the tower visions in almost exclusively allegorical terms,[36] Rüpke argues that not only Hermas's initial instruction but also much of the imagery is imbedded in the real topography of the author's location.[37] He proposes that the round, white stones that Hermas sees in Vis. 3.2.8 (10.8) and the white mountain in Sim. 9.29.1–3 (106.1–3) are drawn from the imagery of salt mining. From the identification of saline imagery in two central passages within the *Shepherd*, Rüpke argues that the text offers insight into the occupational orientation of the audience. The *Shepherd* is a text that was written for a group of Christian tenants working in and around salt mines.[38]

Rüpke's article is fascinating and fits well with description of how salt was obtained in Pliny the Elder, *Nat.* 31.73–92. However, Rüpke's conclusion about the audience is too strong when one considers that it is based on a single constellation of evidence. A similar argument might be made based on the presence of agricultural and botanical imagery in Sim. 2–5 (51.1–60.7) and Sim. 8 (67.1–77.5). Working from this evidence, one might also argue that the *Shepherd* was written for agricultural tenants. The arguments that salt workers and tenant farmers comprise the *Shepherd*'s primary audience are too tenuous to be used as descriptions of the entire audience. Yet they do provide insight into the type of people who might have been included in the *Shepherd*'s audience. Although a precise description of the audience cannot be identified, the *Shepherd* draws on a variety of imagery that may have resonated with the audience. In light of the repeated emphasis on wealth, the audience may be best understood as a diverse collection of working believers in the Roman Empire. Within this audience, there seems to have been issues of economic inequality and, at least from the author's perspective, social commitment to the community. One may still wonder, though, where the text originated.

Location: Where Was the Shepherd Written?

Briefly, everything points to Rome as the place of the *Shepherd*'s composition and the location of the intended audience. Only the reference to Arcadia in Sim. 9.1.4 (78.4) speaks against it.[39] Rome is the place where Rhoda lives and the city

---

35. Rüpke (1999, 150–1).
36. E.g., Dibelius (1923, 459); Brox (1991, 121).
37. Rüpke (1999, 156).
38. Rüpke (1999, 158–60).
39. These sentences closely follow Brox (1991, 22): "Alles spricht für Rom als Abfassungsort des PH, und nur Sim IX 1,4 spricht dagegen." See further Staats (1986, 103).

that Hermas comes to inhabit as her slave. It also appears to be the location in which Hermas is reacquainted with his former owners years later (Vis. 1.1.1 [1.1]). Hermas sees Rhoda bathing in the Tiber, the river that provided the lifeline of ancient Rome (Vis. 1.1.2 [1.2]). In Vis. 4.1.2 (22.2), Hermas is traveling along the Via Campana and comes to a place about ten stadia from the public road. The Via Campana was a public thoroughfare that led southwest out of Rome.[40]

Evidence for an Italian provenance may be enhance if one emends the text from εἰς κώμας to εἰς Κούμας in Vis. 1.1.3; 2.1.1 (1.3; 5.1). This emendation is initially enticing.[41] Cumae was a city set along the Via Campana, so the location can easily be made to fit with the story. If the variant is accepted, Hermas must be imagined to be on a moderately lengthy journey to the sea. Cumae was also the home of a Sibyl, which may explain why Hermas thinks that the woman whom he sees is the Sibyl in the first two visions (Vis. 2.4.1 [8.1]). The Latin translations have also been employed as evidence for the original reading of Cumae. L² provides evidence for a city in Vis. 1.1.3 (1.3) when it reads *apud civitatem Ostiorum* (to the city of Ostia), and it again presupposes a region in Vis. 2.1.1 (5.1) with *apud regionem Cumanorum* (to the regions of Cumae). In Vis. 1.1.3 (1.3), L¹ reads *cum his cogitationibus* (with these thoughts), and the translator again records *cum his* (with these) in Vis. 2.1.1 (5.1). *Cum his* has been understood as an auditory reconstruction of *Cumis*, that is, as evidence for reading Cumae.[42] Cumae may then be regarded as the reading that unites the sounds of the Greek text and L¹ and agrees with L² in Vis. 2.1.1 (5.1).

However, the *Shepherd* offers little evidence for a journey as long as the one that Hermas must have taken if he went to Cumae. Moreover, S, A, and B provide unanimous support for εἰς κώμας in both verses, while the translation in E suggests that the translator made use of a similar Greek text. This provides strong manuscript evidence for reading εἰς κώμας, while the story makes very good sense if Hermas is on a shorter journey into the villages around Rome.[43] By understanding Hermas's journey as one that is taken into the countryside, this reading also provides stronger evidence for a specifically Roman provenance. Finally, Antonio Carlini has proposed that the *Shepherd* follows a similar apocalyptic theme as found in *4 Ezra* 13.57 in which Ezra walks into the field (*in campum*) glorifying God.[44] If so, Hermas's journey into the villages would contribute to the apocalyptic setting along with Hermas's journey into pathless regions (Vis. 1.1.3 [1.3]). On balance,

---

40. Dibelius (1923, 482).

41. The Cumae reading has been accepted by Dindorf (1857, 67–8); Dibelius (1923, 431); Joly (1968, 76, 88); Brox (1991, 80); Holmes (2007, 454, 462).

42. For additional textual witnesses, see Tornau and Cecconi (2014, 42).

43. The reading εἰς κώμας is accepted by Anger and Dindorfius (1856, 3, 7); Körtner and Leutzsch (1998, 146, 154, 377n.13); Osiek (1999, 43); Ehrman (2003, 2.174, 184); Prinzivalli and Simonetti (2010–15, 2.220, 228).

44. Carlini (1985).

then, it seems preferable to stay with the Greek witnesses and to understand Hermas's journey as going εἰς κώμας.

In light of this evidence, it is difficult to avoid the conclusion that the text was composed by someone who lived in Rome and was likely written to people who lived in or near Rome.[45] If Rüpke is correct that the imagery of white stones in the tower visions is imbedded in the topography around Rome and if the discussion of the elm and vine in Sim. 2 were employed in Roman viticulture,[46] these may be taken as supplementary evidence to the already strong indications that the text originated in Rome. Whether or not Hermas's second vision of the tower in Arcadia (Sim. 9.1.4 [78.4]) is meant to designate a real geographical location on the Peloponnesian peninsula,[47] there is no need to emend the text of this verse.[48] It remains unlikely that the *Shepherd* or the text of Sim. 9 originated in Arcadia. All that can be said based on the text of the *Shepherd* is that Hermas is transported to Arcadia in the narrative. It is difficult to say whether Hermas or the author knew this place from experience. Although it is difficult to rule locations other than Rome out definitively due to the way in which historical arguments are made, no other location in the Roman Empire is nearly as strong of an option as Rome when considering the origin of the *Shepherd*.

Date and Authorship: When Was the Shepherd Written and Who Wrote It?

The questions of date and authorship are linked to another issue in critical scholarship on the *Shepherd*, namely, the unity of the text.[49] These three questions are best handled together. If the *Shepherd* was written in stages and later edited,

---

45. Dibelius (1923, 423); Brox (1991, 22-3); Körtner and Leutzsch (1998, 135-6); Osiek (1999, 18); Verheyden (2007, 64); Hellholm (2009, 249; 2010, 237); Grundeken (2015a, 9-11).

46. Rüpke (1999); Osiek (1999, 162). On the elm and vine as a first-century means of farming in Italy, see Columella, *Arb.* 16; Pliny the Elder, *Nat.* 17.35.

47. As argued by Harris (1887; 1896, 1-20).

48. Zahn (1868, 211-18) proposes that the reference to Arcadia (Ἀρκαδίαν) in Sim. 9.1.4 (78.4) originally referred to Aricia (Ἀρικίαν). Aricia was a city southeast of Rome and would tie the text more closely to its Roman origins. However, the textual evidence does not support Zahn's emendation. A, L¹, and L² read Arcadia. Despite its Greek origins, travel by unexplained means occurs not only in Sim. 9.1.4 (78.4) but also, for example, in Vis. 1.1.3 (1.3) and 2.1.1 (5.1).

49. I focus here on the question of unity regarding larger sections of the *Shepherd*. It may be possible that smaller portions of the text were added at different times. For example, Walsh (2019a) has argued that Vis. 3.10-13 (18-21) was added to the Visions to correct the portrayal of the woman in the rest of the Visions. However, the concern of this section of Chapter 4 leaves aside this important but small portion of the text in order to ask questions about the overall unity of the Visions, Mandates, and Similitudes.

several dates must be supposed for the various stages of the text. This decision may also affect how one views authorship. On the other hand, if the *Shepherd* is a unified text that was written at one time, the question of authorship and date may be easier to handle. In either case, questions about the date and authorship of the *Shepherd* are intimately connected to how one understands the unity of its composition.[50]

One of the reasons for positing a text that was compiled from multiple periods and perhaps multiple authors is the enormous amount of material that is covered in the *Shepherd*. The text includes dreams, visions, mandates, allegories, and parables. The repetitions and tensions that arise within these genres have led many to propose multiple authors. The most complex theories of composition involve three or more authors spread over more than fifty years.[51] Adolf Hilgenfeld argued for a tripartite authorship scheme in which an author whom Hilgenfeld designates *Hermas pastoralis* wrote Vis. 5; Mand. 1–12; Sim. 1–7 (25–66) at the end of the first century. *Hermas apocalypticus* then wrote Vis. 1–4 (1–24) at the end of Trajan's reign, perhaps around 117 CE. Finally, *Hermas secundarius*, whom Hilgenfeld regards as the brother of Pius,[52] added Sim. 8–10 (67–114) in the middle of the second century.[53] Perhaps the most famous argument comes from Stanislas Giet, who proposes a tripartite structure that differs radically from Hilgenfeld.[54] According to Giet, Vis. 1–4 (1–24) were written early in the second century, and Sim. 9 (78–110) followed not long after as an addendum to clarify the first author's Christology. During the time of Antoninus Pius, perhaps around 160 CE, Vis. 5–Sim. 8; 10 (25–77; 111–14) were composed by someone who held an adoptionist Christology. In addition to Christological tensions, Giet also cites variations in how the *Shepherd* understands repentance in support of his theory of multiple authorship.[55] Finally, the most complex theory of multiple authorship in recent years has been constructed on linguistic grounds by William Coleborne.[56] Coleborne constructs an *apparatus discernendi* that is based on 162 linguistic items that include things like parts of speech and verbal voices.[57] After analyzing how each part of speech is distributed in the *Shepherd*, he concludes that six authors contributed to the *Shepherd*: V (Vis. 1–4 [1–24]); R and E (Vis. 5 [25];

---

50. See similarly Joly (1993, 527), although Joly only mentions date and unity.

51. For overviews of scholarship outside of the commentaries, see Wilson (1993, 14–23); Soyars (2019, 10–20).

52. See Muratorian fragment, 75–7.

53. Hilgenfeld (1881, xx–xxxi).

54. See the extensive argumentation in Giet (1963; 1966). Osiek (1983, 7; 1986, 114) employed Giet's thesis as a framework for her early studies, but she later argued for single authorship (1999, 10n.90). Single authorship will be discussed below.

55. "Nous disposons d'un certain nombre d'indices qui permettent de la cerner, ce que beaucoup d'auteurs se sont efforcés de faire" (Giet 1961, 215).

56. Coleborne (1969; 1970).

57. Coleborne (1969, 135–7).

Mand. 12.3.3–12.6.5 [46.3–49.5]); M (Mand. 1.1–12.3.3 [26.1–46.3]); S (Sim. 1–7 [50–66]); S.8 (Sim. 8 [67–77]); S.9 (Sim. 9 [78–110]). Nothing is said of Sim. 10 (111–14), because much of the text is preserved only in Latin, and Coleborne's *apparatus discernendi* is based on Greek linguistic markers.[58]

Each of the theories above points to difficulties within the text and narrative of the *Shepherd*.[59] The work is long and nonlinear. Tensions appear in doctrinal teaching as one continues to read through the *Shepherd*. Nevertheless, the absence of agreement among these multiple theories of authorship and the dearth of attestation for any tripartite or sexpartite division of the *Shepherd* that matches the proposals above suggest that these theories, brilliant though they may be, are ultimately unlikely to account for how the *Shepherd* was composed. Moreover, it is unclear that positing multiple authors assists interpreters in explaining the literary tensions and compositional issues with which they are purported to help. After all, if multiple authors wrote various portions of the *Shepherd*, one may still wonder why the texts were combined. If a later author wrote to correct an earlier author, why not write a separate work? Such complicated theories of authorship continue to struggle to explain why the *Shepherd* has come to readers in the form that it has today.[60]

Yet there may be evidence for a bipartite theory of composition.[61] The external evidence for this division is partly based on the manuscripts of the *Shepherd* that are extant. Bonner argued that M circulated without Vis. 1–4 (1–24) based on the spatial limitations of the papyrus.[62] Lefort made a similar argument regarding the manuscript of C², the Sahidic translation of the *Shepherd*.[63] As one examines the internal evidence for such a division in the *Shepherd*, the departure of the woman from Vis. 5–Sim. 10 (25–114) and the absence of the shepherd in Vis. 1–4 (1–24) are striking. Two completely distinct revelatory figures open further the possibility that the *Shepherd* was composed by two authors at different times. One may go on to add further examples of how these sections demonstrate that they were written separately. For example, the shepherd shows Hermas the second tower vision already knowing about the account in Vis. 3 (9–21) and insisting that the shepherd's account will be more accurate (Sim. 9.1.1–3 [78.1–3]). The evidence for two authors working over a period of at least several years is intriguing to consider.

---

58. Coleborne (1969, 135).

59. Although Dibelius (1923, 421) does not presuppose multiple authors, he likewise argues for a composition history that is viewed in stages: Vis. 1–4 (1–24); Vis. 5–Sim. 8 (25–77); Sim. 9 (78–110); Sim. 10 (111–114).

60. For further critiques, see Barnard (1964); Grant (1964); Joly (1967; 1993, 528–9); Brox (1991, 25–33); Körtner and Leutzsch (1998, 130–5); Osiek (1999, 9–10).

61. For further arguments in support of two authors, see Spitta (1896, 241–381); Wilson (1927, 50); Barnard (1968, 32). Maier (1992, 58) argues for a single author but leaves open the possibility for a different editor.

62. Bonner (1925, 117–19; 1934, 7–14).

63. Lefort (1952a, vi–vii).

However, the evidence is not quite as clear-cut as the paragraph above might initially indicate, particularly with regard to the textual evidence. M and C² do not necessarily indicate that the *Shepherd* was composed in separate parts. Rather, they show only that the *Shepherd* could circulate in different formats.⁶⁴ Moreover, both M and C² stem from an Egyptian provenance. The localized nature of the manuscript evidence may suggest that the shepherd's portion of the *Shepherd* had a special influence in Egypt and may be of interest for future reception historical studies of the *Shepherd*, but the manuscripts on their own are not strong evidence for multiple authorship or composition historical studies. The internal evidence for two authors from within the *Shepherd*'s story is somewhat stronger. After all, one may wonder why two revelatory figures are required for Hermas and why there is so little overlap between the two. Even if the revealers do not intersect with one another over the course of the narrative, however, calls for repentance, warnings about sin, and instructions about right living are found throughout the story. The *Shepherd* can be read as a united work, even if it may have been composed by two authors.

Although arguments for two authors cannot be definitively set aside, the unity of the *Shepherd* also pulls hard in discussions of authorship—even if it is a unity that must also allow for tension throughout the text. One reason for inclining toward unified authorship is that, despite their initial promise, it is unclear how many problems multiple authorship hypotheses are able to solve.⁶⁵ Hypothesizing multiple authors does not remove repetition or tension in the text and, on its own, does not describe it. Despite strong minority voices, most scholars today have opted to see the *Shepherd* as a text written by one author.⁶⁶ To be sure, arguing for a single author does not mean that the text was written at one time. The *Shepherd* is an additive text, and Vis. 5.5–7 (25.5–7) and Sim. 9.1.1–3 (78.1–3) suggest that the text is self-consciously agglutinative.⁶⁷

It is not easy to reconstruct the order in which the *Shepherd* may have been composed. Most argue that Vis. 1–4 represent the oldest portion of the text,⁶⁸

---

64. Joly (1967, 203–5). Carlini and Giaccone (1991, 12) have argued that B contained only Vis. 1–4, which could strengthen the case for the *Shepherd* circulating in two parts. However, Carlini (1987, 34) has maintained that B is the work of an excerptor. It thus remains difficult to see how separate circulation of the manuscripts requires multiple authors. In addition, the pagination of the manuscripts that supports some arguments regarding M, C², and B were likely added by a later hand. This may have occurred after pages were already lost (Körtner and Leutzsch 1998, 130).

65. Hillhorst (1976, 186); Brox (1991, 31, 33); Grundeken (2015, 14).

66. For arguments in support of single authorship, see Link (1888); Joly (1967; 1968, 11–16; 1993, 529–30); Staats (1986, 101–2); Brox (1991, 25–33); Henne (1992b); Wilson (1993, 22–3); Körtner and Leutzsch (1998, 130–5); Osiek (1999, 3–4, 8–10); Grundeken (2015a, 11–16).

67. Wilson (1927, 52). For a recent attempt to show the layers of construction in the *Shepherd*, see Rüpke (2016, 142–4).

68. E.g., Dibelius (1923, 421); Osiek (1999, 10); Bandini (2001).

but not all have agreed.⁶⁹ Dibelius and Brox argue for a composition process in which newer portions were added to the sections of the *Shepherd* that were already written.⁷⁰ Thus, the process may be reconstructed in the following way: Vis. 1–4 (1–24); Vis. 5–Sim. 8 (25–77); Sim. 9 (78–110); Sim. 10 (111–114). Brox does not think that it is possible to date the various elements of the *Shepherd* as they were reconstructed. Only the relative chronology within the work can be dated.⁷¹ Although it is difficult to determine definitively, this suggested order of composition is intriguing to consider. It agrees with the order in which the text is read, maintains a straightforwardly additive structure within the text, and provides the simplest solution to the problem of composition. It may be possible to simplify the thesis of Dibelius and Brox so that Vis. 5–Sim. 10 (25–114) can be viewed as a more or less single stage in composition.⁷² In either case, though, the text may be viewed as unified insofar as it comes from a single author, but this unity must be held loosely enough to allow for the difficulties that arise in the text.

A further argument for the unity of the work can be added to counter the argument for separation based on the external evidence provided by M and C². Some of the earliest witnesses to the *Shepherd* suggest that their versions of the text contained both the woman's revelation and the revelation of the shepherd. If so, the most likely conclusion is that they had the entire text before them.⁷³ Clement of Alexandria quotes from Vis. 3.4.3 (12.3); Vis. 3.13.4 (21.4); Vis. 5.5 (25.5); Mand. 7.1–4 (37.1–4), and he may also cite Sim. 9.16.5–7 (93.5–7).⁷⁴ Tertullian's reference to the *Shepherd* as "the apocryphal *Shepherd* of the adulterers" implies knowledge of the text that stretches from Hermas's lustful look at Rhoda (Vis. 1.1.2 [1.2]) to the teaching that an adulterous woman can be taken back by her husband (Mand. 4.1.7–8 [29.7–8]). Origen likewise cites from Vis. 2.4.3 (8.3); Mand. 1.1 (26.1); Sim. 6.3.2–3 (63.2–3); Sim. 6.4.4 (64.4). When one adds the observation that S contained the entire *Shepherd* and that the manuscripts for the earliest translation (L¹) contain no evidence for a break between Vis. 4 and 5 (22–25),⁷⁵ it is difficult to

---

69. E.g., Hilgenfeld (1881, xx–xxxi).

70. Dibelius (1923, 421); Brox (1991, 26–8).

71. Brox (1991, 29).

72. Osiek (1999, 10) points out that Sim. 10.1.1–2 (111.1–2) presupposes knowledge of Vis. 5.1–3 (25.1–3), while Sim. 10.3.1 (113.1) presupposes Sim. 9.10–11 (87–88). Such presumptions of knowledge indicate that Sim. 10 (111–114) must have been written after Vis. 5 (25) and Sim. 9 (78–110). This is surely right. However, a two-stage composition proposal can also account for this observation by recognizing that the author remembered writing Vis. 5 (25) and Sim. 9 (78–110) when they wrote Sim. 10 (111–114).

73. Henne (1992b, 18–21); Osiek (1999, 4); Grundeken (2015a, 15–16).

74. For references and further discussion of Clement, Tertullian, and Origen, see Chapter 3 of this volume.

75. Vis. 1.1.1–Mand. 4.3.6 (1.1–31.6); Sim. 6.5.5–8.2.5 (65.5–68.5); Sim. 9.14.4–9.18.5 (91.4–99.5) are found in S. On the manuscripts for L¹, see further Tornau and Cecconi (2014, 12–19).

avoid the conclusion that the text circulated as a whole from the second century. Despite the tensions, contradictions, and rough transitions that are found in the *Shepherd*, then, the text is best understood as a unity written by a single author.[76]

If the *Shepherd* is to be viewed as a unified text from a single author, when was this text written? It is difficult to date the stages of writing that may have occurred, but three primary pieces of evidence are utilized to frame discussions of the *Shepherd*'s date.[77] The first is the reference to a man named Hermas in Rom 16:14. Origen proposed that this Hermas was the author of the *Shepherd* (*Comm. Rom.* 10.31), and his suggestion would date the text, or at least part of it, to the second half of the first century.[78] The next piece of evidence to consider is the reference to Clement in Vis. 2.4.3 (8.3). Clement was a leader in the Roman church to whom a variety of texts in early Christianity are attributed. Of these, the most likely is *1 Clement*, a letter from the Roman church to the Corinthians that likely dates to the end of the first century.[79] This evidence relies on several suppositions. However, if Hermas's reference to Clement refers specifically to Clement of Rome, if Clement was involved with the writing or transition of *1 Clement*, and if *1 Clement* is dated to the end of the first century, then this portion of the Visions likewise dates from the late first or early second century. The Muratorian fragment provides the final point of data to consider. Since the Muratorian fragment describes the *Shepherd* as having been written "very recently, in our times" (*nuperrim, e temporibus nostri*; 74) and declares that Hermas is the brother of Pius, who was bishop of Rome from approximately 140 until 155,[80] this provides evidence for a date in the middle of the second century. Perhaps one might suggest a date in the 140s.[81]

In order to fit all of these dates, the author of the *Shepherd* would need to have been a younger contemporary of Paul and remained capable of writing for nearly a century. Since such a situation is unlikely, one must weigh the evidence carefully in order to come up with the most likely date. Although Clement was not an uncommon name in the Roman world, the combination of the presence of a leader named Clement in Rome (Vis. 2.4.3 [8.3]) and the traditional ascription of a Roman letter to the Corinthians to Clement suggest that the *Shepherd* was in the process of being written around the end of the first century or early in the

---

76. Verheyden (2007, 65); Hvalvik (2007, 212–13).

77. For an excellent discussion of the *Shepherd*'s date with further references to scholarly literature, see Grundeken (2015a, 2–9).

78. While Chadwick (1957, 276) does not accept Origen's proposal as authentic, he suggests that Origen's suggestion preserves an early Roman tradition.

79. *1 Clement* is often dated around 95. This was classically done by Lightfoot (1889–91, 1.1.346–358). However, Welborn (1984) maintains that the letter should be more broadly dated from 80 to 140.

80. On Pius, see Eusebius, *Eccl. hist.* 4.11.6–7.

81. If one does not accept the Muratorian fragment as a second- or early-third-century document, the citations of the *Shepherd* by Irenaeus, Tertullian, and Clement of Alexandria provide the latest possible dates of composition for the *Shepherd*.

second century.[82] However, there is little basis for Origen's claim that the Hermas who wrote the *Shepherd* is the same Hermas mentioned in Rom 16:14 (*Comm. Rom.* 10.31). Origen similarly attributes *1 Clement* to the Clement mentioned in Phil 4:3 (*Comm. Jo.* 6.36).[83] This suggests a tendency in Origen's writings to link early writings with figures in recognized apostolic letters, such as Romans and Philippians. The lack of corroborating evidence regarding Hermas along with another link between an early Christian text and a person of the same name in a Pauline letter collectively speaks against using Origen as evidence for the *Shepherd*'s date. Finally, the discussion must take up the Muratorian fragment. Although the date of the fragment is disputed, the suggestion that the *Shepherd* stems from around or just before the time of Pius is plausible.[84] A date around 140 allows the text to be cited by authors at the end of the second century. One person could also be linked with the Roman church from the late first century through the middle of the second century and have authored the *Shepherd*.

Although it is difficult to make dogmatic assertions regarding the unity, authorship, and date of the *Shepherd*, the best conclusion based on the available evidence appears to be that the *Shepherd* is a unified text that was written by a single author over a long period of time and was finished around 140.[85] Although the reference to Clement in Vis. 2.4.3 (8.3) likely indicates that portions of the text date to the end of the first or beginning of the second century, it is not possible to date specific portions of the *Shepherd* precisely. This book, then, will interpret the final form of the *Shepherd* as a text that stems from a particular Roman author dating to the middle of the second century.

Conclusion

Chapter 4 has brought Part I to a close by endeavoring to highlight and to answer questions about the *Shepherd* that are asked by critical scholarship. The *Shepherd* is an early Christian apocalypse that addresses a broad audience of Roman Christians whom, among other things, the author perceives as having issues with wealth in the community. Although the *Shepherd* is a winding and occasionally repetitive story that contains various theological tensions, it is best understood as a unified

---

82. Scholars who date the entire text to the first century include Wilson (1927, 54–9); Jeffers (1991, 106–12); Wilson (1993, 9–61). On the attribution of the Roman letter now known as *1 Clement* to Clement of Rome, see Eusebius, *Eccl. hist.* 3.16.1; 4.23.11 as well as the titles and subscriptions in Alexandrinus, Hierosolymitanus, the Latin translation, and the Syriac translations of *1 Clement*.

83. Origen is followed by Eusebius, *Eccl. hist.* 3.15.1.

84. Gonzalez (1984, 1.67); Brox (1991, 23–5); Joly (1993, 529); Osiek (1999, 18–20); Grundeken (2015a, 11).

85. See similarly Brox (1991, 23); Osiek (1999, 20); Hvalvik (2007, 212–13); Hellholm (2009, 249–50; 2010, 237–8).

text from a single author that was written over an extended period of time and was likely finished around 140.

Part I has thus introduced the narrative arc of the lengthy text known as the *Shepherd*. It has also explored the earliest manuscripts, translations, and recent critical editions of the *Shepherd*, while also giving attention to the text's reception prior to the first printed edition in the sixteenth century. This chapter has concluded Part I by considering critical questions regarding the *Shepherd*'s genre, audience, location, date, and authorship. The aim of Part I is to enable readers to engage the text of the *Shepherd* as a whole. The viewpoints on critical questions from Part I will inform the exegetical, literary, historical, and theological discussions that follow in Part II.

Part II

STUDYING THE *SHEPHERD OF HERMAS*

Part II attempts to follow the lead of Part I by focusing on the text of the *Shepherd*. Beginning with a summary of the text rather than topics like authorship and date, the structure of Part I is intended to emphasize the importance of exploring the *Shepherd* itself before and alongside critical introductory issues. Part II likewise opens with a focus on the text by starting with exegesis of the *Shepherd*. Chapter 5 seeks to interpret Similitude 5 in dialogue with other scholarship with a view to both its historical and literary connections. The textual focus is enhanced in Part II by the closing exegesis of the *Shepherd* in Chapter 12. While Chapter 5 maintains its focus on the second-century world of the *Shepherd*, Chapter 12 attempts to show how interpretive engagement with the *Shepherd* can stretch between ancient and contemporary worlds. Chapters 6 and 11 strengthen the chiastic structure of Part II by drawing attention to literary features in the *Shepherd*. Chapter 6 provides a prosopographical study that examines authority, hierarchy, and revelation between the characters, and Chapter 11 explores metaphors related to the tower and household imagery in Vis. 3 and Sim. 9.

Between these exegetical and literary bookends, Chapters 7 and 8 provide a historical lens through which to view the *Shepherd*, and Chapters 9 and 10 offer a theological engagement with the text. Chapter 7 examines the Greco-Roman and early Jewish world in which the *Shepherd* was written and illustrates how knowing texts that are contemporary with the *Shepherd* can make some elements of this second-century apocalypse less surprising. Chapter 8 takes up a similar text with a view to early Christian texts. Since it can be difficult to isolate precisely what is pagan, Jewish, and Christian in the ancient world, the distinctions between Greco-Roman, early Jewish, and early Christian are made for heuristic purposes. These two chapters collectively illustrate both that the *Shepherd* is a text that fits within its second-century world and that it remains a story which is very much its own. Chapter 9 then turns to a theological engagement with the *Shepherd*'s understanding of God. Although the *Shepherd* is an unsystematic text that does not methodically outline its Christology or pneumatology, it maintains an incipient Trinitarian understanding of God in which the Son and spirit are distinguished from the rest of creation by their creative activity, uncontained name, and preexistence. Chapter 10 then takes up sins that the woman and shepherd reveal to Hermas as well as the repentance that should provide the solution to much of what ails the community. A community hampered by double-mindedness and wealth can be restored by a new way of understanding that comes in repentance.

Much like the woman and the shepherd in their revelation to Hermas, each of the chapters in Part II works together with a partner. Chapters 5 and 12, 6 and 11, 7 and 8, and 9 and 10 offer a textually based, literary, historical, and theological engagement with a unique apocalyptic text.

Chapter 5

FASTING AND THE VINEYARD: EXEGETING SIMILITUDE 5

Just as Part I began with a summary that privileged the narrative within the *Shepherd*, Part II opens with a focus on the text by starting with exegesis. Exegesis is the act of interpreting a text. Having briefly summarized Sim. 5 as part of the synopsis of the entire *Shepherd*, this chapter seeks to offer an interpretation of this similitude in dialogue with other scholarship. This parable has an extensive history of interpretation, particularly when it comes to the Christological sections of the parable and the discussion of flesh and spirit (Sim. 5.5.2–5.6.8 [58.2–59.8]).

A key difficulty when interpreting Sim. 5 is the way in which the meaning of the imagery from the original parable (Sim. 5.2.1–11 [55.1–11]) changes over the course of the interpretation. This is an issue when interpreting various metaphors in the *Shepherd*. For instance, the twelve mountains in Sim. 9 (78.1–110.3) are first said to symbolize the twelve tribes that inhabit the world (Sim. 9.17.1–2 [94.1–2]). However, the shepherd's explanation shifts later in the parable when the mountains are interpreted as various kinds of believers (Sim. 9.19.1–9.29.3 [96.1–106.3]). Philippe Henne describes this phenomenon with the term "allegorical polysemy" (polysémie allégorique).[1] Because *polysemy* suggests many meanings, I prefer the word *multisemy* in order to recognize that there are multiple meanings in the allegories of the *Shepherd* without necessarily defining how many. This literary technique is employed elsewhere in the *Shepherd*, but a particularly clear example is found in Sim. 5.[2] Here a single parable is interpreted in three ways. By allowing these three interpretations to stand in multisemous independence, the interpretations that the shepherd offers to Hermas work together to enrich the original parable. While the interpretations are multiform, the various interpretations should not be construed as incoherent. Rather, each interpretation has its own coherence within the parable.

---

1. Henne (1989); Bucur (2007, 132–3). For the example of the mountains, see Henne (1989, 131).

2. In addition to the mountains in Sim. 9 and the interpretations in Sim. 5, the waters on which the tower is built in Vis. 3 are both the waters on which the earth is founded (Vis. 3.2.4 [10.4]) and the waters of baptism (Vis. 3.3.5 [11.5]; 3.7.3 [15.3]).

The interpretation of Sim. 5 will thus be aided by keeping allegorical multisemy in mind. Another helpful matter to recall concerns the literary structure of the parable. The passage opens with a conversation about fasting between the shepherd and Hermas (Sim. 5.1.1–5 [54.1–5]). The shepherd then tells Hermas a parable about a slave and master in response to their conversation (Sim. 5.2.1–11 [55.1–11]). When Hermas does not understand the parable, the shepherd demonstrates its relevance to fasting (Sim. 5.3.1–9 [56.1–9]). Thus, Sim. 5.1–3 [54–56]) hold together in a parabolic unit about what fasting is. Much to the shepherd's chagrin, however, Hermas continues to ask about the meaning of the parable (Sim. 5.4.1–5.5.1 [57.1–58.1]). His persistence leads to continued explanations. The shepherd shows Hermas that the parable is also a Christological allegory (Sim. 5.5.2–5.6.4a [58.2–59.4a]) before continuing to discuss the relationship between flesh and spirit (Sim. 5.6.4b–8 [59.4b–8]). The similitude concludes with ethical exhortations for Hermas and his readers in light of the parabolic material (Sim. 5.7.1–4 [60.1–4]). Sim. 5 can then be usefully organized into the following sections: (1) the discussion of fasting (Sim. 5.1–3 [54–56]); (2) the turn to Christology (Sim. 5.4.1–5.6.4a [57.1–59.4a]); (3) the relation of flesh and spirit (Sim. 5.6.4b–8 [59.4b–8]); and (4) concluding ethical exhortations (Sim. 5.7 [60.1–4]).

Fasting (Sim. 5.1.1–5.3.9 [54.1–56.9])

When Hermas sees the shepherd in Sim. 5, Hermas is described in three ways: fasting, sitting on a mountain, and thanking God for everything God has done with him (Sim. 5.1.1 [54.1]). This breaks from the openings in Sim. 3.1 (52.1) and 4.1 (53.1), in which the shepherd immediately shows something to Hermas. The mundane beginning in Sim. 5.1.1 (54.1) is consistent with the start of Sim. 6.1.1 (61.1) and 7.1 (66.1), in which Hermas meets the shepherd in ordinary circumstances.

The three descriptions can be addressed in reverse order. Although this chapter interprets a single similitude, the reference to what God has done for Hermas prior to this offers a reminder that Hermas has already had multiple interactions with revelatory figures from God. Hermas's location on a mountain is reminiscent of other times when his revelations have come in isolated places or when he is alone (Vis. 4.1.1–2 [22.1–2]; Vis. 5.1 [25.1]; Sim. 2.1 [51.1]).[3] Finally, Hermas is described as fasting. Although fasting will become a focal point of this parable, this is not the first time in which readers have encountered Hermas fasting. After Hermas copies a writing that he cannot understand, he reports in Vis. 2.2.1 (6.1) that he fasted and later receives the meaning of the words. Hermas receives the first vision of the tower after fasting many times (Vis. 3.1.2 [9.2]). Later in the same vision, Hermas fasts again in order to know why the woman appeared to him in three

---

3. Hermas's revelation begins with him being carried to a place where there is no path and where people cannot go (Vis. 1.1.3 [1.3]; Vis. 2.1.1 [5.1]).

forms (Vis. 3.10.6–7 [18.6–7]).[4] Yet in Sim. 5, Hermas is not fasting in order to receive revelation but as part of a regular practice. He has a station (στατίων; Sim. 5.1.2 [54.2]). Hermas employs a Latin loanword, *statio*, in his Greek speech.[5] The regularity of the fasting implicit in Hermas's description coincides with another second-century discussion of fasting.[6] In *Did.* 8.1, the author instructs readers to fast on Wednesdays and Fridays. This twice-weekly practice distinguished the Didachist's fast from Jewish fasts on Mondays and Thursdays.[7] Hermas's routine is not specified further, but station suggests some regularity, even if it is not as regimented as other early Christian writings recommend.[8]

If the description of Hermas's fast is relatively ordinary, his relationship with the shepherd seems to have flipped completely. After Hermas's persistent questionings throughout much of the book, it is surprising to see the shepherd ask the first question. Hermas is thus the one who gives answers in Sim. 5.1.1–2 (54.1–2). Also startling is the quickness with which the shepherd shifts from the singular to the plural in his interview. Although difficult to capture in idiomatic English, the shepherd first asks Hermas, "Why have you (sg.) come here early?" (Sim. 5.1.1 [54.1]) Two questions later, however, the shepherd asks Hermas, "What is this fast that you (pl.) keep?" (Sim. 5.1.2 [54.2]). Hermas answers in the singular, so other people do not appear to be in the narrative. Rather, the shepherd's plural address draws the audience into his conversation with Hermas.

The shepherd continues to speak as he demonstrates that his questions were intended to lead to revelation. The shepherd quickly transitions from a questioner to a revelatory figure when he claims that Hermas's customary fast is useless (Sim. 5.1.3 [54.3]). Through the dialogue with Hermas, the shepherd teaches something both negative and positive. The negative item is that Hermas's station is not a fast that is pleasing before God. The positive element of the shepherd's teaching concerns what a pleasing fast is (Sim. 5.1.3 [54.3]).[9] God does not accept Hermas's

---

4. Joachim also fasts in an isolated place until God visits him (*Prot. Jas.* 1.4; 4.2). Moses (Exod 24:18; 34:28), Elijah (1 Kgs [3 Kgdms] 19:8), and Jesus (Mark 1:12; Matt 4:1; Luke 4:1) likewise fast in deserted lands.

5. On the origin of *statio* in early Christian texts, see Mohrmann (1949, 76; 1953); Hillhorst (1976, 168–79). On the importance of Sim. 5.1.2 (54.2) as one piece of early Christian evidence for the use of Latin in Greek-speaking Christianity, see Houghton (2016, 14).

6. Osiek (1999, 169).

7. Rordorff and Tuilier (1978, 36–8); Wengst (1984, 97nn.64–5); Niederwimmer (1998, 131–3); Wilhite (2019a, 171–3). See also *Did. apost.* 21.

8. In addition to *Did.* 8.1, see the links that Tertullian finds between fasts and stations in *Or.* 19; *Ux.* 2.4; *Jejun.* 10. See also Brox (1991, 308–9). However, Ptolemy warns Flora not to fast on a set day (Epiphanius, *Pan.* 33.5.13).

9. In the midst of the shepherd's speech, the plural returns to a singular as suddenly as the initial change. The shepherd says, "I am telling you (sg.) that this is no fast that you (pl.) think you are fasting, but I will teach you (sg.) what an acceptable and complete fast is before God" (Sim. 5.1.3 [54.3]).

fast on Hermas's terms, because fasting in this way does not lead to acts of justice and righteousness. Accordingly, the fast serves no purpose (Sim. 5.1.4 [54.4]). Although the shepherd will later clarify how fasting can be properly undertaken (Sim. 5.3.5–7 [56.5–7]), the shepherd here focuses on right actions in his positive teaching. Hermas should not commit evil and should serve the Lord with a pure heart. The directives sound like statements which are found at various points in the Mandates.[10] The shepherd says that Hermas can keep a fast that is pleasing to God by focusing on right actions beyond the treatment of food alone.[11] The shepherd's treatment of fasting is reminiscent of the prophetic critique of fasting in Isa 58:1–14, in which the prophet calls for correcting injustice, freeing the oppressed, and housing the homeless. Although the *Shepherd* does not cite Isa 58 directly, the passage is cited clearly in *Barn.* 3.1–6 and Justin, *Dial.* 15.1–11. The *Shepherd* defines fasting for Hermas in a way that keeps with other early Christian conceptions of fasting.

The shepherd next urges Hermas to listen to a parable about fasting (Sim. 5.2.1 [55.1]). The parable involves a master who is leaving on a journey and is told in two parts. In Sim. 5.2.2–8 (55.2–8), the master commands a slave to build a wall around his vineyard while he is away but not to do anything else. If he does these things, the master promises the slave his freedom. The slave obediently fences in the vineyard. He also removes the weeds and cultivates the land. When the master returns to a flourishing vineyard, he not only gives the slave his freedom but also makes the slave coheir with the master's son—a decision with which the son and his friends agree. The second part centers on a banquet (Sim. 5.2.9–11 [55.9–11]). The master sends some of the banquet food to the slave, but the slave takes only what he needs. He distributes the rest to his fellow-slaves, and the slaves pray that he will receive even more favor. By giving away his food, the slave embodies the instructions that were given in Sim. 2.5–7 (51.5–7).[12] Despite his status as a slave, the slave becomes rich relative to his fellow-slaves. He acts as a just wealthy person when he gives away the extra food that he has received, and he also curries favor through his provision for his fellow-slaves, who are poorer than him. When the master hears about this in Sim. 5.2.11 (55.11), he is overjoyed along with his son and the son's friends.

Two matters are worth noting before addressing the shepherd's interpretation directly. First, by telling a story about a vineyard, the shepherd delves into a tradition with deep roots in Jewish prophetic literature and in the Jesus traditions. Perhaps the most notable example of such a parable is found in Isa 5:1–7 where readers discover a parable about God's care for Israel that is told in terms of the

---

10. Osiek (1999, 169).

11. Brox (1991, 310). Rudolph Arbesmann finds an emphasis on "the inner disposition of the soul" and "the spirit of penance and self-denial" in this passage (Arbesmann 1949–51, 38). However, Hermas is called to act, and Arbesmann's priority on the interior risks obscuring the need for actions.

12. Brox (1991, 311); Osiek (1999, 172). See similarly Downs (2016, 253–4).

construction of a vineyard. Jeremiah also reports God's complaint about Israel's worship of other gods by comparing two different types of vines (Jer 2:21), while the Psalmist narrates Israel's exodus and exile by employing the imagery of a vineyard (Ps 79:9–17 [MT 80:9–17]). Likewise, the Synoptic Gospels recall a parable that Jesus told about Israel's leaders in terms of corrupt vineyard tenants (Matt 21:33–46; Mark 12:1–9; Luke 20:9–16), while John describes the relationship between the Father, Jesus, and believers in terms of a vine (John 15:1–6). The story in Sim. 5.2 (55.1–11) draws upon and develops traditions like these.[13]

The second item to observe is the correspondence between the two-part structure of the parable and the two-part explanation by the shepherd. The shepherd's speech can be divided in multiple ways, namely, rhetorically and thematically. The clearest means by which the interpretation can be structured is around Hermas's questions. The explanation begins because Hermas tells the shepherd that he does not understand the parable. The shepherd then teaches him the meaning of the story (Sim. 5.3.1–3 [56.1–3]). After finding that the master's instructions correspond to God's commands, Hermas affirms that he will do whatever the shepherd tells him. Upon hearing this, the shepherd continues his explanation (Sim. 5.3.4–9 [56.4–9]). This twofold division is made based upon rhetorical markers.[14]

Brox observes a second way in which the shepherd's comments are outlined that corresponds more closely with the thematic structure of the parable.[15] The explanation in Sim. 5.3.1–6 (56.1–6) discusses the duties that God's servants have in keeping God's commands. This includes keeping watch against evil and purifying one's heart. The discussion between Hermas and the shepherd here parallels the first section of the parable in which the slave kept the master's commands regarding the vineyard (Sim. 5.2.2–8 [55.2–8]). The second portion of the explanation takes up the way in which money saved on food during a fast should be gathered and given to the poor (Sim. 5.3.7 [56.7]), which is suggested by the slave's giving away of extra food in Sim. 5.2.9–11 (55.9–11). Brox's thematic outline helpfully illustrates how the parable and the explanation fit together.

With this outline in mind, more can now be said about the shepherd's explanation in Sim. 5.3 (56.1–9). After Hermas's declaration of ignorance and the shepherd's corresponding promise to explain matters,[16] the shepherd's interpretation works on an analogy. The shepherd takes important themes and actions from the parable and applies them to the issue at hand, that is, to fasting. The shepherd opens with a fundamental statement: "Keep the Lord's commandments, and you will be pleasing

---

13. Joly (1968, 227n.1); Beavis (2018, 656–8, 665–6).

14. Henne (1988, 572).

15. Brox (1991, 306).

16. Joly (1968, 230n.1) notes a similar phenomenon in *4 Ezra* 5.39. The interaction between Hermas and the shepherd is similar to interactions between apocalyptic visionaries and interpreting angels in other early Jewish apocalypses. See the further discussion about interpreting angels in Chapter 7.

to him and registered in the number of those who keep his commandments" (Sim. 5.3.2 [56.2]).[17] The slave in the parable embodied this statement well in Sim. 5.2.2–8 (55.2–8). The shepherd has given Hermas a series of mandates as God's messenger. If Hermas keeps these, he will please God. To go beyond these commandments like the slave in the vineyard will bring even greater glory for Hermas.[18] If Hermas adds the type of service that he undertakes by fasting while keeping God's commandments, he can thus rejoice even more (Sim. 5.3.3 [56.3]).

When he hears this, Hermas tells the shepherd that he will keep any command that the shepherd gives (Sim. 5.3.4 [56.4]). The shepherd offers two actions that summarize what is required for a proper fast. Hermas must guard himself from every evil word and desire, and he must purify his heart from the empty things in this age. If Hermas does these things, his fast will be deemed complete (Sim. 5.3.6 [56.6]). The shepherd's explanation in Sim. 5.3.5-6 (56.5-6) links back to Sim. 5.1.3-5 (54.3-5). Fasting does not consist in going without food. Rather, the one who is fasting should live in a way that is characterized by keeping God's commandments and abstaining from evil activities.[19] Such an observation does not render the limitation of one's food worthless. Instead, it places physical abstention from food in its proper position relative to acting rightly. The shepherd's more specific instructions about fasting are prefaced with a clause assuming that the fast will be done after Hermas has completed what has already been written (Sim. 5.3.7 [56.7]). Hermas should then refuse to eat anything except bread and water. In the shepherd's description of fasting with basic food rather than a complete rejection of all nourishment, he attests a practice that is similar to other early Christian texts.[20] For example, Tertullian highlights the stories of Daniel, Elijah, Samuel, and Aaron as examples of limited fasts (*Jejun.* 10). Tertullian regards these fasts as inferior to complete abstention from food, but he nevertheless offers evidence for the sort of practice described in the *Shepherd*.[21]

The shepherd does not stop by giving Hermas instructions about how to approach food when fasting. He continues to discuss how Hermas should pass on the money that he saves on food to widows, orphans, and the needy (Sim. 5.3.7 [56.7]). Hermas is instructed to estimate the cost of food from the day of fasting and to give that money away.[22] The purpose of this action is twofold. First,

---

17. Most of this phrase is omitted in A. This is likely due to homeoteleuton—a scribal error due to the similar endings of nearby words. In this case, the scribe's eyes moved from the first mention of "the commandments" (τὰς ἐντολάς) in Sim. 5.3.2 [56.2]) to the second instance of the word later in the verse. The text translated here follows M, to which L¹ and L² are similar. See further Bonner (1934, 49–50).

18. Svigel (2016, 253–4).

19. Blidstein (2017, 79) rightly observes that fasting in the *Shepherd* and other early Christian texts could be linked to actions such as prayer and repentance.

20. Dibelius (1923, 567); Osiek (1999, 174).

21. See also *Acts Paul* 3.25; *Acts Thom.* 20. See further Dunn (1996, 86–8).

22. Similar instructions are found in Aristides, *Apol.* 15.7–8; *Const. ap.* 5.1; *Did. apost.* 19.1; Origen, *Hom. Lev.* 10.2.

the one who receives will be satisfied by this act of humility. Second, that person will pray for Hermas. The shepherd's instructions now bear strong resemblance to Sim. 5.2.9–11 (55.9–11). The slave enjoyed favor and prayer from his fellow-slaves and the approval of his master for his work of supererogation. The shepherd's explanation also corresponds to the parable of the elm and the vine (Sim. 2.5–7 [51.5–7]).[23] When the rich supply the needs of the poor, they trust that their reward comes from God and that the poor will pray for them to be further blessed. The importance of fasting is thus not limited to the individual. The fast is a communal practice not in that everyone fasts as a community but in that one person's fasting benefits others around them.

The conclusion of the parabolic interpretation continues the shepherd's exhortation to act rightly and to obey the commandments (Sim. 5.3.8–9 [56.8–9]). The shepherd expands the emphasis on community in a direction that should be familiar to readers of the *Shepherd* at this point in the narrative. In addition to giving to the poor, Hermas should obey the shepherd's instructions along with his children and his household.[24] The shepherd's interpretation of the parable thus uses the parable as a vehicle by which to urge Hermas and his readers to act rightly. The parable is not interpreted as a description of a fact, event, or situation. It is viewed instead as an ethical example and tool to teach the correct way to follow God's commandments.

Christology (Sim. 5.4.1–5.6.4a [57.1–59.4a])

Thus far in Sim. 5, the shepherd and Hermas have discussed fasting, heard a parable, and interpreted the parable with regard to the initial conversation about fasting. In theory, this could be a good stopping place for Sim. 5. It is startling, then, when Hermas begins feverishly to ask the shepherd to reveal the meaning of the parable. Yet this is precisely what Hermas does in Sim. 5.4.1 (57.1). Hermas lists the characters from the parable about which he desires to know. In resuming this conversation at such a high pitch, Hermas changes markedly from the inquisitive obedience evident in his statements in Sim. 5.3.1, 4 (56.1, 4). His level of intensity has been ramped up. The shepherd's conversation rises to match Hermas's level. In response to Hermas's ardor, the shepherd tells Hermas that he is arrogant.[25] If anything needs to be explained to Hermas, the shepherd informs him that it will be explained (Sim. 5.4.2 [57.2]). The shepherd does not explicitly mention that he has just finished explaining the parable, but the earlier interpretation, along with Hermas's immediate questions, may be part of why the shepherd is so frustrated.

---

23. Brox (1991, 313).

24. For earlier references to children and the household, see Vis. 1.1.9 (1.9); 1.3.1–2 (3.1–2); Mand. 2.7 (27.7); 5.1.7 (33.7); 12.3.6 (46.6).

25. Reiling (1973, 100) notes that, aside from Hermas, such terminology is applied with similar force only to the false prophet in Mand. 11 (43.1–21).

Hermas counters that whatever he sees or hears will have been seen or heard in vain if the shepherd does not explain the meaning (Sim. 5.4.3 [57.3]). Yet the shepherd has another comeback: servants of God should ask for revelation directly from God. Only idle servants hesitate to ask (Sim. 5.4.3 [57.3]). Since God is gracious and compassionate, the shepherd presses Hermas as to why he has not asked God (Sim. 5.4.4 [57.4]). Hermas responds that he has asked the shepherd because the shepherd is there with him. He assures the shepherd that if the shepherd was not there, he would ask the Lord directly (Sim. 5.4.5 [57.5]). The shepherd, perhaps somewhat exasperated, insists that Hermas is sly and arrogant. Yet because he is stubborn, the shepherd will explain the meaning of the parable so that Hermas can make the explanation known to others (Sim. 5.5.1 [58.1]).

Narratively, the conversation provides a transition from one explanation to another. By recording this conversation, the narrator allows for a break between the fasting interpretation and the Christological interpretation. The sharpness of the conversation further emphasizes what follows.[26] Having just heard an explanation of the parable and a pointed exchange between the shepherd and Hermas, readers are now prepared to discover what Hermas wants to know.

The shepherd's explanation interprets the parable as an allegory. He lists ten items and their corresponding meanings in Sim. 5.5.2–3 (58.2–3).

1. Field	This world
2. Lord of the field	Creator, finisher, and empowerer of all things
3. Son	Holy spirit
4. Slave	Son of God
5. Vines	This people
6. Walls	The Lord's holy angels
7. Weeds	Lawless deeds of God's slaves
8. Food	Commandments
9. Friends and counselors	Holy angels
10. Master's journey	Remaining time until his coming

Not everything in the parable is mentioned. For example, the shepherd's allegorical interpretation omits the many slaves whom the master owns and to whom the trusted slave gives food. However, most of the key nouns in the parable have an allegorical equivalent, particularly those in Sim. 5.2.2–8 (55.2–8). The explanation describes God's actions in the world in order to bring the commandments to God's people. This is accomplished by the slave's work in caring for the vineyard and is approved by the master, the son, his friends, and his counselors. Lawless deeds are

---

26. A similar strategy is found in Vis. 3.8.9 (16.9), in which the woman insults Hermas before urging readers to act rightly and wisely until the completion of the tower (Vis. 3.9.1–10 [17.1–10]). See Osiek (1999, 78). Likewise, the shepherd has already been frustrated with Hermas when he began to draw the Mandates to a close and countered Hermas's worries that he is unable to keep the commandments (Mand. 12.3.5–12.4.1 [46.5–47.1]).

removed by the slave, and the slave passes the commandments on to those who serve God.

The shepherd's interpretation brings the parable closer to the type of story that Jesus tells at the temple in the Synoptic Gospels (Matt 21:33–46; Mark 12:1–12; Luke 20:9–16).[27] Both the *Shepherd* and the Synoptics tell a story about God's actions in history that utilizes the vineyard as a setting. Although there is no suggestion of literary dependence, this is not the only way in which the shepherd's interpretation is in keeping with themes found elsewhere in early Christian literature. A field is understood to be a metaphor for the world in the Matthean explanation of the parable of the wheat and the weeds (Matt 13:38).[28] Likewise, the reference to God in terms of the master who created all things echoes widely held Jewish and Christian claims in the centuries surrounding the times of the *Shepherd*'s composition. The shepherd has already emphatically affirmed God's place as creator by placing this claim at the head of the Mandates (Mand. 1.1 [26.1]). In doing so, the *Shepherd* echoes statements also found in early Jewish texts (e.g., Sir 18:1; Wis 1:14; 2 Macc 7:23; 3 Macc 2:3). God's role in creation is similarly attested in Acts 17:24; Rom 11:36; 1 Cor 8:6; Eph 3:9; Rev 4:11.[29] Additionally, that God empowers his creation is found in Ps 67:29 (MT 68:29). While the implication of Sim. 5.5.3 (58.3) that one must be ready for the Parousia is not surprising in early Christian literature,[30] it is more unusual for God to be the one who returns rather than Jesus. Yet this is how the shepherd's interpretation must be read.[31]

What is more surprising is that the son in the parable is identified as the holy spirit,[32] while the slave in the parable is described as the Son of God. Indeed, after Hermas's exclamations of wonder (Sim. 5.5.4–5 [58.4–5]), this is precisely the point about which he inquires: "Why, lord, is the Son of God positioned in the form of a slave?" (Sim. 5.5.5 [58.5]). The shepherd's response begins by rejecting the premise of Hermas's questions. The Son of God is not positioned as a slave but rather has great authority and lordship (Sim. 5.6.1 [59.1]).[33] Hermas, perhaps expressing

---

27. Osiek (1999, 171n.1); Glancy (2002, 104–5); Beavis (2018, 656–7).

28. The parable is found in Matt 13:24–30.

29. See further Joly (1968, 235).

30. E.g., Mark 13:33–37; Matt 25:13.

31. *2 Clement* also speaks of God's appearance rather than Jesus's return (*2 Clem.* 12.1). Joly (1968, 236n.3); Brox (1991, 317–18); Osiek (1999, 178n.22).

32. On the holy spirit in the *Shepherd*, see Chapter 10 of this volume as well as Brox (1991, 541–6); Haas (1992, 552–86); Osiek (1999, 31–4); Svigel (2019, 30–5).

33. There is a textual issue at this point in the manuscript tradition. L^1, L^2, and E attest negative adverbs that can be translated into English as "not." However, A does not include the comparable Greek word, while M is defective at this point in the manuscript. I accept the reading in the translations because they provide the more difficult reading. The shepherd has just said that the Son of God is the slave in the parable (Sim. 5.5.2 [58.2]) but now appears to contradict himself. Because leaving the word "not" out of the text makes more sense in the story, it is more difficult to imagine why a scribe would add "not" to their text than why they would omit the word. This suggests that "not" is more likely to

what most of the audience thinks when recalling the allegorical identifications in Sim. 5.5.2 (58.2), informs the shepherd that he does not understand how this is the case.

The shepherd explains the reason for his claim that the Son of God has authority by observing that the vineyard is handed over to him (Sim. 5.6.2 [59.2]). God planted the vineyard. This action represents God's creation of God's people and recalls the exploration of the Lord of the field in Sim. 5.5.2 (58.2). Yet when God gave the field over to the Son of God, the Son of God established angels to protect the people. The shepherd's explanation is an allegorical interpretation of Sim. 5.2.3 (55.3), in which the slave builds a fence around the vineyard. Using the interpretive key of Sim. 5.5.2–3 (58.2–3), the shepherd depicts the Son of God establishing angels to protect the people, that is, the vines. One may wonder what to make of the slave's next action in Sim. 5.2.3–4 (55.3–4) where he takes the weeds out and cultivates the vineyard. While this extra work was initially interpreted as fasting while keeping God's other commandments (Sim. 5.3.5–6 [56.5–6]), the shepherd now tells Hermas that the slave's clearing of the weeds also represents the act of cleansing the people from their sins. The Son of God's actions demand hard work, "for no one is able to cultivate a vineyard without toil or labor" (Sim. 5.6.2 [59.2]). After purifying their sins, the shepherd reveals that the Son of God next showed people the paths of life. In other words, the Son of God gave them the law that he received from his father (Sim. 5.6.3 [59.3]). The law that Jesus brings is best understood as including the moral teaching in the *Shepherd*, particularly in the Mandates.[34] Referring again to the identifications of Sim. 5.5.2–3 (58.2–3), the shepherd tells Hermas about the slave's act of passing along bread to the other slaves (Sim. 5.2.9 [55.9]). However, since the other slaves were not mentioned in Sim. 5.5.2–3 (58.2–3), the shepherd does not refer to the other slaves by name. Rather, the shepherd uses a pronoun (αὐτοῖς) in Sim. 5.6.3 (59.3) and thereby merges the people represented by the vines with the other slaves alongside the Son of God. The shepherd concludes that the Son of God is in fact the Lord of the people because he has received all authority from his Father (Sim. 5.6.4 [59.4]).[35]

The interpretation in Sim. 5.5.2–5.6.4a (58.2–59.4a) thus moves in three parts that correspond to the slave's three primary movements. In the parable, the slave (1) fences in the vineyard as instructed, (2) cultivates the vineyard by removing the weeds, and (3) gives his surplus food away. The Son of God correspondingly (1') established angels to watch over the people, (2') cleansed the people from their sins, and (3') showed them the paths of life by giving them the law.[36]

---

be the older reading. See further Hilgenfeld (1881, 84); Joly (1968, 237n.6); Brox (1991, 318); Lindemann and Paulsen (1992, 446); Osiek (1999, 177); Ehrman (2003, 2.332–333); Holmes (2007, 578–9); Prinzivalli and Simonetti (2010–15, 2.360).

34. Osiek (1999, 179).

35. See the similar language in Matt 28:18; 1 Cor 15:24–25; Eph 1:20–23.

36. Svigel (2016, 253–61) takes Sim. 5 to be evidence for an incarnational narrative about Jesus that held together early Christian communities not only in Rome but in much of the ancient Mediterranean world.

Before moving further into Sim. 5.6.4b–8 (59.4b–8), one further matter should be highlighted in this section. The shepherd's interpretation interprets the Son of God in terms of a slave. Similar interpretive moves are found elsewhere in early Christian literature. Paul describes Jesus as emptying himself and taking on the form of a slave. Jesus humbled himself to accept death on a cross and was exalted to the place of honor at the Father's right hand (Phil 2:6–11).[37] The Johannine Jesus demonstrates his servanthood by washing the disciples' feet in John 13, then urging them to likewise become slaves because "a slave is not greater than his master" (John 13:14–16; see also John 15:20).[38] Justin understands Jacob's marriage to Leah and Rachel (Gen 29:1–30) as types for the synagogue and the church. Yet Christ is a slave of both and restores all who keep his commandments (*Dial.* 134.1–5).[39] Without referring to any of these passages directly, the shepherd follows a similar interpretive trajectory in Sim. 5.5.2–5.6.4a (58.2–59.4a) by describing Jesus as the servant whose actions provided salvation. The *Shepherd* portrays the Son as a slave, but the slave has authority over the vineyard and works for the salvation of the vines that the master has planted.

Flesh and Spirit (Sim. 5.6.4b–8 [59.4b–8])

After finishing his allegorical interpretation, the shepherd shifts directions. He instructs Hermas, "Hear why the Lord took his son and the glorious angels as a counselor concerning the slave's inheritance" (Sim. 5.6.4 [59.4]). Along with Sim. 5.5.2–5.6.4a (58.2–59.4a), Sim. 5.6.4b–8 (59.4b–8) has attracted scholarly attention because of what it says about Jesus. Joly observes that some scholars find the *Shepherd*'s Christology to be adoptionist and binitarian.[40] A key reason for this is that the slave in the parable, who is identified as the Son of God (Sim. 5.5.2 [58.2]), receives his reward on the basis of what he has done. His reward is to be welcomed as an heir into the family of the master (God) and the son (holy spirit). Although much of Sim. 5.5.2–5.6.4a (58.2–59.4a) focuses on the slave's work in the vineyard, Sim. 5.6.4b–5.6.8 (59.4b–59.8) discusses the slave's reward. There is a twist in the plot, however. The slave is no longer identified as the Son of God. Rather, the slave

---

37. Joly (1968, 237n.5). Brox (1991, 319) thinks that the *Shepherd*'s use of slave imagery does not fit well with the other use of δοῦλος as a title for Jesus in Phil 2:7, while Henne (1992a, 190) acknowledges that "l'identification du Christ à l'esclave en Phil 2,7 a une toute autre valeur." The point is not that these two passages are identical. Rather, both rely on a depiction of Jesus as a slave who is exalted from his humble position. For further discussion, see Beavis (2018, 665–6); Soyars (2019, 153–63).

38. Bennema (2014, 266) divides John 13:4–17 into four stages: showing, knowing, doing, and being. John 13:14–16 include portions of Jesus's rationale (knowing) and the instruction to imitate him (doing).

39. See further Origen, *Comm. Matt.* 12.29 and the references listed in Bauer (1909, 316).

40. Joly (1968, 32). See also Wilson (1927, 45).

now stands for the flesh (Sim. 5.6.5 [59.5]). Yet the question of whose flesh is in view must be raised. Since the allegorical interpretation described the salvific work that the Son of God accomplished in the vineyard, it seems initially plausible to consider the flesh under discussion in Sim. 5.6.4b–5.6.8 (59.4b–59.8) to belong to Jesus. Thus Dibelius concludes that an adoptionist Christology is in view at least insofar as Christ's fleshly nature is elevated because of his work.[41] Wilson understands the parable to mean that God has a natural son, the holy spirit, and an adopted son, the Son of God. The Son of God, who is represented by the slave in the parable, was a celestial entity that advised God at the beginning of creation but was only related to God as an heir after the incarnation.[42]

The adoptionist interpretation accounts for each of the characters in the parable as separate entities. The parabolic master, son, and slave are consistently interpreted as distinctly identifiable characters. Osiek likewise acknowledges that the *Shepherd* seems to attest a "pneumatic adoptionist Christology."[43] But if this is the case, one wonders why the *Shepherd* was not condemned during the Christological controversies of the fourth and fifth centuries.[44] Chapter 3 highlighted the popularity of the *Shepherd* among figures such as Eusebius, Athanasius, Didymus, Jerome, Rufinus, and John Cassian. The current chapter has also highlighted Henne's admonition to be aware of polysemous or, better, multisemous images in the *Shepherd*.[45] Perhaps it is better, then, to think of Sim. 5.5.2–5.6.4a (58.2–59.4a) and 5.6.4b–5.6.8 (59.4b–59.8) as completely separate interpretations of the parable.

Henne argued for such an understanding in his study of Christology in *1 Clement* and the *Shepherd*. He interprets the son in the parable as the Trinitarian holy spirit in Sim. 5.5.2 (58.2).[46] The *Shepherd* thus presents an incipient Trinitarianism in Sim. 5.5.2–5.6.4a (58.2–59.4a). When the shepherd shifts to an alternative explanation of the parable in Sim. 5.6.4b–5.6.8 (59.4b–8), Henne understands the emphasis of the parable to lie on the ethical reformation of the believer's life. He thus divides the focus of the two explanations into Christology and soteriology, respectively.[47] Moreover, the identity of the slave differs in each interpretation. In the first, the slave represents the Son of God. In the second, however, the flesh has no relation to the Son of God. The flesh is discussed solely with reference to believers in the audience. Bogdan Bucur separates the shepherd's explanations in a similar fashion. The identity of the Son of God is taken up in Sim.

---

41. Dibelius (1923, 573).
42. Wilson (1993, 132–4).
43. Osiek (1999, 179).
44. Osiek (1999, 179–80); Bucur (2007, 120).
45. Henne (1989).
46. Henne (1992a, 225).
47. Henne (1988; 1989, 132). Hurtado (2003, 604) likewise sees a focus on how believers should live in Sim. 5.6.4–8 (59.4–8). For more on the outline of this parable, see Stewart-Sykes (1997, 275–6); Svigel (2016, 260–1).

5.5.2–5.6.4a (58.2–59.4a), while the right way for the audience to employ their flesh as believers is discussed in Sim. 5.6.4b–5.6.8 (59.4b–8).⁴⁸ However, Bucur understands the reference to "the preexistent holy spirit who created all creation" (τὸ πνεῦμα τὸ ἅγιον τὸ προὸν τὸ κτίσαν πᾶσαν τὴν κτίσιν; Sim. 5.6.5 [59.5]) to be a reference not to the Trinitarian holy spirit but rather to the Son of God. He compares the phrase in Sim. 5.6.5 (59.5) to language in Vis. 2.4.1 (8.1); Sim. 9.1.1 (78.1); Sim. 9.12.1–2 (89.1–2) along with other instances of early Jewish and early Christian angelomorphism.⁴⁹

This brief overview of scholarship illustrates the difficulties that readers of Sim. 5.4–5.6 (57.1–59.8) have encountered and the highly disputed nature of the text. The primary issue to settle is how the shepherd's interpretations in Sim. 5.5.2–5.6.4a (58.2–59.4a) and Sim. 5.6.4b–5.6.8 (59.4b–8) relate to each other. Does the latter interpretation develop the former? Or are these passages better understood as completely separate from one another? Phrased in this way, the options form a false dichotomy. Either option could be right, but there is no reason to exclude a third option from the outset. Another way of reading these passages could view Sim. 5.6.4b–5.6.8 (59.4b–8) as both a continuation of the Christological interpretation that precedes it and as an expansion of the parable so that it applies to the audience. Two preliminary reasons for the plausibility of this way of reading can be offered before turning to a closer reading of Sim. 5.6.4b–5.6.8 (59.4b–8). First, the passage is not obviously disconnected from what came before. This suggests continuity between the two explanations. Although the shepherd introduces this passage by instructing Hermas to listen, he employs the same characters from the parable and the Christological interpretation (Sim. 5.6.4b [59.4b]).⁵⁰ Moreover, the parable's master, son, and angels are given the same interpretive identifications as in Sim. 5.5.2–3 (58.2–3). Second, however, the audience expands by the end of this passage. Although it is not clear whose flesh is under discussion in Sim. 5.6.5 (59.5), the shepherd refers to all people at the end of the explanation (Sim. 5.6.7 [59.7]). These two observations suggest both continuity and discontinuity in the shepherd's interpretation. Recognizing both elements may allow for a resolution in the tension regarding how to understand the relationship of Sim. 5.5.2–5.6.4a (58.2–59.4a) and Sim. 5.6.4b–5.6.8 (59.4b–8).

It is helpful to start by considering elements of discontinuity in the shepherd's final interpretation of the parable. In the conclusion of the explanation, Hermas is told that "all flesh" (πᾶσα σάρξ) will be paid (Sim. 5.6.7 [59.7]). The wage that the shepherd refers to is payment for a job well done. However, two qualifications are given in order that this flesh might receive a reward. First, the flesh must be

---

48. Bucur (2007, 135–8).

49. Bucur (2007, 127–9). See also Marshall (2005, 14–15). Bucur follows a suggestion in Levison (1995a) to consider the *Shepherd*'s use of *spirit* alongside other early Jewish usages, which sometimes employ the word with reference to angels. See further Levison (1995b; 1997, 27–55).

50. So also Lona (1993, 70n.180).

found undefiled and spotless. Second, the holy spirit must dwell in the flesh. All flesh in which these two qualities obtain will receive a reward. The shepherd's third interpretation is thus not only a Christological interpretation of the parable. Nevertheless, the Son of God is not far removed from the interpretation. The transition in Sim. 5.6.4b (59.4b) uses most of the same identifications from Sim. 5.5.2–3 (58.2–3) so that the flesh in which God chose to make his holy spirit dwell can be understood as belonging to the Son of God. The flesh then takes the role of the slave in the parable (Sim. 5.2 [55.1–11]) and serves the holy spirit well (Sim. 5.6.5 [59.5]). The flesh becomes a willing collaborator with the spirit in everything so that God chose the flesh to be a partner with the holy spirit (Sim. 5.6.6 [59.6]). The parable illustrates God's choice of the flesh in the Son of God who became a slave. In this work, the Son of God united his flesh to the spirit perfectly (Sim. 5.6.4b–7 [59.4b–7]), just as his labor to remove the weeds was interpreted as the removal of lawless deeds in Sim. 5.5.2–5.6.4a (58.2–59.4a).[51] Through the slave's actions, the flesh may now have a dwelling place and not lose its reward (Sim. 5.6.7 [59.7]).

Although the slave symbolizes the flesh in Sim. 5.6.4b–5.6.8 (59.4b–59.8), an overview of scholarship indicates that the question of whose flesh is in view is more difficult to answer. There appears to be some fluidity in the shepherd's interpretation. The flesh is described in some ways that befit the Son of God in Sim. 5.5.2–5.6.4a (58.2–59.4a). However, the Son of God is not the only one in view in the shepherd's last explanation (Sim. 5.6.7 [59.7]). The audience is invited to participate in the parable by submitting their flesh to God's spirit. Put another way, they are invited to imitate the Son of God, who subjected his flesh to God's spirit so that the spirit labored with and through him. This reading best accounts for the ambiguities in Sim. 5.5.2–5.6.8 (58.2–59.8).

While the interpretation pertains to both the Son of God and the *Shepherd*'s readers, the *Shepherd* does not lay out a fully developed Christological statement in Sim. 5.6.4b–5.6.8 (59.4b–8). Rather, the shepherd's interpretation must be understood alongside the concerns in the rest of the work.[52] The *Shepherd* is concerned about how believers can live in a divided world, that is, a world that is externally divided into two spirits and a world divided inside people who struggle with double-mindedness. The slave in the parable, who is variously understood as the Son of God and the flesh of both God's Son and believers, provides a way to unify the flesh with God's Spirit. Because the Son of God subjected his flesh to the holy spirit, the *Shepherd*'s readers are enabled and encouraged to live in the same

---

51. See similarly Hauck (1993, 196–7).

52. "The Christology of Hermas can only be understood when the questions, that is, the problems of human nature and salvation, is addressed" (Hauck 1993, 188). Although one might nuance Hauck's view of what the *Shepherd* is about differently, at least as it is phrased in this sentence, his admonition to read the *Shepherd* on its own terms is worth heeding.

way.⁵³ The shepherd finally tells Hermas, "You also have the explanation of this parable" (Sim. 5.6.8 [59.8]).

The Challenge of the Parable (Sim. 5.7 [60.1–4])

Hermas tells the shepherd that he is happy to have heard this explanation (Sim. 5.7.1 [60.1]). His response links both to the shepherd's conclusion of his explanation and to the dialogue that he had with the shepherd in Sim. 5.4.1–5.5.1 (57.1–58.1). Hermas's gladness upon hearing the explanation coincides with his previous pleas for the shepherd to explain the parable further. Hermas's request has been granted, and he is happy.⁵⁴ Yet the shepherd is not quite finished. He again tells Hermas to listen. Hermas is instructed to keep his flesh pure and undefiled so that the spirit that dwells in the flesh may testify for it and so that the flesh may be justified (Sim. 5.7.1 [60.1]).⁵⁵ The justification of the flesh is not Hermas's responsibility. The verb is passive, which signifies that another must act in order for the flesh to be justified.⁵⁶ Yet Hermas is called to be active in keeping his flesh pure. His response to the parable's interpretation is thus not merely acceptance or belief. Nor is it enough for Hermas to transmit the revelation, although readers can presume that Hermas has done precisely this because they are reading the text. In order to respond properly to the shepherd's teaching, Hermas must actively keep his flesh pure.

This instruction follows closely along the lines of what has been said already in the *Shepherd*. For example, the shepherd instructed Hermas in Mand. 5.1.1–2 (33.1–2) to be patient and understanding so that the holy spirit that dwells in him will not be defiled by another spirit.⁵⁷ Instructions to keep the flesh pure are likewise found in Ign. *Phld.* 7.2; *Acts Paul* 3.5; *2 Clem.* 9.3. The *Shepherd* is hardly alone in this instruction. Yet the *Shepherd*'s teaching follows a parable explaining the way in which the flesh and spirit should relate to one another. Although the instruction to keep the flesh pure sounds ambiguous when read on its own, the meaning becomes clearer after reading Sim. 5.6.4b–5.6.8 (59.4b–8). Hermas is to submit his flesh to the holy spirit that dwells in him. Likewise, the reward mentioned in Sim. 5.6.7 (59.7) receives some clarification in the shepherd's instruction to Hermas. The reward is the immortality of the flesh. Hermas is told not to ascent to the idea

---

53. Svigel (2016, 260), borrowing from Kuruvilla (2013), usefully refers to Sim. 5 as "'christiconic,' that is, Christ's life as a true, ideal man becomes a pattern to follow for all Christians."
54. Brox (1991, 324–5).
55. Blidstein (2017, 155).
56. Thus Osiek (1999, 182) notes that justification is God's work.
57. See further Brox (1991, 325); Rothschild (2017).

that the flesh is merely mortal. Because the flesh and the holy spirit should work together, Hermas will not live if the flesh is defiled (Sim. 5.7.2 [60.2]).[58]

Hermas then inquires about the means by which someone who has already defiled their flesh before hearing what the shepherd says may be saved (Sim. 5.7.3 [60.3]). The shepherd's response does not allow ignorance to be an excuse for sin. Rather, God's power is able to heal ignorance because all authority belongs to God.[59] Hermas's responsibility is simply to keep himself pure (Sim. 5.7.4 [60.4]). As he does this, the Lord will heal earlier acts of ignorance because the Lord is always compassionate. However, neither the flesh nor the spirit can be defiled from now on. As in the interpretation of Sim. 5.6.4b–5.6.8 (59.4b–8), the shepherd is emphatic that the flesh and spirit belong together. Because of this, the shepherd reasons that flesh and spirit cannot be defiled separately. If one is defiled, both will ultimately be defiled. Hermas must therefore keep both the flesh and the spirit pure. In Sim. 5.7.1 (60.1), the shepherd told Hermas to keep his flesh pure. The shepherd clarifies that he must keep both flesh and spirit from becoming stained in keeping with the earlier discussion of the flesh and spirit in the parable (Sim. 5.7.4 [60.4]; see Sim. 5.6.4b–5.6.8 [59.4b–8]). If Hermas obeys what the shepherd has told him and properly relates his flesh to his spirit, he will live to God.

Conclusion

The shepherd's instructions in Sim. 5.7 (60) are thus offered in light of the parabolic interpretation of Sim. 5.6.4b–5.6.8 (59.4b–8). A similar thing was found in the shepherd's instructions during the first interpretation of the parable in Sim. 5.3 (56). In the earlier passage, Hermas is to follow the shepherd's commandments by doing good, staying away from evil, and purifying his heart from meaningless things in this age. Added to this, Hermas may fast and give away the money for that day's food to the poor. In the latter passage, Hermas is urged to submit his flesh to the holy spirit that dwells in him so that he can live. The revelation that the shepherd offers to Hermas in the form of a parable and a series of interpretations

---

58. The *Shepherd* may refer here to the resurrection of the flesh, but it is not clear that the flesh's immortality includes the notion that the flesh will rise again. See further Lehtipuu (2015, 112–13). A clearer statement of the resurrection of the flesh is found in *2 Clem.* 9.3 Although the *Shepherd* clearly maintains the dignity of the flesh (Joly 1968, 241n.3), there is not enough evidence to assert that the *Shepherd*'s statements are polemically oriented. For claims that the *Shepherd* here polemicizes against gnostic claims see Lake (1912–13, 2.171); Dibelius (1923, 574). Reiling (1973, 66) and Brox (1991, 326) rightly correct this view.

59. Osiek (1999, 183). Ignatius claims that the ignorance of evil began to be destroyed in Ign. *Eph.* 19.3. Schoedel (1985, 94) rightly notes that the tense of the verbs should be interpreted as inceptive (i.e., began to x). On the interpretation of Ign. *Eph.* 19.2–3, see further Lookadoo (2017b, 74–7). For further links between ignorance and sin in ancient literature, see Körtner and Leutzsch (1998, 267n.125).

should thus result in Hermas living rightly. By living in accordance with the shepherd's instructions, Hermas will be blessed (Sim. 5.3.9 [56.9]) and will live to God (Sim. 5.7.4 [60.4]). Yet if Hermas's lifestyle is called to change along with that of his household and readers, the basis for the change is found in the reality of what the shepherd has revealed. The Son of God has been revealed in power by taking on the role of a slave, clearing the vineyard of lawless deeds, and submitting his flesh perfectly to the holy spirit. In the hands of the shepherd who has been sent to Hermas from God, a simple story about a slave's work in a vineyard reveals not only the truth about fasting but also the scope of the salvific work of the Son of God and the way in which the flesh and spirit relate to one another. In so doing, Sim. 5 illustrates well the multiple ways in which the *Shepherd*'s imagery and parables can be interpreted within the same text.

Chapter 6

THE CHARACTERS IN THE *SHEPHERD*

After undertaking an exegetical reading of one passage in the *Shepherd*, Chapter 6 turns now to a broader perspective on the work as a whole. This chapter examines the characters of the *Shepherd* in order to understand more clearly who is in the story. By viewing characters as a group, it will become easier to track the convoluted relationships within the story.[1] Yet this chapter aims to accomplish more than simply a list of characters. By exploring who the characters are and what they do in the story, this chapter hopes to contribute to discussions of the social dynamics in the text and audience. By reflecting on the revelatory characters in the text, the author's depiction of how revelation is given may also be better understood. To accomplish these goals, this chapter will attempt a prosopographical study of the *Shepherd* with similar aims to Paul Foster's prosopography of Colossians.[2]

> It is perhaps useful to explain what the term prosopography means. It is derived from the Greek word for "created face," *prosōpoeia* (προσωποεία). A prosopography is not simply a list of *dramatis personae* in a literary work such as Colossians. Rather, it seeks to gain insight into a collective group of historical characters, where details about certain individuals might be minimal or non-existent. Therefore, prosopographical research has the aim of learning about group dynamics and patterns of social relationships through the study of collective biography.[3]

The remainder of the chapter divides into three broad sections. The initial sections will explore the characters in the *Shepherd*. Although the prosopography will attempt to be thorough in its examinations, two caveats should be noted from the outset. First, only characters who are seen, discussed, or interacted with will appear in the prosopography. Groups of people represented, for example, by stones, branches, or mountains will not be considered here.[4] Second, more space

---

1. On prosopography, see further Stone (1971); Cameron (2003); Eck (2010).
2. Foster (2016, 90–105).
3. Foster (2016, 90).
4. More will be said about some of these symbolic groups in the study of imagery in Chapter 11.

will be given to major characters, such as Hermas, the woman who reveals the visions to him, and the shepherd. After identifying what the *Shepherd* says about various literary characters, the closing section of the chapter synthesizes these observations in order to learn more about group dynamics and revelation in the *Shepherd*. In so doing, the final section moves a prosopographical description of literary characters to a fuller study of what these relationships say about the world of the text and the second-century Roman audience.

Major Characters

Hermas

As the narrator, Hermas is the character through whose eyes one reads the *Shepherd*. He is mentioned in the opening sentences of the story in which he tells readers that the person who raised him (ὁ θρέψας) sold him to a woman named Rhoda in Rome.[5] It is not clear if Hermas was sold to Rhoda as a child or a young man. Hermas says that he was "reacquainted" (ἀνεγνωρισάμην) with Rhoda after many years (Vis. 1.1.1 [1.1]), which indicates that Hermas was later freed.[6] At this point, Hermas may have been able to meet his former owner again. When he was sold to Rhoda, Hermas may have already lived in Rome or he may have come to Rome at the time that he was sold. It is unclear how the preposition εἰς should be understood in this context (Vis. 1.1.1 [1.1]), and Hermas does not say much about his life before Rhoda.[7] Wherever Hermas was born, he is living in Rome again at the time of the story because he has remade the acquaintance of Rhoda, whom he loves "like a sister" (ὡς ἀδελφήν; Vis. 1.1.1 [1.1]).[8] Later in the *Shepherd*, the first vision of the tower takes place in the field where Hermas is involved in the production and refinement of raw materials (Vis. 3.1.2 [9.2]). Although both the text and translation of χονδρίζεις are disputed,[9] this remark suggests that Hermas is currently employed in an agrarian business.

---

5. One meaning attributed to the verb τρέφω is "to care for children by bringing them up" (BDAG s.v. 2). The participle is also used on two Jewish funerary inscriptions from Acmonia and Acroenus. Trebilco (1991, 70–1) translates the participles as "foster-parents" and "slaves" respectively. In the case of Hermas, the term likely refers to the man who raised him as a boy while he was a slave. See further Glancy (2002, 74–5); Weiß (2009, 193–4); Rüpke (2016, 147–8).

6. Osiek (1999, 42); Verheyden (2007, 64).

7. Brox (1991, 77); Körtner and Leutzsch (1998, 375 n.4).

8. Wilson (1927, 23n.2) notes that there are similarities between the opening of the *Shepherd* and ancient comedies. However, he is also correct to point out that Hermas's love for his owner is not sexual in nature.

9. The text is found only in S. L¹ contains a different translation, namely, *ubi uis*. The correctors of S, A, B, and L² read χρονίζεις. The multiple attestation for χρονίζεις may lie behind Körtner and Leutzsch's (1998, 160) preference for this reading. Yet it is precisely the

6. *The Characters in the* Shepherd

While Hermas's love for Rhoda is nonphysical, he also notices her beauty and thinks that someone would be fortunate to be married to such a woman (Vis. 1.1.2 [1.2]). There may be an implicit contrast between Rhoda and Hermas's wife. Hermas is married with children, and the sins of his family are a key reason why God calls Hermas to repentance through the revelatory figures in the *Shepherd* (Vis. 1.3.1 [3.1]; Sim. 7.2–3 [66.2–3]). Hermas is taught so that he can teach his family. Moreover, he appears to have been unable to raise them up properly prior to the revelations in this book. Hermas's character is described in some detail in Vis. 1.2.2–4 (2.2–4) by the woman who comes to him from God. When she comes to him, Hermas is crying because he has been visited by the heavenly Rhoda, who informs him that he has sinned.[10] The woman describes Hermas as patient, not easily angered, and always laughing. If the woman's description can be accepted as accurate, Hermas seems to be a cheerful character who is willing to wait for things to go as they should. These characteristics may also be hinted at when Hermas thanks the Lord for what has been revealed to him. Yet when he meets the woman, his face is downcast and unhappy. After a conversation in which Hermas explains his distress and the woman warns him against evil, she again describes Hermas as self-controlled (ἐγρατής; Vis. 1.2.4 [2.4]). He abstains from evil desires while also being full of single-mindedness and great innocence. The combination of self-controlled, single-minded, and innocent is also found in the virtue list of Vis. 3.8.7 (16.7). Indeed, many of the woman's descriptions are repeated elsewhere in the text. This gives rise to a tension in the *Shepherd*. Hermas is both a man who seeks to do right and a man who has sinned with regard to his family and to Rhoda.[11] Neither the good nor the bad traits in Hermas can be disregarded without ignoring parts of the narrative.

The same tensions arise when one considers the trait that Hermas might embody most consistently throughout the *Shepherd*, namely, curiosity. Hermas's curiosity is exemplified most clearly in his persistent questions. Some requests are

---

difficulty of χονδρίζεις that results in different translations. In light of the difficulty of the reading, S should be followed (Prinzivalli and Simonetti 2010–15, 2.555n.40).

Broadly speaking, one may follow BDAG in understanding this word in relation to grain production: "to make coarsely crushed grain, *make groats*" (BDAG, s.v.). This is the option chosen by Weiß (2009, 201) and may be implicit in the references to farming in Ehrman (2003, 2.193) and Holmes (2007, 469). On the other hand, Jörg Rüpke (1999, 155–7) notes etymological connections between the verb in the *Shepherd* and the noun χόνδρος, meaning salt. Using this and other clues from the text, Rüpke understands Hermas to be involved in salt mining rather than grain production. He is followed by Maier (2015, 148).

10. This is not the only time that Hermas cries in the *Shepherd*. He weeps when he sees the beast (Vis. 4.1.7 [22.7]) and is moved to tears because of his deceptive lifestyle when he is told to love truth (Mand. 3.3 [28.3]).

11. *Tension* seems to be a better word than *contradiction*. Although it is not always easy to see how Hermas's sin and his right actions fit together, Dibelius (1923, 437) speaks too strongly when he refers to the woman's description in Vis. 1.2.4 (2.4) as "ein Widerspruch."

basic and simply further the conversation. For example, Hermas's first question in the *Shepherd* is directed to Rhoda, and he simply asks her why she has come (Vis. 1.1.5 [1.5]). At other times Hermas is worried about his life. After talking with Rhoda, Hermas fears for his salvation and asks how he can be rescued (Vis. 1.2.1 [2.1]).[12] He asks the shepherd a similar question when he is commanded to speak truth (Mand. 3.1–2 [28.1–2]). Since Hermas is unsure of whether he can be saved since he has lived deceitfully with everyone, he asks the shepherd how he can live after his previous actions (Mand. 3.3 [28.3]).

Hermas often asks questions in response to what he has seen or been told. His curiosity about the tower visions leads him to question both the woman and the shepherd for further information. He insists to the lady that his vision will be for naught if she does not explain its meaning to him (Vis. 3.3.1 [11.1]). He then inquires about why the tower was built on water (Vis. 3.3.5 [11.5]), the identity of the six men (Vis. 3.4.1 [12.1]), and the significance of the various stones that are put into the tower (Vis. 3.5.2 [13.2]).[13] Hermas also expresses his desire to know things in a statement: I would like to know (ἤθελον γνῶναι; Vis. 3.4.3 [12.3]; see also 3.8.6 [16.6]; 3.11.4 [19.4]).[14] When he sees the second vision of the tower, Hermas is likewise pertinacious when questioning the shepherd. Hermas's curiosity is evident to the shepherd before he asks a question, and Hermas is told that everything will be explained later (Sim. 9.2.5–7 [79.5–7]). Hermas again declares his desire to know more about the tower and the building using the same language that he employed with the woman (ἤθελον ... γνῶναι; Sim. 9.5.3 [82.3]).[15] When the shepherd allows him to ask questions freely (Sim. 9.11.9 [88.9]), Hermas first inquires about the rock, the door, and the discrepancy in their age (Sim. 9.12.1–3 [89.1–3]). Yet his continued questions keep the dialogue moving throughout Sim. 9.12.1–9.33.3 [89.1–110.3]).[16]

The way in which the woman and the shepherd perceive Hermas's curiosity is also noteworthy because it changes throughout the text. At times, Hermas is lauded for his eagerness to learn and for his persistence in demanding answers. The woman reveals the tower to Hermas because he is eager to know everything, even if he is poorly instructed (Vis. 3.1.2 [9.2]). Similarly, when Hermas wants to inquire further about purity, the shepherd's response is a single but affirmative, "Speak" (λέγε; Mand. 4.1.4 [29.4]). Yet both revealers tire of Hermas's questions at points

---

12. Brox (1991, 5) perceptively remarks that Hermas here becomes "das Paradigma auch von Einsicht und Reaktion."

13. See further Vis. 3.1.3 (9.3); 3.2.1 (10.1); 3.4.2, 3 (12.2, 3); 3.5.4, 5 (13.4, 5); 3.6.3, 5, 6 (14.3, 5, 6); 3.7.5 (15.5); 3.8.5, 6, 9 (16.5, 6, 9); 4.3.1 (24.1).

14. Tagliabue (2017, 235).

15. See also Mand. 5.1.7 (33.7); 12.3.1 (46.1); Sim. 2.2 (51.2); 6.3.4 (63.4).

16. Sim. 9.12.5 (89.5); 9.13.1, 2, 3, 6 (90.1, 2, 3, 6); 9.14.1 (91.1); 9.15.1, 4, 5 (92.1, 4, 5); 9.16.1, 5 (93.1, 5); 9.17.1, 3 (94.1, 3); 9.18.1, 5 (95.1, 5); 9.19.3 (96.3); 9.28.3 (105.3); 9.29.4 (106.4). See further Mand. 4.1.4, 6, 7 (29.4, 6, 7); 4.3.1 (31.1); 4.4.1 (32.1); 5.1.7 (33.7); 10.3.3 (42.3); Sim. 2.4, 5 (51.4, 5); 3.2 (52.2); 5.4.1, 3 (57.1, 3); 8.3.1 (69.1).

and refer to him as foolish. Hermas's continued questions about the stones in the tower lead the woman to ask him how long he will continue to be foolish (μωρός) and lack understanding (ἀσύνετος; Vis. 3.6.5 [14.5]). The shepherd also grows frustrated with Hermas, at one point remarking that his stupidity (ἀφροσύνη) is persistent (Sim. 6.5.2 [65.2]).[17] Despite the frustrations with Hermas's curiosity, Osiek correctly notes:

> The praise for theological curiosity here, which Hermas obviously exemplifies, does not conflict with commandments to simplicity and belief (such as *Mandates* 1; 2) or against doubt (*Mandate* 9), or the reminder that humanity can have only limited understanding of God (*Sim.* 9.2.6–7); nor is it evidence of Gnosticism; the goal is not even knowledge, but understanding (v. 6). It simply indicates the author's conviction that worldly distractions block the full life of faith and that that life necessarily includes the desire to understand more about the things of God.[18]

Or, to use the *Shepherd*'s words, Hermas's curiosity is not an "empty eagerness" (κενόσπουδος; Sim. 9.5.5 [82.5]). Hermas's curiosity as well as his embodiment of imitable and inimitable traits make Hermas a complex character. In some ways, Hermas mirrors what is found in the textual description of his community. Just as Hermas is both self-controlled (Vis. 1.2.4 [2.4]) and accused of having illicit desires for what is wicked (Vis. 1.1.8 [1.8]), so also the parable of the tower depicts Self-Control as a woman who lives in the tower (Sim. 9.15.2 [92.2]) while some of the branches in the parable of the willow struggle for a time with misplaced desires (Sim. 8.10.1 [76.1]). Hermas is not only portrayed as a member of the community that he addresses. He also mirrors and represents this community. Moreover, his curiosity leads him to increased understanding in ways that are suggestive of how the text describes repentance. While he can annoy his interlocutors with the number of questions that he proffers, Hermas's curiosity allows the revealers to teach in more detail. Their revelation and Hermas's understanding are thus enhanced by his curiosity. Repentance can likewise be portrayed as a dialogical act.[19] Hermas is moved to confess his sin when he finds himself alone in the field prior to the first tower vision. In the midst of this discursive act, the woman urges him to move beyond a prayer of confession to intercede for righteousness on behalf of himself and his family (Vis. 3.1.5-7 [9.5-7]). Hermas's curiosity can be valued because it leads to an increased understanding. Likewise, Hermas's repentance leads to further understanding (Mand. 4.2.2 [30.2]). In all these things, Hermas serves as a complicated member and model of his community.

---

17. See further Vis. 3.3.2 (11.2); 3.6.5 (14.5); 3.8.9 (16.9); Mand. 10.2.1 (41.1); Sim. 5.4.2, 3 (57.2, 3); 9.14.4 (91.4).
18. Osiek (1999, 137). The reference to "v. 6" in the commentary is to Mand. 10.1.6 (40.6).
19. See further Lipsett (2011, 41–2).

The Woman

After Hermas talks with Rhoda, he meets another woman. Not unlike the woman whose wit Sherlock Holmes admires in "A Scandal in Bohemia,"[20] the woman in the *Shepherd* is also cunning and unnamed. Her identity is not fully revealed until Vis. 3.10.1–3.13.4 (18.1–21.4), although something is said about who she is in Vis. 2.4.1 (8.1). When Hermas first encounters the woman, he describes a great white chair that is made out of snowy-white wool (Vis. 1.2.2 [2.2]).[21] The woman to whom the chair belongs is described as elderly (πρεσβῦτις), and her clothing is shining. Along with the white chair, the shiny clothing paints a bright picture. The woman has a book in her hands and sits alone on the chair. After greeting the distressed Hermas, she asks him why he is sad, downcast, and unhappy (Vis. 1.2.3 [2.3]). The woman is not severe with Hermas when he tells her about his conversation with Rhoda.[22] However, she acknowledges Hermas's misguided thought while also revealing the sins of his family (Vis. 1.2.4–1.3.2 [2.4–3.2]).

The woman is variously described, illustrates her authority by different means, and responds to Hermas in unexpected ways. Two conversations shed further light on the woman's identity. First, after the meaning of the words that Hermas copied is revealed (Vis. 2.2.2–2.3.4 [6.2–7.4]), Hermas is visited by an attractive young man while he is sleeping (Vis. 2.4.1 [8.1]).[23] The young man asks Hermas if he knows who the elderly woman is. Hermas answers, "The Sibyl." Although his answer turns out to be incorrect, Hermas's assumption is not completely out of place. The Sibyl was often depicted as an elderly woman who offered divine prophecies.[24] Hermas's declaration that the woman is the Sibyl is thus an understandable mistake. The young man corrects Hermas by informing him that the woman is the church.[25] When Hermas asks why the church appears as an elderly woman,[26] Hermas reports the young man's answer: "'Because,' he said, 'she was created first of all.

---

20. Doyle (1891; 1892, 3–28).

21. Similar descriptions occur in Dan 7:9–10; *1 En.* 46.1–2; 47.3; Rev 20:11. See further Baynes (2012, 173).

22. On the dynamic juxtaposition of the woman and Rhoda in Vis. 1.1–2 (1–2), see Harkins (2020, 60).

23. The *Shepherd* highlights aesthetic beauty at several points throughout the work. For example, the wild women in Sim. 9.9.5 (86.5) are described as beautiful, while the fruits on the eleventh mountain in the same Similitude can be compared in terms of beauty (Sim. 9.28.3 [105.3]). Rhoda's beauty is also mentioned in Vis. 1.1.2 (1.2). For references to aesthetically pleasing young men in Greco-Roman literature, see Körtner and Leutzsch (1998, 401n.209).

24. E.g., Ovid, *Metam.* 14.129–153; Clement of Alexandria, *Strom.* 1.108.1 (21). The Sibyl will be discussed in further detail in Chapter 7.

25. Tagliabue (2017, 229–34).

26. The depiction of God's people as a woman may find its roots in Jewish scriptures and other literature that depicts Israel as a woman. E.g., Isa 54:1–10; Jer 2:2–3; Hos 1:1–3:5; *4 Ezra* 9.26–10.59.

On account of this, she is an elderly woman and the world was created for her sake'" (ὅτι, φησίν, πάντων πρώτη ἐκτίσθη. διὰ τοῦτο πρεσβυτέρα καὶ διὰ ταύτην ὁ κόσμος κατηρτίσθη; Vis. 2.4.1 [8.1]). This identification creates circularity in how the message of the Visions is to be understood. The woman-church reveals God's messages to Hermas, who is to give these messages to others in the church. The young man has adequately explained the elderly appearance of the woman, but the statement about the world's creation is more surprising. Not only has the church been placed in the world, but the world was indeed created for the church.[27]

Hermas asks to learn more about the woman's identity at the end of the vision of the tower (Vis. 3.10.1–3.13.4 [18.1–21.4]).[28] As she leaves, he begins to ask her to reveal something about the three forms in which she appeared to him.[29] The woman tells him that he must ask for further revelation (Vis. 3.10.2 [18.2]). Hermas then retroactively explains to readers that the woman appeared to him in different forms in each vision (Vis. 3.10.3–5 [18.3–5]). After Hermas fasts, a young man appears to him in order to reveal the significance of the woman's three forms.[30] In the first vision, she was extremely old and was seated in a chair (Vis. 3.10.3 [18.3]).[31] She appeared old because Hermas's spirit was withered, double-minded, and powerless (Vis. 3.11.2–3 [19.2–3]). She was seated on a chair so that her weak body might be supported (Vis. 3.11.4 [19.4]). In the second vision, her face appeared younger. Although her body and her hair appeared elderly, she was able to talk with him while standing and was more joyful than before (Vis. 3.10.4 [18.4]). The young man tells him a parable about an old man who is awaiting death. When the old man receives an inheritance, however, he finds that he becomes stronger, more joyful, and is able to stand (Vis. 3.12.1–3 [20.1–3]).

The woman was seated again in the third vision, but she appeared younger, exquisitely beautiful, and joyful (Vis. 3.10.5 [18.5]).[32] The young man draws a comparison between the woman's appearance and someone who has received good news that helps them to forget their sorrow. The person becomes more joyful and looks forward to the future. "So also you received the renewal of your spirits because you saw these good things" (οὕτως καὶ ὑμεῖς ἀνανέωσιν εἰλήφατε τῶν πνευμάτων ὑμῶν ἰδόντες ταῦτα τὰ ἀγαθά; Vis. 3.13.2 [21.2]). Regarding the woman's seated posture, the young man explains that her seated posture is now

---

27. For further connections between this passage and the *Shepherd*'s teachings about creation, see O'Brien (1997, 474–6, 487–94).

28. On the possibility that this portion of the text is a secondary addition, see Walsh (2019a, 523–32).

29. It seems best to understand the imperfect verb ἠρώτων as an inceptive imperfect. I have thus translated the word as "begins to ask."

30. When the young man's explanations in Vis. 3.10.1–3.13.4 (18.1–21.4) are combined with Vis. 2.4.1 (8.1), one may find here another example of allegorical multisemy. See similarly Henne (1993, 133–4).

31. See similarly Vis. 1.2.2 (2.2).

32. See also Vis. 3.1.2, 7–9 (9.2, 7–9).

a position of strength. The reason for the change in explanation has to do with what the woman is seated on. The bench (συμψέλιον) on which the woman sits in Vis. 3 has four legs and is able to stand strong.[33] Moreover, the young man finds significance in the symbolism between the four legs on which the bench stands and the four elements of which the world is established (Vis. 3.13.3 [21.3]). Although the bench in the third vision is significant for reasons outside of Hermas, the primary reasons given for the woman's changing appearance lie in the changes that occur in Hermas or in Hermas and his community. The variations in the woman take place because Hermas's spirit revives, and her appearance becomes correspondingly youthful in recognition of Hermas's changes. The way in which the woman looks thus holds up a mirror by which readers can discover more about Hermas's repentance. In so doing, the woman's polymorphic alterations may also draw the audience's attention to their own need for repentance.

It is also worth noting in a prosopographical study that the woman's appearance is described in the next vision. Following the identification of the woman as the church (Vis. 2.4.1 [8.1]) and the explanation of her varied appearances (Vis. 3.10.1–3.13.4 [18.1–21.4]), Hermas meets a young woman (παρθένος). She is dressed in white as if she was coming out of a bridal chamber (Vis. 4.2.1 [23.1]). Because of his previous interactions with the woman, he immediately recognizes her as the church (Vis. 4.2.2 [23.2]). Although their greetings in Vis. 4.2.2 (23.2) are not exactly identical, they recall the greetings with which their story began in Vis. 1.2.2 (2.2). This time there is a familiarity in their greetings, not only for the readers, who recognize the similarities in how they speak, but also for the characters, who are meeting one another in the world of the text. Yet the woman is never completely familiar to Hermas. She disappears unexpectedly when Hermas looks away at a loud noise because he thinks that the beast is returning (Vis. 4.3.7 [24.7]).

The woman appears as a revelatory figure throughout her work with Hermas in the Visions. She reveals divine matters to Hermas not only with her words but also by embodying the people of God, the topic of many of her revelations.[34] She also guides Hermas in his prayers, not only by urging him to pray and fast more (Vis. 3.10.2 [18.2]) but also by suggesting how to pray (Vis. 3.1.6 [9.6]).[35] She speaks to Hermas in a way that is reminiscent of a wise teacher, addressing Hermas and his readers as her "children" (τέκνα; Vis. 3.9.1 [17.1]).[36] The woman's

---

33. The word συμψέλιον is used in the *Shepherd* at Vis. 3.1.4, 7 (9.4, 7); 3.2.4 (10.4); 3.10.1, 5 (18.1, 5); 3.13.3 (21.3).

34. In addition to personifying the people of God, the woman is set in a narrative within the *Shepherd*. For a discussion of the *Shepherd*'s narratival teaching alongside other similar early Christian teachings in non-narrative texts, see Tagliabue (2020, 122–3).

35. Walsh (2017) perceptively observes that the woman also communicates by touching Hermas (Vis. 1.4.2 [4.2]; 3.1.6 [9.6]). Thus her "relationship with Hermas is dynamic and multisensory, and meaning is revealed in a relational context that leads to spiritual growth and action" (Walsh 2017, 80).

36. Lookadoo (forthcoming).

role continues in Vis. 4 (22–24) where she reveals to Hermas that the beast that he has seen indicates a coming tribulation and that the colors of the beast symbolize the time of the world from Hermas's present until the coming age (Vis. 4.2.3–4.3.6 [23.3–24.6]). Yet despite the increasing familiarity with Hermas throughout the woman's portion of the story, she appears and disappears at will and remains a mysterious and otherworldly revealer throughout the narrative.

The Shepherd

After the woman's disappearance, readers next find Hermas after he has prayed in his house and sat down on the bed (Vis. 5.1 [25.1]). Vis. 5 introduces the title character of the *Shepherd* as he meets Hermas in his house. When Hermas sees the shepherd, he initially fails to recognize him. This man is described by the narrator as "glorious in appearance" (ἔνδοξος τῇ ὄψει; Vis. 5.1 [25.1]). Yet he also comes dressed like a shepherd, wearing a white skin, with a bag on his shoulder and a rod in his hand. The first exchange between Hermas and the shepherd reflects Hermas's confusion. After greeting each other, the shepherd tells Hermas that he has been sent by the most holy angel (Vis. 5.2 [25.2]). Since Hermas does not recognize the shepherd, he is hesitant to accept the shepherd's claim.[37] He asks the shepherd who he is (Vis. 5.3 [25.3]), and the shepherd's appearance suddenly changes (Vis. 5.4 [25.4]). Although the shepherd's appearance can change rapidly, the text does not specify in what manner the shepherd changes or in what ways he looks different. Nevertheless, the change allows Hermas to recognize the shepherd clearly, even if the shepherd's polymorphy is not given interpretive significance in the same way that the woman's is.[38] While his appearance must be coherent with earlier descriptions of the shepherd so that Hermas can identify him throughout the rest of the *Shepherd*, the combination of humble, pastoral dress, glorious appearance, and variable manifestations marks the origin and status of the shepherd as different from Hermas.

The shepherd first states the purpose of his visit to Hermas in Vis. 5.2 (25.2): "I was sent by the most holy angel to live with you for the rest of the days of your life."[39] However, the shepherd says more about his purpose as the dialogue continues in Vis. 5. The shepherd was sent to show again to Hermas everything that he saw earlier (Vis. 5.5 [25.5]). The second part of the *Shepherd* is significantly longer than the first, but the shepherd claims that everything that Hermas will learn from him was already taught to him by the woman. The shepherd's role is to expand and clarify. This connects the portions of the *Shepherd* in which Hermas interacts with different revelatory figures and suggests that literary connections

---

37. Brox (1991, 187) rightly points out that Hermas's belief that the shepherd might be a test contrasts with Hermas's actual testing in Sim. 7.1 (66.1).
38. See especially Vis. 3.10.1–3.13.4 (18.1–21.4).
39. ἀπεστάλην ἀπὸ τοῦ σεμνοτάτου ἀγγέλου ἵνα μετὰ σοῦ οἰκήσω τὰς λοιπὰς ἡμέρας τῆς ζωῆς σου (Vis. 5.2 [25.2]).

should be expected between these portions of the work. The shepherd's role is thus to show "the most important and useful points to you [Hermas]" (αὐτὰ τὰ κεφάλαια τὰ ὄντα ὑμῖν σύμφορα) from what Hermas has already been shown by the woman (Vis. 5.5 [25.5]).[40] Because of the importance of what the shepherd shows Hermas, Hermas is instructed to write and seems only too willing to do so (Vis. 5.5–6 [25.5–6]). Yet the shepherd is also identified by Hermas's own narration in which Hermas designates him not only as the shepherd but also as the angel of repentance (ὁ ἄγγελος τῆς μετανοίας; Vis. 5.7 [25.7]).[41] The opening dialogue in Vis. 5 starts a new section in the *Shepherd* by introducing readers to the shepherd, who is identified by his appearance, his role, and his names.

The shepherd interacts with Hermas in two primary ways. After his introduction in Vis. 5.1–7 (25.1–7), the shepherd begins by instructing Hermas to act in certain ways and to train himself in particular patterns of thought. Hermas does not speak in the first two Mandates (Mand. 1.1–2.7 [26.1–27.7]). An introductory formula indicates that the shepherd is still speaking at the beginning of Mand. 2.1 (27.1), but the first two Mandates otherwise consist solely of the shepherd's speech to an unquestioning Hermas. The shepherd also teaches without a response from Hermas in Mand. 9 (39.1–12) and Sim. 1 (50.1–11). In these passages, the shepherd's authority is evident because it is allowed to stand as it is without the need for further modification or explication.

Yet this is not the only way in which the shepherd talks to Hermas. More often, Hermas speaks back to the shepherd. The shepherd thus becomes the teacher in a discursive teacher–student relationship.[42] Hermas often reacts to the shepherd's teaching with questions. Hermas's first question arises from a recognition that he has not followed what the shepherd is now saying to him. After the shepherd urges Hermas to love truth and not defraud or deceive others (Mand. 3.1–2 [28.1–2]), Hermas weeps bitterly. The shepherd draws Hermas's concern out of him with a series of interrogatives that leads to Hermas's key question: " 'Sir, how then,' I said, 'can I live when I have done these things' " (πῶς οὖν, φημί, κύριε δύναμαι ζῆσαι ταῦτα πράξας; Mand. 3.3 [28.3]). The shepherd's response is encouraging and clarifies how Hermas should live from this point forward (Mand. 3.4–5 [28.4–5]).

---

40. Osiek (1999, 101).

41. The same term is used of the shepherd at Mand. 12.4.7 (47.7); 12.6.1 (49.1); Sim. 9.1.1 (78.1); 9.14.3 (91.3); 9.23.5 (100.5); 9.24.4 (101.4); 9.31.3 (108.3); 9.33.1 (110.1). Repentance is a major theme in the *Shepherd*. On μετάνοια in the *Shepherd* and its connections with manliness even when exhibited by female figures, see Lipsett (2011, 19–53). On the angel of repentance in early Jewish and early Christian literature, see van Henten (1999, 52).

42. Perhaps the preeminent example of such relationships in antiquity is to be found in the interactions of Socrates and his interlocutors. Wolfsdorf (2017, 43–5), however, is right to refer to Socrates's dialogues as an attempt to expose an inconsistency in someone else's beliefs. The shepherd's interactions with Hermas may be more similar to dialogues between revelatory figures and their charges in other Second Temple apocalypses (e.g., *1 En.* 17.1–36.4; *Apoc. Abr.* 10.1–17.21).

The following commandment is written similarly. The shepherd instructs Hermas about holiness and inappropriate uses of sex (Mand. 4.1.1–3 [29.1–3]). Hermas tells the shepherd that he has questions (Mand. 4.1.4 [29.4]). He then repeats similar statements in Mand. 4.2.1 (30.1); 4.3.1 (31.1); 4.4.1 (32.1). The remainder of Mand. 4 proceeds in largely dialogical fashion so that the shepherd's initial commandment is clarified, qualified, and accurately applied for Hermas and his community. This mode of speaking is particularly evident in the lengthy visions of Sim. 8–9 (67.1–110.3).

Although these two modes of speaking are primary for the shepherd, this division is not exhaustive. The shepherd tires and is occasionally angered by Hermas's questions. When Hermas confesses his uncertainty about his capacity to keep the commandments, the shepherd insists that Hermas must make his own choice to guard the commandments (Mand. 12.3.4–6 [46.4–6]). Part of keeping the commandments is a matter of the will. Yet Hermas is afraid of the shepherd because the shepherd says these things angrily (Mand. 12.4.1 [47.1]). In response, the shepherd begins to speak more gently to Hermas and to explain God's commandments in more detail to this "foolish, uncomprehending, double-minded" man (ἄφρον, ἀσύνετε, καὶ δίψυχε; Mand. 12.4.2 [47.2]).[43] The shepherd also flips the tables on Hermas and asks him questions. This is evident as early as Mand. 3.3 (28.3), in which the shepherd first asks Hermas why he is crying. Yet it is Hermas's weeping that invites the shepherd's inquiry. A clearer example can be found in Sim. 2.1 (51.1).[44] The shepherd appears to Hermas while he is walking in a field and asks him why he is thinking about the elm and vine. The shepherd's question gives way to an allegorical interpretation of the rich and poor based on the symbiosis of elms and vines. Still, it is the shepherd's question, rather than Hermas's persistent interrogation, that enables the shepherd to share his message.

Although the shepherd's presence dominates the text, his place with Hermas is somewhat complicated at the end. In Sim. 10, the shepherd's place in an angelic hierarchy becomes apparent when the angel who handed Hermas over to the shepherd appears. When the angel leaves, he takes the shepherd with him (Sim. 10.4.5 [114.5]). However, the shepherd will return at a later time to live with Hermas, thereby fulfilling what the shepherd said he was sent to do in Vis. 5.2 (25.2).[45] In this way, the shepherd's place in a hierarchy, need to respond to authority, and particular connection to Hermas are clarified as the *Shepherd* draws its story to a close. The combination of the shepherd's revelations, inquiries, and place in a chain of authority provides the audience with a complicated picture of

---

43. Another example of the shepherd's anger is found in Sim. 5.4.1–5.5.1 (57.1–58.1).

44. See also Sim. 5.1.1–2 (54.1–2).

45. Moxnes (1974, 51–2) draws attention to the similarities between the language of Vis. 5.2 (25.2) and theophanic appearances in the Hebrew Bible. In the *Shepherd*, the use of such language to describe both the Most Holy Angel and the Lord need not require the two characters to be identical to one another.

teaching, even while the words that the shepherd utters offer readers a vision of how to live well before God.

Minor Characters

Otherworldly Characters

In addition to the woman and the shepherd, Hermas encounters a variety of otherworldly characters during his transformation process. These include several other angelic figures who are sent to Hermas or seen by Hermas as part of his revelation. It is not always clear if each of the angels who are named in the *Shepherd* refers to different figures or whether some angels go by different names. For example, the shepherd is also referred to as "the angel of repentance," while the woman is simultaneously identified as the church. Nevertheless, there are hints of hierarchy throughout the work, even if it is not always easy to reconstruct this hierarchy in its entirety. The woman and the shepherd are both sent by someone else, while they are able to command some of the other characters when they meet.

The first angelic figures that Hermas meets after the woman are the four young men who carry the woman's chair and two others who take the woman east (Vis. 1.4.1, 3 [4.1, 3]). These six men return in the third vision and are commanded by the woman to build the tower (Vis. 3.1.6-8 [9.6-8]). Although they are not finally in charge of the tower, these young men take a leading role in the construction and are helped by other unnamed and unnumbered men (Vis. 3.2.5 [10.5]).[46] The men are identified as angels, whom God created first and placed in charge of creation (Vis. 3.4.1-2 [12.1-2]).[47] One young man takes a particularly active role in the Visions when he explains who the woman is and why her appearance changes (Vis. 2.4.1 [8.1]; Vis. 3.10.7-3.13.4 [18.7-21.4]). It is not clear if this young man is one of the six who builds the tower. In light of the proximity of the young man to the other young men and his special knowledge of the woman, however, he is likely one of the six men who has been given an additional revelatory responsibility.

The virgins are superior to the young men when it comes to building the tower. Yet it is not clear how many virgins are at the construction of the tower or what they should be called.[48] When the woman shows the vision to Hermas, he sees seven women (γυναῖκες) who support the tower and offer a place to anyone who serves them (Vis. 3.8.2-8 [16.2-8]). Their names are virtues and qualities that should characterize Hermas and his community. When the shepherd ushers Hermas to this vision, he sees twelve virgins (παρθένοι) who must carry the stones into the tower for their placement to be accepted (Sim. 9.2.3-4 [79.3-4]; 9.3.2 [80.2]; 9.4.1 [81.1]). Hermas stays with the virgins overnight in the tower and sleeps with

---

46. See also Sim. 9.3.1 (80.1); 9.4.4-9.5.1 (81.4-82.1).

47. Osiek (1999, 69). The fences in Sim. 5.2.2-3 (55.2-3) are also identified as angels in Sim. 5.5.3 (58.3). Their responsibility is to keep the people of God together.

48. On this topic, see Walsh (2019b, 476-82).

them like a brother rather than a husband. Their relationship is platonic and filled with joy (Sim. 9.10.6–9.11.9 [87.6–88.9]). Moreover, these virtuous virgins are juxtaposed against other women in black garments who are named for vices (Sim. 9.15.1–3 [92.1–3]). Although there is some continuity across the Shepherd, the number and roles of the women shift throughout the text.

As the inclusion of the women of vice indicates (Sim. 9.15.1–3 [92.1–3]), references to otherworldly figures are not only to virtuous angels. In addition to the women of vice, Hermas meets a huge beast with locusts coming out of its mouth in Vis. 4.1.5–10 (22.5–10). Hermas is able to pass by the beast because he trusted in the Lord and because the Lord sent Thegri, the angel who is over the beasts, to close its mouth (Vis. 4.2.4 [23.4]).

Other angelic figures include the most holy angel, the angel of the Lord, and the glorious angel.[49] All of these figures appear to have authority over the shepherd. The most holy angel sent the shepherd to Hermas (Vis. 5.2 [25.2]), while the angel of the Lord instructs the shepherd to examine carefully the willow branches that people received (Sim. 8.2.5 [68.5]). The shepherd informs Hermas that the punishing shepherd was sent to him at the command of the glorious angel or, in other words, by an authority higher than the shepherd (Sim. 7.1 [66.1]).[50] The shepherd also describes the glorious angel as the one who assigned the shepherd to live in Hermas's house (Sim. 9.1.3 [78.3]). The great and glorious angel is named Michael in Sim. 8.3.3 (69.3) after the angel in Sim. 8.1.2–8.2.5 [67.2–68.5]) is described as the angel of the Lord. The final references to an angel who outranks the shepherd are found in Sim. 10 when "the angel who handed me over to this shepherd" (*nuntius ille, qui me tradiderat huic pastori*; Sim. 10.1.1 [111.1]) speaks directly with Hermas.

There is a slippage in terminology when discussing otherworldly figures in the Shepherd that complicates precise identification of each figure. Nevertheless, the hierarchical elements of the angelic order remain clear throughout the text. It may also be the case that some of the angels referred to here by separate terms are in fact to be identified with one another. Although it is not possible to draw precise connections between all angels in the Shepherd, clear demarcations of good and evil as well as hierarchical tendencies suggest a well-defined, though not fully revealed, otherworldly life.

Hermas's Family

Hermas does not receive his visions for himself alone but also for the community in which he finds himself. Among those with whom Hermas lives is his family, who

---

49. On the most holy angel, see Vis. 5.2 (25.2); Mand. 5.1.7 (33.7). On the angel of the Lord, see Sim. 7.5 (66.5); 8.1.2–8.2.5 (67.2–68.5). On the glorious angel, see Sim. 7.1 (66.1); 8.3.3 (69.3); 9.1.3 (78.3); 9.7.1 (84.1).

50. Hermas first sees the punishing shepherd and the shepherd of luxury in Sim. 6 (61.1–65.7).

are a source of difficulty in this text. Although Hermas's wife and children are most problematic, his relationship with Rhoda provides a link between otherworldly and this-worldly figures because Hermas knows her in both realms. She is Hermas's master, lives in Rome, and bought Hermas as a slave (Vis. 1.1.1 [1.1]).[51] Although little is said about Rhoda as an earthly character, Hermas notices her beauty (Vis. 1.1.2 [1.2]). Moreover, her ability to purchase a slave suggests at least modest means for her or her family. Yet Rhoda appears to Hermas after her death. She comes to warn Hermas that she will be his heavenly accuser, but she is not yet playing that role (Vis. 1.1.5-6 [1.5-6]). Instead, she is the first revelatory figure in the *Shepherd*, informing Hermas that God is angry with him (Vis. 1.1.6-7 [1.6-7]) and describing the difference between evil and righteous desires (Vis. 1.1.8-9 [1.8-9]).[52] Although she upsets Hermas, he thinks carefully over her words (Vis. 1.2.3 [2.3]). Rhoda's revelations are important in Hermas's development, but they are incomplete (Vis. 1.3.1 [3.1]).

As the woman who interprets Hermas's visions reveals to him, another reason for God's anger at Hermas is so that Hermas's family will turn away from their sin (Vis. 1.3.1 [3.1]). Hermas's children are spoiled and undisciplined (Vis. 1.3.1-2 [3.1-2]), have blasphemed the Lord (Vis. 2.2.2 [6.2]), and have betrayed their parents (Vis. 2.2.2 [6.2]). Hermas's children are also described as sexually promiscuous (Vis. 2.2.2 [6.2]).[53] Hermas's desire for a wife like Rhoda suggests that his relationship with his wife may not be ideal. His wife is reported to have little control over what she says, but she is able to find mercy (Vis. 2.2.3 [6.3]). Despite their problems, none of Hermas's family is beyond salvation. They are instead in need of correction. Thus Hermas must observe the commandments that he receives along with his children (Mand. 12.3.6 [46.6]; Sim. 5.3.9 [56.9]; 7.6 [66.6]).

Community Leaders

Although the revelations to Hermas suggest a privileged place for him in the community, he is not the only leader mentioned in the *Shepherd*. Hermas is instructed to write two little books that he will send to Clement and Grapte.[54]

---

51. Slaves could be counted as part of the family in which they served. Thus Rhoda can be placed in this section on Hermas's family, since Hermas would have been placed in her family at an earlier point in his life. Slaves could also be counted as property as evidenced in the will recorded in P.Mich. 5.323. See further Glancy (2002, 10-11) on the blurring of lines that could occur when discussing slaves as persons, family, and property. For more on slave families, see Martin (1990, 2-7).

52. Osiek, MacDonald, and Tulloch (2006, 41).

53. Osiek, MacDonald, and Tulloch (2006, 39).

54. On the books for Clement, Grapte, and Hermas, see Baynes (2012, 177-9). On the question of whether the little books are "letters" or "books," see Dibelius (1923, 443); Brox (1991, 96-7); Baynes (2012, 178-9).

Clement is then to be responsible for sending the books to believers in other cities, while Grapte will teach the widows and orphans (Vis. 2.4.3 [8.3]). Although neither Clement nor Grapte is given a title, the roles that are given to them suggest that they have a significant place in the community of those who first read the *Shepherd*. The close connection between their names and the elders to whom Hermas should read his book also indicates a leading position for Clement and Grapte. However, not all of the people who are named in the *Shepherd* are given respectable tasks. Maximus may also be a prominent person in the community, but he is not as favored as Clement or Grapte. Rather, it appears that he has denied something intrinsic to the community or the community's beliefs.[55] Hermas warns Maximus that a struggle is coming and reminds him that "the Lord is near to those who turn to him" (Vis. 2.3.4. [7.4]).[56]

In addition to sending two books with Clement and Grapte, Hermas is also instructed to read to "the elders who preside over the church" (Vis. 2.4.3 [8.3]). The elders refer to a group of ecclesial leaders in Rome who were earlier instructed to live righteously (Vis. 2.2.6–7 [6.6–7]).[57] Along with the elders, the *Shepherd* also refers to bishops and deacons.[58] All of these terms are also found in the Pauline corpus.[59] Although these references may suggest a hierarchical arrangement among the leadership in the Roman church, the hierarchy remains ambiguous throughout the *Shepherd*. Moreover, it is not clear that each reference to a leadership position corresponds with actual leaders in Rome. For example, references to deacons occur in conjunction with the construction of the church in Vis. 3.5.1 (13.1), with servants of God whose chronological placement is unclear (Sim. 9.15.4 [92.4]) and with deacons who have served for their own profit (Sim. 9.26.2 [103.2]).[60] Such references make it difficult to use the *Shepherd* to reconstruct Roman church order in the second century.[61]

---

55. Dibelius (1923, 449–50).

56. Hermas reports that this is a quotation from the otherwise unknown Book of Eldad and Modat. See further Zahn (1868, 317–18); Dibelius (1923, 450); Seitz (1944); Joly (1968, 95n.3); Leiman (1974); Levine (1976); Martin (1983–5); Brox (1991, 103); Körtner and Leutzsch (1998, 400n.206); Osiek (1999, 57); Allison (2011); Bauckham (2013).

57. See the references to elders (πρεσβύτεροι) in Vis. 2.4.2–3 (8.2–3); 3.1.8 (9.8). Note also the reference to "those who preside over the church" (οἱ προϊστάμενοι τῆς ἐκκλησίας; Vis. 2.4.3 [8.3]).

58. Bishops (ἐπίσκοποι) are mentioned in Vis. 3.5.1 (13.1); Sim. 9.27.2 (104.2), while deacons (διάκονοι) are referred to in Vis. 3.5.1 (13.1); Sim. 9.15.4 (92.4); Sim. 9.26.2 (103.2).

59. Osiek (1999, 22).

60. Grundeken (2018).

61. Jeffers (1991, 186), however, overstates the case when he claims that "Hermas rejects the notion of a clergy set apart." On ecclesial leadership in the *Shepherd*, see Joly (1968, 40–1; 1993, 541); Brox (1991, 533–41); Batovici (2011, 305–7, 313–14); Trebilco (2013, 309–10); Grundeken (2018).

Bringing the Observations Together

This chapter has highlighted what can be known of various characters in the *Shepherd*. What, then, can be said in light of these statements? Based on the observations highlighted thus far regarding particular characters, something can be said about authority, revelation, and wealth in the *Shepherd*.

The clearest indications of hierarchical authority lie in the references to angels being sent by another. The shepherd introduces himself by telling Hermas that he was sent by the most holy angel to show Hermas what he had seen earlier with the help of the woman (Vis. 5.2, 5 [25.2, 5]). The shepherd's promise is completed in Sim. 9 when he shows Hermas the vision of the tower from Vis. 3 and provides a more detailed explanation.[62] Yet the most holy angel remains in a position of authority not only over Hermas but also over the shepherd. The shepherd's subordinate place is evident again in Sim. 10.1.1 (111.1) when the angel who handed Hermas over to the shepherd visits him and temporarily calls the shepherd and virgins to return with him (Sim. 10.4.4 [114.4]). The woman revealer likewise has a place in a hierarchy. Although the one who sent her is never named, her identification as the church who was created before all things (Vis. 2.4.1 [8.1]) reveals her significant and pretemporal, but ultimately subordinate, position before the God who creates.[63] Thegri is likewise sent by the Lord to protect Hermas from the beast (Vis. 4.2.4 [23.4]).

Although a full map of the angelic orders cannot be drawn from the *Shepherd* and such a sketch was obviously not intended by the author, the theme of authority becomes particularly evident with the characters in Sim. 7 (66.1-7).[64] The punishing angel is also sent by the glorious angel (Sim. 7.1 [66.1]), and the shepherd does not have the authority to order the punishing angel to cease his work on Hermas (Sim. 7.5-6 [66.5-6]). Hermas recognizes the shepherd's authority and asks the shepherd to intercede for him. However, it is not clear that Hermas acknowledges the authority of the punishing angel. In the shepherd's explanation for Hermas's punishment, the shepherd must thus outline these connections for Hermas. A reading of the *Shepherd* that is sensitive to the narrative and dialogue may catch the theme of authority in Sim. 7. However, a prosopographical awareness of otherworldly characters clarifies that the interactions between the shepherd and Hermas is part of a theme that arises regularly in connection to angels in the *Shepherd*. Human figures who have authority, such as the elders, are mentioned less often than otherworldly figures and play a less significant role in the *Shepherd*.

---

62. Dibelius (1923, 601).

63. On God as creator in the *Shepherd*, see Vis. 1.1.6 (1.6); 1.3.4 (3.4); Mand. 1.1 (26.1). See further O'Brien (1997, 474-6).

64. Osiek (1999, 193) highlights authority in this passage in a slightly different way, namely, by showing how Hermas has been delivered from angelic authority to angelic authority: "Hermas has been passed from hand to hand, from the great angel to the Shepherd (who is the angel of conversion, *Vis.* 5.2, 7) to the shepherd-angel of punishment."

As in the case of otherworldly figures, however, a strict hierarchy of Hermas's church cannot be drawn from the information in the *Shepherd*.

While authority is not likely to be called a dominant theme in the *Shepherd* and a full hierarchical list of authoritative figures cannot be compiled, this prosopographical study has highlighted ways in which this theme is repeated throughout the work.[65] What, then, does authority do for those who have it in the *Shepherd*? In brief, authority legitimizes the message that is shared. Clement and Grapte will be empowered to share what they have read in part because their place in the community is important enough for them to be named. Because they have been sent by beings greater than them, the woman and the shepherd should be trusted when they speak. Finally, since Hermas was instructed to write by both the woman and the shepherd, the book that he offers to readers should be regarded as legitimate and trustworthy—at least in narrative terms. In the *Shepherd*, authority offers legitimacy for messages that ultimately derive from God.

There is also a close connection throughout the *Shepherd* between revelation and teaching. Although the woman helps Hermas to see the tower (Vis. 3.2.4 [10.4]; Sim. 9.1.2 [78.2]) and the shepherd goes with Hermas on journeys in the countryside (Sim. 2.1 [51.1]; 6.1.5 [61.5]), both the woman and the shepherd spend much of their time revealing new things to Hermas through teaching. After greeting each other, the woman's first act is to teach Hermas why God is angry with him (Vis. 1.2.4–1.3.2 [2.4–3.2]). Moreover, she instructs Hermas near the end of the tower vision about the peace that should characterize Hermas's community (Vis. 3.9.1–10 [17.1–10]).[66] A noteworthy element in the woman's revelations is their didacticism. Something similar can be said of the shepherd, who begins his discussion with Hermas with a series of commandments that Hermas is to copy (Vis. 5.5–7 [25.5–7]). These are related in the Mandates where Hermas primarily listens to what the shepherd says and does not travel to new realms with the shepherd (Mand. 1.1–12.6.5 [26.1–49.5]).[67] The shepherd continues to instruct in the Similitudes, reflecting with Hermas about fasting (Sim. 5.3.2–9 [56.2–9]), double-mindedness and repentance (Sim. 6.1.1–4 [61.1–4]), and the importance of keeping the spirit at peace (Sim. 9.32.1–5 [109.1–5]). These discussions run alongside the shepherd's explanations of what Hermas sees. Revelation in the *Shepherd* is, then, intimately linked with teaching. Based on these characters, one could even say that teaching is revelation. Hermas does not merely see and understand. The revelatory figures must teach him the meaning of what is revealed and discuss additional topics along the way.

---

65. On hierarchy in the *Shepherd*, see Hellholm (2009, 245–6; 2010, 234).

66. Walsh (2019a, 536–8) sheds light on the multifaceted relationship between the woman's teaching and her authority by deploying the term "spiritual director."

67. Although visions are not a primary feature of the Mandates, the shepherd shows Hermas true and false prophets who are seated on a bench and chair, respectively (Mand. 11.1 [43.1]).

The link between revelation and education obtains with respect to characters other than these central revealers. Although readers first encounter Rhoda as Hermas's owner, she reveals to Hermas that God is angry with him by teaching him that he sinned against her. She goes on to describe the aims and actions of the wicked and righteous (Vis. 1.1.4–9 [1.4–9]). Rhoda's revelation not only sets the stage for everything that follows in the *Shepherd*, her words contribute to Hermas's tutelage from the beginning of the work. The young man who reveals the woman's identity and the significance of her multiple forms undertakes his task by teaching Hermas what he has already seen (Vis. 2.4.1 [8.1]; 3.11.1–3.13.4 [19.1–21.4]). The virgins likewise play a revelatory role in the second tower vision. They inform Hermas that the shepherd will not return that day and apprise him that they will live with him like a brother from that point on (Sim. 9.11.1–3 [88.1–3]). Finally, the angel who sent the shepherd to Hermas concludes the entire work with a series of instructions for Hermas. Hermas will now be protected by the shepherd (Sim. 10.1.2 [111.2]), must keep his house clean (Sim. 10.3.2 [113.2]), and should rescue people from distress and hardship (Sim. 10.4.2–3 [114.2–3]). Hermas himself may then teach others by telling them what he has learned through his revelations (Sim. 10.2.2–4 [112.2–4]). By paying attention to the characters and their words, the link between revelation and teaching becomes clearer.[68] Teaching is a primary means by which Hermas receives what God has revealed.

Finally, the *Shepherd*'s portrayal of wealth has been a topic of discussion among other scholars.[69] Although wealth has not been a significant topic in this prosopographical study, some of the findings may nevertheless suggest the importance of the topic within the *Shepherd*. For example, a study of Hermas's character must begin by noting that he was a former slave in Rome (Vis. 1.1.1 [1.1]). Because not all slaves were poor, Hermas's enslavement need not require him to have been destitute. However, it is likely the case that he has fewer means than Rhoda because she was able to purchase him (Vis. 1.1.1 [1.1]). If Hermas's undisciplined treatment of his children is put together with the references to sexual misbehavior (Vis. 1.3.1–2 [3.1–2]; Vis. 2.2.2 [6.2]), Hermas's children may also be wasteful with their money, spending it on activities that take them away from the paths of righteousness that the revealers go to such great lengths to teach Hermas. Finally, the woman describes Grapte's duty to instruct the widows and orphans (Vis. 2.4.3 [8.3]). Although not all widows and orphans were poor, references to these groups suggest a marginalized place in the community. Yet Grapte is called to go precisely there. On their own, these references to wealth do not constitute a great deal of interest in the topic within the *Shepherd*. However, when these observations are coupled with the teachings of the woman and the shepherd, they

---

68. Rüpke (2016, 144–6) helpfully outlines both the multiple levels of mediation in the *Shepherd* and their function.

69. See especially Osiek (1983); Leutzsch (1989, 113–37). See also Verheyden (2007, 69).

may complement the findings of other scholarship regarding the importance of wealth in this text.[70]

Conclusion

By paying attention to how the characters in the *Shepherd* are described, a prosopographical study enables one not only to list the persons in the narrative but also to note motifs that may otherwise be easily overlooked. The thematic studies that arise as a result of prosopographical engagement with the *Shepherd* may offer fresh insights into the text. Two examples from this chapter include the importance of authority among otherworldly characters and the connections between the legitimation of a message and the authoritative status that one has. Alternatively, prosopographical study may complement the findings of other scholars by offering further evidence, as the case of references to wealth among the characters in the *Shepherd*.

In focusing on the details found in verbal depictions of the characters, this chapter has thus offered a close examination of the *Shepherd* that explores the text as a whole. Such analyses, however, should be complemented by exploring the literary-historical environment in which the *Shepherd* finds itself. By looking outside of the text, one may further contextualize the findings of this literary prosopography of the *Shepherd*. It is to this task that Chapters 7 and 8 turn.

---

70. On wealth in the *Shepherd* and in scholarship on the *Shepherd*, see Chapter 10 and the literature cited there.

Chapter 7

THE *SHEPHERD* IN ITS GRECO-ROMAN AND EARLY JEWISH SETTINGS

The *Shepherd* contains numerous reminders that it is a text that originates from a particular time and place. These signs may be easiest to see in mundane references to daily life. Rhoda bathes in the Tiber River rather than, for example, the Nile or the Han (Vis. 1.1.2 [1.2]). The shepherd comes to Hermas dressed in white with a staff in his hand (Vis. 5.1 [25.1]). A twenty-first-century shepherd might appear to Hermas in different clothes. These details should serve as a reminder of what L. P. Hartley so memorably wrote: "The past is a foreign country: they do things differently there."[1] The *Shepherd* is a document from the past. As such, it will serve readers well to know something about the historical and literary milieus out of which the text originated.

This chapter will highlight some of the ways in which the *Shepherd* fits well within its surrounding Greco-Roman and early Jewish environments, focusing primarily on literary settings. Like other early Christian literature from the first two centuries CE, the *Shepherd* originated within the Roman Empire. Rome's influence extended across Europe, throughout most of North Africa, and across much of western Asia. Where Rome did not rule directly or where its rule was sometimes contested, its power was evident in its military supremacy and economic dominance. The immense geographical scope of Roman rule during the first two centuries CE meant that Roman occupation was not everywhere the same. However, Rome was a major political, economic, cultural, and religious force during the time when the early Christian movement was developing. Within this Roman environment, Jews had a particularly strong influence on early Christians. Jewish scriptures continued to be read by early Christians as their authoritative texts. The earliest Christians were active in the synagogues and are best seen as a sect within Judaism during the earliest days. A separate early Christian identity was beginning to form among many in the second century, but this identity was often formed against the backdrop of Judaism.[2] Although the relationship between particular communities of early Jews and early Christians could range

---

1. Hartley ([1953] 2002, 17). Hartley's reference has become famous, but the statement was made earlier by Cecil (1949).

2. This phenomenon can be clearly seen in Ign. *Magn.* 8.1–10.3; *Phld.* 6.1–9.2.

from harmonious to contentious, early Judaism and its texts are vital resources for students of early Christianity and readers of the *Shepherd* in particular.

Three caveats may be given at the start. First, as is the case with many textual comparisons, the examples in these chapters could be expanded. Although the passages highlighted here are designed to situate the *Shepherd* historically within its literary contexts, they are by no means intended to be exhaustive. Second, the comparison of passages in the *Shepherd* and other texts is made for the sake of highlighting similarities in the literature but do not imply a direct literary relationship. Literary dependence may be argued in some cases, but such arguments remain a task for other studies. Third, although Greco-Roman and Jewish texts have been separated from one another in this chapter, this division is only for heuristic purposes. The way in which the *Shepherd* shares literary motifs with multiple texts from throughout the early Roman Empire indicates that these cultural backgrounds were closely intertwined in the *Shepherd*. Hellenism was a cultural force in Palestinian Judaism from the third century BCE.[3] The lines between Greco-Roman and Jewish literary culture are likely to have been even further blurred, crossed, and rearranged in Rome during the second century CE. While the division of Greco-Roman and Jewish may be useful for studying this and other early Christian texts, such a split ceases to be helpful if it becomes fixed in interpreters' minds. With these provisions in mind, Chapter 7 can now take up the *Shepherd* in its Greco-Roman and early Jewish settings.

The Shepherd *in Its Greco-Roman Setting*

When considering the *Shepherd* within its Greco-Roman setting, perhaps the first matter to consider is the teaching that Hermas receives for how to engage with authorities outside of Hermas's community.[4] The opening Similitude contrasts two cities: your city (ἡ πόλις ὑμῶν) and this city (ἡ πόλις αὕτη; Sim. 1.1 [50.1]). The discussion of alternative cities by an author in Rome led Zahn to identify "this city" as Rome.[5] Although the passage should be read more generally as a contrast between the life ordered by God and the life that ignores or opposes God,[6] understanding Rome as a type of "this city" opens an intriguing interpretive

---

3. For a thorough presentation of evidence to be considered on this issue, see Hengel (1973, 108–95; 1974, 58–106). For an updated statement of the same position with particular regard to Christian origins, see Hengel and Schwemer (2007, 21–36; 2019, 23–38).

4. As Grundeken (2015a, 85) has observed, the *Shepherd* is often left aside in discussions of early Christianity and the Roman Empire. See also Grundeken (2015b).

5. Zahn (1868, 121–4).

6. Dibelius (1923, 551); Joly (1968, 210n.2, 432–3); Brox (1989a, 273–4; 1991, 286). Grundeken (2015a, 86) notes that the force of any direct comparisons with Rome is blunted by the recognition that believers not only live in a city (Sim. 1.1–3, 5–6 [50.1–3, 5–6]) but also a "land" (Sim. 1.4 [50.4]) and "a foreign place" (Sim. 1.1, 6 [50.1, 6]).

avenue. If Rome is included as part of life within "this city," then the shepherd urges Hermas to be mindful of the true Lord rather than the lord of this city. The shepherd does not call for active opposition against political authorities but prepares Hermas for a difficult relationship in which Hermas may passively dissent from them in favor of keeping God's commandments (Sim. 1.7-8 [50.7-8]). Such a conflict is likely to involve suffering. The rationale for this instruction follows partly from the fickleness of the ruler of this city; the ruler may insist that Hermas and his fellow-believers either follow his laws or leave (Sim. 1.4 [50.4]). More than this, however, the rationale stems from the *Shepherd*'s insistence on God's authority (Sim. 5.7.3 [60.3]; 9.23.4 [100.4]). There is only one God who created the world (Mand. 1.1 [26.1]), and this God is the Almighty (Vis. 3.3.5 [11.5]). By describing God's power in such all-encompassing terms, the *Shepherd* implicitly circumscribes the authority of all other human authorities.[7]

The *Shepherd* thus delimits the power granted to human authorities and provides at least an implicit contrast with how some in the Roman Empire may view the emperor. The portrayal of prophecy may also be fruitfully set alongside Hellenistic texts. Not all Greco-Roman authors viewed prophecy positively. Lucian (*Peregr.* 11) and Celsus (Origen, *Cels.* 6.24, 41) both looked at Christian prophets skeptically. The *Shepherd* takes up the subject of prophecy most fully in Mand. 11 (43). As part of the discussion of false prophecy, the *Shepherd* identifies false prophets as those who seek places of honor and receive money for their prophecy (Mand. 11.12 [43.12]).[8] In Lucian's satirical depiction of Peregrinus as a Christian prophet, Peregrinus receives honor and is worshipped like a god (*Peregr.* 11).[9] He likewise receives substantial monies after he is imprisoned (*Peregr.* 13).[10] Although there are substantial differences between Lucian's *Peregrinus* and the *Shepherd*, they share similar views about how deceptive prophets seek places of honor for themselves and receive payment for their oracles.

At the end of the first century or in the second century,[11] Apuleius also records tales of a prophetic huckster in *Metam.* 2.12-14. While staying as a guest in Milo's house, Lucius, who is the protagonist in Apuleius's narrative, has a conversation with his host over dinner. The topic of prophecy comes up at dinner, and Lucius describes what he considers to be the impressive work of the prophet Diophanes at Corinth.[12] Diophanes is described as a Chaldean (*Chaldaeus*; *Metam.* 2.12,

---

7. Grundeken (2015a, 94).

8. The *Shepherd* also describes false prophets as diviners who tell people what they want to hear, something which Aune (1978) points out is also found in Greco-Roman literature. See further Aune (1983, 34-47).

9. He also recommends himself and his abilities (Lucian, *Peregr.* 12), something that Dibelius (1923, 540) associates with syncretistic prophecy. See further Reiling (1973, 51-2).

10. Bremmer (2017, 59-61) argues that Lucian portrays Peregrinus as a second Jesus. On this passage, see also Hurtado (2016a, 28-9; 2016b, 71-2).

11. On the date of Apuleius's *Metamorphoses*, see Tilg (2014, 2-3).

12. As Harrison (2015, 14) points out, however, Lucius is already an asinine character even before his transformation into an ass in *Metam.* 3.24. Thus it is not clear within the

14), who is "somewhat brown" (*suffusculus*; *Metam.* 2.13). As Diophanes's ethnic origins lie at the borders of Roman influence, so Lucius believes that his prophetic powers stem from the edges of human knowledge. Diophanes will tell people their fortunes if they will pay him. In this way, residents of Corinth learn what days are most propitious for them to marry, build, or travel (*Metam.* 2.12). The *Shepherd*'s objection to prophets who take money in Mand. 11.12 (43.12) is again usefully read alongside the story of Diophanes. However, Lucius has no objection to Diophanes's payments. He only mentions the effects that Diophanes had on Corinth. Milo is not as impressed with Diophanes as Lucius is. He knows another portion of Diophanes's story. When a man named Cerdo comes to Diophanes to find when he should travel, Diophanes is greeted by a friend before Cerdo can pay (*Metam.* 2.13). Without thinking, Diophanes tells his friend the truth about his journey to Corinth. He was shipwrecked and lost everything. After watching his possessions vanish in the sea, Diophanes received some support from the pity of strangers. Yet even this was taken from him when he was robbed and his brother murdered by the same group of bandits (*Metam.* 2.14). After Cerdo hears this story, he picks up his money and runs away. Diophanes has revealed his own deception and incompetence. Or, as the shepherd tells Hermas, Diophanes proves to be a false prophet and is thus like an empty jar in a storeroom (Mand. 11.15 [43.15]).[13]

Two elements of the Diophanes story can be elaborated further with reference to other texts. First, Diophanes's prophecies are related to ordinary matters like building and travel (*Metam.* 2.12–13). In Plutarch, *Def. orac.* 413b, a Cynic philosopher named Didymus Planetiades complains about the shameful questions that people bring to the gods. Their questions about treasure, inheritance, and marriage are said to disprove Pythagoras's claim that people behave their best around the gods. Rather, they expose the illnesses of their souls to the gods when they ought to keep these things hidden not only from deities but also from their elders.[14] The *Shepherd* likewise describes the double-minded who come to false prophets to ask what will happen to them (Mand. 11.2 [43.2]).[15] Conversely, the prophet whom God has chosen speaks from divine power and not under consultation (Mand. 11.5 [43.5]).

Second, a second-century papyrus (P.Berol. 11517 [LDAB 4554]) contains fragments of a novel about Daulis.[16] The story includes Daulis's sack of Delphi,

---

story how reliable Lucius's narration is. Nevertheless, Lucius's views were recognizable during the second century in the Roman Empire.

13. For additional comparison of this story and Mand. 11, see the excellent discussion in Reiling (1973, 81–4).

14. For further examples of questions that were asked of oracles, see the literature cited in Körtner and Leutzsch (1998, 229n.240).

15. Dibelius (1923, 537).

16. On the date of the papyrus, see Schubart (1920, 188). See also the English translation in Stephens and Winkler (1995, 375–88). The papyrus was a book roll, of which three columns of text survive.

including its famous oracle through which Apollo spoke. Just as Milo delighted in pointing out the deceptions and downfall of Diophanes (Apuleius, *Metam.* 2.14),[17] so Daulis gloats that the oracle who had foretold what would happen to others did not know its own fate (P.Berol. 11517, col. 2, lines 35–36). The shepherd likewise tells Hermas that a prophet filled with the earthly spirit is empty (Mand. 11.3, 13, 15 [43.3, 13, 15]). Although the empty prophet most often spends time with the double-minded, they may be unaware of what happens when they enter a righteous gathering. In such circumstances, their earthly prophetic spirit flees, and they are left speechless and broken (Mand. 11.14 [43.14]). Their falsehood is exposed.

The incident that leads to Lucius and Milo's conversation about Diophanes comes about as Lucius reflects on the spontaneous prophecy of Pamphile in Milo's house. While looking at the light of a lamp, Pamphile predicts that it would rain heavily the next day. Milo laughs at her and refers to her as a Sibyl (Apuleius, *Metam.* 2.11). Hermas initially identifies the woman who comes to him as a Sibyl (Vis. 2.4.1 [8.1]), although he seems to have been more sincere in his attribution than Milo. Hermas's naming of the woman as a Sibyl may have had particularly strong resonance in a Roman or more generally Italian setting. Tarquinius Priscus gathered oracular collections of the Sibyl's utterances and thereby established Rome as a collector of Sibylline materials long before Hermas (Dionysius of Halicarnassus, *Ant. rom.* 4.62).[18] The Roman poet Ovid also recounts the story of Aeneas's interactions with the Sibyl as he journeyed through the underworld (Ovid, *Metam.* 14.101–153). The Sibyl describes how, when she was chosen to be a Sibyl by Apollo, she was granted a wish. Her desire was for long life, but she did not specify that she wanted to be young while she lived long. Thus she had lived for 700 years and had many more years to live. She laments her dwindling size and weakening limbs (Ovid, *Metam.* 14.129–153). Her description contains some resonance with the woman's early appearances to Hermas.[19] The woman is described as elderly in Hermas's initial encounters with her (Vis. 1.2.2 [2.2]; 2.1.3 [5.3]; 2.4.1 [8.1]). After the fact, readers find that the woman was seated in the first vision because she was weakened from old age (Vis. 3.11.3–4 [19.3–4]). In the second vision, her hair and body still appear elderly (Vis. 3.12.1 [20.1]). The early descriptions of the woman in the *Shepherd* thus fit well with Greco-Roman depictions of the Sibyl.

Perhaps the best-known description of the Sibyl comes from Vergil's *Aeneid*. The Sibyl serves as Aeneas's guide through the underworld in *Aen.* 6.42–901.[20]

---

17. Reiling (1973, 84).

18. For more on the Sibyl, see Collins (1983–5, 1.317–20); Walde (2008, 411–12).

19. Another reference to Sibylline prophecies in second-century Christian literature can be found in Clement of Alexandria, *Strom.* 1.108.1 (21).

20. Anchises had already warned Aeneas that he must meet the Sibyl and visit the underworld in *Aen.* 5.721–742 so that Book 6 opens with Aeneas on the coast of Cumae, seeking "the distant shrine of the dreadful Sibyl" (*horrendaeque procul secreta Sibyllae*; *Aen.* 6.10).

However, the *Shepherd*'s agricultural imagery can also be explored well alongside the Roman poet's other verse, particularly in the *Georgics* and *Eclogues*. For example, the image of the vine and the elm that the *Shepherd* allegorizes in Sim. 2 (51) is alluded to as a matter of agrarian life in *Ecl.* 2.70. Corydon's vine is only half-pruned on the elm. Mars weaves the elms in happy vines in *Georg.* 2.221, while Vergil opens the *Georgics* by including a question about when it is best to bring the elm and vine together in marriage (*Georg.* 1.2-3).[21] The shepherd's discussion with Hermas employs vine and elm imagery to reflect on relations between the rich and poor rather than marriage. Yet both the *Shepherd* and Vergil utilize an image from Italian grape production. Another plant that is prominently described in the *Shepherd* is the willow tree of Sim. 8 (67-77). Vergil's poetry also makes reference to willow trees (*salices*) in these poems. The willow is connected to the vine at the end of the *Eclogues* (*Ecl.* 10.40).[22] One of the things that willows provide is shade for the shepherds (*Georg.* 2.434-435). The willow in the *Shepherd* likewise provides shade for all who call on the name of the Lord (Sim. 8.1.1 [67.1]).[23] Although these similarities are not strong enough to suggest literary dependence,[24] it is striking that the *Shepherd* employs similar imagery to Vergil's earlier poetry. Vergil's place in Rome and the value that he places on the Italian countryside are also noteworthy in view of the repetition of botanical imagery in the *Shepherd*.

The *Shepherd* also contains striking similarities to the *Tabula Cebetis*, or *Tablet of Cebes*. The *Tabula* is a popular philosophical dialogue that was known to Tertullian (*Praescr.* 39.4) and is usually dated from the first century BCE to the first century CE.[25] Indeed, these similarities have been such that some researchers have argued that the *Shepherd* employed the *Tabula* as a model.[26] It is not clear that the similarities are such as would allow one to conclude that one text definitively knew the other, but both stories come from similar literary and rhetorical backgrounds. The *Tabula* narrates a tale about an encounter that Cebes and some acquaintances had while in the Temple of Cronus. As they look at the offerings dedicated to Cronus, they come across a complex work of art that they cannot interpret. An elderly man appears and interprets the various scenes that are depicted in the

---

21. See also Catullus 62.48-57; Ovid, *Am.* 2.16.41; *Metam.* 14.661-668; Commodian, *Instr.* 30.16. For further discussion, see Gleede (2016, 253-4).

22. This passage is particularly interesting, since they are found in Pan's closing song to the Arcadians (*Ecl.* 10.31-77; see Herm. Sim. 9.1.4 [78.4]). See further Schwartz (1965, 244).

23. Willow trees also provide a place for Galatea to flee as she waits to be found (Vergil, *Ecl.* 3.64-65).

24. *Pace* Schwartz (1965, 245-7), who argues that the author of the *Shepherd* knows Vergil's poetry.

25. See further Fitzgerald and White (1983, 3-4); Hirsch-Luipold (2005a, 29).

26. E.g., Taylor (1901-3; 1903); Cotterill and Taylor (1910). Taylor's thesis was correctly challenged early on by Stock (1903); Weinel (1904). On the possibility of the *Tabula*'s direct influence on the *Shepherd*, see further Joly (1963; 1968, 51-3); Lampe (1989, 195; 2003, 231); Brox (1991, 52-4); Hirsch-Luipold (2005a, 26n.49).

work.[27] An extended dialogue ensues in which Cebes and those with him learn how to understand the intricately designed episodes in the table. Each scene is an allegorical depiction of life.

To take one example, the old man describes a scene in which all the people hear how to live well but must then drink a cup that causes them to forget and be deceived (*Tab. Ceb.* 5.1–6.3). The cup varies in its effectiveness on individuals. Some forget more than others and are thus more vulnerable to being deceived. The old man's allegory is clear. There are two ways to live.[28] Some recall how to live a eudaimonistic life better than others, yet all have been estranged from how they were meant to live. Although specific teachings may differ between the texts, similar descriptions are found throughout the *Shepherd*, particularly in the discussion of the tower (Vis. 3; Sim. 9), the elm and the vine (Sim. 2), the vineyard (Sim. 5), and the willow tree (Sim. 8). The dialogue about Tychē (Τύχη), or Fate, illustrates additional similarities between the two narratives. Like the woman and the shepherd, the old man maintains a certain authority as the most knowledgeable character in the dialogue. As such he plays a revelatory role, even if he does not reveal heavenly secrets.[29] The dialogue is then driven by Cebes's questions. He asks about the woman and the round stone on which she stands (*Tab. Ceb.* 7.1–3). This allows the old man to identify her as Tychē and to describe the sudden unstable changes that she causes. Likewise, Hermas asks both the woman and the shepherd about the construction process by which the tower is built (e.g., Vis. 3.3.1, 4 [11.1, 4]; Sim. 9.11.9 [88.9]). He asks specifically about the foundation for the towers (Vis. 3.3.5 [11.5]; Sim. 9.12.1–2 [89.1–2]), and his questions allow the revelatory figures to demonstrate their knowledge to Hermas and the readers (e.g., Vis. 3.3.2–5 [11.2–5]; Sim. 9.11.9–9.12.3 [88.9–89.3]).

Further similarities arise between the *Tabula* and *Shepherd* when one considers the imagery that both texts employ to discuss virtues and vices. For example, the old man appears to Cebes and his friends with a rod that he uses to point to the picture (*Tab. Ceb.* 4.2), while the woman employs a rod to point out the tower to Hermas (Vis. 3.2.4 [10.4]).[30] Both texts make use of feminine, familial language to illustrate connections between virtues. The old man highlights connections between education, truth, and persuasion by telling Cebes that Education (Παιδεία) has two daughters: one is called Truth, while the other is Persuasion (ἡ δὲ Ἀλήθεια, ἡ δὲ Πειθώ; *Tab. Ceb.* 18.2). Likewise, Hermas learns from the woman that the seven women in the tower are daughters of one another (Vis. 3.8.5 [16.5]). They follow from one another because they were born in a certain order

---

27. Trapp (1997) rightly observes the similarities between the scene in the *Tabula* and the shields given to Achilles and Aeneas (Homer, *Il.* 18.478–608; Vergil, *Aen.* 8.625–731).

28. Feldmeier (2005, 150–1).

29. This differs from Socratic dialogues, at least as portrayed by Plato (Trapp 1997). On Socrates's dialogues, see Wolfsdorf (2017, 41–3).

30. Joly (1968, 105n.1).

(Vis. 3.8.7 [16.7]).³¹ In contrast to Tychē, who stands on a round stone (*Tab. Ceb.* 7.1–3), Paideia is positioned upon a four-cornered stone (τετράγωνος; *Tab. Ceb.* 18.1–3). She is thus stable and unmovable. The shepherd points out that the tower is likewise built upon a four-cornered rock (τετράγωνος) that is able to contain the whole world (Sim. 9.2.1 [79.1]).³² The rock is later identified as the Son of God (Sim. 9.12.1 [89.1]), and he provides stability for the tower that is built upon it. Finally, *Tab. Ceb.* 28.3 describes people who have a desire for vices but refer to them as virtues. The old man summarizes their desires in terms of extravagance and a lack of control. The shepherd likewise tells Hermas about people who live in pleasure and luxury under the control of the angel of luxury and deception (Sim. 6.2.1–2 [62.1–2]). The passages are further alike in that both groups of people are described using zoological imagery. The old man describes them as cattle to Cebes, while the shepherd portrays them as sheep when talking to Hermas.³³

The *Tabula* and the *Shepherd* both contain extended dialogues with allegorical interpretations that draw upon similar imagery and are offered by characters whose knowledge far exceeds the knowledge of the listeners. The questions from those who receive and record the dialogue drive both the story and the ongoing interpretation forward. These similarities, along with references to outsiders, Sibyls, and dubious prophets, illustrate that the *Shepherd* should be read alongside other Greco-Roman literature.³⁴ This remains true even if one cannot go so far as to call the *Tabula* "one of the main sources of the *Pastor*."³⁵ The *Shepherd* is a text that is fully at home in a Greco-Roman literary setting.

The Shepherd *in Its Early Jewish Setting*

While the *Shepherd* can be well-placed alongside other Greco-Roman literature, it also fits well alongside early Jewish texts in the way that it employs motifs such as revelatory figures, wisdom teaching, and instructions about the spirits or two ways. Similarities to Jewish literature pervade the *Shepherd* so much that Friedrich Spitta argued that "the original of the 'Shepherd' is not from a Christian but a Jewish

---

31. Lampe (1989, 195; 2003, 230); Hirsch-Luipold (2005b, 131n.83). The *Shepherd* later employs the same terminology for double-mindedness (Mand. 9.9 [39.9]) and desire (Mand. 12.2.2 [45.2]).

32. Taylor (1901–3, 306). Joly (1968, 51) points out that the woman, that is, the church, is also said to have been seated on a couch with four legs (Vis. 3.13.3 [21.3]; see Vis. 3.1.4, 7–9 [9.4, 7–9]).

33. Hirsch-Luipold (2005b, 140n.127). For additional similarities between the *Tabula* and Sim. 6, see Dibelius (1923, 579–80).

34. A good example of how to read the *Shepherd* in this way can be found in Rüpke (2016) as he incorporates the *Shepherd* into a study of the role of the lived experiences of individuals in Roman religious texts.

35. Cotterill and Taylor (1910, 14).

source."³⁶ Helmut Köster follows in a similar tradition, seeing the *Shepherd* as a reworking of an originally Jewish text.³⁷ Although Joly opposes such arguments for an originally Jewish *Grundschrift*,³⁸ he nevertheless attends to "l'arrière juif" of the *Shepherd*.³⁹ In light of this scholarly history, it is worth considering carefully some of the ways in which the *Shepherd* might be situated alongside other early Jewish literature.

The *Shepherd* shares several features with Jewish apocalyptic literature.⁴⁰ As in other apocalypses, Hermas receives unique revelations from God that are mediated through otherworldly beings. In light of the prominence of dialogue in the *Shepherd*, one of the key elements to highlight concerns similarities between the shepherd and interpreting angels in other early Jewish apocalypses. Interpreting angels are often given the responsibility of clarifying confusing messages, visions, or dreams. They are sent to a particular person with whom they are to speak and whose questions they usually answer. They sometimes serve as guides on journeys through terrain that was previously unknown. Apocalyptic texts that utilize such angelic figures include *3 Baruch*, *4 Ezra*, the *Apocalypse of Abraham*, and the *Book of the Watchers* (*1 En.* 1–36).⁴¹ These texts draw upon the depiction of revelatory figures in Ezek 8–11; 40–48; Zech 1:7–6:8 as sources of vocabulary and imagery.⁴²

The description of the shepherd's appearance fits well alongside other interpreting angels in early Jewish apocalypses. The shepherd comes to Hermas while he is at home sitting on a couch.⁴³ The text simply says that "a certain man entered" (εἰσῆλθεν ἀνήρ τις; Vis. 5.1 [25.1]). The description of an angelic revealer as a man can also be found in Ezek 8:2 (LXX) and *Apoc. Abr.* 10.4. Ezekiel describes

---

36. "[D]as Original des 'Hirten' nicht christlichen, sondern jüdischen Ursprungs ist" (Spitta 1896, 342). See further Spitta (1896, 342–81).

37. Köster (1957, 254–5).

38. Joly (1993, 537–8).

39. "Hermas est pétri de culture juive" (Joly 1993, 533). See further Joly (1993, 533–5) and the literature referred to in the footnotes of Joly's text (Joly 1968).

40. As discussed with regard to the *Shepherd* in Chapter 4, the definitions and boundaries of apocalyptic literature remain a disputed matter. While the Second Temple texts referred to here as *apocalyptic* may be loosely grouped together, their relationship to one another, their precise location on a conceptual map of apocalyptic literature, as well as the particular traits that mark them out as apocalyptic remain disputed. For additional discussion, see the section on the genre of the *Shepherd* in Chapter 4 and the literature cited there.

41. For more on the interpreting angel, see Nickelsburg (2001, 294–5); Wright (2010, 329); Reynolds (2013). On similarities between Jewish apocalyptic texts and the angelology of the *Shepherd*, see Hvalvik (2007, 214).

42. Since it is unclear precisely how many angels are mentioned in Zech 1:7–17, the topic of angels in Zechariah has received more attention. E.g., Tigchelaar (1987); Delkurt (1999); Schöpflin (2007); Hallaschka (2010).

43. Osiek (1999, 99) is correct in arguing that Hermas's bed (κλίνη) is probably a dining couch and that this appearance is not a nocturnal vision.

"the likeness of a man" who appeared to him with fire. Likewise, after Abraham hears a voice telling Iaoel to go, Iaoel appears "in the likeness of a man" and takes Abraham by the right hand (*Apoc. Abr.* 10.4).[44]

Hermas's revelatory angel appears glorious and comes dressed like a shepherd. He wears a white skin with a bag on his shoulder and a rod in his hand. The angelic interpreters in Ezekiel are also described gloriously, though not with precisely these terms. Like the interpreting angel in Ezek 9:2, the shepherd wears a white garment, though its material composition is not disclosed. Like the interpreters in Ezek 9 and 40,[45] what the shepherd has in his hand is indicative of how the shepherd is described and apparently important enough to mention from his first appearance. The instrument in his hand gives further insight into both the shepherd's identity and role.

The role of interpreting angels in some apocalypses includes guiding their charges on journeys. The woman and the shepherd do not guide Hermas along heavenly journeys in the way that the seven angels accompany Enoch (*1 En.* 17.1–36.4) or that Phanuel assists Baruch in his journey through the heavens (*3 Bar.* 1.3–17.1).[46] The *Shepherd* is driven by dialogue in a way that is more comparable to the first four episodes of *4 Ezra* (3.1–10.59). Yet it is important to note that Hermas does not stay completely still when he is with the woman and the shepherd. The woman meets Hermas while he is traveling along the road (Vis. 2.1.1–3 [5.1–3]). In order to show him the tower, she meets Hermas in a secluded portion of a field where the vision is revealed (Vis. 3.1.2–4 [9.2–4]). When she comes to him again, she meets him along the Via Campania (Vis. 4.1.2 [22.2]; 4.2.1 [23.1]). The shepherd meets Hermas in his house (Vis. 5.1 [25.1]). While Hermas is fasting, the shepherd sits next to him on a mountain and restarts their discourse (Sim. 5.1.1 [54.1]). Although the two of them begin Sim. 6 by meeting again in Hermas's house, they decide to go to the plain to observe the shepherds (Sim. 6.1.1, 5 [61.1, 5]). The shepherd also leads Hermas to Arcadia for the second tower vision (Sim. 9.1.4 [78.4]). While being a guide for Hermas is not a significant part of the role that the woman and shepherd play, they move with Hermas in a way that is not altogether different from the guiding role played by interpreting angels in other Jewish apocalypses.

Both the shepherd and the woman exhibit at least one more characteristic that is familiar from early Jewish portrayals of interpreting angels: an emphasis on their ability to speak. Although little is said about their eloquence, their ability to speak is emphasized in the repetition of verbs of speech (e.g., λέγει; φησί[ν]). Verbs of speech tend to interrupt the discourse of both revealers. For example, as the shepherd explains the importance of fasting in Sim. 5.3 (56), his speech

---

44. Like the *Shepherd*, the *Apocalypse of Abraham*, the *Book of the Watchers*, and *3 Baruch* suggest a hierarchy of angels. See further *Apoc. Abr.* 10.3–4; *3 Bar.* 4.7 (Slav.); 11.4–9; *1 En.* 20.1–7.

45. See further Blenkinsopp (1990, 57–8); Joyce (2007, 102).

46. On angels in *3 Baruch*, see Kulik (2010, 52–3).

is interrupted three times over a brief period with the phrase, "he said" (φησι; Sim. 5.3.4–5 [56.4–5]). Verbs of speech are also interspersed among the woman's speech in her explanation of the tower. The narrator employs four such verbs in Vis. 3.3 (11) alone (Vis. 3.3.1, 2, 4, 5 [11.1, 2, 4, 5]). The ability to speak is likewise highlighted in Zechariah in the consistent reference to "the angel who spoke to me" (e.g., Zech 1:9, 13, 14; 2:3)[47] and again in *4 Ezra* by a similar narrative frame to the *Shepherd*.[48] The revealers in the *Shepherd* are characterized not only with an ability to speak but also with a consistent emphasis on their capacity to communicate with the person to whom they are sent.

In addition to general similarities in how the *Shepherd* and *4 Ezra* employ interpreting angels, another intriguing resemblance between these two texts is their use of a woman to represent the people of God. This tradition has roots that extend to depictions of Israel as a woman in texts, such as Isa 54:1; Jer 2:22; Ezek 16:3; Hos 2:19–20. A similar custom can be found in the practice of personifying cities in certain goddesses, such as the metonymical use of Roma for Rome. In the central vision of *4 Ezra* (9.26–10.59), the prophet encounters a woman who is grieving the loss of her son (*4 Ezra* 9.38–10.4). Ezra is incensed at the mother's weeping over a single son when Jerusalem, "the mother of us all" (*mater nostra omnium*; *4 Ezra* 10.7) has been destroyed.[49] As she listens to Ezra's anger, the woman's face begins to shine. She cries out, the earth shakes, and a city with enormous foundations appears where the woman had been (*4 Ezra* 10.25–27). Uriel, Ezra's interpreting angel, then explains that the woman was Zion and interprets the woman's story as an allegorical history of God's people in Jerusalem (*4 Ezra* 10.40–54).[50]

The woman in the *Shepherd* is likewise identified with the people of God. Although Hermas mistakes her for a sibyl, the young man with whom he speaks corrects him by informing him that the woman is the church. While the woman in *4 Ezra* allegorizes Zion's history in a narrative, the woman communicates something about God's people through her appearance. Although he only discovers this message in the course of a conversation with the young man, the woman's elderly appearance represents her place in creation.[51] She was created before all things (Vis. 2.4.1 [8.1]). Her transformations in the first three visions mirror the changes in Hermas's soul as he interacts with her (Vis. 3.10.1–3.13.4 [18.1–21.4]).[52] As in *4 Ezra*, the woman reveals more about herself by allowing Hermas to look at a building project. Ezra sees a city, while Hermas sees a tower (Vis. 3 [9–21]). Uriel informs Ezra what he is looking at. The woman-church is in the unique position to interpret herself in the tower-church (Vis. 3.3.3 [11.3]).[53] The woman remains with

---

47. For further references, see Schöpflin (2007, 190n.8).
48. Stone (1990, 82–3).
49. On the destruction of Jerusalem in *4 Ezra* and *2 Baruch*, see Sulzbach (2014, 146–8).
50. Ezra thus changes his attitude toward Jerusalem's destruction. See further Willett (1989, 61–2).
51. Brox (1991, 105–6); Osiek (1999, 58).
52. Humphrey (1995, 141–4).
53. Zahn (1868, 369).

Hermas as they look at the tower, but she exits from the story in as surprising a manner as the weeping woman in *4 Ezra*. After she explains the beast that Hermas has seen, Hermas hears a noise, looks away, and she vanishes (Vis. 4.3.7 [24.7]).

Additional points of convergence may be drawn between certain statements in the *Shepherd* and those in *4 Ezra*.[54] As the woman departs from Hermas following the first vision, she tells him to be courageous, or, playing on the Greek etymology, to "be a man" (ἀνδρίζου; Vis. 1.4.3 [4.3]). Near the end of the document, the shepherd tells Hermas to conduct himself "courageously" or, again translated with an eye to etymology, "manfully" (*uiriliter*; Sim. 10.4.1 [114.1]). After Ezra's encounter with the woman, Uriel likewise tells Ezra to "stand up like a man" (*sta ut vir*; *4 Ezra* 10.33). If Ezra does this, Uriel will teach him.[55] Ezra had fainted after the first vision and Uriel had strengthened him and set him on his feet. He is elsewhere told to stand and not to be afraid as Uriel tells him about the end of the age (*4 Ezra* 6.13–17). The connection between masculinity and standing in *4 Ezra* 10.33 is suggestive for the characterization of Ezra in this apocalypse. Since Ezra appears to be afraid after meeting the woman in the fourth vision, he is challenged to be more courageous and more masculine as he was earlier in the text. In the *Shepherd*, on the other hand, Hermas's masculinity increases as he takes up his position as a leader and provides a model for all early Christian readers.[56] Gender thus plays an understated but surprising role in both apocalypses.

Both Hermas and Ezra receive revelation in conjunction with their fasting and prayer. When Hermas is carried away to pathless regions for a second time, he immediately falls to his knees and prays (Vis. 2.1.2 [5.2]). Soon after, he fasts for fifteen days (Vis. 2.2.1 [6.1]). The woman shows Hermas the tower vision after he fasts many times and prays to the Lord (Vis. 3.1.2 [9.2]). Hermas discovers more about the woman's identity after he fasts for a day (Vis. 3.10.6–7), while the shepherd tells Hermas the parable of the vineyard when he finds him fasting on a mountain (Sim. 5.1.1. [54.1]). Ezra likewise receives instructions from Uriel to fast so that further instructions can be given to him (*4 Ezra* 5.13). After he fasts for seven days (*4 Ezra* 5.20),[57] he complains to God and prompts Uriel to come to him (*4 Ezra* 5.21–32). A similar pattern is found at the transition from the second to the third visions (*4 Ezra* 6.31–7.2).[58] Although Ezra is not instructed to fast

---

54. Jachmann (1838, 63–7) even proposed that the *Shepherd* was literarily dependent upon *4 Ezra*, going so far as to call it "an imitation" (eine Nachahmung) of *4 Ezra* (1838, 66–7). Although one need not posit literary dependence, Jachmann's argument begins from the observation of similarities like these.

55. Stone (1990, 330) points out that the command for Ezra to stand is given prior to receiving revelations. This becomes clearest in *4 Ezra* 14.2 where Ezra stands to hear God's direct address.

56. Young (1994, 250–3).

57. Seven-day fasts are also found in *2 Bar.* 9.2; 12.5.

58. See similarly *2 Bar.* 20.5–22.8. *2 Baruch* takes up similar themes to *4 Ezra*. For further similarities, see the synopsis in Berger (1992).

before meeting the woman in the fourth vision, his diet is carefully regulated. He should eat only flowers, not consume meat or wine, and pray continually (*4 Ezra* 9.24–25).[59] Links between fasting, prayer, and revelation are not limited to the *Shepherd* and *4 Ezra*,[60] but such connections illustrate how the *Shepherd* can be usefully viewed within the literary environment of early Jewish apocalyptic.

The word "apocalyptic" is popularly associated with catastrophic predictions of the future.[61] The futuristic orientation of apocalyptic literature may lead one to think of prophecy, although neither apocalyptic nor prophecy are exclusively future-telling endeavors in the biblical and early Jewish traditions. Nevertheless, apocalyptic literature may be viewed in some similarities to prophetic literature,[62] and the *Shepherd* deals with true and false prophecy in ways that fit not only a Greco-Roman background but also scriptural and early Jewish backgrounds (Mand. 11 [43]).[63] Yet this is not the only stream of thought from which apocalyptic may be viewed. Early Jewish apocalypses also draw from wisdom traditions, and the *Shepherd* is no exception.[64] As sometimes exemplified in the wisdom genre,[65] there is a concern for books in apocalyptic literature. At the beginning of Daniel's apocalyptic dreams, he sees books opened in the heavenly court (Dan 7:10). On the other hand, Ezra is instructed to seal seventy books whose contents are secret and to give them only to the wise.[66] "For in them is the spring of understanding, the fountain of wisdom, and the river of knowledge" (*in his enim est uena intellectus et sapientiae fons et scientiae flumen*; *4 Ezra* 14.47). The woman likewise gives a book to Hermas, but Hermas is unable to read it until the meaning is revealed to him after fasting (Vis. 2.1.3–2.3.4 [5.3–7.4]).[67] The meaning of the words is initially

---

59. Jonathan Moo (2011, 146–7) rightly notes that Ezra's change in diet marks a change in Ezra's shift of how Jerusalem's destruction is perceived.

60. E.g., Dan 9:3; 10:3, 12; *2 Bar.* 43.3; 47.2; *Apoc. Abr.* 17.1–18.14. See further the literature cited in Körtner and Leutzsch (1998, 155nn.155–7).

61. Note, for example, the definition given in Oxford Dictionaries online: "describing or prophesying the complete destruction of the world" (https://www.lexico.com/definition/apocalyptic; accessed August 29, 2020).

62. Najman (2014).

63. See further Joly (1968, 192–9); Reiling (1971; 1973, 97–8).

64. Lebram (1978, 192–3).

65. E.g., Eccl 12:12; Sir 50.27. On links between the wisdom and apocalyptic genres, see Goff (2014).

66. Metzger (1983–85, 1.555n.o).

67. On heavenly books in Vis. 2, see Baynes (2012, 174–9). Wright (2017, 217) rightly includes the reference to the readings of Hermas, Clement, and Grapte as evidence for communal reading practices, since Hermas is instructed to read the book "to this city" (εἰς ταύτην τὴν πόλιν; Vis. 2.4.3 [8.3]). Within "this city," a reference to Rome, the woman also makes specific reference to the elders as an important audience to which Hermas should read. On the other hand, Clement will read to the cities outside of Rome, while Grapte will instruct the widows and orphans.

mysterious, but their significance is ultimately revealed thanks to the woman's interpretive and literary skill.

The woman's speech in Vis. 3.9.1–10 (17.1–10) contains motifs that are reminiscent of how wisdom is described in Proverbs, Ben Sira, and the Wisdom of Solomon.[68] To begin with, the speeches in Prov 8 and Sir 24 are extended monologues given by female characters about the right way to live and to know God. After she allegorizes the tower for Hermas, the woman also offers a speech that is addressed to Hermas and to his community about how they should live without discord in the community.[69] She starts by calling for her children to listen to her (Vis. 3.9.1, 2 [17.1, 2]). At the end of her speech in Prov 8, Lady Wisdom likewise urges her son to listen to her (Prov 8:32; see also Prov 8:34). Wisdom acts like a mother who trains people up in how they are to live. In the *Shepherd*, the woman describes how she raised her children in single-mindedness, innocence, and holiness (Vis. 3.9.1 [17.1]). Wisdom nourishes her participants like a canal in a garden so that they grow into a river (Sir 24:30–31). The Wisdom of Solomon reports that, although Solomon was born without any special privileges (Wis 7:1–6), he rejoiced and learned from how wisdom led him (Wis 7:12–14), recognizing that wisdom is led by God (Wis 7.15–16). The woman tells Hermas that she wants to stand joyfully (ἱλαρά) before God (Vis. 3.9.10 [17.10]). She will be able to do this if the people live peaceably with one another. Wisdom's speech in Sir 24 is given in an "assembly of the Most High" (ἐν ἐκκλησίᾳ ὑψίστου; Sir 24:2). She further describes in the speech how she "ministered before him" (ἐνώπιον αὐτοῦ ἐλειτούργησα) when she was sent to Israel (Sir 24:10).[70]

Based on the connections between wisdom and the woman in Vis. 3.9 (17), one may recognize additional links in how the woman's place in creation can be compared to scriptural and early Jewish portrayals of wisdom's role in creation. Wisdom describes how she was created by God at the beginning of his ways (Prov 8:22). In Prov 8, wisdom was the first entity that God created and is thus older than the springs of water and the mountains (Prov 8:23–25). Although wisdom in Ben Sira is closely connected to Israel (Sir 24:8–12), wisdom again describes how she was created before the age (Sir 24:9). Following this claim to supratemporality, wisdom's description of her service in the tent of God likewise reads most naturally as a service that extends before the current age. Solomon describes wisdom as a breath of God's power and an emanation of the Almighty's glory (Wis 7:25). Such a close connection to God along with the statements about wisdom's pretemporal

---

68. Osiek (1999, 80) writes that the woman "speaks as mother who instructs her children in virtue, a wisdom motif." As Osiek (1999, 80) rightly notes, wisdom motifs do not negate prophetic elements of the woman's speech. On the genre of Vis. 3.9 (17), see Walsh (2019a, 540).

69. The addressees in Vis. 3.9 (17) are plural.

70. Wisdom is closely linked to both Israel and the Torah in Sir 24:9–12, 23–27. See further Sauer (2000, 182).

place with God suggest that Wis 7:25 should be understood in the same vein.[71] In these strands of wisdom literature, wisdom was the first thing created by God and is thus prior to visible creation.[72]

The *Shepherd* claims something similar about the church and, by extension, about the woman who represents the church. In addition to correcting Hermas's mistaken identity of the woman as the sibyl, the young man who speaks with him informs him that she was created as the first of all things (Vis. 2.4.1 [8.1]). This is offered as the reason for the woman's elderly appearance at the end of Vis. 2. In the first vision, the woman had likewise told Hermas that God had created the church along with everything else that is visible (Vis. 1.3.4 [3.4]). The church's place as one of God's created entities and the special temporal relationship that God has granted to the church over and against the rest of the universe fits well with how wisdom is described in other early Jewish wisdom texts. That wisdom and the church are both personified by women further supports reading the *Shepherd* within this environment.[73] Although the church is not depicted as an agent in the creative process, God created all things for the sake of his church (Vis. 1.1.6 [1.6]). Hermas also describes how he heard that all things will become level for the elect if they keep his commandments (Vis. 1.3.4 [3.4]).[74] These early passages suggest that creation responds in some ways to the church and further illustrates the close relationship between the church and creation that is similar in some ways to the relationship between wisdom and creation described in writings such as Proverbs, Ben Sira, and the Wisdom of Solomon.

The *Shepherd* shares a way of speaking about two ways with other scriptural and early Jewish texts.[75] This is perhaps clearest in Mand. 6.1.1–2 [35.1–2]) where the shepherd tells Hermas that two ways divide the lives of those who are righteous and unrighteous.[76] Although the two-ways pattern is by no means exclusively Jewish,[77] this manner of speaking is found in Jewish scripture. Psalm 1:6 contrasts the way of the righteous and the ungodly, while Prov 4:10–19 relies on similar imagery to distinguish between wisdom and righteousness, on the one hand, and foolishness and unrighteousness, on the other.[78] This language is developed and extended in the Testaments of the Twelve Patriarchs and in some Qumran literature. The *Community Rule* sets out the paths of light and darkness in 1QS

---

71. On the creation and personification of wisdom, see further Blischke (2007, 173–8); Reiterer (2015, 184–6).

72. In addition, wisdom aided in God's creation of the rest of the world according to Prov 8:26–31; Wis 7:22; *2 En.* 30.8.

73. Brox (1991, 525).

74. O'Brien (1997, 484–5).

75. For recent discussion of the Two Ways, see Wilhite (2019a, 99–103; 2019b, 75–140).

76. Brox (1989a, 271); Hvalvik (2007, 213).

77. The two-ways pattern is likewise evident in Hellenistic literature (e.g., Xenophon, *Mem.* 2.1.21–39; Hesiod, *Op.* 287–92). See further Taylor (1893).

78. See also Deut 30:15; Josh 24:15; Ps 139:24; Prov 2:8–22; Jer 21:8; Bricker (1995).

III, 13–IV, 26.[79] Although all things were created by God (1QS III, 15, 25–26), he placed two spirits within human beings: the spirits of truth and deceit (1QS III, 18).[80] The spirit of truth or light is characterized by following God's laws and acting both truly and justly (1QS IV, 2–6). This path leads to healing, peace, and life (1QS IV, 6–8). The deceitful spirit is greedy, prideful, irreverent, and dishonest (1QS IV, 9–11). Ultimately, it leads to destruction (1QS IV, 11–14). These two ways of living are overseen by angelic figures: the Prince of Lights and the Angel of Darkness (1QS III, 20–21). In the Testament of Asher, Asher reports that God has granted two ways to human beings (*T. Ash.* 1.3–5). Those who love evil show no mercy and cheat their neighbor, while those who are good are righteous, repentant, and single-minded. Similar to the Angel of Darkness in 1QS, Asher describes those who give themselves up to the evil way as overmastered by Beliar (*T. Ash.* 1.8).[81] Asher also describes the twofold nature of virtues and vices (*T. Ash.* 2.1–6.8).

In addition to telling Hermas that there are two ways, namely, righteousness and unrighteousness, he also shows Hermas two angels in Mand. 6.2.1–10 (36.1–10); Sim. 6.2.1–6.5.7 (62.1–65.7). The two ways and two angels represent alternative ways of living and keeping God's commandments. The crooked way has many obstacles and comprises uneven ground (Mand. 6.1.3 [35.3]). The wicked angel is bitter, foolish, and turns people away from God (Mand. 6.2.4 [36.4]). The angel of luxury and deception crushes empty souls and turns them away from the truth by tantalizing them with their desires (Sim. 6.2.1 [62.1]). Conversely, the righteous way is smooth (Mand. 6.1.4 [35.4]), reflects on virtue, purity, and contentment (Mand. 6.2.3 [36.3]), and provokes repentance in people by subjecting them to painful experiences (Sim. 6.3.2–6 [63.2–6]). Moreover, the *Shepherd* also describes the virtues of faith, fear, and self-control in twofold terms (Mand. 6.1.1–8.12 [35.1–38.12]). For example, fear of the Lord keeps one from doing evil, while fear of the devil is worthless since the devil has no power in him (Mand. 7.2–4 [37.2–4]). Likewise, one should be self-controlled regarding evil, but there is no need for self-control regarding what is good (Mand. 8.2 [38.2]). The *Shepherd's* use of the two-ways teaching can thus be usefully situated within an early Jewish literary environment.

A final matter to note is the way in which the *Shepherd* utilizes the designation "the gentiles" (τὰ ἔθνη) to refer to outsiders. Drawing from the way τὰ ἔθνη are sometimes portrayed in the Septuagint,[82] early Jewish texts employ the term to distinguish Israel from other nations.[83] The *Shepherd* likewise uses τὰ ἔθνη

---

79. The imagery of ways or paths can also be found in Sir 15:11–17; CD II, 6; Philo *Agr.* (101); *2 En.* 30.15; *4 Ezra* 7.3–12; m. 'Abot 2.1.

80. Philo also speaks of two powers that indwell human beings (*QE* 1.23).

81. See also 1QM XIII, 12; *T. Levi* 3.2–3; *1 En.* 1.9; 54.3–5; 63.1; *2 En.* 10.1–3.

82. E.g., Exod 15:14; Deut 7:1; Ps 2:1. See further Lust, Eynikel, and Hauspie (2003, 172); Muraoka (2009, 190).

83. E.g., *Ep. Aris.* 139; *T. Levi* 9.10; *Pss. Sol.* 9.9; *3 Macc.* 6.9; Wis 14:11; 15:15. See further Trebilco (2017, 151–4).

as a term for outsiders, thereby distinguishing the addressees who keep God's commandments from those who are external to the community. When the woman finishes reading to Hermas for the first time, he finds her last words pleasing but her initial words difficult. The woman explains that the last words are for the righteous, while the earlier words are "for the gentiles and apostate" (τοῖς ἔθνεσιν καὶ τοῖς ἀποστάταις; Vis. 1.4.2 [4.2]). In Sim. 8.9.3 (75.3), some who were formerly in the community and who are described as returning their willow branches with two parts withered and one part green continued living with the gentiles, rejected God, and are thus counted with the gentiles. This portion of the *Shepherd*'s parable indicates that "gentiles" does not refer only to non-Jews. Nevertheless, the word relies on this earlier meaning for its force as it distinguishes τὰ ἔθνη from the true people of God. The *Shepherd* extends the negative connotations that the word has in some early Jewish texts in order for the word to have its effect on readers.[84] Although the *Shepherd*'s readers are nowhere explicitly referred to as Israel, the usage of τὰ ἔθνη as a reference for outsiders suggests that insiders to the community are no longer to be regarded as gentiles. The *Shepherd* is not the only early Christian text to employ τὰ ἔθνη in this way. "That this usage occurs across a whole range of quite different and disparate NT texts shows that the expectation of undergoing such a linguistic re-learning process, and hence the 'Judaising' of language by 'Gentiles' was quite common."[85]

The Shepherd: *Greco-Roman or Early Jewish?*

In light of these comparisons with literary texts in the surrounding world, it should be clear that the *Shepherd* is a document that can be viewed as part of this environment. This chapter has not argued that the *Shepherd* has borrowed directly from any of these documents. Rather, the goal has been to show that the *Shepherd* contains images, phrases, and dialogues that have precedents in other ancient literature. The *Shepherd* should thus be situated alongside these traditions. Yet the author has written the *Shepherd* in such a way that the work stands on its own. Even if literary borrowing is allowed in some instances, the author has incorporated any traditions that were utilized from elsewhere into a visionary and dialogical story that does not require knowledge of any other ancient texts in order to be understood. The arguments by Spitta and Köster for an originally Jewish apocalypse that was reworked by a Christian editor are unlikely and in any case without sufficient evidence.[86]

---

84. For other instances of τὰ ἔθνη in the *Shepherd*, see Vis. 2.2.5 (6.5); Mand. 4.1.9 (29.9); 10.1.4 (40.4); 11.4 (43.4); Sim. 1.10 (50.10); 4.4 (53.4); 8.9.1 (75.1); 9.17.2, 4 (94.2, 4); 9.18.5 (95.5); 9.28.8 (105.8). The adjective ἐθνικός is used in Mand. 10.1.4 (40.4).

85. Trebilco (2017, 175). See further Trebilco (2014, 194–200; 2017, 150–76).

86. Spitta (1896, 342–81); Köster (1957, 254–5).

Nor does this comparison make it easier to say much more about who the author was or what social or literary movements might have been influential than was already said in Chapter 4. The *Shepherd* is sometimes described as a "Jewish Christian" text.[87] Although it is certainly the case that the author has employed motifs found in Jewish apocalypses, depicted the woman in a way that is similar to portrayals of Lady Wisdom, and spoken of τὰ ἔθνη, the author nowhere explicitly identifies as Jewish Christian. Moreover, Jewish identity markers do not play a significant role in the text. On the basis of the comparison in this chapter, there are no strong grounds for identifying the *Shepherd* as a Jewish Christian text.[88] The *Shepherd* is better seen as a text coming out of the diverse early Christian movement of the second century. It is to further discussion of the *Shepherd* alongside early Christian literature that the book turns next.

---

87. E.g., Daniélou (1964, 36–9); Holmes (2007, 442).
88. See further Grundeken (2015a, 24–52).

Chapter 8

THE *SHEPHERD* AND EARLY CHRISTIAN LITERATURE IN THE FIRST TWO CENTURIES

Following from the previous chapter, this chapter attempts to place the *Shepherd* alongside early Christian literature in the first two centuries CE. This chapter again refrains from engaging in questions about literary borrowing. The question of how the *Shepherd* received New Testament documents has been given attention both with a focus on the whole New Testament and with a focus on particular parts.[1] The issue is particularly complicated because the *Shepherd* contains no explicit citations from other extant early Christian documents.[2] Although these studies will be cited throughout the chapter, the point of this chapter is only to show how the *Shepherd* may be read as a text that is enmeshed in the early Christian literary environment. Canonical New Testament divisions are used for the sake of convenience, but the goal is ultimately to view the *Shepherd* holistically within the early Christian literary environment. It is, therefore, necessary to move beyond the boundaries of the New Testament. Chapter 8 thus begins by exploring the *Shepherd* alongside the Gospels, Pauline Epistles, the Catholic Epistles, and Revelation. It then lifts its gaze beyond the New Testament to look at the *Shepherd* alongside extra-canonical literature.

The Shepherd *and the Gospels*

In an 1892 study of the Gospels and the *Shepherd*, Charles Taylor argues that the *Shepherd* contains early references to an argument employed by Irenaeus regarding why there could only be four Gospels.[3] Irenaeus appeals to the four principal minds, four living creatures (Ezek 1:6; Rev 4:7), and four universal covenants

---

1. On the reception of the New Testament in the *Shepherd*, see Drummond (1905); Verheyden (2005). On the reception of the Gospels in the *Shepherd*, see, e.g., Köster (1957); Massaux (1986, 261–325). Jefford (2017, 49–52) and Soyars (2019) helpfully examine the reception of Paul in the *Shepherd*.

2. In other words, there are no citations that are introduced by a clear quotation formula. The only explicit citation comes from the Book of Eldad and Modat (Vis. 2.3.4 [7.4]).

3. Taylor (1892, 4) conveniently states his thesis as follows:

to show that there must be only four Gospels (Irenaeus, *Haer.* 3.11.8–9).[4] After looking for uses of the term εὐαγγέλιον in the *Shepherd*, Taylor interprets ἀγγελία ἀγαθή as a reference to good news about the story of Jesus. He then looks for usages of the number four, such as the woman's position of strength when she is seated on the four-legged couch (Vis. 3.13.3 [21.3]) and the four sets of stones that are placed in four rows at the foundation of the tower (Sim. 9.4.3 [81.3]; 9.15.4 [92.4]).[5] Although there are good reasons to read the *Shepherd* and the Gospels alongside one another, Drummond is diplomatic to say that he "cannot place much confidence" in Taylor's interpretation of the number four in the *Shepherd*.[6] There is nothing to suggest that the number four has anything to do with the canonical Gospels except for Irenaeus's later testimony.

How, then, might the Gospels and the *Shepherd* be fruitfully read alongside one another? There are loose terminological similarities between the *Shepherd* and some of the Gospels. Both the *Shepherd* and Matthew make reference to a "great king" (βασιλεὺς μέγας; Vis. 3.9.8 [17.8]; Matt 5:35), while the reference to tribulations leading believers to deny the Lord or choking them like thorns (Vis. 3.6.5 [14.5]; Sim. 9.20.1–2 [97.1–2]) shares imagery that is found in the Parable of the Sower (Matt 13:20–21; Mark 4:18–19; Luke 8:14). Although they are small in scope, such verbal parallels indicate that the *Shepherd* and the Gospels are literary texts that originated within the early Christian movement.

Parallel themes and imagery may be more helpful to interpreters of the *Shepherd*. Sim. 3–4 tell corresponding parables about trees in winter and trees in summer. Although trees are difficult to distinguish in winter, they are easy to distinguish once their fruits and leaves appear in summer (Sim. 3.1–4.8 [52.1–53.8]). The righteous and unrighteous may look similar now, but the shepherd urges Hermas and his readers to act rightly so that their fruits may be known "when the Lord's mercy appears" (ὅταν ... ἐπιλάμψῃ τὸ ἔλεος τοῦ κυρίου; Sim. 4.2 [53.2]). The shepherd's analogy is reminiscent of the Matthean Jesus's parable of the farmer who plants good seed only to have his neighbor sneak in at night to plant weeds. While the good plants cannot now be easily separated from the

> It is a prevalent opinion that the work of Hermas is of little or no value for the history of the Canon. But I have been led to think that its testimony, especially to the Gospels, is strong and convincing, although it does not lie on the surface: that it says in effect that the number of the Gospels was actually and necessarily four, as Irenaeus said after it: and that Irenaeus was indebted to Hermas in respect of that important and remarkable statement, for which the later writer is always taken to be the independent and original authority.

4. See further Campenhausen (1972, 176–201); Skeat (1992); Foster (2012, 105).
5. Taylor (1892, 3–21).
6. Drummond (1905, 118). For evaluation of Taylor's study, see Köster (1957, 253–4); 46; Brox (1991, 46n.6); Osiek (1999, 88n.32); Verheyden (2005, 299–300).

weeds, Jesus compares the kingdom of heaven to the harvest, at which time the former will separate the weeds from the grain (Matt 13:24–30, 36–43).[7]

The shepherd also employs botanical imagery in the following Similitude when he tells a story about a slave who works in a vineyard (Sim. 5.2.1–11 [55.1–11]). The shepherd introduces his story by instructing Hermas to "listen to the parable" (ἄκουε τὴν παραβολήν; Sim. 5.2.1 [55.1]). He then narrates the story of a faithful slave who goes beyond his master's instructions. The master rewards the slave's hard work not only with the freedom that he promised but also by making him coheir with his son (Sim. 5.2.7–8, 11 [55.7–8, 11]). The Synoptic Gospels record a parable that Jesus spoke in Jerusalem (Matt 21:33–46; Mark 12:1–12; Luke 20:9–19).[8] The story likewise contains an introductory statement that refers to the parable (Matt 21:33; Mark 12:1; Luke 20:9). As in the Shepherd, a man plants a vineyard and leaves it in the care of others. As in the Shepherd, the man has a son. However, those in charge of the vineyard do not obey the man's instructions. They beat the slaves who are to collect the owner's portions of the harvest and eventually kill his son. The farmers who are left in charge of the vineyard in the Synoptic parables are irresponsible and contrast with the slave in the Shepherd.[9] The slave's newfound position not only as freedman but as coheir with the owner's son is startling in light of how Roman freedmen were viewed by their freeborn neighbors.[10] The extraordinary work that the slave in the Shepherd's parable offers is also reminiscent of the faithful slave who actively watches over the master's affairs while the master is away (Matt 24:45–51; Luke 12:41–45).

In the second interpretation of Sim. 5, the shepherd notes that the Son of God cleansed people from their sins after he received control of the vines, which represent the people of God (Sim. 5.6.1–2 [59.1–2]). The shepherd explains that the Son is Lord over all people "because he received all authority from his Father" (ἐξουσίαν πᾶσαν λαβὼν παρὰ τοῦ πατρὸς αὐτοῦ; Sim. 5.6.4 [59.4]). The Matthean Jesus likewise tells his disciples that "all authority" (πᾶσα ἐξουσία) has been given to him (Matt 28:18). The shepherd informs Hermas in the same Similitude that the Son gives the law to his people and that he received that law from his Father (Sim. 5.6.3 [59.3]). In John, Jesus similarly tells his people that he received the commandment from his Father (John 10:18; 12:49; 14:31). Such similarities between how the Son is described in the Shepherd, the Synoptics, and John suggest that one's reading of the Shepherd may also be aided by knowledge of John.

---

7. A similar parable is also told in Gos. Thom. 57. On the similarities between Sim. 3–4 (52–53) and Matt 13:24–30, 36–43, see Dibelius (1923, 558); Snodgrass (2018, 193–4).

8. On the interpretive framework to be used for the similar parable in Gos. Thom. 65, see Gathercole (2014, 461–2).

9. For additional contrasts between the Synoptics and the Shepherd, see Glancy (2002, 104–5). On Sim. 5.2 (55) and the Synoptic Gospels, see Drummond (1905, 122); Dibelius (1923, 562); Joly (1968, 227n.1); Staats (1986, 103); Leutzsch (1989, 145); Osiek (1999, 171n.1); Beavis (2018, 656–8).

10. Glancy (2002, 105); Beavis (2018, 661–5).

Johannine similarities to the *Shepherd* may be clearest in Sim. 9 (78–110). The Son of God is referred to as the gate (πύλη) of the tower in Sim. 9.2.2 (79.2); 9.12.1–3 (89.1–3). The Son is both the rock on which the tower stands and the newly chiseled door that represents the Son's revelation in the last days. Jesus likewise describes himself as the door (θύρα) in John 10:7, 9.[11] His description of how he acts as the door is intertwined with his description of himself as the shepherd (John 10:1–5).[12] Anyone who enters by means of another way than the door is a thief (John 10:8). Only those who enter through the door will be saved (John 10:9). Likewise, only stones that are brought through the gate may be set in the tower that Hermas sees (Sim. 9.12.4–5 [89.4–5]). The use of the door image in both the *Shepherd* and John envisions an exclusivity surrounding the Son whereby the Son is the only means of entry into God's realm. The gate "is the one entrance to the Lord" (μία εἴσοδός ἐστι πρὸς τὸν κύριον; Sim. 9.12.6 [89.6]). In John, no one can come to the Father except through Jesus (John 14:6).[13] One must receive the seal of baptism in order to receive the Son's life and enter into God's kingdom (Sim. 9.16.4 [93.4]). The Johannine Jesus tells Nicodemus that no one can enter God's kingdom unless that person is born of water and the Spirit (John 3:5). For both texts, Jesus's significance is found in the unique way in which he grants access into the Father's life and realm.[14]

The Shepherd *and the Pauline Epistles*

Although knowledge of the Pauline letters may inform one's reading of the *Shepherd* alongside other early Christian literature,[15] the clearest example comes in Mand. 4.1 (29). The shepherd's instructions to Hermas to guard purity suggest that divorce is not the norm (Mand. 4.1.1 [29.1]). An exception is given for cases of adultery (Mand. 4.1.4–6 [29.4–6]).[16] If the adulterous partner repents, however, the wronged partner is obliged to take them back (Mand. 4.1.7–8 [29.7–8]).[17] For

---

11. See *1 Clem.* 48.2–4 (Ps 117:19–20 [LXX]) and Ign. *Phld.* 9.1 for other early Christian references to Jesus as the door. See also Nagel (2000, 243–9); Hill (2004, 376–8, 438–9); Lookadoo (2018, 90–3).

12. Whatever the pre-Johannine history of these images, the author brings them together in a way that fits well within John 10:1–18 so that the shepherd and the door should be read together. For further discussion, see Beasley-Murray (1999, 166–7); Michaels (2010, 578n.3); Frey (2013, 318).

13. Drummond (1905, 123); Hill (2004, 377).

14. For more on exclusivity and inclusivity in John, see Koester (2008, 209–14).

15. For similarities between how Ephesians and the *Shepherd* describe the church, see Muddiman (2005).

16. One may here note similarities to the Jesus tradition in Matt 19:3–9 (Drummond 1905, 121; Massaux 1986, 284–5).

17. Niederwimmer (1975, 167–8).

this reason, the shepherd tells Hermas that divorced persons should not marry someone else. Paul likewise instructs the Corinthians not to divorce (1 Cor 7:10), but he rules that those who are divorced are not to marry someone else (1 Cor 7:11). The correspondence between these passages is noteworthy and indicates that, in this instance at least, the *Shepherd* and Paul's letters may be placed within similar streams of Christian tradition.[18] Nevertheless, the *Shepherd* differs from Pauline instructions when the text clarifies that only one repentance is allowed in situations of adultery (Mand. 4.1.8 [29.8]). This instruction fits well with the *Shepherd*'s other instructions on repentance, but no such teaching is found in the Pauline letters.

Finer verbal similarities are also worth observing in order to show how language and themes from the Pauline letters compare to the *Shepherd*.[19] When the shepherd interprets the tower vision for Hermas, he describes the unity of the stones in terms of incorporation into the tower. They have become one spirit, one body, and one garment with one color for their clothing (Sim. 9.13.5, 7 [90.5, 7]). The repetition of the number one is likewise found in Eph 4:4–6, where believers are urged to be unified in one body and one spirit because they have been called in one hope, one Lord, one faith, one baptism, and one God.[20] The believers in the tower even think the same things (Sim. 9.13.7 [90.7]; see also Sim. 9.29.2 [106.2]), which is reminiscent of Paul's instruction that the Philippians should have the same mind in themselves (Phil 2:2, 5; 4:2; see also Rom 15:5; 2 Cor 13:11).[21] When Hermas inquires why the stones came up from the deep, the shepherd tells Hermas that they had come through the water in order to be made alive. Baptismal imagery is employed to signify the difference between life and death (Sim. 9.16.1–4 [93.1–4]). Paul likewise contrasts life and death using baptismal imagery (Rom 6:1–11).[22] If one follows the text of B, L¹, and L² in Vis. 2.3.1 (7.1),[23] the contrast between

---

18. Note also the resemblance between Mand. 4.4.1–2 (32.1–2) and 1 Cor 7:39–40. On Mand. 4 and 1 Cor 7, see Dibelius (1923, 513); Brox (1991, 214); Osiek (1999, 116); Verheyden (2005, 322–9).

19. Jonathan Soyars usefully expands the data to consider in the *Shepherd* to include not only extended verbal citations but also the adoption, adaptation, and synthesis of Pauline literary phenomena (2019, 222–3). In his conclusion, he considers a further possibility: "The *Shepherd* might even be said to represent the emerging development of a Pauline sociolect or, more specifically, a Pauline rheterolect, in second-century Rome" (Soyars 2019, 224).

20. See also Sim. 9.17.4 (94.4); 9.18.4 (95.4). Similar repetition of the number one is found elsewhere in early Christian literature at Ign. *Magn.* 7.1–2; *Phld.* 4; Justin, *Dial.* 63.5; Clement of Alexandria, *Strom.* 5.113.2–5.114.1 (14). For further background, see Maier (2005, 316).

21. Soyars (2019, 189–91).

22. For further discussion, see Osiek (1999, 238); Jefford (2017, 50).

23. S, A, and E contain a shorter text that only mentions death: μνησικακία θάνατον κατεργάζεται. B, L¹, and L² read μνησικακία θάνατον κατεργάζεται, τὸ δ' ἀμνησίκακον ζωὴν αἰώνιον κατεργάζεται (*memoria enim malorum mortem operatur, oblivio enim malorum vitam aeternam cooperatur*). One of the manuscripts in L¹ contains the shorter reading, but

life and death is furthered. Bearing a grudge leads to death, while forgetting a grudge results in eternal life. In a similar way, Paul distinguishes grief that leads to repentance and results in salvation from grief that leads to death (2 Cor 7:10).[24]

One further conceptual comparison will also be helpful to note when considering the *Shepherd* alongside Pauline literature. Some have found the *Shepherd*'s articulation of salvation and focus on right living to contrast with Pauline understandings of grace.[25] One of the most robust statements of this view comes from Thomas Torrance. Torrance finds "confusion" in the *Shepherd* between creation and redemption and sees few, if any, references to the atoning work of Christ.[26] He argues that the *Shepherd*'s conception of grace is "Judaistic,"[27] while the place of moral activity and works is out of sync with the way in which the Pauline letters articulate such teachings.[28]

Torrance is correct that the *Shepherd* places more emphasis on God's creative work than on Christ's atoning work at the cross. This contrasts to some degree with Paul's letters, which regularly speak of Christ's death and the work that he accomplished for believers.[29] Paul also insists that salvation is not by works of the law but by grace through faith in Christ.[30] However, the Son of God in the *Shepherd* works on behalf of believers in Sim. 5.6.2 (59.2). The Son's work for the vines makes them into a vineyard. Afterward, he shows them the paths of life and gives them the law (Sim. 5.6.3 [59.3]). The Son's work precedes any activity on the part of God's people. The woman and the shepherd elsewhere inform Hermas that justification comes from outside of believers (Vis. 3.9.1 [17.1]; Mand. 5.1.7 [33.7]), although believers are obliged to live rightly so that they may be justified (Sim. 5.7.1 [60.1]). "In Hermas's imagination it is repentance, itself flowing from faith, that results in justification."[31] The judgments in the tower visions and in the vision of the willow tree are closely connected to believers' actions while being brought into the tower or when they held their willow branch (Vis. 3 [9–21]; Sim. 8–9 [67–110]). Yet a simplistic contrast between the Pauline letters and the *Shepherd*

---

the overwhelming majority of manuscripts contain the longer reading. See further Tornau and Cecconi (2014, 44). The shorter reading is accepted by Lindemann and Paulsen (1992, 340); Ehrman (2003, 2.188); Holmes (2007, 466). The longer reading is accepted by Carlini (1988, 237); Carlini and Giaccone (1991, 73); Prinzivalli and Simonetti (2010–15, 2.232).

24. Carlini (1988).
25. E.g., Hückstädt (1889, 6n.7); Harnack (1891, 86–7); Bigg (1909, 81).
26. Torrance (1948, 112–15).
27. Torrance (1948, 115–16).
28. Torrance (1948, 116–19).
29. E.g., Rom 3:21–26; 5:6–8; 1 Cor 1:23; 15:3–5; 2 Cor 5:21; Gal 3:1; Phil 2:8. See further Dunn (1974); Breytenbach (1999; 2010b).
30. E.g., Rom 3:21–4:25; Gal 3:6–4:31; Eph 2:8–9; Phil 3:9. See further Barclay (2014; 2018); Breytenbach (2003; 2010a); McFarland (2013, 156–9; 2016, 183–91).
31. Soyars (2019, 102). One might also note that endurance in faith leads to salvation in Vis. 3.8.5 (16.5; see further Schliesser 2017, 43).

does not seem to fit the evidence. The *Shepherd*'s lexicon for means to salvation may be larger than the traditional Pauline statement that salvation comes through faith, but the relationship between the *Shepherd*'s way of speaking and the Pauline idiolect cannot be described in terms of opposition.[32]

The Shepherd *and the Catholic Epistles*

The Pauline letters are not the only epistles in the New Testament or in early Christian literature more broadly. As in 1 Peter, Hermas is instructed regarding his worries (μέριμνα). When Hermas meets the beast that sends forth flaming locusts, the woman commends him for not being double-minded and for casting his worry on God (Vis. 4.2.4 [23.4]). Hermas is then to go and tell others that a time of suffering is coming and that they should likewise cast their worries on the Lord (Vis. 4.2.5 [23.5]). This contrasts with the state of Hermas's soul in the first vision in which he was weakened by preoccupations with the ordinary matters of life and refused to cast his worries the Lord (Vis. 3.11.3 [19.3]). 1 Peter employs similar language when urging the audience to humble themselves. They should cast all their worry upon God because he cares for them (1 Pet 5:7).[33] The *Shepherd* also speaks of suffering in similar ways to 1 Peter. In the *Shepherd*, attention that is placed on the suffering of God's elect overwhelms any glimpses that may be given to the suffering of the unrighteous. Hermas is instructed to tell believers that the beast that he saw foreshadows suffering that will not come upon them (Vis. 4.2.5–6 [23.5–6]; 4.3.6 [24.6]).[34] When 1 Peter discusses suffering, the emphasis likewise falls upon believers (1 Pet 4:17–19). For this reason, 1 Peter urges believers to live as strangers in the world (1 Pet 2:11–12), something which the shepherd also hints at when he describes the two cities to Hermas (Sim. 1.1–11 [50.1–11]).

The Petrine letters, Hebrews, and the *Shepherd* acknowledge an important place for the prophets who lived before Jesus. 1 Peter regularly cites the prophets, particularly Isaiah. The author thus suggests that the message of the prophets and the events that happened in Christ are coherent. Yet there is a sense in which the prophets' message was only completed in Christ. This places the audience of 1 Peter in a privileged position (1 Pet 1:10–12). The audience of 2 Peter is exhorted to remember the words of the prophets (2 Pet 3:2).[35] The author of Hebrews likewise notes the importance of the prophets and the various ways in which God spoke through them (Heb 1:1). The author cites the prophets (e.g.,

---

32. For a nuanced perspective of faith in Sim. 8 (67–77) and more broadly in the *Shepherd*, see the still valuable study of Zahn (1868, 184–90).

33. Similar language is also found in Ps 55:23 (54:23 LXX); Wis 12:13. On this language in the *Shepherd* and 1 Peter, see Drummond (1905, 115); Osiek (1999, 87n.22).

34. Bauckham (1974, 36).

35. For additional similarities between the *Shepherd* and 2 Peter, see Zahn (1868, 430–8); Grünstäudl (2013, 193–7); Frey (2018, 199–200).

Heb 2:6–8; 8:7–12) and commends their faithful lives as models for his audience (Heb 11:32–40).³⁶ Yet God has spoken freshly through the Son (Heb 1:2). Because God has spoken through his Son, the Son's message is more powerful than the prophets. The *Shepherd* similarly gives a prominent role to the prophets. When the *Shepherd* allegorizes the tower vision to Hermas, he identifies the third group of stones as the prophets and ministers of God (Sim. 9.15.4 [92.4]). These thirty-five stones precede the forty stones that represent the apostles and teachers and who proclaim the Son of God. The order suggests that the prophets whom the shepherd describes are pre-Christian. Additionally, the first three sets of stones add up to 10 + 25 + 35 = 70, which may be taken as a complete way of referring to the church's foundation before the Son's appearance in the flesh.³⁷ Yet the prophets are simply incorporated into the tower. For the *Shepherd*, there is no strong distinction between the prophets and the church in the way that Hebrews and 1 Peter differentiated them. The prophets are even brought through the door by the virgins (Sim. 9.15.5–6 [92.5–6]).

There is a particular affinity between the *Shepherd* and James. This may be clearest in the repeated use of "double-mindedness" (διψυχία) in the *Shepherd*.³⁸ Double-mindedness is associated with doubt in James. James instructs someone who lacks wisdom to ask for it from God. However, they should ask without doubting that God will give it to them (Jas 1:5–7). A doubting person is described as "double-minded" (δίψυχος) and "unstable in all their ways" (ἀκατάστατος ἐν πάσαις ταῖς ὁδοῖς αὐτοῦ; Jas 1:8). The word double-minded is employed again in Jas 4:8 as a substantive. Double-minded people stand parallel to the sinners and are instructed to purify their hearts. Double-mindedness is used as a noun, adjective, and verb more than fifty times in the *Shepherd*.³⁹ The shepherd instructs Hermas about double-mindedness in prayer in Mand. 9.1 (39.1). Double-mindedness manifests itself in an interior dialogue that doubts whether God will grant a request because of sin in a person's life. The shepherd emphasizes that God will answer a person's prayer if that person does not doubt because God is richly compassionate (Mand. 9.2 [39.2]).⁴⁰ A persistent and trusting faith is thus the antidote to double-mindedness (Mand. 9.6–7, 10–12 [39.6–7, 10–12]). Double-mindedness is also connected to repentance when the woman tells Hermas that

---

36. On citations of scripture in Hebrews, see Docherty (2009); Steyn (2011). For the prophets as exemplary, see Alexander (2009); Dyer (2017, 157–60).

37. See further Dibelius (1923, 624–5); Brox (1991, 397n.10, 429–30); Osiek (1999, 237); Grundeken (2018, 96–7).

38. For double-mindedness in early Christian literature, see Seitz (1944; 1947; 1958); Porter (1990).

39. Osiek (1999, 30). For references, see Kraft (1964, 113–14).

40. The shepherd acknowledges that prayers take time and instructs Hermas to keep praying when requests are delayed (Mand. 9.7–8 [39.7–8]). No instruction is given about when requests might be answered negatively. The shepherd seems to assume that the requests that a person asks of God come from a righteous disposition.

he must inform his family about their sins (Vis. 2.2.2–4 [6.2–4]). The woman's instruction for all the saints is that their sins will be forgiven if they repent and drive away double-mindedness (Vis. 2.2.4 [6.4]). Double-mindedness is then set opposite to remaining firm (Vis. 2.2.7 [6.7]). The fourth mountain of the second tower parable symbolizes the double-minded who are somewhere between alive and dead, have green leaves at the top but cracked foundations at the root, and turn to idolatry when persecution comes. Nevertheless, there is hope that they might repent (Sim. 9.21.1–4 [98.1–4]).

The *Shepherd* employs the concept of double-mindedness in a more thoroughgoing and elaborate manner than James. Yet the two texts appear to be participants in the same early Christian language game. Other similarities between the two texts suggest that they may be fruitfully read together. For example, James is addressed "to the twelve tribes in the Diaspora" (ταῖς δώδεκα φυλαῖς ταῖς ἐν τῇ διασπορᾷ; Jas 1:1). The shepherd describes the twelve mountains surrounding the tower as the twelve tribes that inhabit the whole world (δώδεκα φυλαί εἰσιν αἱ κατοικοῦσαι ὅλον τὸν κόσμον; Sim. 9.17.1 [94.1]). Although James may maintain more explicit ties to Jewish wisdom traditions, both James and the *Shepherd* signify that their texts are written to all believers using the image of twelve tribes that are dispersed.[41] James additionally refers to the tongue as unstable (ἀκατάστατον) and evil in Jas 3:8, while the *Shepherd* refers to slander as "an unstable demon" (ἀκατάστατον δαιμόνιον; Mand. 2.3 [27.3]). The links between speech and instability are noteworthy.

Perhaps the most significant parallels are between the *Shepherd* and James 4. Both texts mention God's power to save and to destroy (Jas 4:12; Mand. 12.6.3 [49.3]). In addition to the reference to double-mindedness in Jas 4:8 and throughout the *Shepherd*, Jas 4:7 urges believers to resist the devil. If they do, the devil will flee from them. The shepherd discusses the devil using wrestling imagery. If someone opposes the devil, the devil will be defeated and flee from them in shame (Mand. 12.5.2 [48.2]). If someone draws near to God, God will also draw near to that person (Jas 4:8). Similarly, in the *Shepherd*'s quotation from the Book of Eldad and Modat, readers find that the Lord draws near to those who turn to him (Vis. 2.3.4 [7.4]). The similarities between the quotation from the Book of Eldad and Modat and Jas 4:8, along with the other similarities between James and the *Shepherd*, have led to reflections on the unidentified quotation in Jas 4:5. Richard Bauckham and Dale Allison have argued that the Book of Eldad and Modat is quoted not only in Vis. 2.3.4 (7.4) but also in Jas 4:5; *1 Clem.* 23.3; *2 Clem.* 11.2.[42] Even if the precise origins of these citations remain uncertain, the presence of such similarities is further evidence that readers of the *Shepherd* may also profit from knowing James and other texts now collected in the Catholic Epistles.

---

41. Bauckham (2017, 108–10).
42. Bauckham ([2004] 2008; 2013; 2017, 109); Allison (2011).

The Shepherd and Revelation

Reading the *Shepherd* and Revelation together may make the most sense prima facie out of any of the books now contained in the New Testament because they are both examples of the apocalyptic genre.[43] In both texts, the recipients of the revelation that comes to them receive previously hidden information from God in special ways. Both texts utilize the sight of the recipients in order to allow reads to experience the text.[44] John and Hermas see sights that overwhelm and surprise them (Rev 1:12; 4:1; 15:1–2, 5; 18:1; Vis. 1.2.2 [2.2]; 2.1.3 [5.3]; 3.1.4 [9.4]; Sim. 3.1 [52.1]; 9.7.4 [84.4]). Both texts also employ interpreting angels in order to clarify the meaning of a vision or statement. When John finds that the destruction of Babylon has given way to the Lamb's wedding feast, a voice confirms that these words are faithful and true. After this, John even bows down to worship the angelic voice, but he is quickly alerted to the fact that his homage is misplaced (Rev 19:9–10).[45] The woman and the shepherd serve as interpreting angels in the *Shepherd*.[46]

One may also point to similarities between Revelation and the *Shepherd* in the way in which both texts make use of books within the texts that they are composing. Both John and Hermas are instructed to write (Rev 1:11; 14:13; 19:9; Vis. 2.4.3 [8.3]; 5.5–7 [25.5–7]),[47] and readers are left thinking that the words that they have arranged have come together in the books that they are now reading. John's experience with books goes beyond reading and writing. He is told to eat a book (Rev 10:2) and finds that the book is sweet in his mouth but bitter in his stomach (Rev 10:8–11).[48] John also has experiences with heavenly books. After John's letters to the churches (Rev 2–3), the opening vision of Rev 4–5 not only astounds readers with its spectacular view into heaven but also highlights the Lamb's importance as the only one who is able to unseal the book (Rev 5:6–9). The Lamb opens the book in Rev 6:1, and the contents of the book unleash the judgments in the rest of the chapter. John also refers to a Book of Life that is kept

---

43. On viewing the apocalyptic genre in terms of prototypes and examples, see Collins (2014, 5; 2016, 32–3). This is not to say that Revelation or the *Shepherd* is a necessarily prototypical apocalypse but that they can nevertheless be classified as examples of the apocalyptic genre. See the discussion of genre in Chapter 4.

44. Berger (2018, 22–32) correctly observes that meaning is often communicated in Revelation sight and sensory perception.

45. A similar event happens when the angel shows John the river of life that flows from God's throne (Rev 22:8–9). See further Bauckham (1993a, 120–40).

46. The women and shepherd's roles as interpreting angels were discussed in Chapter 7. On interpreting angels in apocalyptic literature, see Nickelsburg (2001, 294–5); Wright (2010, 329).

47. It is worth noting, however, that John is restricted from writing some things. For example, he is told not to write what the seven thunders say (Rev 10:4).

48. Berger (2018, 15–22) highlights the importance of senses other than sight and hearing in Revelation.

with the Lamb and records the names of the Lamb's followers (Rev 3:5; 13:8; 17:8; 20:12, 15; 21:27). The woman in the *Shepherd* tells Hermas about the book of life, in which those who repent will have their names inscribed alongside the saints (Vis. 1.3.2 [3.2]). He once hears the woman read from a book (Vis. 1.3.3–4 [3.3–4]), while at another time he sees her reading from a book as she walks (Vis. 2.1.3 [5.3]). Hermas is allowed to copy the book, but the book is mysteriously snatched away from him as soon as he finishes writing (Vis. 2.1.3–4 [5.3–4]). Moreover, he cannot understand what he has copied but has only copied the syllables. The meaning comes to Hermas only after he fasts for fifteen days (Vis. 2.2.1–2.3.4 [6.1–7.4]). Both Revelation and the *Shepherd* speak about the book of life. Yet while Hermas can only understand what he reads with the woman's aid, John watches events unfold when he sees a heavenly scroll unsealed and experience another book through ingestion.

Women also play a key role in both texts, although their roles are not exactly the same.[49] The woman in the Shepherd of Hermas was already characterized in Chapter 6 and described in Chapter 7 in conjunction with the woman in *4 Ezra* and with wisdom texts. The woman is closely identified with the people of God, was created before all things, and transforms her appearance as Hermas's soul undergoes changes. She communicates with Hermas by speaking to him directly. One key means of revelation is thus the woman's speech. She is also closely connected to the construction of the tower in Vis. 3 (9–21) not only because she reveals the tower's meaning in her conversation with Hermas but because both the woman and the tower represent the people of God. The woman's speech near the end of the tower vision (Vis. 3.9 [17]) is reminiscent of descriptions of Lady Wisdom in scriptural and early Jewish wisdom collections.

Women are key characters in the New Testament Apocalypse, but John does not receive revelation directly from the women in his visions. Rather, his sight leads to increased understanding. The woman that John sees in Rev 12 takes part in a vision that John describes as a "great sign" (σημεῖον μέγα; Rev 12:1).[50] The woman is about to give birth to a son, while a dragon waits in front of the woman in order to devour the son. The boy, who represents the messiah,[51] is snatched away when he is born, while the woman flees to the desert (Rev 12:1–6). After the dragon wages war against Michael and the other angels (Rev 12:7–12), he returns to his pursuit of the woman in Rev 12:13. The woman is given two wings so that she can fly to her place until the right time. When the dragon attempts to drown the woman with water from its mouth, the ground absorbs the water and enables

---

49. See further Lookadoo (forthcoming).

50. This is the first place in Revelation that John employs the word σημεῖον. The term is also used in Rev 12:3; 13:13, 14; 15:1; 16:14; 19:20.

51. The description of the boy as one "who is about to shepherd all the nations with an iron rod" recalls language from Ps 2:9, a psalm which was given a messianic interpretation not only in early Christian texts but also in early Jewish texts. See, e.g., 4Q174 I, 18–19; *1 En.* 48.8; *Pss. Sol.* 17.24; Acts 4:25–26; 13:33; Heb 1:5; Rev 2:27.

the woman to flee (Rev 12:14–17). The woman represents both the mother of the messiah and the people of God.[52] Her place in the desert uses imagery that is reminiscent of the Exodus narrative. This differs from the portrayal of the woman in the *Shepherd* as an instantiation of wisdom. The woman in Rev 12, like Israel, has been protected by God and given a place in the desert in which to wait for her final redemption.

Women are also connected to buildings or cities in the *Shepherd* and Revelation.[53] As the woman and the tower are both identified as the people of God in the *Shepherd*, so the people of God are portrayed as a bride who is closely connected to the New Jerusalem in Revelation. The messianic Lamb is her groom, and she has prepared herself for him (Rev 19:6–10). After this description of the people as a bride, John sees a new city coming down from heaven that has also prepared itself as a bride that is adorned for her husband (Rev 21:2).[54] Nor are the women in the *Shepherd* and Revelation entirely good. In Revelation, another woman is connected to another city, namely, the harlot and Babylon. These are particularly prominent in Rev 16–18, and both the evil of this woman/city and their destruction are described in vivid terms.[55] In Sim. 9, Hermas spends the night with twelve women who represent twelve holy spirits or virtues (Sim. 9.10.4–9.11.9 [87.4–88.9]; 9.13.2 [90.2]; 9.15.1–2 [92.1–2]). His stay with them is marked by prayer and dancing but is not sexual in nature. However, other women are described who dress in black clothes, have bare shoulders, and loosened hair (Sim. 9.13.8 [90.8]). These represent unclean spirits or vices (Sim. 9.15.3 [92.3]). The feminine imagery in these early Christian apocalypses portrays women in the revelation that the text wishes to communicate, offers a central role to women who function positively in the revelation, and juxtaposes other women who represent that which opposes God. The women are complex figures in both apocalypses, but their roles are key to understanding what the text means.

The Shepherd *and Wider Early Christian Literature*

Discussions of the *Shepherd* within early Christian literature should not be limited to texts within the New Testament or to texts that predated the *Shepherd*. Regardless of how many individual books within the New Testament that the *Shepherd* may have known, the *Shepherd* offers no hint of recognizing a New Testament canon. Texts that were written at around the same time as the *Shepherd* or perhaps slightly

---

52. Koester (2018, 123–4).

53. Humphrey (1995, 84–149).

54. Muddiman places Eph 5 alongside Rev 21 in his analysis of the *Shepherd*'s ecclesial imagery (2005, 119).

55. On the contest between Babylon and Jerusalem as well as the harlot and the bride, see Bauckham (1993b, 131–2); Zimmermann (2003, 178–82); Huber (2007, 185–9; 2013, 56–88); Koester (2014, 642–3).

later may bear witness to the same theological and literary environment within which the *Shepherd* was composed. The comparison of the *Shepherd* within its early Christian literary environment must extend beyond the bounds of the New Testament canon. One might begin by comparing the *Shepherd* to various authors or texts that were written in the second or early third centuries. An alternative way to consider the *Shepherd* alongside other literature would reflect on themes that the *Shepherd* shares with other early Christian texts. These themes can be explored with a particular eye to geography and the Roman origins of the *Shepherd* and certain other early Christian texts. Some attempt will be made here to blend these methods of comparison, though a thematic organization provides the controlling focus.

The *Shepherd* devotes a significant amount of time to the topic of repentance (μετάνοια).[56] Repentance is linked to several themes, and one of the practices with which repentance is linked in the Similitudes is hope. In particular, the shepherd shows Hermas that there is hope for some people to repent. On three instances, the shepherd employs very similar language in order to convey his message. In Sim. 8.7.2 (73.2), the shepherd discusses the double-minded and slanderers but says that repentance remains open for them. Indeed, some have already repented, "and there is still hope for repentance among them" (καὶ ἔτι ἐλπίς ἐστιν ἐν αὐτοῖς μετανοίας). The shepherd returns to the double-minded later in the similitude, but he insists that there is still "hope for repentance" (μετανοίας ἐλπίς; Sim. 8.10.2 [76.2]). In his discussion of the two angels, the shepherd also refers to the hope for repentance for those who enjoy a luxurious life but who have not blasphemed. They may be able to live by repenting (Sim. 6.2.4 [62.4]). Zahn and Lightfoot recognized long ago that Ignatius of Antioch employs similar language when he writes to the Ephesians.[57] He instructs his readers to pray unceasingly for all people to find God, "for there is hope for repentance in them" (ἔστιν γὰρ ἐν αὐτοῖς ἐλπὶς μετανοίας; *Eph.* 10.1). Both Ignatius and the *Shepherd* utilize the language of the "hope for repentance" without using definite articles. They also employ similar language to refer to the target audience of repentance when each text uses the preposition ἐν.[58] The *Shepherd* and Ignatius are part of the same environment to such an extent that they can utilize similar language when discussing repentance.[59]

---

56. The varied ways in which the *Shepherd* discusses repentance will be considered more fully in Chapter 10.

57. Zahn (1873, 620); Lightfoot (1889–91, 2.2.58). See also Joly (1993, 539–40).

58. Joly (1993, 540). The textual evidence is split in Ignatius's letter. I am inclined to accept the evidence of the Greek and Latin middle recensions, which include the preposition. However, the Greek long recension, the Syriac translation, and the Armenian translation omit the preposition. Lightfoot (1889–91, 2.2.58) places the Greek preposition in brackets. Camelot (1969, 78), Fischer (1981, 148), Lindemann and Paulsen (1992, 184), Ehrman (2003, 1.228), Holmes (2007, 190), and Prinzivalli and Simonetti (2010–15, 1.352) include the preposition in the text.

59. Contrary to Joly (1993, 540), the close similarities in language do not require one text to cite the other. However, Joly (1993, 540n.115) rightly points out additional similarities

The *Shepherd*'s references to two ways of living were discussed in Chapter 7 but present another opportunity to reflect on the degree to which the *Shepherd* is enmeshed within the Greco-Roman, early Jewish, and early Christian literary world. The shepherd tells Hermas that there are two ways to live in Mand. 6.1.1–4 (35.1–4). One way of living leads to righteousness and allows for smooth passage, while the other is unrighteous and is strewn with obstacles.[60] In addition to referring to two paths, the shepherd uses the image of two angels (Mand. 6.2.1–10 [36.1–10]; Sim. 6.1.5–6.5.7 [61.5–65.7]). As in the case of the two ways, one angel is described as the angel of righteousness, while the other angel is referred to as the angel of evil (Mand. 6.2.1 [36.1]). The righteous angel is modest, gentle, and quiet (Mand. 6.2.3 [36.3]). However, the punishing angel is also placed on the side of righteousness, while simultaneously being depicted as a shepherd who uses thorns and briars to punish the sheep (Sim. 6.2.6–7 [62.6–7]). The punishing angel receives the sheep who have wandered away from God in order to pursue the pleasures of this age (Sim. 6.3.3 [63.3]). These angels stand over and against the angel of evil, who is linked with bitterness and foolishness (Mand. 6.2.4 [36.4]), and the angel of luxury and deception (Sim. 6.2.1 [62.1]), whose pleasant treatment of the sheep ends up crushing them because they live indulgently. The angel of luxury and deception ultimately leads the sheep to death or corruption.

The early Christian provenance of the two ways has a long history in scholarship because of the similarities between the two-ways tradition in the *Didache* and the *Epistle of Barnabas*.[61] While the tradition of dividing life into two ways was widespread in ancient Mediterranean literature, the *Shepherd*'s bifurcated understanding of life should also be explored in connection with these early Christian texts. For example, the *Didache* likewise refers to two ways, one of which leads to life while the other leads to death (*Did.* 1.1). The *Epistle of Barnabas* likewise introduces two ways of teaching and authority (*Barn.* 18.1–2). Although the paths in this text are characterized by light and darkness rather than life and death,[62] it is important to note that the *Epistle of Barnabas* refers to angels who are given authority over one path (*Barn.* 18.1). The path of darkness belongs to "the black one" (ὁ μέλας; *Barn.* 20.1).[63] As one compares the two-ways tradition in the

---

when it comes to the temple metaphor that Ignatius uses in Ign. *Eph.* 9.1 and the botanical imagery in, e.g., Ign. *Trall.* 11. On Jesus as door in Ign. *Phld.* 9.1 and in Sim. 9, see Legarth (1992, 331); Lookadoo (2018, 86–93, esp. 92–3).

60. Jefford (2006, 91).

61. See the studies in, e.g., Robinson (1920); Vokes (1938, 27–61; 1993, 213–16); Barnard (1966, 87–107); Layton (1968); Rordorff ([1972] 1986). On the study of the two ways within recent scholarship on the *Didache*, see Wilhite (2019c).

62. However, it is worth noting that two-ways terminology related to life and death appears in *Barn.* 5.4. On the significance of two-ways terminology throughout the epistle and not just in *Barn.* 18–21, see Rhodes (2011).

63. On "the black one" in the *Epistle of Barnabas*, see Prostmeier (1999, 219–20, 555–7); Rothschild (2019). Didymus the Blind identifies the black one in the *Epistle of Barnabas* as Satan and claims that the *Shepherd* likewise refers to Satan as black (*Comm. Zach.*

Shepherd, *Didache*, and the *Epistle of Barnabas*, further similarities illustrate the origins of the text in a similar milieu. The angel of righteousness is described as "gentle and quiet" (πραΰς καὶ ἡσύχιος; Mand. 6.2.3 [36.3]). Likewise, the *Didache* and *Epistle of Barnabas* urge their readers to be "gentle" (πραεῖς [*Did*. 3.7]; πραΰς [*Barn*. 19.4]) and "quiet" (ἡσύχιος [*Did*. 3.8]; ἡσύχιος [*Barn*. 19.4]). The shepherd's teaching to Hermas about sincere giving (Mand. 2.4–7 [27.4–7]) is loosely paralleled by the briefer instructions in the traditions of the *Didache* and the *Epistle of Barnabas*, in which the audience is taught to be sincere in heart and rich in spirit (*Barn*. 19.2) and to give freely to anyone who asks (*Did*. 1.5–6).[64] Although such connections do not require one to posit a literary connection between any of these texts, the texts can be read alongside one another as examples of early Christian paraenesis. Moreover, they represent part of a tradition that continued to be used in early Christian texts through at least the fourth century.[65]

Thus far the consideration of the *Shepherd* has focused largely on similarities in the language of select early Christian texts, particularly Ignatius's letters, the *Didache*, and the *Epistle of Barnabas*. In addition to linguistic parallels, another way to explore the *Shepherd* alongside early Christian literature is to examine thematic resemblances between various works. The *Shepherd*'s discussion of prophecy can be placed alongside other early Christian texts to offer insights into understandings of prophecy during the first two centuries CE.[66] In particular, the *Shepherd*'s warnings against false prophets are part of a larger set of warnings in early Christian texts against false prophecy. These warnings do not stem from a common source, but they do represent a recurrent theme in a variety of early Christian texts.

The shepherd teaches Hermas that false prophecy comes from an earthly spirit which has no power (Mand. 11.11 [43.11]). Thus, the false prophet has no place among the righteous, cannot deceive the righteous, and flees from the presence of righteous people (Mand. 11.1–2, 13–14 [43.1–2, 13–14]). False prophets only speak when they are consulted by double-minded people to tell their fortune (Mand. 11.2, 4, 6 [43.2, 4, 6]).[67] However, the false prophet will be proved to be

---

355.20–24). Didymus may have in mind Sim. 9.19.1 (96.1) where the black mountain of the second tower vision represents apostates and blasphemers. See also Ehrman (1983, 12–13).

64. Niederwimmer (1993, 108–16); Prostmeier (1999, 539–40).

65. E.g., Matt 7:13–14; Ign. *Magn*. 5.1–2; Clement of Alexandria, *Strom*. 5.5.31 (5); Lactantius, *Inst*. 6.3; *Const. apost*. 7.1.1–19; Aldridge (1999); van de Sandt and Flusser (2002, 55–111); Jefford (2006, 88–91, 217); Stewart-Sykes (2011, *passim*).

66. Another intriguing topic of study may consider the relationship between life, death, and baptism in texts that are associated with Rome or its environs. This list would arguably include at least Paul's Romans, Hebrews, 1 Peter, *1 Clement*, Ignatius's *Romans*, the *Shepherd*, and the writings of Justin. One might also add the Gospel of Mark and the writings of Marcion, insofar as the latter can be reconstructed.

67. On the other hand, the divine spirit does not need to be consulted. Rather, when a prophet is filled by a spirit that comes from God, that prophet speaks freely on the spirit's initiative (Mand. 11.5 [43.5]).

empty when they encounter righteous people just like empty jars in a storeroom are found to be empty when one has not filled the jars (Mand. 11.15 [43.15]). A false prophet is self-exalting and desires to sit in the place of honor (Mand. 11.12 [43.12]). They enjoy a luxurious lifestyle, and their prophecy is contingent upon payment. A true prophet of God, on the other hand, regards themselves as poorer than other people and cannot receive money for their prophecy (Mand. 11.8, 12 [43.8, 12]). After hearing the descriptions of true and false prophets, Hermas and the audience are instructed to test the person who claims to be a "spirit-carrier" (πνευματοφόρον) by their words and lifestyle (Mand. 11.16 [43.16]).

Chapter 7 illustrated examples elsewhere in Greco-Roman literature of skepticism regarding diviners who make their fortunes through prophecy in a way that is analogous to Mand. 11.1–6 (43.1–6). However, concerns about fortune-making by fortune-telling are also found in early Christian texts. Near the end of the second century, Irenaeus accuses Marcus of propagating Valentinian doctrine through magic and false prophecy (Irenaeus, *Haer.* 1.13.1–7).[68] Marcus is said to be a disciple of Valentinus, who claims to have improved upon the Valentinian system (Irenaeus, *Haer.* 1.13.1).[69] The primary way in which Marcus understands himself to have further clarified Valentinus's thought is through a better grasp of precisely how letters and syllables function to bring further enlightenment. According to Irenaeus, Marcus portrays himself with a particularly strong connection to Σίγη (Irenaeus, *Haer.* 1.14.1–1.15.6). Irenaeus's critique of Marcus's lifestyle is most relevant to readers of the *Shepherd*.[70] He argues that Marcus preys upon wealthy women in Asia Minor and attracts them to his way of teaching through magical signs performed on cups of wine (Irenaeus, *Haer.* 1.13.2). Irenaeus accuses him of being possessed by a demon through which he is able to prophecy (Irenaeus, *Haer.* 1.13.3).[71] In addition to his own prophecy, Marcus is said to urge women to prophecy by using invocations to confuse the woman who then prophecies out of her vanity (Irenaeus, *Haer.* 1.13.3).[72] Irenaeus is writing a polemical treatise, and Marcus would have articulated his practices differently. Yet regardless of whether this is an accurate description of Marcus's practices, Irenaeus records an instance of early Christian skepticism toward prophecy that is used to make money—in this case, from the purses of wealthy women in Asia Minor. He also traces the

---

68. Reiling (1973, 64–5, 85–6).

69. On Marcus's place in the Valentinian school, see Dunderberg (2005, 82–3).

70. It is possible that Irenaeus's depiction of Marcus's lifestyle is based upon rumor or exaggerated for polemical reasons. For the purposes of this chapter, the early Christian awareness of and skepticism toward fortune-telling are what is important. The question of how the historical Marcus lived can be left to one side for this discussion. See further Förster (1999, 123–6); Dunderberg (2005, 83).

71. Note that the *Shepherd* similarly speaks of prophets being filled by an earthly spirit (Mand. 11.11–15 [43.11–15]).

72. Förster (1999, 116–17).

origins of Marcus's prophecy to a demon, something which is perhaps not so far removed from the earthly spirit in the *Shepherd*.

The testing of prophecy is a phenomenon that is likewise attested elsewhere in early Christian texts. These texts are found as early as the Pauline letters. For example, Paul urges the Thessalonians not to be contemptuous of prophecy but to "test everything" (1 Thess 5:20–21). Although they should keep what is good, they should also stay away from every form of evil (1 Thess 5:21–22). In a lengthier discussion of prophecy in 1 Cor 14, Paul instructs the Corinthians to test the prophetic words uttered in the congregation (1 Cor 14:29). 1 John instructs readers to test whether the spirits are from God precisely because there are so many false prophets at work in the world (1 John 4:1–3). Ignatius's own prophetic speech may have been tested by the Philadelphians when he visited (Ign. *Phld.* 7.2).[73] Finally, the *Didache* warns its readers to test prophets who speak in the community (*Did.* 11.7–12). The community is specifically warned against prophets who demand payment for their prophecy (*Did.* 11.12). Prophets should be welcomed and also examined (*Did.* 12.1).[74] If a prophet is only passing through for a few days, the community is instructed to provide for their needs (*Did.* 12.2). However, a prophet who wishes to settle in the community should work for their living (*Did.* 12.3). This appears to be targeted at prophets such as the satirical portrait painted of Peregrinus by Lucian, who becomes rich because other Christians offer him money (Lucian, *Peregr.* 13). The *Shepherd*'s skepticism of false prophets, fortune-telling, and prophecy for hire is thus not unusual in early Christian literature.[75]

One may further contextualize the *Shepherd*'s discussion of prophecy by looking to Roman debates surrounding Montanism at the end of the second and beginning of the third centuries. The best-known form of this debate centers around a Montanist adherent named Proclus and his proto-catholic counterpart by the name of Gaius. The story is recorded by Eusebius and dated to the Zephyrinus's episcopacy (199–217 CE; *Hist. eccl.* 2.25.6; 6.20.3).[76] However, the New Prophecy's influence can be detected in Rome during the time of Eleutherus (174–189 CE),[77] and the role of the holy spirit in the New Prophecy was debated with unique vigor in Rome.[78] Writing in the third century, the author of the Hippolytan *Refutation of*

---

73. Trevett (1983, 9). However, this is only one way in which to understand the passage. For further discussion of this passage, see Lookadoo (2018, 103–6).

74. Although the language of *Did.* 12.1–5 does not have to be interpreted with regard to travelling prophets or apostles, Wilhite (2019a, 204–5) correctly notes that the discussion of prophets and apostles in both *Did.* 11 and *Did.* 13 indicates that the prophets are still in view in *Did.* 12.

75. On prophecy in the *Didache*, Ignatius, and *Shepherd*, see Jefford (2010).

76. Zephyrinus was bishop of Rome in 199–217 CE. The New Prophecy seems to have moved to Rome by the 170s. On the origins of Montanism in Rome, see Trevett (1996, 55–62).

77. Marjanen (2005, 191).

78. Heine (1989).

All Hereies asserts that the founders of the movement claimed to be inhabited by the holy spirit (*Ref.* 8.19.1).⁷⁹ The *Shepherd* makes the same declaration on behalf of true prophets (Mand. 11.9 [43.9]). Both the *Shepherd* and Hippolytus's report about the Montanists thus locate the authority of a prophet in their inhabitation by the spirit. Yet Hippolytus dismisses the Montanists precisely because of their prophecies (*Ref.* 10.25.1). By the third century, views about prophecy are transitioning. The *Shepherd*'s views appear to have been marginalized in favor of alternative ways of constructing authority. While descriptions of the false prophets and instructions for the communities affected differ based on the author, audience, dates, and environments in the texts that have been mentioned, the *Shepherd*'s portrayal of false prophets can nevertheless be mapped thematically alongside other early Christian discussions of false prophecy.

Conclusion

Chapter 8 has explored ways in which the *Shepherd* can be usefully read alongside other early Christian texts. Along with Chapter 7, this chapter hopes to have illustrated that the *Shepherd* is a text that can be located within the Greco-Roman, early Jewish, and early Christian literary worlds of the second-century Roman Empire. These chapters have not attempted to demonstrate examples of literary borrowing between the *Shepherd* and any of the other texts that have been mentioned. Rather, the exploration of the *Shepherd* alongside other ancient literature in this book is designed to highlight connections between the *Shepherd* and the literary environment out of which the text comes. By doing this, the strangeness that strikes readers when initially encountering the *Shepherd* can be placed in perspective. The *Shepherd* is an intriguing early Christian apocalypse from the second century CE that should be studied on its own terms, but its motifs are not absolutely sui generis. Readers should attempt to make sense of the *Shepherd* in a way that respects the text's integrity. Yet they may also recognize ways in which the *Shepherd* can be located alongside literary practices attested elsewhere in the Roman Empire. Implicitly, these chapters may also help to demonstrate ways in which, though these classifications may be useful for analytic purposes, the Greco-Roman, early Jewish, and early Christian literary worlds of the second-century Roman Empire cannot be easily disentangled. The *Shepherd* is a text that is fully enmeshed in the complex literary environment of the second-century Roman Empire, and these chapters have provided specific examples of ways that this cross-pollination is not only evident but potentially beneficial for interpreters of the *Shepherd*.

---

79. Regarding the Paraclete and Roman Montanism, see further Trevett (1996, 62–6). On the authorship of the *Refutation*, see the discussion in Litwa (2016, xxxii–xl).

Chapter 9

GOD IN THE *SHEPHERD*

The previous two chapters have attempted to set the *Shepherd* within the historical world of the Greek-speaking Roman Empire by comparing the *Shepherd* to texts from what may loosely be termed Greco-Roman, Jewish, and Christian provenances. Chapters 9 and 10 turn to doctrinal issues in the *Shepherd*, that is, to questions about what the *Shepherd* teaches. The matters taken up for discussion will primarily be theological and ethical. Chapter 9 begins by exploring what the *Shepherd* says about God. The traditional Christian belief about God understands God as Father, Son, and holy spirit. Although Trinitarian dogmatics have developed over the course of church history,[1] Irenaeus's description of what had been handed down to him at the end of the second century is structured in Trinitarian terms. Believers were baptized "in the name of God the Father, and in the name of Jesus Christ, the Son of God, [who was] incarnate, and died, and was raised, and in the holy spirit of God" (*Epid.* 3). Although the councils of the fourth and fifth centuries clarified how Christians should speak of God and this project of seeking clearer understanding of God is ongoing in Christian systematic theology, incipient Trinitarian thought goes back to some of the earliest Christian documents still extant.[2]

The *Shepherd* likewise speaks about God, the Son of God, and the Spirit or spirit, but readers have disagreed about precisely how the *Shepherd* employs such language, describes each person, and identifies their interrelatedness. Agreement has been particularly difficult to find when considering how the *Shepherd* talks about the Son, and the Christology of the *Shepherd* has thus been a topic of much reflection in scholarship. It has been variously characterized as adoptionist, angelomorphic, or proto-orthodox. Chapter 5 began to address the question with regard to Sim. 5 (54.1–60.7), but this chapter will consider how the Son is described in the *Shepherd* as a whole. Questions about the nature of the holy spirit in the *Shepherd* have also been taken up in scholarship. Ambiguity occurs regarding whether τὸ ἅγιον τὸ πνεῦμα should be understood as the "holy spirit" or the "Holy Spirit." This chapter will thus consider the *Shepherd*'s use of pneumatic language alongside the question of how the Son is described. A final section will

---

1. Collins (2008, 27–51); Phan (2011).
2. E.g., Matt 28:19; 2 Cor 13:13; Ign. *Magn.* 13.2; *Mart. Pol.* 14.3.

reflect on Trinitarian beliefs in the *Shepherd*. Yet before going further, it will be helpful to consider the more general, and seemingly mundane, question of how God is described in the *Shepherd*. It is to this task that the chapter first turns.

God

The shepherd offers one of the most fulsome statements about who God is in Mand. 1.1 (26.1). Hermas must believe that "God is one, who created and arranged all things, who made all things to be from that which is not, and who contains all things but is alone uncontained."[3] As is typical in early Jewish and early Christian writings,[4] the shepherd emphasizes that there is only one God in whom Hermas is called to believe. Of particular interest to the shepherd is God's activity in creation. He highlights that God created (κτίσας) and arranged (καταρτίσας) all things. The *Shepherd*'s insistence that God created all things is likewise shared with other early Christian and early Jewish texts,[5] and this claim sets God apart from the rest of God's creation as the sole creator. The language of arrangement indicates that God did not create matter and leave it a mess. Rather, God set the world in order.[6] God's power in creation is further evident in the fact that he made everything that exists out of nothing. Finally, the *Shepherd* makes the additional claim that God contains all things but is alone uncontained (πάντα χωρῶν, μόνος δὲ ἀχώρητος ὤν). This language becomes increasingly prominent in second-century Christian texts as a way of describing God in a unique fashion.[7] The shepherd not only identifies God by God's actions in creation. He makes a further claim about the type of being that God is, namely, that while God is found in all creation because God contains all creation, God alone is uncontained by anything else. The true God is thus the sort of being that cannot be contained. Although the *Shepherd* does not make much of this language, there is an implicit claim of God's infinitude in Mand. 1.1 (26.1).

The language of creation is found elsewhere in the *Shepherd* as mentions of God's creation are made throughout the text. Before Hermas is carried away to meet the celestial Rhoda, he is exulting over "God's creatures" (τὰς κτίσεις τοῦ

---

3. πρῶτον πάντων πίστευσον ὅτι εἷς ἐστιν ὁ θεός, ὁ τὰ πάντα κτίσας καὶ καταρτίσας, καὶ ποιήσας ἐκ τοῦ μὴ ὄντος εἰς τὸ εἶναι τὰ πάντα, καὶ πάντα χωρῶν μόνος δὲ ἀχώρητος ὤν (Mand. 1.1 [26.1]).

4. E.g., Deut 6:4; Zech 14:9 (LXX); *Sib. Or.* 3.11; *Ep. Aris.* 132–138; Josephus, *Ant.* 4.201; Mark 10:18; 12:32; 1 Thess 1:9; Gal 3:20; 1 Cor 8:4, 6; Jas 2:19; Ign. *Magn.* 8.2.

5. *Jub.* 31.29; Eph 3:9; Col 1:16; Rev 4:11; *Did.* 10.3. See also Sim. 5.5.2 (55.2); 7.4 (66.4).

6. See the similar language in Ps 73:16 (MT 74:16); 88:38 (89:38 MT); Heb 11:3; *Barn.* 16.6.

7. E.g., *Ker. Petr.* 2 (in Clement of Alexandria, *Strom.* 6.39.2-3 [5]); Justin, *Dial.* 127.2; Athenagoras, *Leg.* 10.1; Theophilus, *Autol.* 1.5; 2.22. See similarly Philo, *Migr.* 192; Theophilus, *Autol.* 2.3; Irenaeus, *Haer.* 2.1.2, 5; 4.20.1; O'Brien (1997, 481–3); Pratscher (2018, 235); Briggman (2019, 80–7).

θεοῦ; Vis. 1.1.3 [1.3]). Similar references to God's creation or creatures are found in Vis. 3.9.2 (17.2); Mand. 8.1 (38.1); 12.4.3 (47.3); Sim. 9.1.8 (78.8); 9.12.2 (89.2); 9.25.1 (102.1). Rhoda identifies God as "the one who dwells in the heavens and created the things that are from that which is not" (ὁ ἐν τοῖς οὐρανοῖς κατοικῶν καὶ κτίσας ἐκ τοῦ μὴ ὄντος τὰ ὄντα; Vis. 1.1.6 [1.6]). The woman notes that God created the world through his wisdom and that God clothed creation with beauty (Vis. 1.3.4 [3.4]).[8] As the shepherd begins with God's creative activity at the start of the Mandates, he likewise emphasizes God's creation of the world near the end (Mand. 12.4.2 [47.2]). Indeed, God can be identified with reference to his creation when the shepherd describes "the one who created them" (τὸν κτίσαντα αὐτούς; Sim. 4.4 [53.4]).[9] This action includes the creation of the people of God (Sim. 5.6.2 [59.2]). Since God created everything, God has ruling authority over the world. Yet God did not create to remain in power as a petty tyrant. God hands authority of creation over to others, including the holy angels (Vis. 3.4.1 [12.1]), God's people (Mand. 12.4.2 [47.2]), and the Son of God (Sim. 5.6.2 [59.2]).

The *Shepherd* describes God by referring to additional traits and actions that characterize God. God rules over the powers (τῶν δυνάμεων), and the woman describes God as invisible, powerful, and strong (ὁ ἀοράτῳ δυνάμει καὶ κραταιᾷ; Vis. 1.3.4 [3.4]). God can also be identified simply by "the name" (τὸ ὄνομα).[10] Another key description of God comes in terms of glory. The will that led God to clothe creation with beauty is described as glorious (Vis. 1.3.4 [3.4]). God's name is likewise described as glorious (Vis. 3.3.5 [11.5]; 4.1.3 [22.3]; 4.2.4 [23.4]; Sim. 9.18.5 [95.5]). By extension, things that come from God or lead to God may also be described as glorious.[11] God has also chosen the people with whom God is identified. These descriptions of God are found throughout the Visions. Hermas is charged to report what he writes to God's elect (Vis. 2.1.3 [5.3]). Similar descriptions of God's people can be found in Vis. 1.3.4 (3.4); 2.2.5 (6.5); 2.4.2 (8.2); 3.5.1 (13.1); 3.8.3 (16.3); 3.9.10 (17.10); 4.2.5 (23.5); 4.3.5 (24.5). The *Shepherd* also describes God's capacity for compassion. The action that moves God to compassion most often in the *Shepherd* is repentance (e.g., Vis. 1.1.9 [1.9]; Sim. 9.23.4 [100.4]). God's compassion is also provoked by the questions of Hermas and all who make requests to God (Sim. 5.4.4 [57.4]). Indeed, God's compassion is even cited as a trait that sets

---

8. O'Brien (1997, 484–5).

9. See similarly Sim. 5.5.2 (58.2); 7.4 (66.4).

10. E.g., Vis. 3.1.9 (9.9); 3.2.1 (10.1); 3.3.5 (11.5); 4.1.3 (22.3); 4.2.4 (23.4); Sim. 6.2.3 (62.3); 8.6.4 (72.4); 8.10.3 (76.3); 9.13.2–3 (90.2–3); 9.17.4 (94.4); 9.18.5 (95.5); 9.27.2–3 (104.2–3). As will be discussed in the following section, the Father and the Son are closely identified by their "name." This list has included instances in which the name may refer to either the Father or the Son for the sake of being expansive.

11. E.g., the shepherd (Vis. 5.1 [25.1]); angels (Sim. 5.6.4, 7 [59.4, 7]; 7.1–3 [66.1–3]; 8.1.2 [67.2]; 8.3.3 [69.3]; 9.1.3 [78.3]; 9.2.3 [79.3]; 9.3.1 [80.1]; 9.7.1 [84.1]; 9.12.6–8 [89.6–8]); fear of the Lord (Mand. 7.4 [37.4]); the commandments (Mand. 12.3.4 [46.4]; Sim. 6.1.1 [61.1]).

God apart from human beings. The shepherd tells Hermas that God does not bear grudges like human beings. Instead, God acts compassionately toward creation (Mand. 9.3 [39.3]). Although this way of identifying God seems to be a matter of degree, it complements the absolute claims about God's difference from creation in Mand. 1.1 (26.1). God thus differentiates Godself from creation because God serves as its creator, is uncontained, and demonstrates more compassion than human beings can show toward one another.

The Son

A coherent, systematic, and widely agreed upon approach to interpreting the Son's place in the *Shepherd* has proven difficult to come by. As mentioned in Chapter 5, the way in which to understand Sim. 5.5.2–5.6.7 (58.2–59.7) is a key place of disagreement. Another difficulty lies in the way that the *Shepherd* often focuses on parenetic teaching rather than dogmatic instruction. The words Ἰησοῦς and χριστός are unlikely even to have appeared in the earliest text.[12] Scholars have thus argued that the *Shepherd* offers an adoptionist Christology,[13] a spirit Christology,[14] or an angelomorphic Christology.[15] Referring to the Christology in Sim. 5 (54–60), Grillmeier concludes that "the confusion is great and cannot be put right."[16] Discussions of what the *Shepherd* has to say about Jesus thus encounter a number of challenges, most of which arise from the unsystematic and sometimes apparently contradictory nature of the *Shepherd*'s portrayal of the Son. If there is any hope for a coherent picture of the *Shepherd*'s understanding of the Son, though, it must be found in a study that allows each statement about the Son to stand on its own.[17]

---

12. Brox (1991, 486); Osiek (1999, 34); Grundeken (2015a, 13). S reads XN (χριστόν) in Vis. 2.2.8, but a corrector has changed this to KN (κύριον) in keeping with A and the likely Vorlagen of L² and E. L¹ reads *filium*. See further Batovici (2014, 459–60). In Vis. 3.6.6 (14.6), A appears to support the reading χριστῷ. However, the manuscript, at least as it appears in Lake (1907), plate 3, is smudged and difficult to read at this point. Finally, A again supports χριστόν at Sim. 9.18.1 (95.1). Although L¹ reads *dominum*, S and L² support the reading θεόν and most likely provide the earliest reading.

13. Harnack (1888, 160n.4); Kelly (1968, 93–5).

14. Dibelius (1923, 574); Abramowski (1984, 431–3); Stewart-Sykes (1997).

15. Moxnes (1974); Hengel (1995, 221, 376); Gieschen (1998, 214–28); Hannah (1999, 187–92); Papandrea (2012, 30–2; 2016, 28–30). For definitions of angelomorphic Christology, see Fletcher-Louis (1997, 14–15); Gieschen (1998, 27–8).

16. Grillmeier (1975, 56). Joly combines several such descriptions when he says that it is "clair que la théologie d'Hermas est binitaire et pneumatique, mais aussi adoptianiste et nettement subordinatianiste" (1993, 542).

17. Moreover, it must come in a study that follows the order of the *Shepherd*. "Die Reihenfolge, in der man die Texte liest, ist nicht beliebig" (Brox 1991, 486).

The first matter to consider is the way in which the *Shepherd* most commonly designates this person, namely, as the Son. The *Shepherd*'s uses of υἱός are found primarily in Sim. 5 (54–60), 8 (67–77), and 9 (78–110), and a study of this term will allow for a fresh look at other elements of how the *Shepherd* characterizes the Son.

However, the first use of the term υἱός is found earlier in the *Shepherd*. When the meaning of the book that Hermas copies is revealed to him, Hermas hears a report of what God has said (Vis. 2.2.2–2.3.4 [6.2–7.4]). In the midst of this speech, Hermas is told that "the Lord swore by his Son" (ὤμοσεν γὰρ κύριος κατὰ τοῦ υἱοῦ αὐτοῦ) that those who deny the Lord will lose their life (Vis. 2.2.8 [6.8]). The Son (υἱός) is differentiated here from the Lord (κύριος). In this passage at least, the Lord refers to the being who is elsewhere known as θεός, while the Son designates a different person. Although swearing an oath by one's eldest child is a practice known from the Greco-Roman world,[18] the presence of a similar oath earlier in the same address warns against pressing the differentiation between the Son and the Lord too far in this instance. For in Vis. 2.2.5 (6.5), Hermas has already heard the Lord swear by his glory (ὤμοσεν γὰρ ὁ δεσπότης κατὰ τῆς δόξης αὐτοῦ). An oath in which God swears by Godself is not surprising in an early Christian apocalypse. Such oaths have precedent in scriptural tradition.[19] Since God has no higher authority by which to swear, God provides the guarantee of the oath that God swears. What is more remarkable is that the Son likewise provides the basis on which God makes an oath.

The Son in Sim. 5 (54–60)

The Lord is again differentiated from the Son in the second interpretation of the parable in Sim. 5.5.2–5.6.4 (58.2–59.4).[20] While the lord of the vineyard is identified as the one who created all things, the slave in the parable depicts the Son of God (Sim. 5.5.2 [58.2]). The remainder of the shepherd's interpretation explores the salvific work that the Son of God undertook on behalf of God's people.[21] While Hermas wonders why the Son is portrayed as a slave, the shepherd shows that the Son "is presented in great authority and leadership" (εἰς ἐξουσία μεγάλην κεῖται καὶ κυριότητα; Sim. 5.6.1 [59.1]). The shepherd's support for this claim lies in salvation historical claims couched in the terms of the earlier parable. God handed the vineyard, that is, the people whom he planted, over to the Son (Sim.

---

18. E.g., Lucian, *Philops.* 27; Pliny the Younger, *Ep.* 2.20.5; Vergil, *Aen.* 9.299–302.

19. E.g., Gen 22:16; Isa 45:23; Jer 22:5; 49:13; Heb 6:13. See also Philo, *Leg. all.* 3.203–208 (3.72–73), the references in Körtner and Leutzsch (1998, 157n.174), and the discussion in Svigel (2016, 266).

20. The word υἱός appears three times in the parable and once in Hermas's dialogue with the *Shepherd* (Sim. 5.2.6, 8, 11 [55.6, 8, 11]; Sim. 5.4.1 [57.1]), but these have been left aside because their referent is the parabolic son and proves to be malleable within interpretations.

21. Brox (1991, 489).

5.6.2 [59.2]). The Son is thus in charge of and responsible for the people of God. The Son's authority is sufficient for him to appoint angels to protect the people, while the Son himself cleansed their sins. Afterward, the Son gave them the Law so that they might know the right way to live (Sim. 5.6.3 [59.3]; see also Sim. 5.5.3 [58.3]).[22] The shepherd does not appeal to metaphysical claims in Sim. 5.5.2–5.6.4 (58.2–59.4) but makes much of the Son's work on behalf of the people. The Son is ruler, caretaker, protector, cleanser, and means to life for the people of God.

Filial language continues to be used in Sim. 5.6.4–8 (59.4–8), but the emphasis shifts from the Son's salvific work to the unity of the spirit and flesh in the person of the Son and the impact this has for other believers. As the brief overview of scholarship in Chapter 5 suggests, this has been an ongoing *crux interpretum* in scholarship on the *Shepherd*.[23] A key question concerns the identity of the υἱός at each point that he is mentioned in the final interpretation of the parable. While the reference to "all flesh" in Sim. 5.6.7 (59.7) gives the interpretation an expansive trajectory, the identity of the Son as slave in Sim. 5.5.2–3 (58.2–3) still lies in the background of the parable's third interpretation.[24] The son in Sim. 5.6.4 (59.4) is a reference to the parabolic son who was earlier identified as the holy spirit (Sim. 5.5.2 [58.2]).[25] The Lord is said to have consulted with the holy spirit and the angels about the slave's, that is, the Son of God's, inheritance. The identification holds true when the shepherd again refers to the Lord taking the parabolic son to be a counselor (Sim. 5.6.7 [59.7]). These statements sound adoptionist when read on their own. The Son's flesh is accepted because he served the spirit blamelessly. His inheritance can thus be viewed as a reward (μισθός). It is not hard to imagine how such a picture of Jesus's earthly life could be employed as a model for the audience to follow, and this picture could lead to the reference to "all flesh" (πᾶσα σάρξ) that is found at the end of the explanation (Sim. 5.6.7 [59.7]).

If this is the Christology of Sim. 5.6.4–8 (59.4–8), however, it is difficult to imagine why the *Shepherd* continued to be popular well into the period of the Christological debates of the fourth and fifth centuries.[26] The expansive ethical application that is made clear only at the end of the shepherd's interpretation also informs the understanding of the parabolic son and slave earlier in the

---

22. Henne observes the mediating role played by the Son in giving the law to the people (1990, 195, 202).

23. On the heavily disputed Christology in Sim. 5, see Zahn (1868, 245–81); Adam (1906, 42–4); Walter (1913); Cirillo (1973); Henne (1988; 1990); Brox (1989a, 276–8; 1991, 486–9); Hauck (1993); Stewart-Sykes (1997); Osiek (1999, 35–6); Hurtado (2003, 603–4); Bucur (2007; 2009, 126–36); Svigel (2016, 253–61); Beavis (2018).

24. Henne makes too sharp a distinction between the different levels of interpretation (1988, 575–6). Stewart-Sykes rightly points out that the interpretations must be read in their narrative order (1997, 276–8).

25. Stewart-Sykes (1997, 278).

26. Osiek (1999, 179–80). See, e.g., the citations from Eusebius, Athanasius, Didymus, and Jerome in Chapter 3.

interpretation. Moreover, it is worth recalling that the second explanation was given with reference to Jesus's salvific activity in the incarnation. The same time frame appears to be operative in Sim. 5.6.4–8 (59.4–8). The union of the spirit and flesh is discussed with references to Jesus's incarnation. The *Shepherd* does not make an exclusive, ontological claim about Jesus's eternal relationship to the holy spirit. The eternal relationship of the Son and spirit is not in view. Rather, Sim. 5.6.4–8 (59.4–8) describes Jesus's fleshly union with the spirit during the incarnation. The third explanation (Sim. 5.6.4–8 [59.4–8]) is thus not completely dissociated from the second (Sim. 5.5.2–5.6.4 [58.2–59.4]) while also looking forward to the exhortation in Sim. 5.7.1–4 (60.1–4).

Yet something more can be said about the means by which the union is described. The *Shepherd*'s account of this union is analogous to two elements of philosophical teaching about union that are found in certain Stoic philosophers. First, the spirit and flesh are unified at the incarnation in the person of the Son, but the spirit and flesh, though unified when God causes the spirit to dwell within the flesh, can still be identified separately from one another. The way in which the *Shepherd* describes the relationship between spirit and flesh is similar to Stoic accounts of mixture (κρᾶσις).[27] Stoic teaching about mixture can be differentiated from juxtaposition, in which two objects remain unaltered as they exist side by side (e.g., rice and beans), and fusion, in which two objects combine to form a new entity (e.g., flour and yeast become bread).[28] Mixture does not allow for particular portions of the mixed elements to be localized. They are entirely coextensive. The elements nevertheless preserve their original substance and qualities when they are mixed.[29] Arius Didymus uses an example from smithing, that of fire and glowing iron (frag. 28; *SVF* 2.471), while Alexander of Aphrodisias employs the example of water and wine to show how two entities can be mixed (*Mixt.* 4, 217.31–32; *SVF*

---

27. Tertullian speaks similarly with regard to Jesus's flesh and spirit in *Prax.* 27. On Tertullian, *Prax.* 27, see Cantalamessa (1962, 168–76); Osborn (1997, 139–41). On Stoic mixture more broadly in early Christianity, see Buch-Hansen (2010, 75–84); Dunderberg (2010, 233–6); Briggman (2019, 140–52).

28. Alexander of Aphrodisias associates these two accounts of mixture with Democritus and Epicurus, respectively (*Mixt.* 2, 214.18–215.8). See further Sambursky (1962, 27–8).

29. Thus Alexander of Aphrodisias writes about Chrysippus's theory of mixture, "Certain mixtures, he says, result in a total interpenetration of substances and their qualities, the original substances and qualities being preserved in this mixture; this he calls specifically *krasis* of the mixed components" (τὰς δέ τινας γίνεσθαι μίξεις λέγει δι' ὅλων τινῶν οὐσιῶν τε καὶ τῶν τούτων ποιοτήτων ἀντιπαρεκτεινομένων ἀλλήλαις μετὰ τοῦ τὰς ἐξ ἀρχῆς οὐσίας τε καὶ ποιότητας σώζειν ἐν τῇ μίξει τῇ τοιᾷδε, ἥντινα τῶν μίξεων κρᾶσιν ἰδίως εἶναι λέγει; Alexander of Aphrodisias, *Mixt.* 3, 216.25–28; *SVF* 2.473). Translation from Sambursky (1959, 121–2). See also the translation of Todd (1976, 117). Whereas Sambursky translates ἀντιπαρεκτεινομένων as "interpenetration," I have followed Todd (1976, 117), Buch-Hansen (2010, 76), and Briggman (2019, 140) in using a form of "coextend" or its cognate noun or adjective when referring to this phenomenon in the main text.

2.473).³⁰ Arius notes that water and wine can be separated after mixture by using a sponge that has been dipped in oil to draw out the water (frag. 28; *SVF* 2.471).³¹ On the Stoic account of mixture, water and wine mix to become coextensive but do not form a new entity in the way that flour and yeast become bread when baked. The mixture retains the particular qualities of the original substances.

The second matter to observe is the place of the active and passive principles in mixtures. The active principle is god, the λόγος, or the πνεῦμα. The passive principle is matter (Diogenes Laertius, *Lives* 7.1 Zeno [134]). The two relate to one another as the active principle causes the passive to mix with it. Alexander thus articulates Chrysippus's understanding of the world as a unified mixture resulting from the spirit's pervading presence in the material world (*Mixt.* 3, 216.14–17; *SVF* 2.473). It is only through the mixture of active and passive principles that the world is held together.³² The active principle acts upon passive principles to form and move passive principles. Although the active principle can be described in corporeal terms because Stoic philosophy believed that only a body could be acted upon, Stoic philosophers could also regard the spirit "as something not akin to matter, but rather to force."³³ Although the passive principle cannot act on the active principle, the active principle may remain quiescent when mixed with the passive principle.³⁴

These two points allow one to read *Sim.* 5.6.4–8 (59.4–8) more coherently. The mixture of spirit and flesh that takes place in the incarnation is complete as the spirit dwells within the flesh. The two are made coextensive and work together.³⁵ They are not juxtaposed next to one another, nor are they fused together. Both the flesh and the spirit can be identified and remain as flesh and spirit, even while they are mixed and united perfectly. Nevertheless, the spirit is the active principle. Although the flesh can act, it cannot act on the spirit or defile the spirit. A rebellion of the flesh would not lead to the destruction of the spirit but to the spirit's abandonment of the flesh. In the case of the incarnation described in Sim. 5.6.4–7 (59.4–7), the flesh's actions not only fail to defile the spirit, they take part in a good and holy collaboration (Sim. 5.6.6 [59.6]) and blameless service (Sim. 5.6.7

---

30. Alexander's choice of example appears to counter Aristotle's earlier use of water and wine as substances that do not mix (*Gen. cor.* 328a 23–31). See Sambursky (1959, 12–13); Sorabji (1988, 102–4).

31. Richard Sorabji confirms that he saw this experiment performed and that Arius Didymus's proposal is efficacious (1988, 103n.101).

32. "All phenomena are, as parts of the Whole, in touch with one another" (Buch-Hansen, 2010, 78). It is for this reason that Cicero claims that the study of physics and ethics cannot be separated (*Fin.* 3.72).

33. Sambursky (1959, 36).

34. See similarly Briggman (2019, 171) regarding Irenaeus.

35. Alexander writes similarly of the mixture of body (σῶμα) and soul (ψυχή; *Mixt.* 4,217.32–218.1). For further discussion of Alexander's arguments in *Mixt.* 3–4 alongside other Stoic accounts of blending, see Sambursky (1959, 15–17); Todd (1976, 30–49).

[59.7]). Unlike the second explanation (Sim. 5.5.2–5.6.4 [58.2–59.4]), however, the third explanation moves beyond a description of the Son of God. The ultimate goal is for "all flesh ... in which the Holy spirit dwells" (πᾶσα σάρξ ... ἐν ᾗ τὸ πνεῦμα τὸ ἅγιον κατῴκησεν [Sim. 5.6.7 [59.7]]) to receive the same reward that the Son did. The Son of God thus provides an example that other believers should follow.[36] They should seek to be unified with the spirit in the same way that the Son's flesh united and submitted to the spirit. By following the Son's example, they are to keep their flesh pure and blameless so that the spirit will testify about it and the flesh will be justified (Sim. 5.7.1 [60.1]). Although the Christology in Sim. 5.6.4–8 (59.4–8) may appear adoptionist at first glance, the author of the *Shepherd* has employed something akin to Stoic mixture theory to portray the Son of God as an example for the people of God.[37]

The Son in Sim. 8 (67–77)

Filial language is employed twice in Sim. 8 (Sim. 8.3.2 [69.2]; 8.11.1 [77.1]). The second usage is important for providing a sketch of the *Shepherd*'s understanding of the Son, but it may be regarded as noncontroversial. It will thus be useful to start with Sim. 8.11.1 (77.1). Two matters are worth observing. First, the Son is again differentiated from the Lord. Although it may not be absolute, the dominant way in which the *Shepherd* identifies the Son is as υἱός rather than κύριος. Son and Lord are again distinguished in the *Shepherd*'s language. The Lord is described as compassionate and has sent the shepherd so that people have a chance to repent. The Lord's desire is for "those who are called through his Son to be saved" (τὴν κλῆσιν τὴν γενομένην διὰ τοῦ υἱοῦ αὐτοῦ σωθῆναι; Sim. 8.11.1 [77.1]). This leads to the second matter in this verse. The *Shepherd* employs salvation language at the end of this parable. This salvation comes through the Son. The Son is thus an intermediary by which salvation is made available to the people of God.

Although the language at the end of Sim. 8 may be traditional, the precise relationships described in the earlier instance of filial language are more difficult to unravel. The concept of multisemy was introduced in Chapter 5 and will again be helpful in reflecting on the willow in Sim. 8.[38] As the shepherd explains the significance of the willow from Sim. 8.1.1 (67.1), he attributes two meanings to the tree. First, the tree "is God's law that is given to the whole world" (νόμος

---

36. On the ethical implications of the *Shepherd*'s Christology in Sim. 5.6.4–8 (59.4–8), see Haas (1993, 572); Hauck (1993, 197–8); Barnes (2001, 5); Svigel (2016, 260).

37. This is not to say that the author of the *Shepherd* borrowed directly from any of the texts on mixture that have been cited so far or that the author was even consciously articulating a Christology in terms of Stoic mixture theory. Rather, the postulation put forward here is that Sim. 5.6.4–8 (59.4–8) engage in a popular philosophical attempt to articulate the relationship between the Son of God and the spirit that indwelled him.

38. See Henne (1989).

θεοῦ ἐστιν ὁ δοθεὶς εἰς ὅλον τὸν κόσμον).[39] Second, "this law is the Son of God who was proclaimed to the ends of the earth" (ὁ δὲ νόμος οὗτος ὁ υἱὸς τοῦ θεοῦ ἐστιν ὁ κηρυχθεὶς εἰς τὰ πέρατα τῆς γῆς; Sim. 8.3.2 [69.2]). The Son and law are both represented by the willow. They are styled in similar terms as the shepherd emphasizes the universality of both the law and the Son. The law is for "the whole world," while the Son was preached "to the ends of the earth." As in the description of the willow overshadowing the plains and the mountains (Sim. 8.1.1 [67.1]), the willow-law-Son has a universal reach.

Multisemy is a useful concept with which to analyze both the law and the Son. The law is represented not only by the willow but also by the branches that are given to each of the people (Sim. 8.3.4 [69.4]). The law is both universal insofar as the tree dominates the scenery in the parable and particular as various branches are given directly to each of the people. More pertinent to this chapter, however, is the way in which the Son is portrayed. When this parable is read after Sim. 5.5.2–5.6.4 (58.2–59.4), the Son appears as both the one who gives the law to the people (Sim. 5.6.3 [59.3]) and as the law itself (Sim. 8.3.2 [69.2]). One might argue that the *Shepherd* presents the Son as offering himself to God's people.[40] However, since these interpretations occur in different parables and the shepherd does not draw attention to any relationship between the two, it is best not to make a strong theological reading at this point. The identification of the Son and law is employed for the purpose of illustrating the way in which the Son and the law work together for the good of the people, a point that is most pertinent to this parable. In referring to Jesus as the law, the *Shepherd* takes part in a broader early Christian discourse in which Jesus was interpreted in legal terms.[41] When the identification of the Son as the willow is accounted for, the *Shepherd*'s depiction of the Son as the law in Sim. 8 draws attention to his role as shelter and protector of God's people. As the willow provides shade under which the people take shelter (Sim. 8.1.1 [67.1]), so the Son provides shelter for those who have believed in him.[42]

This, however, is not the end of the difficulty with Sim. 8. Immediately following the identification of the tree as the law and son, the shepherd says that the angel of the Lord standing by the tree is Michael (Sim. 8.3.3 [69.3]). The close association between the Son and Michael can be seen as supporting those who

---

39. The law's enormous size may function similarly to the size of the angel who stands next to the tree (Sim. 8.1.2 [67.2]), namely, it provides "an indication of their celestial status" (Bucur 2009, 119).

40. A similar motif may be found in Hebrews, where Jesus is both the high priest (Heb 5–7) and the sacrifice (Heb 9). See Attridge (1989, 248–9); Johnson (2006, 236–7); Small (2014, 184–6).

41. E.g., *Ker. Petr.* 1a (in Clement of Alexandria, *Strom.* 1.182.3 [29]); 1b (in Clement of Alexandria, *Strom.* 2.68.2 [15]); Justin, *Dial.* 11.2; 43.1; Clement of Alexandria, *Strom.* 7.16.5 (3). See further Dobschütz (1893, 28–9); Brox (1991, 361); Hvalvik (2006, 418–24).

42. The Son similarly protects the people as the slave in Sim. 5.6.2 (59.2). However, there the Son's protection comes in the form of angelic defenses.

argue that the *Shepherd*'s Christology is angelomorphic, particularly if Michael and the Son are to be identified with one another.⁴³ Dibelius went so far as to argue that Michael is a vestige of an originally Jewish source and that Michael plays the same role as the Son in the Christianized interpretation.⁴⁴ Michael gives the law to the people under the tree and is also described as one "who has authority over and guides this people" (ὁ ἔχων τὴν ἐξουσίαν τούτου τοῦ λαοῦ καὶ διακυβερνῶν; Sim. 8.3.3 [69.3]). These roles are not out of place in the shepherd's descriptions of the Son elsewhere.⁴⁵ One may also add to this that Michael is characterized as "great and glorious" (μέγας καὶ ἔνδοξος), a description that can also be employed with regard to the Son (Sim. 9.12.7 [89.7]). Yet the depiction of the Son in Sim. 9 must be examined to understand why this description of Michael might lead some to suspect the presence of angelomorphy in the *Shepherd*.

The Son in Sim. 9 (78–110)

The most extensive discussion of the Son occurs in the retelling of the tower vision. The shepherd describes six angels who play leading roles in the construction of the tower (Sim. 9.12.6 [89.6]). Yet they are not the supreme characters. In the midst of these six, there is a "great and glorious man" (ἔνδοξον καὶ μέγαν ἄνδρα) walking around the tower to inspect the stones (Sim. 9.12.7 [89.7]). This man is then identified as the Son of God (Sim. 9.12.8 [89.8]). The presence of the same adjectives, μέγας and ἔνδοξος, to describe Michael and the Son may provide further support for those who perceive an angelomorphic Christology in the *Shepherd*. In Sim. 8–9, then, there are three primary reasons why one might interpret the *Shepherd* on angelomorphic terms: the close association between Michael and the Son in Sim. 8, the similar roles that Michael and the Son play in Sim. 8, and the kindred descriptions of Michael and the Son in Sim. 8.3.3 (69.3); 9.12.7 (89.7).

While it is interesting to note the similarities between the descriptions of Michael and the Son, the use of the same adjectives is not enough to identify the two beings.⁴⁶ The words μέγας and ἔνδοξος are used elsewhere in the *Shepherd* to modify the name (Vis. 4.1.3 [22.3]; 4.2.4 [23.4];⁴⁷ Sim. 9.18.5 [95.5]), the fear of the Lord (Mand. 7.4 [37.4]), the commandments (Mand. 12.3.4 [46.4]), the Lord's rich compassion (Sim. 8.6.1 [72.1]), and the things that Hermas has seen

---

43. As is done by, e.g., Dibelius (1923, 576); Daniélou (1964, 119–27); Kelly (1968, 95); Hannah (1999, 187–8); Papandrea (2016, 29).

44. Dibelius (1923, 588–9, 592).

45. E.g., the Son has great authority in Sim. 5.6.4 (59.4). See also Sim. 9.12.6–7 (89.6–7) and the discussion below.

46. Svigel (2019, 34–5).

47. Following the text of A, L¹, and L². S reads ἁγίου ἀγγέλου καὶ ἐνδόξου ὀνόματος instead of μεγάλου καὶ ἐνδόξου ὀνόματος (*magnum et honorificum nomen*).

(Sim. 9.2.5 [79.5]; 9.14.4 [91.4]).[48] Nor is it the exclusive property of the Son to have authority or to give the law.[49] God has given human beings authority to rule over creation (Mand. 12.4.2 [47.2]), while the commandments belong to the Lord (Vis. 3.5.3 [13.3]), are given by the angel (Vis. 5.5 [25.5]), and are to be kept by the people (Mand. 1.2 [26.2]; Sim. 1.7 [50.7]). Moreover, Michael is distinguished both in the shepherd's explanation and in the parable. The Son is represented by the tree in the explanation, while Michael is the name of the angel (Sim. 8.3.2–3 [69.2–3]). Although the angel works in proximity to the tree, these two entities are not confused in the parable (Sim. 8.1.1–2 [67.1–2]).

In thus linking this discussion of the Son in Sim. 8–9, however, one risks missing yet another controversial Christological statement in the *Shepherd*. Near the beginning of Sim. 9, the shepherd says to Hermas, "For that spirit is the Son of God" (ἐκεῖνο γὰρ τὸ πνεῦμα ὁ υἱὸς τοῦ θεοῦ ἐστιν; Sim. 9.1.1 [78.1]). The apparent identification of the Son and spirit along with the close association of the Son and spirit elsewhere in the *Shepherd* has led some to describe the text in terms of a spirit Christology or pneumatic Christology.[50] Yet this is not necessarily the case. After all, the spirit that the shepherd refers to in Sim. 9.1.1 (78.1) is the spirit that spoke to Hermas in the form of the church. Since the woman is identified as the church (Vis. 2.4.1 [8.1]), she seems to be in view. Moreover, she has already identified herself with the tower (Vis. 3.3.3 [11.3]). This leads to a complex set of relationships. If all of these identifications are strictly held, it is difficult to see how one can avoid the conclusion that woman=church=tower=spirit=Son of God.[51] To follow this set of identifications would make Vis. 3 and Sim. 9 nearly inscrutable. In view of this, it is better to hold that these are not all strict identifications. Rather, the *Shepherd* indicates a set of relationships with this form of speech. The woman, church, tower, spirit, and Son of God are intimately connected with one another as God reveals God's ways to Hermas and works them out in Hermas's community. This is particularly relevant to the interpretation of the spirit and Son of God in Sim. 9.1.1 (78.1), since they are introduced in a later Similitude.[52] Instead of understanding the shepherd to be identifying the spirit and Son with the church, the text can be read more profitably by understanding the spirit and Son to be closely related to the church. As the remainder of Sim. 9 will show, the Son is particularly active in and through the church.

---

48. Svigel (2016, 263–5) makes a similar point in dialogue with Gieschen (1998, 226). Since the *Shepherd* refers to "glorious angels" in the plural (Sim. 9.2.3 [79.3]), this point could also be brought to bear on the arguments of Hannah (1999, 187).

49. *Pace* Moxnes (1974), who argues for an angelomorphic Christology on the basis of shared functions between God and his angel.

50. E.g., Abramowski (1984, 431–3); Stewart-Sykes (1997, 282). Vermes (2013, 173–4) also notes the association between the spirit and the Son.

51. See further the discussion in Dibelius (1923, 602).

52. Osiek rightly points out that this verse "is typical of the additive style of the author" (1999, 212). See also Svigel (2016, 261–3).

Although Sim. 9.1.1 (78.1); 9.12.6–8 (89.6–8) have received the most scholarly attention, Sim. 9 has more to say about the Son of God. The tower parable includes a vision of a large white rock and a door that is newer than the rock (Sim. 9.2.1–2 [79.1–2]). The shepherd's interpretation adds a new twist to these traditional early Christian Christological images.[53] The rock and the door both represent the Son of God (Sim. 9.12.1 [89.1]). The rock appears older in order to represent the Son as older than creation. The Son is preexistent and was thus able to serve as the Father's counselor in creation (Sim. 9.12.2 [89.2]).[54] The door is younger to represent the Son's revelation in the last days (ἐπ' ἐσχάτων τῶν ἡμερῶν; Sim. 9.12.3 [89.3]). Moreover, all the stones that go into the tower must enter through the door. The Son is thus the access point through which one can enter the kingdom of God, and the Son alone provides this means of access (Sim. 9.12.4–5 [89.4–5]).[55]

The powers that the Son of God has and gives to his people are represented in the parable by twelve virgins (Sim. 9.13.2 [90.2]). It is not enough simply to bear the Son's name. One is also given to the virgins in order to be clothed in the traits that they represent just as the Son likewise bears the names of these virgins (Sim. 9.13.3 [90.3]).[56] The work of the Son and the virgins makes the tower appear as a single rock. The stones that enter are fully incorporated into the tower. The same is true of "those who have believed in the Lord through his Son and are dressed in these spirits" (οἱ πιστεύσαντες τῷ κυρίῳ διὰ τοῦ υἱοῦ αὐτοῦ καὶ ἐνδιδυσκόμενοι τὰ πνεύματα ταῦτα) as they become one spirit and one body (Sim. 9.13.5 [90.5]).[57] Although θεός is most often the one designated by ὄνομα, the Son is closely associated with God in that God's people are said to have received the name of the Son of God (πάντες τὸ ὄνομα τοῦ υἱοῦ τοῦ θεοῦ ἔλαβον; Sim. 9.13.7 [90.7]).

The Son's name is not only described as great (μέγα) but also as uncontained (ἀχώρητον). The Son sustains the entire creation (τὸν κόσμον ὅλον βαστάζει; Sim. 9.14.5 [91.5]).[58] Since he sustains creation, the shepherd concludes that the Son is able to sustain those who carry his name (Sim. 9.14.6 [91.6]). However, the shepherd uses two descriptions that are characteristic of God elsewhere in the *Shepherd* in order to support the point. The Son is uncontained (ἀχώρητος) and active in creation, just as God was described in Mand. 1.1 (26.1). To be sure, the Son is not described as the creator (ὁ κτίσας), but the Son's role in sustaining creation (Sim. 9.14.5 [91.5]) or serving as counselor at creation (Sim. 9.12.2 [89.2])

---

53. On the door, see, e.g., John 10:1–10; *1 Clem.* 48.2–4; Ign. *Phld.* 9.1; Clement of Alexandria, *Exc.* 26; Hippolytus, *Ref.* 5.8.20–21; 5.9.21; 5.17.9; Ps.-Clem. *Hom.* 3.18.3.

54. Brox (1991, 493).

55. See also Sim. 9.15.2 (92.5); Brox (1989a, 272–3).

56. Osiek (1999, 235).

57. Two things are worth noting in this phrase. First, υἱός is again distinguished from κύριος. Second, the repetition of the number one in Sim. 9.13.5, 7 (90.5, 7) is reminiscent of similar repetitions in Eph 4:4–6; Ign. *Magn.* 7.1–2; *Phld.* 4.

58. On the use of ὅλος in the *Shepherd*, see Verheyden (2015, 590–3).

indicates a relationship between the Son and God that is not found between God and God's creatures.[59] The Son's relationship is thus unique.

When Hermas asks about the stones that have come up from the deep (Sim. 9.16.1 [93.1]),[60] the shepherd tells Hermas that they came from the deep to symbolize their need for baptism. Baptism is described as "the seal of the Son of God" (ἡ σφραγὶς τοῦ υἱοῦ τοῦ θεοῦ; Sim. 9.16.3 [93.3]) and provides the means by which they are able to enter into God's kingdom.[61] The Son's role is linked to baptism but involves mediation or the provision of access as in the description of the Son as door. The forty stones, which represent the apostles and teachers who proclaim the Son (Sim. 9.15.4 [92.4]), also proclaim the Son to the other stones and enable them to come to know the name of the Son of God (Sim. 9.16.5–7 [93.5–7]). The apostles announce the Son to the twelve mountains that represent the twelve tribes inhabiting the world (Sim. 9.17.1 [94.1]). The stones that come from the twelve mountains are called by the name of God's Son (Sim. 9.17.4 [94.4]),[62] and the Son rejoices when he receives these people unified and purified (Sim. 9.18.4 [95.4]). It is thus a reward to dwell with the Son (Sim. 9.24.4 [101.4]), although for some this reward comes at the cost of suffering on account of the Son's name (Sim. 9.28.2–3 [105.2–3]).

The Spirit

The *Shepherd* is a text that is filled with spirits as Hermas reports on the visions that he has seen.[63] References to the Holy spirit or to spirits that come from God thus occur throughout the text. Yet it is not always clear when the *Shepherd* refers to the supreme spirit that comes from and is closely associated with God or when the *Shepherd* refers to other spirits that are holy. In Sim. 5.5.2 (58.2) and Sim. 9.1.1 (78.1), there are two references to the holy spirit in ways that approach what Christians would later term a divine hypostasis. However, Sim. 9.13.2 (90.2) mentions holy spirits in the plural. The difficulty can be shown orthographically in English in the choice one makes regarding capitalization, that is, holy spirit or Holy Spirit.[64] However, these distinctions in capitalization were not available to the

---

59. Following Grillmeier (1975, 42–4) and Brox (1991, 427), the Son may also be ascribed some form of preexistence.

60. See also Sim. 9.3.3–5 (80.3–5); 9.4.3–4 (81.3–4); 9.5.3–5 (82.3–5); 9.15.4–6 (92.4–6).

61. Ferguson (2009, 218–19); Grundeken (2015a, 131). On the kingdom of God in the *Shepherd*, see Windisch (1928, 171–2).

62. See further Grundeken (2015a, 131–2).

63. For a thorough terminological analysis of πνεῦμα in the *Shepherd*, see Martín (1978, 297–308).

64. A similar phenomenon is described with reference to German in Brox (1991, 542). The issue becomes more acute when one observes that πνεῦμα can also refer to human spirits without any particular reference to the divine spirit. See Vis. 1.2.4 (2.4); 3.8.9 (16.9); 3.11.2 (19.2); 3.12.2 (20.2); 3.12.3 (20.3); 3.13.2 (21.2).

Shepherd's author or earliest reader. I have thus written all instances of *spirit* in the *Shepherd* in lowercase letters.⁶⁵

Despite the difficulty of determining precisely which spirit is in view at some points, the *Shepherd* goes on to describe the holy spirit in ways that indicate a special relationship to God. Like the Son, the spirit is both differentiated from God, who is most commonly known as θεός or κύριος, while simultaneously being intimately associated with God. The spirit is identified as the master's parabolic son in Sim. 5.5.2 (58.2). As the shepherd enters into the third interpretation of the parable, he links the holy spirit to the act of creation by referring to the spirit "that created all creation" (τὸ κτίσαν πᾶσαν τὴν κτίσιν; Sim. 5.6.5 [59.5]). The shepherd has already programmatically named God as creator in Mand. 1.1 (26.1).⁶⁶ The potential for the spirit's unique connection to God is enhanced when one notices that the spirit is also described as preexistent (προόν; Sim. 5.6.5 [59.5]). The holy spirit likewise plays a revelatory role. The shepherd reminds Hermas that the spirit spoke with him in the form of the church in Vis. 3 (Sim. 9.1.1 [78.1]).⁶⁷ The spirit employed the woman-church as the means by which to show the vision that was intended. The spirit now utilizes the shepherd to show Hermas a more detailed vision of the tower (Sim. 9.1.2 [78.2]). The shepherd emphasizes that both he and the woman are empowered to show Hermas the tower visions "through the same spirit" (διὰ τοῦ αὐτοῦ μὲν πνεύματος; Sim. 9.1.2 [78.2]).

In the first two Visions, the spirit carries Hermas into regions that are not traversable under ordinary circumstances (Vis. 1.1.3 [1.3]; 2.1.1 [5.1]). The spirit carries him while sleeping the first time. Hermas is awake and recalling his previous experience when he carried the second time. The shepherd also speaks about a divine spirit (πνεῦμα θεῖον) in the context of prophecy. The divine spirit does not empower false prophets (Mand. 11.2 [43.2]). The divine spirit does not speak when consulted; it is not a soothsayer's spirit (Mand. 11.5 [43.5]). Rather, the divine spirit that rests on a prophet answers the prayers of righteous people who trust the divine spirit. The prophetic spirit then fills the prophet so that the prophet speaks to the people in the holy spirit (Mand. 11.9 [43.9]). The divine spirit is thus powerful and can force the earthly spirit to flee (Mand. 11.10, 14 [43.10, 14]).

The passage in Mand. 11, however, simultaneously illustrates the difficulties in clarifying the portrayal of the spirit in the *Shepherd*. The shepherd mentions a divine spirit (Mand. 11.2, 9 [43.2, 9]), earthly spirit (Mand. 11.2, 14 [43.2, 14]), holy spirit (Mand. 11.9 [43.9]), spirit given by God (Mand. 11.5 [43.5]), prophetic spirit (Mand. 11.9 [43.9]), and a spirit belonging to the devil (Mand. 11.3 [43.3]).

---

65. Holmes (2007, 444). See also Osiek (1999, 33).

66. On links between the spirit and creation in the *Shepherd*, see further Martín (1978, 336–8).

67. This spirit is identified as the "holy spirit" (τὸ πνεῦμα τὸ ἅγιον) in A and L². However, L¹ reads only *spiritus*, perhaps indicating the difficulties that Sim. 9.1.1–2 (78.1–2) created for early interpreters and translators.

Leaving aside the spirits whose origins are described as earthly or diabolical, are all other spirits mentioned in Mand. 11 a reference to the holy spirit that is elsewhere described in relation to creation and preexistence? The reference to holy spirits (ἅγια πνεύματα; Sim. 9.13.2 [90.2]) in the plural indicates that the *Shepherd* knows of multiple spirits that are holy. Thus, when the rest of the *Shepherd* is accounted for, it becomes clear that the text also envisions spirits that come from God, are somehow associated with the unique holy spirit, and can nevertheless be differentiated.

The shepherd speaks of two different kinds of spirits in Mand. 5 and 10. The shepherd describes "the holy spirit that dwells in you" (τὸ πνεῦμα τὸ ἅγιον τὸ κατοικοῦν ἐν σοί) as a spirit that remains pure when someone is patient (Mand. 5.1.1–2 [33.1–2]). On the other hand, when an irascible spirit appears, it chokes the holy spirit. The holy spirit is forced to flee because it is delicate (τρυφερόν; Mand. 5.1.3 [33.3]).[68] Distress likewise crushes the holy spirit (ἐκτρίβει τὸ πνεῦμα τὸ ἅγιον; Mand. 10.1.2 [40.2]). Although distress has the capacity to bring people to salvation (Mand. 10.1.2 [40.2]; 10.2.3–4 [41.3–4]), the shepherd urges Hermas to take up cheerfulness (Mand. 10.3.1 [42.1]). The holy spirit is characterized by cheerfulness when it is given to people, so they should not grieve the holy spirit (Mand. 10.3.2 [42.2]).[69] In addition to dovetailing with the *Shepherd*'s description of two ways and two angels (Mand. 6.2 [36]; Sim. 6.2–5 [62–65]), the spirits in Mand. 5; 10; 11 broadly have two origins. These are the earthly and diabolical,[70] on the one hand, and the holy spirit that comes from above, on the other. In these texts, then, it is difficult to identify τὸ πνεῦμα τὸ ἅγιον as the holy spirit who is uniquely identified with God. Rather, the holy spirit that dwells in the person is an agent that manifests itself in the work to which God calls it. The indwelling holy spirit is thus closely related to the holy spirit that is uniquely connected to God but not to be strictly identified with that spirit.

The shepherd describes the spirit somewhat differently in Mand. 3.[71] While the holy spirit in Mand. 5; 10 is described as delicate and can leave a person when it encounters a heavier spirit, the spirit in Mand. 3 functions more like collateral that gives testimony regarding how people have lived.[72] The spirit is described as "the one that God caused to dwell in this flesh" (ὃ ὁ θεὸς κατῴκισεν ἐν τῇ σαρκὶ ταύτῃ; Mand. 3.1 [28.1]). Hermas is told to love truth so that everyone will recognize that the spirit is true. The spirit has the same characteristics as the Lord. Since the Lord speaks truly (Mand. 3.1 [28.1]), the spirit that believers receive from the Lord likewise does not lie (Mand. 3.2 [28.2]). For Hermas or others in his community to lie results in the defilement of the Lord's commands and prevents them from

---

68. Morgan-Wynne (1989).
69. Bautista (2014, 6).
70. See also Mand. 9.11 (39.11).
71. See Haas (1993, 569).
72. Haas rightly observes that the spirit in Mand. 3 plays a similar role to the spirit in Sim. 5.6.7 (59.7) insofar as both give testimony (1993, 572–3).

returning the spirit to God in the way that it was given to them. When Hermas weeps because of his previous lack of truthfulness, the shepherd consoles him by reminding him that a wicked conscience should not dwell with the spirit of truth and that distress should not afflict the holy and true spirit (Mand. 3.4 [28.4]). Although the need to keep the spirit in the right way and the presence of the spirit within Hermas and believers is similar to Mand. 5; 10, the spirit in Mand. 3 does not flee at the presence of falsehood. Instead, it becomes a defiled deposit and reports back to God.[73]

As alluded to already, the shepherd's description of the spirit shifts again in Sim. 9.13.2 (90.2) when he tells Hermas about the holy spirits. The shepherd offers an interpretation of the women in the tower that is much expanded from the woman's description in Vis. 3.8.2–8 (16.2–8). The most obvious expansion is in the number of the women from seven (Vis. 3.8.2 [16.2]) to twelve (Sim. 9.2.3 [79.3]; 9.15.2 [92.2]).[74] The virgins in Sim. 9 are also given a more prestigious role in the interpretation. They are powers of the Son of God (Sim. 9.13.2 [90.2]). One must be found in their clothing in order to enter the tower, and it is this clothing that makes each stone in the tower appear the same (Sim. 9.13.2, 5 [90.2, 5]). When one wears the spirit's clothing, they can then enter the tower through the waters of baptism (Sim. 9.16.1–2 [93.1–2]). The spirits thus unify the people of God (Sim. 9.17.4 [94.4]; 9.18.4 [95.4]; 9.31.4 [108.4]). The names of the twelve spirits are opposed by twelve evil spirits (Sim. 9.15.1–3 [92.1–3]).[75] While the holy spirits' interactions are described in terms of love and piety, the evil women seduce believers to come out of the tower. Finally, two examples of those who have received the spirit can also be found in the shepherd's description of the mountains. The single-minded believers on the seventh mountain wear the holy spirits and have received a portion of the Son's spirit (Sim. 9.24.2, 4 [101.2, 4]). The teachers on the eighth mountain are said to have lived in righteousness and truth "just as they also received the holy spirit" (καθὼς καὶ παρέλαβον τὸ πνεῦμα τὸ ἅγιον; Sim. 9.25.2 [102.2]).

These examples provide a fitting way to conclude this section on the spirit. Although the *Shepherd* is by no means systematic in its discussion of the spirit and is thus not always absolutely consistent, the text is nevertheless largely coherent.

---

73. A similar way of thinking is evident in Sim. 9.32.2 (109.2). Believers are instructed to return their spirit to the Lord "whole as you received [it]" (*integrum sicut accepistis* [L¹]; ὡς παρελάβετε [F]; see Bandini 2000, 112). See further Sim. 9.32.3–5 (109.3–5).

74. On the way in which the second tower vision multiplies and divides the number of women, see Walsh (2019b, 476–82).

75. The twelve virgins are Faith, Self-Control, Power, Patience, Single-Mindedness, Innocence, Holiness, Joy, Truth, Understanding, Harmony, and Love. These correspond to but are identified differently from the women in Vis. 3.8.3–5 (16.3–5) who are Faith, Self-Control, Single-Mindedness, Knowledge, Innocence, Reverence, and Love. The twelve women who wear black garments are Faithlessness, Lack of Self-Control, Disobedience, Deceit, Grief, Evil, Licentiousness, Anger, Falsehood, Foolishness, Slander, and Hate. On the relationship between spirits and virtues/vices, see Adam (1906, 41–2).

Examples can be found in the description of the inhabitants of the mountains. The teachers who return the spirit as they received it because they live in truth (Sim. 9.25.2 [102.2]) embody the instructions given to Hermas in Mand. 3.1–2 (28.1–2). The single-minded believers on the seventh mountain do not wear the virgins' clothes or even the holy spirits. Rather, they wear the holy spirit. This indicates a strong link between the holy spirit who is uniquely associated with God and the holy spirit(s) that live in the flesh and of whom believers receive a portion. Lastly, the contrast between the twelve holy spirits and twelve women dressed in black in Sim. 9 vividly enacts the depictions of the two spirits that the *Shepherd* describes acting elsewhere, especially in Mand. 5; 10. None of this precludes the *Shepherd* from referring to the holy spirit who created all things and is thus involved in activities that can only be undertaken by a divine person (Sim. 5.6.5 [59.5]). Although one may wish for more guidance from the *Shepherd* about the precise relationships between the holy spirit and other spirits, there is strong evidence for a single holy spirit associated with God who is active through other spirits that dwell in believers.

Reflections on Incipient Trinitarianism

What, if anything, can be said to draw this chapter to a close in light of the study of the *Shepherd* discusses God, Jesus, and the spirit? One may begin by noting that there is a loosely triadic shape to the way in which God's actions are described in the *Shepherd*. However, it is not always clear precisely how the Son and spirit relate to God. Some argue that there is a binitarian orientation to how the *Shepherd* describes God. Bucur understands the *Shepherd* to set forth a binitarian understanding of God that has been modified with pneumatological content, particularly in Mand. 6; Sim. 9.[76] Although it appears that "the *Shepherd* is aware of Trinitarian formulae," the text is markedly binitarian, that is, "concerned mostly with God and the supreme 'holy spirit'—the Son of God."[77] Michele Rene Barnes likewise interprets the *Shepherd* in binitarian terms and cites Sim. 5.6.5–7 (59.5–7) as an example of "Spirit inhominization."[78] Not all, however, are convinced that binitarianism is the lens through which the *Shepherd* is best viewed. Michael Svigel acknowledges that there are puzzling and peculiar elements to how the *Shepherd* portrays God, but the *Shepherd* "does not present an insurmountable problem for nascent trinitarianism."[79]

The *Shepherd* is an unsystematic text that does not always consistently describe the Son or the spirit. The uneven accounts cause tension in the text's depiction of

---

76. Bucur (2007).
77. Bucur (2007, 141).
78. Barnes (2001, 5). See also Adam (1906, 42–9, 60–1); Gieschen (1998, 222, 225).
79. Svigel (2019, 35). Svigel (2016, 267) makes a similar point with regard to the *Shepherd*'s Christology.

God. Yet these inconsistencies do not result in an incoherent understanding of God. The Son and spirit are portrayed as God because they are involved in tasks that only God can do. The clearest example of this is in creation. The shepherd's imperative that Hermas believe that God is one is qualified by the participial phrase "the one who created and ordered all things and made everything that is from what is not" (ὁ τὰ πάντα κτίσας καὶ καταρτίσας, καὶ ποιήσας ἐκ τοῦ μὴ ὄντος εἰς τὸ εἶναι τὰ πάντα; Mand. 1.1 [26.1]). Yet the Father was not alone at creation. The Son served as the Father's counselor at creation (Sim. 9.12.2 [89.2]), and his name sustains the entire creation (Sim. 9.14.5 [91.5]). The spirit is likewise said to have been involved in creation (Sim. 5.6.5 [59.5]). In light of the widespread early Jewish and early Christian outlook that only God can create the world,[80] these descriptions strongly suggest that the Shepherd is governed by an underlying Trinitarian structure.

When the link between creation and the Father, Son, and spirit has been made, one may add more tentative connections into the mix. Of particular note is the adjective ἀχώρητος, uncontained. The shepherd claims that God contains all things "but is alone uncontained" (μόνος δὲ ἀχώρητος ὤν; Mand. 1.1 [26.1]). The Son is described in similar terms. His name is "uncontained" (ἀχώρητος; Sim. 9.14.5 [91.5]). Although this word is not used elsewhere in the Shepherd, it could be employed in other early Christian texts as a description for God. The Son is thus intimately connected to the Father. The spirit is not said to be uncontained, and its capacity, or the capacity of closely related holy spirits, for dwelling in human beings may have hindered the application of this term to the spirit. However, the spirit is said to be preexistent (προόν; Sim. 5.6.5 [59.5]). When the spirit's preexistence is viewed alongside its activity in creation, such language creates further links between the Father, the Son, and the spirit within the text of the Shepherd.

The Shepherd's occasionally unsystematic terminology and unwieldy structure make it difficult for interpreters to provide an exhaustive analysis of the text's doctrine of God. However, there are hints of incipient Trinitarianism throughout the Shepherd, even if these hints do not coalesce into a complete picture. The Shepherd presents a loosely proto-orthodox view of God as Father, Son, and spirit that challenges its readers to live rightly in response to God's constructive and salvific activity that has been ongoing since before time could be measured and which continues into the readers' present.

---

80. See especially Bauckham (1998, 9–13; 2008, 7–11).

Chapter 10

SIN AND REPENTANCE

While the *Shepherd* presents God's work on behalf of creation and the church as both continual and also as originating from before time could be measured, the present reality of Hermas and his community is one that is marred by less than ideal circumstances. The Son's work in the vineyard has taken away the sins of God's people (Sim. 5.6.2 [59.2]), but Hermas is nevertheless warned against wrongdoing. Double-mindedness (διψυχία) is a key term in the *Shepherd*, and Hermas is urged instead to be single-minded (ἁπλοῦς) in his faithfulness toward God. Hermas receives instructions about how he and his community should utilize wealth. They are also warned against mistreating those in the community who are poor. The parables of the willow tree and the tower warn that some members of the community may not be included in the people of God when all things come to an end because of problems in their faith or their actions. Although the *Shepherd* presents an early Christian vision that can at times be stunning, it makes equally clear that all is not yet well among those who first wrote and read the text.

It is for this reason that the *Shepherd* calls believers to repent. The goal of the text is for believers to change the way in which they are currently acting and opt for the way recommended by the woman and the shepherd. Hermas provides a key example of what it means to repent and to change the course of one's life. Although his path to transformation is not linear and his communications with revelatory figures can be tense at times, Hermas progresses to live and speak in ways that are in line with what he has been taught over the course of the narrative. Along the way, the text raises questions about how many times believers may repent, tests the boundaries of what is expected in an apocalyptic text, closely relates repentance to baptism, and describes repentance as a means by which one can come to a better understanding of God and God's ways.

This chapter takes up the topics of sin and repentance in the *Shepherd*. Following the previous chapter's study of how the *Shepherd* describes God, this chapter starts with depictions of the community that highlight problems and ongoing difficulties within and among believers. The chapter next explores how the community is instructed to change its ways. Along with changing their actions, the *Shepherd* presents believers with a vision of changed people. The chapter thus closes by examining the literary and theological significance of sin and repentance within the *Shepherd*, taking up Hermas as the central exemplar of what a life tarnished by sin looks like as it is transformed through repentance.

Sin

Perhaps the most notable way in which the *Shepherd* describes what is wrong with the community centers around descriptions of it as double-minded. The words δίψυχος, δισταγμός, and διαλογίζομαι along with cognate verbs and nouns appear roughly sixty times in the *Shepherd*.[1] Although the most extended instructions regarding double-mindedness are found in Mand. 9.1-12 (39.1-12),[2] Hermas is told early in the *Shepherd* that everyone who receives the message in the pages of his book will be forgiven if they repent and "drive double-mindedness away from their heart" (ἄρωσιν ἀπὸ τῆς καρδίας αὐτῶν τὰς διψυχίας; Vis. 2.2.4 [6.4]). Hermas himself is instructed not to be double-minded (Vis. 3.3.4 [11.4]; 4.1.4, 7 [22.4, 7]), but he nevertheless serves as an example of double-mindedness in his interactions with the shepherd (Mand. 12.4.2 [47.2]; Sim. 1.3 [50.3]). A good example of one way in which double-mindedness manifests comes in Sim. 6.1.1-2 (61.1-2). Hermas is contemplating the commandments in his house. While he notices their beauty, he claims that he will be blessed if (ἐάν) he walks in them. This suggests that Hermas may have at least a hint of doubt regarding his ability to keep the commandments. Such, at least, seems to be the shepherd's interpretation. When the shepherd appears next to Hermas,[3] he affirms that the commandments are beautiful but asks Hermas why he is behaving in a double-minded manner. Double-mindedness doubts either the commandments or one's ability to keep the commandments even though these commandments have come from God. Hermas is called simply to walk in the commandments.

Double-mindedness causes further difficulties in the lives of believers. It makes believers susceptible to false prophets (Mand. 11.1-2 [43.1-2]).[4] It also creates difficulties for believers when they pray (Mand. 9.1 [39.1]),[5] and double-minded people are easily affected by distress when they fail at an action that they have undertaken (Mand. 10.2.2 [41.2]). For this reason, double-minded people are particularly vulnerable to suffering (Vis. 4.2.6 [23.6]) and are urged to believe in the Lord.[6] Before Hermas sees the beast that signifies the coming tribulation, he is

---

1. For references see Kraft (1964, s.v).
2. On early Christian reception of Mand. 9, see Dibelius (1923, 528-9).
3. Brox (1991, 332-3) cites Sim. 6.1.2 (61.2) along with Vis. 5.1 (25.1) as examples of the way in which revelatory figures can appear suddenly beside Hermas.
4. Reiling (1973, 32-33).
5. See also Sir 7:10; *Barn*. 19.5; *Did*. 4.4. Faith and prayer are linked closely in Jas 1:6; 5:17 (Körtner and Leutzsch 1998, 221n.186).
6. Schliesser (2017, 43) refers to the call for the double-minded to believe as a "paradigmatic plea."

warned by a voice not to be double-minded (Vis. 4.1.4 [22.4]). He recalls this voice and is encouraged when he sees the beast (Vis. 4.1.7–8 [22.7–8]). The woman informs him that he was able to pass the beast because he was not double-minded (Vis. 4.2.4 [23.4]).[7] Double-mindedness hinders believers from repentance (Vis. 2.2.4 [6.4]), which, as will be discussed later in this chapter, is key to understanding the practices that the *Shepherd* recommends. One cannot be double-minded and repent at the same time. Double-mindedness is also linked to a lack of faith and a lack of understanding (Vis. 3.10.9 [18.9]). The double-minded will thus struggle to accept fully the message that is given to them through Hermas and the revealers. Provisions have been made to assure them that these things are true (Vis. 3.4.3 [12.3]).

The seriousness with which the *Shepherd* takes up double-mindedness is evident in Mand. 10.1.1 (40.1), in which double-mindedness is described as the sister of distress and irascibility. The inability to trust the messages that ultimately come from God or to follow his commandments has consequences for the double-minded. They are represented by stones that are thrown far from the tower and may or may not land on a road because they are seeking a better way than what God has given (Vis. 3.7.1 [15.1]).[8] Their sticks are represented as half-green and half-withered in the parable of the willow (Sim. 8.7.1–3 [73.1–3]; 8.8.3, 5 [74.3, 5]). The shepherd repeats that there is hope for the double-minded to repent. However, if they do not repent, they will lose their life and remain outside of the tower. Similar stark warnings continue in the next Similitude, in which the shepherd groups the double-minded with hypocrites and blasphemers (Sim. 9.18.3 [95.3]). The double-minded are further described as people who are neither alive nor dead; they have the Lord on their lips but not in their hearts (Sim. 9.21.1–3 [98.1–3]). Hope remains, however, for the double-minded to repent (Sim. 9.21.4 [98.4]).

Double-mindedness is thus a broadly used concept that is related to a variety of ways in which believers can act wrongly in the community.[9] Is there anything that is at the heart of this concept? To answer this question, it is important to recognize that double-mindedness in the *Shepherd* relies upon a relational understanding of faith. Divided allegiance lies at the heart of what it means to be double-minded.[10] This is clearest in Mand. 9, in which a key example of double-mindedness involves a question about prayer from a sinful person. The proper response should recognize

---

7. On the place of double-mindedness in Vis. 4, see Bauckham (1974, 31–2). For further connections between double-mindedness and suffering, see Vis. 2.2.7 (6.7); Sim. 9.21.3 (98.3).

8. Osiek (1999, 73–4) rightly points out the similarities between the double-minded in Vis. 3.7.1 (15.1) and the stones that represent people who have known the truth but did not dwell in it in Vis. 3.6.2 (14.2).

9. For summaries that illustrate the variety of ways in which double-mindedness is discussed in the *Shepherd*, see Brox (1991, 551–3); Körtner and Leutzsch (1998, 221n.186); Osiek (1999, 30–1).

10. Reiling (1973, 32–4). See also Osiek (1999, 31).

that God is not like human beings, so the person who is praying ought to turn to God with their whole heart (Mand. 9.2–3 [39.2–3]). Double-mindedness thus threatens the exclusivity of the relationship that God demands with people because it pictures God with the same fickle traits as other people.

The *Shepherd* also connects double-mindedness to matters of wealth and business. When interpreting the significance of those who returned their sticks half-green and half-withered, the shepherd informs Hermas that such people are mixed up in their business affairs (αἱ πραγματεῖαι; Sim. 8.8.1 [74.1]). Those who refuse to heed the commandments will fall away completely, "for they blasphemed the Lord because of their business affairs and denied him" (διὰ τὰς πραγματείας γὰρ αὐτῶν ἐβλασφήμησαν τὸν κύριον καὶ ἀπηρνήσαντο αὐτόν; Sim. 8.8.2 [74.2]).[11] Similar language is used in Sim. 9 to describe the third mountain, which represents those who are wealthy and actively mixed up in business (Sim. 9.20.1 [97.1]), while the stones that are too round to be placed in the tower of Vis. 3 represent those who deny the Lord because of their wealth and business affairs (Vis. 3.6.5 [14.5]). For the *Shepherd*, there is a connection between wealth and the denial of the Lord in times of suffering. However, this connection is not drawn as tightly as the link between double-mindedness and suffering in Vis. 4.

Business affairs and wealth are linked to warnings against other sins in the *Shepherd*. Desire to work at one's business is set alongside irascibility, bitterness, luxurious food and drink, illicit desires for women, boasting, and greed as signs that the evil angel is present in a person (Mand. 6.2.5 [36.5]). Wealth and business affairs are also connected to gentile friendships (φιλίαι ἐθνικαί; Mand. 10.1.4 [40.4]),[12] while Hermas is elsewhere warned against participating in many business dealings because such people become enmeshed in sin (Sim. 4.5 [53.5]). These statements offer a clue about what the *Shepherd* finds wrong in business. It does not seem to be the business itself. Rather, business leads the readers of the *Shepherd* away from their place as servants of the Lord (Sim. 4.5 [53.5]) and to various other dealings that run contrary to the commandments that have been received.[13] Hermas's life prior to writing the *Shepherd* is alluded to as an example of how wealth and business can distract believers from God and from the people of God (Vis. 3.6.5–7 [14.5–7]; Mand. 3.3–5 [28.3–5]). The comments about luxurious food and drink, boasting, and greed may also remind readers that the *Shepherd*'s comments should be understood in the context of urban life in Rome. Increased

---

11. The pronoun at the end of this clause is redundant. This may partially account for the reading of λοιπόν in A. The reading αὐτόν is much more strongly attested in the manuscript tradition and is found in M, P.Oxy. 13.1599, L¹ and L². It has been followed here because of its stronger attestation and redundant nature.

12. Note the similar language about friendship with outsiders in Jas 4:4. Brox (1991, 244) defines gentile friendship in terms of living with the Gentiles instead of the Christian community. The adjective is thus used to denote outsiders. See also Sim. 8.9.1–3 (75.1–3); Trebilco (2017, 150–76).

13. Maier (1997, 135).

wealth made it possible for people to buy high-end foods and to throw lavish parties wherein such foods could be consumed. This provided a means by which to display one's wealth in front of one's friends and others in the community.[14] It thus promoted a culture that the author seems to have found boastful. The desire for such a lifestyle and the money required to live it are deplored in the *Shepherd* in large part because they are fleeting and quickly forgotten (Sim. 6.4.4 [64.4]; 6.5.3–4 [65.3–4]). Instead, believers are called to live their lives in service to the God who created the world and who acted on their behalf to bring them into the tower under construction.

This is not to say that wealth is inherently evil or has no place in the community. Early in the Similitudes, the shepherd comes to Hermas as he is contemplating the relationship between the vine and the elm tree.[15] He informs Hermas that they "are set as an example for God's servants" (εἰς τύπον κεῖνται τοῖς δούλοις τοῦ θεοῦ; Sim. 2.2 [51.2]). The shepherd highlights the way in which the fruitless elm bears fruit through the vine, while the vine is only able to bear fruit because it is attached to the elm (Sim. 2.3–4 [51.3–4]). "This parable, then, is set for God's servants, for poor and rich" (αὕτη οὖν ἡ παραβολὴ εἰς τοὺς δούλους τοῦ θεοῦ κεῖται, εἰς πτωχὸν καὶ πλούσιον; Sim. 2.4 [51.4]). Rich and poor act in complementary ways toward one another. Indeed, they are "both partners in the righteous work" (ἀμφότεροι κοινωνοὶ τοῦ ἔργου τοῦ δικαίου; Sim. 2.9 [51.9]). The rich have a great deal of wealth, but their money distracts them from the things of the Lord.[16] They are thus impoverished in matters that pertain to God, and what little prayer they do manage remains weak (Sim. 2.5 [51.5]). When the rich give to the poor, they benefit from the prayers of the poor because the poor are rich in prayer and confession. This results in a flourishing symbiotic relationship as the rich care for the needs of the poor and the poor pray even more for the rich (Sim. 2.6–7 [51.6–7]). While wealth is a topic about which the *Shepherd* has much to say, the text nevertheless maintains a place for the rich and their money as long as it is used benevolently.

Given the prevalence with which the *Shepherd* discusses wealth and the links that it makes between wealth and double-mindedness,[17] one may wonder if this focus on wealth can be further contextualized.[18] To begin with, the issue of wealth in the *Shepherd* raises questions regarding the economic status of believers in

---

14. If one follows Downs (2019), Paul may respond to a similar situation in 1 Cor 11:17–34 in describing the weakness, sickness, and death (1 Cor 11:30) of some wealthy believers who suffer from overconsumption.

15. On the way in which elms and vines were used in the Roman Empire, see Fuentes-Utrilla, López-Rodríguez, and Gil (2004, 9–11).

16. See also Mand. 10.1.5 (40.5).

17. Leutzsch handily refers to the topic of rich and poor as a "Dauerthema" throughout the *Shepherd* (1989, 113).

18. This has been an important topic of study elsewhere in scholarship on the *Shepherd*. See further Osiek (1983); Leutzsch (1989, 113–37); Lampe (2003, 90–9); Grundeken (2015a, 114–27, 152–9); Downs (2016, 250–6).

Rome during the second century. Next, the teachings about wealth in this text ask for reflection on the connections between wealth, prestige, and patronage among early Christians living in the Roman Empire.

The *Shepherd* presents a challenge to anyone who would flatly portray all early Christians as impoverished or from the lowest classes.[19] The repeated warnings to the rich indicate that there was at least some economic diversity. Yet *rich* and *poor* are not particularly specific classifiers, and the *Shepherd* does not provide historians with an exhaustive account of exactly who was present when Roman believers gathered together. A more nuanced scale for evaluating wealth in the *Shepherd* is required.[20] While the *Shepherd* suggests that there were disparities in wealth among Roman believers during the first half of the second century, it is unlikely that many, if any, in the *Shepherd*'s audience would be among the elite of the Roman Empire.[21] Nevertheless, at least some in the community seem to have lived above subsistence level. This allows them to give their money to those who live at or below subsistence level, and this is precisely the practice that the shepherd's parable about the elm and vine recommends to Hermas and the community (Sim. 2.1–10 [51.1–10]). Certain bishops are lauded for providing shelter for those in need (Sim. 9.27.2 [104.2]).[22] Moreover, the *Shepherd* suggests that collections were taken up from Roman believers in order to give to the needy. Certain deacons are accused of mishandling their ministries and "raiding the livelihoods of widows and orphans" (διαρπάσαντες χηρῶν καὶ ὀρφανῶν) for their own profit (Sim. 9.26.2 [103.2]).[23] While this indicates that all was not well in the Roman community and that exploitable divisions existed between rich and poor, it also suggests that there were at least some organized efforts to collect money—and perhaps food, goods, and services—on behalf of those in need.[24]

---

19. This is the tendency of, e.g., Deissmann (1925, 212–17).

20. For attempts to provide a more nuanced scale with a particular focus on Paul and the Roman Empire of the mid-first century, see Barclay (2004); Friesen (2004); Oakes (2004; 2009); Longenecker (2009). See also the discussion in Horrell (2019, 50–63).

21. One figure who is often named as a candidate for an early Christian member of at least the municipal elite class is Erastus (Rom 16:23). For recent discussions of his place in Corinth, see Meggitt (1996); Friesen (2010); Goodrich (2010; 2011); Weiß (2010; 2015, 106–46); Brookins (2013).

22. Note also the general instructions to be hospitable in Mand. 8.10 (38.10) as well as the description of those who are hospitable in Sim. 8.10.3 (76.3); 9.27.2 (104.2). See further Brox (1991, 234–5).

23. Osiek (1999, 249). The evidence is too scant to assume that deacons were the primary officials in charge of the collection (so Alikin 2010, 271). This position is rightly questioned by Grundeken (2015a, 152). Although referred to as a *presbyter*, the example of Valens and his love of money may provide a comparable example from the first half of the second century. See Pol. *Phil.* 11.1–4; Maier (1993); Lookadoo (2017a: 372–3).

24. Grundeken (2015a, 152–9).

However, one may ask what it is that made at least some comparatively wealthy Roman believers hesitant to follow the instructions outlined by the *Shepherd*. One could appeal to self-interest on the part of the rich. Doubtless, this plays a role, but it proves to be a rather bland response. In order to set the interest of wealthier members more precisely in the context of second-century Rome, it is helpful to reflect on connections between wealth and prestige. For residents of the Roman Empire, wealth brought with it certain expectations. In addition to an increased sense of security, the expectation was that those with means would utilize their money in ways that benefited others. One way in which this might be done is by hosting banquets in one's home and inviting others to it. Such affairs could be extravagant, and the question of precisely how extravagant any early Christian celebration might have been must remain an open question. It is worth noting, however, that the woman describes people who make themselves sick by overeating (Vis. 3.9.7 [17.7]).[25] This could indicate a banquet setting or a similar environment in which lavish meals were consumed over the course of an entire evening. The woman understands this as an instance in which the community lacks a sense of sharing or community spirit (ἀσυνκρασία; Vis. 3.9.4 [17.4]) since the poor suffer due to lack of food while the rich suffer due to excess. Rather than using their wealth to increase their own prestige through lavish foods (Mand. 6.2.5 [36.5]; 8.3 [38.3]; 12.2.1 [45.1]), the rich are instructed to care for the poor with a view to the overall well-being of the whole community.[26]

Patronage was another way in which the rich could both display their wealth and demonstrate their benevolence. As an extension from such patronage, wealthy people might also give loans with terms of interest attached. They could thus turn from benevolent patrons to harsh creditors. The shepherd appears to allude to such a phenomenon when he says that the good do not oppress debtors or those in need (Mand. 8.10 [38.10]).[27] Yet the shepherd reverses even the expectation that the wealthy should be good patrons in Sim. 2. Admittedly, the wealthy are called to provide generously for the needs of the poor. However, the rich are simultaneously indebted to the poor for their intercessions on behalf of the wealthy. The poor thus serve as patrons of the rich using prayer as their currency (Sim. 2.5–7 [51.5–7]). The gifts of the rich may be viewed as meritorious, but they are only indirectly effective because their efficacy comes through the prayers of the poor.[28] The rich and

---

25. On Vis. 3.9 (17), see further Downs (2019, 584–6).

26. Mayo (2016, 184–5). The references to the bodies of the have-nots wasting away (Vis. 3.9.3 [17.3]) and to community spirit (Vis. 3.9.4 [17.4]) indicate that the community is in view. This is not purely an altruistic action by the rich on behalf of the poor. The rich benefit from their charity as they avoid the harmful effects of overindulging and as they are included in the tower (Vis. 3.9.4–6 [17.4–6]). See further Grundeken (2015a, 116). On the role of reciprocity in the Greco-Roman world and the emergence of the concept of a "pure" gift, see Barclay (2015, 24–63).

27. E.g., Lampe (2003, 91) understands Mand. 8.10 (38.10) as a reference to giving loans for interest. On translation and textual issues in this verse, see Grundeken (2015a, 119n.21).

28. Downs (2016, 252).

poor are not called to be in patron–client relationships. Instead, they are partners (κοινωνοί; Sim. 2.9 [51.9]), and the primary allegiance of both rich and poor is to God rather than any human patron.[29] Following the description in Sim. 2, these relationships appear to hold for those who are within the believing community in Rome. Care for those who are poor, needy, or in distress is extended to "every person" (*omnis homo*) in Sim. 10.4.2–4 (114.2–4).[30] Moreover, the shepherd's inclusion of giving away the money that would ordinarily be spent for food when fasting opens the possibility of who might be able to give (Sim. 5.3.7 [56.7]). Not only are the rich expected to give. If people fast, all may be able to give at least some. While the *Shepherd* devotes much attention to divisions between rich and poor, the text also problematizes facile attempts to make such a distinction.

Double-mindedness and wealth take an important place when considering what the *Shepherd* sees as wrong within the community to which it is addressed. However, these are not the only issues that are mentioned. When Hermas meets Rhoda in the opening vision, he is accused of having an evil desire against her (Vis. 1.1.8–9 [1.8–9]). His lust is confirmed by the woman in Vis. 1.2.4 (2.4) and is juxtaposed against single-mindedness and innocence. Such evil desires are savage in their ability to entangle and destroy people (Mand. 12.1.1–3 [44.1–3]). Lust (ἐπιθυμία) is a characteristic of those who rebel against God and remain outside of the tower (Vis. 3.7.2–3 [15.2–3]), is a trait found in the works of the evil angel (Mand. 6.2.5 [36.5]; Sim. 6.2.2–3 [62.2–3]), and desires not only someone else's wife or husband but also others' wealth, extravagant food, and luxury (Mand. 12.2.1 [45.1]). It thus includes but is larger than misplaced sexual desires.

Hermas's family likewise exhibits traits that the *Shepherd* considers sinful. Hermas's children are described in terms that suggest sexual promiscuity (Vis. 2.2.2 [6.2]). They are corrupt, undisciplined, and in need of instruction (Vis. 1.3.1 [3.1]). They have thus betrayed their parents (Vis. 2.2.2 [6.2]). Hermas's children have blasphemed the Lord, while his wife acts wickedly when she speaks (Vis. 2.2.2–3 [6.2–3]). Although not attributed directly to Hermas's family, evil speech (καταλαλιά) is likewise described as an evil over which it is necessary to exercise control (Mand. 8.3 [38.3]). It is depicted by one of the women dressed in black in the second tower vision (Sim. 9.15.3 [92.3]). Finally, irascibility and distress are described as traits that should not characterize the holy spirit (Mand. 5; 10). Although individual acts of anger or grief may not necessarily be described as sinful by the *Shepherd*, lifestyles that are characterized by such traits choke the holy spirit so that the holy spirit must flee and believers' lives are directed by another spirit (Mand. 5.1.3–4 [33.3–4]; 10.2.2 [41.2]). Of course, it is worth noting that distress can also play a positive role because it may lead people to repentance (Mand. 10.2.3 [41.3]). The connection between sin—or at least a lifestyle that is more prone to be characterized by sin—and repentance leads naturally to the next section.

---

29. Jeffers (1991, 133–4); Jensen et al. (2014, 394–5); Mayo (2016, 184).
30. Lampe (2003, 93).

Repentance

The history of scholarship has a long-standing interest in the topic of repentance within the *Shepherd*.[31] This interest is well-placed, since the *Shepherd* uses forms of the verb μετανοέω and its cognate noun roughly 145 times in the text.[32] In some ways, this historical interest may be traced back to Tertullian, whose characterization of the *Shepherd* as "the apocryphal *Shepherd* of the adulterers" (*illus apocryphus Pastor moechorum*; *Pud*. 20.2) owes something to the *Shepherd*'s allowance of repentance between a couple after adultery (*Mand*. 4.1.7–8 [29.7–8]). Tertullian's rigorist practices led him to disavow the *Shepherd*'s teachings on repentance, at least in the case of adultery. More recent scholarship has also inquired about whether the *Shepherd* allows for multiple instances of repentance after baptism.[33] If one had to characterize matters along these lines, it is difficult to do better than the description from Holmes:

> The answer, which seeks to balance both God's justice and mercy (cf. *4 Ezra*), is yes, once—but only for a limited time, so one must repent quickly before the opportunity passes.[34]

Another matter of scholarly interest concerns the mechanisms by which one repents in the *Shepherd*. Given the consistent interest in repentance throughout the text, some have wondered whether it is possible to find preludes of a full-fledged sacrament of repentance.[35] While these two areas of scholarship may be interesting to consider, this section aims to show both that repentance is a key concern throughout the *Shepherd* and that there are other questions to investigate regarding the *Shepherd*'s understanding of repentance.[36] The *Shepherd* may not be absolutely homogeneous in how it describes repentance throughout the entire text, but it is consistent insofar as it depicts repentance as a continual and thoroughgoing concern in the life of the community and in the lives of believers.

Before continuing further, though, one may begin by asking precisely what it is that the *Shepherd* has in mind when discussing μετάνοια. Osiek argues that the

---

31. Dibelius (1923, 423), for example, refers to "der Predigt von der Buße" as the "Verkündigung, die dem Verf. wirklich am Herzen liegt." Similarly Brox (1991, 476) writes, "Das hauptsächliche Thema des PH ist die Rettung der Getauften trotz postbaptismaler Sünden, das Mittel dazu die Buße." See also the helpful study by Zahn (1868, 327–60).

32. This count is based on Kraft (1964, s.v.). The ambiguity in this number (i.e., "roughly") comes from instances of textual discrepancies within the transmission of the *Shepherd*.

33. E.g., Poschmann (1940, 134–205); Wiles (1967, 153–4); Joly (1968, 22–7; 1993, 530–3). For a comparison of Tertullian and the *Shepherd* on second repentance, see D'Alès (1905, 339n.5); Adam (1906).

34. Holmes (2007, 443).

35. E.g., D'Alès (1914); Poschmann (1940, 134–205); Rahner (1983, 57–113).

36. On the centrality of repentance in the *Shepherd*, see Blidstein (2017, 120).

text envisions "a fundamental personal change" rather than a ritual change.[37] With this in mind, she argues that it is better to translate μετάνοια as "conversion" rather than "repentance." By using this word, she intends to evoke personal and corporate transformation rather than a ritual or repeated discipline.[38] Osiek captures well the transformative nature of μετάνοια both with regard to the individual and with regard to the community. Repentance involves a change that takes up the entire life and results in a change in the person. This is well illustrated in the transformation of the woman's form described in Vis. 3.10.1–3.13.4 (18.1–21.4). The changes in the woman mirror alterations that have occurred in Hermas's own spirit (Vis. 3.11.1 [19.1]; 3.12.3 [20.3]; 3.13.2 [21.2]). "Therefore, those who repent through and through are made new and set on a foundation—those who repent with their whole heart" (οἱ οὖν μετανοήσαντες ὁλοτελῶς νέοι ἔχονται καὶ τεθεμελιωμένοι, οἱ ἐξ ὅλης καρδίας μετανοήσαντες; Vis. 3.13.4 [21.4]). The woman's transformation continues in Vis. 4.2.1–2 (23.1–2) when the narrator describes the woman in terms that draw upon bridal imagery.[39] Insofar as the woman represents the entire church, one may also see the changes to her in corporate terms.[40] Yet the individual is clearly in the process of changing, since the woman's rejuvenation represents what is happening within Hermas himself.

One should also add that instances of renewal in the lives of believers as a result of repentance are not found only in connection with the woman. Hermas later speaks about the mercy that God gives to those who call upon God's name and gives thanks for the angel of repentance. For it is through the angel of repentance that "our spirit" (ἡμῶν τὸ πνεῦμα) was renewed and "our life" (τὴν ζωὴν ἡμῶν) restored (Sim. 9.14.3 [91.3]).[41] Repentance and baptism are closely linked together as actions that bring about restoration in the lives of believers. Baptism is linked to forgiveness of sins in Mand. 4.3.1 (31.1), and one should not sin again after receiving forgiveness of sins (Mand. 4.3.2 [31.2]).[42] Their lives should instead be characterized by purity.[43] Like repentance, baptism is required for entry into the tower. While baptism is a one-time event, the shepherd informs Hermas that provisions have been made for repentance after baptism (Mand. 4.3.3–7 [31.3–7]). Although a notion of repentance that allows for it to occur only a limited number of times during the life of a believer may sound restrictive, it is clear from Mand.

---

37. Osiek (1999, 29).

38. So Osiek (1999, 28–30).

39. Muddiman (2005, 119) points out that this image bears striking similarities to the description of the church in Eph 5:25.

40. Osiek (1999, 30). *Pace* Dibelius (1923, 485–6); Grundeken (2015a, 136).

41. Grundeken (2015a, 139).

42. One should note that these views represent the position that Hermas has heard "from certain teachers" (παρά τινων διδασκάλων; Mand. 4.3.1 [31.1]). The shepherd modifies what Hermas has heard in the following dialogue (Mand. 4.3.1–7 [31.1–7]). See further Blomkvist (2011, 854); Grundeken (2015a, 128).

43. Blidstein (2017, 144–6) even characterizes repentance in terms of purification.

4.3.1–7 (31.1–7) that this special allowance is due to God's grace. The shepherd thus explains that the Lord is "exceedingly compassionate" (πολυεύσπλαγχνος) and "showed compassion on what he made" (ἐσπλαγχνίσθη ἐπὶ τὴν ποίησιν αὐτοῦ) by establishing and granting the shepherd authority over repentance (Mand. 4.3.5 [31.5]). Although there is a close link between baptism and repentance, repentance stands apart as something that is possible to do after one's initial conversion and baptism.

Thus, although Osiek's preference for the word "conversion" as a translation for μετάνοια in the *Shepherd* rightly captures the transformative impact that it should have in the life of believers, the usefulness of the term to capture all of what the *Shepherd* means when referring to μετάνοια remains somewhat limited. The primary reason for this has to do with the connotations of an initial change that come about when one uses the word "conversion" as an English gloss for μετάνοια. The word too often connotes an initial transition from one religion or set of religious practices to another. A good example of this lies in the way in which "conversion" is used by Evangelical Christians to describe the initial confession and repentance that are made when turning to Christ in faith. "The call to conversion has been the content of the gospel. Preachers urged their hearers to turn away from their sins in repentance and to Christ in faith."[44] However, the *Shepherd* means more than simply an initial conversion by the word repentance and, while Osiek does not define conversion so simply,[45] the term risks being misheard and misused too easily when applied to the *Shepherd*. Despite ambiguities in using the term, it is preferable to maintain *repentance* as a gloss for μετάνοια. Nevertheless, it is important to remember that the *Shepherd* views repentance as a transformative action that affects both the entire person and the community in which they live.

Insofar as repentance is an answer to the problem of double-mindedness in the community, it maintains at least loose connections to single-mindedness and its cognates, at least within the textual world of the *Shepherd*. Single-mindedness (ἁπλότης) is paired with innocence (ἀκακία) in ways that create a memorable and somewhat regularly repeated assonance.[46] Hermas is initially described by the woman as full of single-mindedness and innocence (Vis. 1.2.4 [2.4]). The woman declares to her addressees in Vis. 3.9 (17) that she has raised them up "in much single-mindedness and innocence and dignity" (ἐν πολλῇ ἁπλότητι καὶ ἀκαίᾳ καὶ σεμνότητι; Vis. 3.9.1 [17.1]). The shepherd likewise tells Hermas to possess single-mindedness and to be innocent so that he will be like children who do not know evil (Mand. 2.1 [27.1]). Single-mindedness is further defined by how believers

---

44. Bebbington (1989, 5). For further discussion of conversionism among Evangelical Christians, see Bebbington (1989, 5–10); Noll (2003, 15–18). For a broader discussion of conversion in sociology and the wider history of Christianity, see Bremmer, van Bekkum, and Molendijk (2006).

45. Osiek (1999, 28–30).

46. Vis. 1.2.4 (2.4); 2.3.2 (7.2); 3.8.5, 7 (16.5, 7); 3.9.1 (17.1); Mand. 2.1, 7 (27.1, 7); Sim. 9.15.2 (92.2); 9.24.2 (101.2).

give to others. Giving to the needy single-mindedly involves not wavering (Mand. 2.4 [27.4]). A person who gives in this way will be regarded as innocent and will live to God (Mand. 2.6–7 [27.6–7]).[47] Single-mindedness is likewise one of the women in the tower visions. She follows self-control as the second daughter of faith in the first tower vision (Vis. 3.8.5 [16.5]). The progression thus goes from faith to self-control to single-mindedness. Innocence follows single-mindedness in the progression (Vis. 3.8.7 [16.7]). Single-mindedness and innocence are again placed next to each other in the second tower vision, though this time they occur in places five and six out of twelve (Sim. 9.15.2 [92.2]). Single-mindedness is thus closely connected to innocence and proves to be the opposite of the hesitation that comes from double-mindedness. Since repentance provides a solution to the double-mindedness that the *Shepherd* regards as so problematic, repentance should lead Hermas and his community to an innocent and single-minded faith in God that does not waver in its generosity toward neighbors.

The focus on repentance in the *Shepherd* has also been scrutinized with regard to the genre of the text. As discussed in Chapter 4, the *Shepherd* is best classified as an apocalyptic text, but its focus on the spatiotemporal world commonly experienced by all human beings has led some to argue that the text is not truly representative of the genre.[48] Although the *Shepherd* does not indulge in much speculation about the future or about other worlds, the teachings in the text are presented to Hermas by two otherworldly mediators, the woman and the shepherd.[49] Batovici identifies repentance as one of the teachings that are mediated through the woman and the shepherd.[50] He highlights three elements of repentance in connection to the apocalyptic genre: the mediation through which Hermas learns about repentance, the exchange between God and believers that results from repentance, and the layered meanings of repentance that unfold throughout the text.[51] These elements can be explored in order.

Various teachings are mediated to Hermas by the woman and the shepherd throughout the *Shepherd*. Although these teachings concern a variety of topics, the shepherd addresses repentance explicitly when showing Hermas the angel of punishment (ὁ ἄγγελος τῆς τιμωρίας; Sim. 6.3.2 [63.2]). This angel, who is likewise depicted as a shepherd, receives those who have wandered from God and directs them back to God by afflicting them in response to their desires for this age (Sim. 6.3.3–5 [63.3–5]). This is designed to bring about repentance. When they repent, they glorify God because they see that God is a righteous judge who has acted justly (Sim. 6.3.6 [63.6]). The woman is likewise instrumental in teaching

---

47. On atonement and almsgiving in Mand. 2.4–7 (27.4–7), see Downs (2016, 254–5).
48. E.g., Hefele (1839, 179); Lake (1912–13, 2.2); Joly (1993, 527); Wilson (1995, 41).
49. This is a key element in defining and identifying apocalyptic literature. See, e.g., Collins (1979, 9; 2016, 24–5); Yarbro Collins (1979, 75). See also the discussion in Chapter 4 of this volume.
50. Batovici (2015d).
51. Batovici (2015d, 168–9).

10. Sin and Repentance

Hermas about repentance as she encourages Hermas and his family to repent (Vis. 1.3.2 [3.2]) and expands this instruction to the entire community in response to the coming tribulation (Vis. 4.2.5 [23.5]).[52]

This mediation is not an end in itself, however. The teaching about repentance does not originate from the woman or the shepherd, nor is this teaching directed toward them. Rather, their teaching about repentance makes possible an exchange between God and the believers. It is not just that repentance makes it possible for believers and God to interact with one another. Even the origins of repentance start with God. When Hermas asks the shepherd to explain why not all of the branches in Sim. 8 repent and turn green, the shepherd tells him that God "gave repentance" (ἔδωκε τὴν μετάνοιαν) to those whose hearts were about to become pure. However, God withholds repentance from those whose hearts remain mired in deceit (Sim. 8.6.2 [72.2]).[53] Prior to Hermas's vision of the beast, he asks God to complete his visions so that he can give repentance to his servants who had stumbled (Vis. 4.1.3 [22.3]). The shepherd, that is, the angel of repentance (Vis. 5.7 [25.7]), appears to be sent as an answer to this request. Hermas thus gives thanks for God's gift of the shepherd and the repentance that the shepherd brings (Sim. 9.14.3 [91.3]).[54] In so doing, he mentions other themes that are closely associated with repentance or are the results of repentance. These include the renewal of the spirit and the restoration of life, particularly when there is no other hope for life (Sim. 9.14.3 [91.3]).

Human beings are not passive in this exchange but have a significant part to play in the repentance that originates with God and is mediated to them by the woman and the shepherd. At the end of Sim. 8, Hermas is instructed to tell those in his community to repent and live to God. There is something for both Hermas and his hearers to do. While the shepherd again reminds Hermas that this repentance is sent by God through the shepherd because of God's compassion (Sim. 8.11.1 [77.1]), believers should respond to the call that they have received while there is still hope for repentance (Sim. 8.7.2 [73.2]; 8.8.3 [74.3]). If believers do not repent quickly, they may end up either with a less desirable place in the tower or being excluded from the tower altogether (Sim. 8.8.3 [74.3]; see also Vis. 3.7.5–6 [15.5–6]; Vis. 5.7 [25.7]). The different possible responses to repentance suggest that repentance has various meanings and is a multifaceted process.[55] For example,

---

52. On the blurring of lines between Hermas's family and the community, see Osiek, MacDonald, and Tulloch (2006, 38–40).

53. Repentance is likewise something that comes from God in Mand. 4.3.4–5 (31.4–5). This teaching about repentance mirrors comments that the shepherd makes elsewhere about God's control and activity in human affairs in Sim. 1.9 (50.9); 4.6 (53.6). The phrase "to give repentance" (διδόναι τὴν μετάνοιαν) is found elsewhere in early Christian and early Jewish literature (e.g., Wis 12.19; Sib. Or. 4.168; 2 Tim 2:25; Barn. 16.9). See further Körtner and Leutzsch (1998, 291n.235).

54. Batovici (2015d, 167).

55. On the complicated nature of μετάνοια in the Shepherd, see the nuanced study in Lipsett (2011, 19–53).

Hermas's repentance involves both confession of sin (Vis. 1.1.3 [1.3]; 3.1.5 [9.5]) and glorification of God (Vis. 2.1.2 [5.2]). Nevertheless, his sin continues to trouble him throughout the story even though he has confessed his sin and glorified God (Vis. 1.2.1–3 [2.1–3]; 5.4 [25.4]; Mand. 3.3–5 [28.3–5]).[56]

Although the *Shepherd* contains several passages that suggest that a special time of repentance has been opened up for believers as a onetime act of grace on God's part (see esp. Mand. 4.3.2–7 [31.2–7]),[57] Hermas's experience of repentance complicates this picture. He learns about repentance at multiple times and through various means as the story continues. Further complicating this picture is the *Shepherd*'s nuanced treatment of desire (ἐπιθυμία) and restraint (ἐγκράτεια). Lipsett terms these "the workhorse words within this text's register of virtue language."[58] While other virtues and vices are important, desire and restraint take on a significant place in this text. Despite the fact that ἐπιθυμία is often a negative term in early Christianity,[59] the *Shepherd* nevertheless leaves open a positive role for ἐπιθυμία. There is a "good and holy desire" (τὴν ἐπιθυμίαν τὴν ἀγαθὴν καὶ σεμνήν) in which the shepherd instructs Hermas to clothe himself (Mand. 12.1.1 [44.1]).[60] Likewise, ἐγκράτεια is a twofold matter, despite the positive role that it often plays in other early Christian texts.[61] Hermas is told that there are some things in which it is necessary to exercise restraint but that self-control is not needed with regard to everything (Mand. 8.1 [38.1]). Specifically, the shepherd tells Hermas to be self-controlled regarding things that are evil, but there is no corresponding recommendation to restrain himself from doing what is good (Mand. 8.2 [38.2]). The nuanced interplay between ἐπιθυμία and ἐγκράτεια mirrors the complicated transformation that is envisioned when the *Shepherd* describes repentance.[62]

One additional matter should be mentioned with regard to the *Shepherd*'s discussion of repentance, namely, the link between repentance and understanding. After Hermas admits his lack of understanding in Mand. 4.2.1 (30.1), the shepherd sets repentance and understanding parallel to one another at the start of his answer: "'I,' he said, 'am over repentance and give understanding to all who repent'" (ἐγώ, φησίν, ἐπὶ τῆς μετανοίας εἰμὶ καὶ πᾶσιν τοῖς μετανοοῦσιν σύνεσιν δίδωμι; Mand. 4.2.2 [30.2]). While it may not be exactly right to say that "the shepherd ties the gift of understanding to the performance of repentance,"[63] there

---

56. Batovici (2015d, 168–9).

57. In addition to the passage quoted earlier from Holmes (2007, 443), see also Snyder (1992, 148).

58. Lipsett (2011, 20–1). See similarly Blidstein (2017, 146).

59. E.g., Rom 7:7–8; Gal 5:24; 1 Thess 4:5; Jas 1:14–15; 2 Pet 1:4; 1 John 2:16; *1 Clem.* 28.1; 30.1; *Did.* 1.4; *Barn.* 10.9.

60. See also Mand. 12.2.5 (45.5); 12.3.1 (46.1).

61. E.g., Acts 24:5; 1 Cor 7:9; 9:25; Gal 5:23; 2 Pet 1:6; *1 Clem.* 35.2; Pol. *Phil.* 4.2; *Barn.* 2.2; Theophilus, *Autol.* 3.15.

62. See further Wudel (2004, 42–4); Lipsett (2011, 36–42).

63. Dibelius (1921, 107): "da knüpft der Hirt die Gabe der Einsicht an die Leistung der Buße."

10. Sin and Repentance

is clearly a close link between repentance and understanding. This connection appears to become an equation as the shepherd continues to speak in Mand. 4.2.2 (30.2).

> Or does it not seem to you, he said, that this repentance is understanding? Repentance, he said, is great understanding. For the one[64] who sins understands that he has done evil before the Lord, and the act that he did comes over his heart. And he repents and no longer does evil. But he does what is good completely, and he humbles his own soul and tortures it because he sinned. You see, then, that repentance is great understanding.[65]

To say that repentance is great understanding is to say more than that one gains understanding through the act of repentance. Indeed, repentance itself is defined in terms of understanding. "The angel of repentance gives understanding, the act of repentance 'is' understanding."[66] Repentance provides a way to know God and comprehend God's actions. Repentance is thus not only an important indicator of the text's moral theology,[67] it also provides the epistemological key by which Hermas can understand everything that is revealed to him.

More can be said about the connections that the *Shepherd* makes between repentance and understanding. Like repentance, understanding is mediated to Hermas (Sim. 5.4.2–5 [57.2–5]; 5.5.4 [58.4]; 9.2.6 [79.6]). Although the shepherd tells Hermas to ask the Lord directly so that he can receive insight, the amount of understanding that Hermas can achieve on his own is limited. For this reason, a mediator must make things known to Hermas. Understanding is one of the women in the second tower vision that helps in the construction of the tower (Sim. 9.15.2 [92.2]). On the other hand, a lack of understanding is associated with lust and evil desire (Mand. 12.1.2 [44.2]). Two examples illustrate the connection between repentance and understanding well. The fifth mountain in the second tower

---

64. This translation follows A and L in reading ὁ ἁμαρτήσας. S reads ὁ ἀνὴρ ὁ ἁμαρτήσας. It is not easy to explain the duplication in S, and the longer reading is tentatively followed by Holmes (2007, 512). My translation follows the more widely attested text as well as Joly (1968, 156), Lindemann and Paulsen (1992, 384), Ehrman (2003, 2.248), and Prinzivalli and Simonetti (2010–15, 2.284) in preferring the shorter reading. The meaning of the passage is not changed drastically on either decision.

65. ἦ οὐ δοκεῖ σοι, φησίν, αὐτὸ τοῦτο τὸ μετανοῆσαι σύνεσιν εἶναι; τὸ μετανοῆσαι φησίν σύνεσίς ἐστιν μεγάλη. συνίει γὰρ ὁ ἁμαρτήσας ὅτι πεποίηκεν τὸ πονηρὸν ἔμπροσθεν τοῦ κυρίου, καὶ ἀναβαίνει ἐπὶ τὴν καρδίαν αὐτοῦ ἡ πρᾶξις ἣν ἔπραξεν, καὶ μετανοεῖ καὶ οὐκέτι ἐργάζεται τὸ πονηρόν, ἀλλὰ τὸ ἀγαθὸν πολυτελῶς, ἐργάζεται καὶ ταπεινοῖ τὴν ἑαυτοῦ ψυχὴν καὶ βασανίζει, ὅτι ἥμαρτεν. βλέπεις οὖν ὅτι ἡ μετάνοια σύνεσίς ἐστιν μεγάλη (Mand. 4.2.2 [30.2]). On the humbling of one's soul in the *Shepherd*, see van Unnik (1952–3, 252–4).

66. Brox (1991, 209): "Der Bußengel schenkt Einsicht, das Bußetun 'ist' Einsicht." See similarly Dibelius (1923, 508).

67. So Osiek (1999, 114).

vision represents believers who are faithful but also slow to learn, arrogant, and self-satisfied (Sim. 9.22.1 [99.1]). The shepherd tells Hermas that understanding has left them because of their arrogance, but these believers foolishly continue to praise their own understanding (Sim. 9.22.2 [99.2]). Some, however, have repented, believed, and subjected themselves to those who had understanding because they recognize their own foolishness. The shepherd calls those who are outside of the tower to repent. Upon doing this, their limited understanding can be rectified, and they may live (Sim. 9.22.3-4 [99.3-4]). The fifth mountain and the paraenesis that follows illustrate the connection between repentance and understanding. Their understanding will vivify via repentance. Moreover, the shepherd has already linked understanding to patience in Mand. 5.1.1 (33.1). The holy spirit dwells with people who are characterized by patience and, by extension, with those who are understanding. Patience and understanding are spoken of like housemates. When living with patience and understanding, one can also rule over evil and act righteously (Mand. 5.1.1 [33.1]). When the shepherd later elaborates on the relationship between patience, double-mindedness, and distress, Hermas admits that he does not understand (Mand. 10.1.3 [40.3]). The shepherd then tells Hermas that those who believe but are distracted by their business activities lose their understanding and fail to comprehend what it means to act righteously (Mand. 10.1.5 [40.5]). However, those who have understanding fear God and inquire about truth and divine matters (Mand. 10.1.6 [40.6]). Dialoguing and inquiring about the truth is a mark of people with understanding.

Given the links between repentance and understanding elsewhere in the *Shepherd* and the example of Hermas and his two celestial interlocutors, it is not unreasonable to suggest that there is a dialogical element to repentance. Repentance involves seeking what is right and is thus, at least in part, an epistemological exercise through which one seeks revelation and is held accountable to God through self-scrutiny.[68] Yet repentance is also a transformative activity in which one's entire life must be altered.[69] It is in the process of transformation that one's understanding is developed. Understanding in the *Shepherd* is thus not a purely mental activity. Rather, understanding takes place through the renewal of the individual's life who is part of, is joined by, and is encouraged with the community of believers. This comprehensive interpretation of repentance originates with God, is mediated to human beings, and demands human action. In so doing, the community's issues with wealth along with their faltering and double-minded commitment to God can be put right, and their lives may be single-mindedly dedicated to the God who created them.

---

68. Cox Miller (1988, 332) goes so far as to suggest that one way of translating μετάνοια in the *Shepherd* is as a "change of consciousness." See also Lipsett (2011, 19-53); Blidstein (2017, 146).

69. Osiek (1999, 28-30); Batovici (2015d, 163-9).

Hermas as a Model of Repentance

Double-mindedness, wealth, and repentance are key ways in which the *Shepherd* addresses the community. Yet the transformation that the text envisions for its readers in repentance is modeled within the narrative by Hermas himself.[70] This may be most clearly indicated by Hermas's interactions with women at the beginning and end of the text. When Hermas meets Rhoda, he begins to love her as a sister (Vis. 1.1.1 [1.1]). When he sees her bathing and helps her out of the Tiber, however, he notices her beauty and thinks that he would be happy to have such a wife of similar beauty and character (Vis. 1.1.2 [1.2]). For this, Rhoda accuses him of a desire for evil (Vis. 1.1.8 [1.8]). Although the observance of beauty and character may be benign on its own, the desire to do evil brings death and captivity upon oneself. The focus on desire is confirmed in Hermas's first conversation with the woman-revealer (Vis. 1.2.4 [2.4]). Despite the severity of Rhoda's critique, however, she holds out hope that God will heal Hermas's sins if he prays to God (Vis. 1.1.9 [1.9]).

Hermas's repentance appears to be complete, or at least nearly so, when he interacts with the twelve virgins in the tower of Sim. 9. He is instructed to stay with the virgins in the tower by the shepherd in order to free the shepherd to go elsewhere (Sim. 9.10.5 [87.5]). This ensures that Hermas is not utterly alone (Sim. 9.10.6 [87.6]), but it leaves him alone with the virgins (Sim. 9.10.7 [87.7]). Although he is initially ashamed to stay with them (Sim. 9.11.3 [88.3]), Hermas begins to play with the virgins and enjoys their singing and dancing (Sim. 9.11.4–5 [88.4–5]). He spends the night with them beside the tower. He sleeps in the midst of the virgins on their linen tunics and joins them in unceasing prayer throughout the night (Sim. 9.11.7 [88.7]). While he is with the virgins overnight, he takes the words of the Lord as his meal (Sim. 9.11.8 [88.8]). Whereas Hermas loved Rhoda as a sister but seems to have wanted more when seeing her in the river (Vis. 1.1.1–2 [1.1–2]), the virgins look at Hermas as a brother (Sim. 9.11.3 [88.3]).[71] The close connections between these scenes of Hermas interacting with women and their placement at the start and near the end of the *Shepherd* suggest that these scenes play something like the role of an *inclusio*. This is closely connected with the quest for manliness on which Hermas is sent. He is instructed to "be a man" or "be courageous" in Vis. 1.4.3 (ἀνδρίζου; 4.3), and the commandment to carry out his ministry "in a manly way" or "courageously" (*viriliter*) is one of the last things that Hermas hears in this story (Sim. 10.4.1 [114.1]).[72] Although Hermas's thoughts about Rhoda give rise to her accusations against him, his night with the virgins demonstrate the transformation that repentance effects in one's life both by

---

70. Maier (1997, 142).

71. See similarly Young (1994, 251).

72. On the resolution of manliness in the *Shepherd*, see Young (1994, 250–3); Lipsett (2011, 34–6).

showing the different actions that may occur (e.g., prayer without ceasing) and the transformed judgments that result from repentance.

Hermas's interactions with women at the beginning and end of the narrative encourage one to see Hermas as a model. Elsewhere in the *Shepherd*, he exhibits other sins that the *Shepherd* emphasizes. Most importantly, Hermas is characterized as double-minded and has been involved in business practices that may have been dishonorably executed. Even after seeing the first tower vision and hearing the shepherd's mandates, Hermas doubts whether he is able to keep the commandments. As a result, the shepherd castigates him for his double-mindedness (Sim. 6.1.1–2 [61.1–2]; see also Mand. 12.4.2 [47.2]). He has also been wealthy (Vis. 3.6.7 [14.7]), and the dishonesty that now makes him weep may be connected to his previous business practices (Mand. 3.3, 5 [28.3, 5]). For this reason, Hermas may be able to speak most effectively to the double-minded (Vis. 3.4.3 [12.3]). Yet Hermas also exemplifies what it means to repent throughout the *Shepherd*. When he confesses his deceit, he is told to live honestly so that he does not grieve the spirit of holiness and truth (Mand. 3.4 [28.4]). Hermas's prayer of confession is also recorded before the first tower vision, and the woman listens to his prayer when she comes. She is not content simply to allow Hermas to confess his sins, however, but also encourages Hermas to pray for righteousness (Vis. 3.1.5–6 [9.5–6]). Hermas's repentance grows as he dialogues with the woman and the shepherd.[73] The result of his repentance and the revelations that result from these visions include an increase in Hermas's understanding.

Repentance alters Hermas's way of thinking and goes on to transform the essence of his entire being.[74] The transformation that repentance brings about may be described most powerfully by the transition from old age to youth in the tower visions. The change in the woman's appearance at the end of Vis. 3 mirrors changes within Hermas's own person, and "those who have repented through and through are made new" (οἱ οὖν μετανοήσαντες ὁλοτελῶς νέοι ἔσονται; Vis. 3.13.4 [21.4]). Likewise, when Hermas is with the virgins, his youth is demonstrated by playing and dancing with the virgins (Sim. 9.11.5 [88.5]). The potency of repentance is such that the best metaphor with which to describe it is a reversal of the very process of aging that is common to all human beings. Hermas provides a model that should be used by readers in order to inspire and instruct their own repentance as they seek to be transformed into people who unite flesh and spirit as they are clothed in holiness with the power of the virgins.

---

73. Lipsett (2011, 41–2) draws particular attention to the conversations with the shepherd when she writes: "The dialogic elements in the *Mandates* work to remind the reader that Hermas is not merely receiving instruction, but undergoing transformation—an active, though erratic, discursive process."

74. For a narrative reading of Vis. 1–4, see Tagliabue (2020).

10. Sin and Repentance

Conclusion

The imagery of age reversal in the woman and in Hermas is illustrative of the power that the author of the *Shepherd* attributes to repentance. The community suffers from double-mindedness, economic inequality, misplaced longings for prestige and growth in business practices, and misdirected desires that result in improper speech, irascibility, and grief. The chief salve that the woman and the shepherd offer for these ailments is repentance—a reordering of desires that results in epistemologically fresh ways of understanding and is borne out through transformations that are evident throughout the apocalypse. Hermas's transformation is apparent even in the Visions and is mirrored by the woman who teaches Hermas. The changes that occur to him become even more drastic when his interactions with the virgins in the tower of Sim. 9 are compared to what is said about Hermas and Rhoda at the beginning of the work. The use of such imagery in the text's depiction of repentance leads to the topic of the next chapter: imagery and metaphors within the *Shepherd*.

Chapter 11

METAPHORS AND IMAGERY IN THE *SHEPHERD*: THE TOWER AND THE HOUSE

The *Shepherd* is a rich text that can be studied with a view to multiple elements in and around the story, including its literary, historical, and theological significance. This chapter returns to a more explicit literary study such as was taken up in Chapter 6. It does so by exploring the way in which metaphors are utilized within the *Shepherd* and takes two metaphors as exemplary of the consistent and thoroughgoing use of images throughout the *Shepherd*. In order to explore the importance of metaphors and imagery in the *Shepherd*, the chapter unfolds in three primary sections. It opens by reflecting on other metaphor studies in the study of Christian origins and comparing these to the *Shepherd*. The plethora of images found in the text mean that the *Shepherd* can contribute much to our knowledge of early Christians' use of metaphors. The chapter continues with a study of the tower visions as examples of pedagogy through images. The woman and the shepherd both present Hermas with visions of a tower (Vis. 3; Sim. 9) and use this image to instruct Hermas about the construction of the church, its component parts, and its relation to God. The tower visions make use of additional imagery that can be profitably compared to other metaphors employed in early Christian texts, while the illustrations in the *Shepherd* can be examined with a view both to how they contribute to the *Shepherd* literarily as well as how Roman readers might interact with such pictures. The chapter concludes by bringing the tower visions into conversations with the multifaceted way in which the *Shepherd* makes use of household language. Of particular interest to this chapter is the way in which household imagery blurs the lines between Hermas's immediate family and his fellow Roman believers who read this text. Domestic idioms along with the tower imagery form a rich tapestry of metaphorical language related to physical spaces in which readers are invited to dwell.

Metaphors in Early Christian Literature

The study of the tower and house in the *Shepherd* can be placed within a larger, ongoing exploration of metaphors in early Christian literature. These studies in Christian origins are, in turn, participants in larger discussions of metaphor that have taken place in the humanities following the linguistic turn. Although there are a number of important philosophical studies of metaphor to which scholars of early Christianity regularly make reference,[1] the definition of a metaphor with the most enduring impact on early Christian studies likely comes from Janet Martin Soskice. She usefully defines a metaphor as "that figure of speech whereby we speak about one thing in terms which are seen to be suggestive of another."[2] Metaphors are an evocative mode of communication that often make use of images or concepts from daily life. These are at least the types of images and metaphors that are explored in this chapter. As will be evident as the chapter progresses, towers and households are set in bewildering locations in the *Shepherd* and yet the images draw on objects known to readers from their everyday lives.

Lest one think that metaphors are merely decorative elements placed into literary works, however, it is worth recalling the ways in which imagery can function within the lives of individuals and communities. Metaphors have the capacity to shape the way in which cognitive meaning is made and reality is understood. As Lakoff and Johnson have so memorably put it, "Metaphors have the power to create a new reality."[3] This reality-shaping potential is worthy of consideration as one reflects on the variety of images that Hermas is given by the revelatory agents that he encounters. Moreover, if metaphors are widely used within particular social gatherings, they come to shape group identity.[4] This capacity is enhanced when images are used prominently within a text or assembly.[5] Given the amount of space that is allotted to Hermas's tower visions and the consistent repetition of household language throughout the *Shepherd*, this chapter seeks to analyze the function of these images within the world of the text. Such a study can be extended by considering how these images might affect early readers of the text, although the limited evidence for how second-century readers received the *Shepherd* should caution one against being overly certain in such a speculative enterprise.

The study of metaphors in early Christianity has occurred within this broad scholarly environment. In addition to methodological studies of metaphors in documents that are pertinent to Christian origins,[6] scholars have explored the ways in which metaphors interact within early Christian texts. Only a few examples can be noted here. The study of cultic metaphors has received attention with a particular focus on temple imagery and the ways in which cultic language contributes to

---

1. E.g., Richardson (1936); Black (1962); Ricoeur (1978); Booth (1979). Nor is it only recent scholars who have been interested in how to define metaphors. For Greco-Roman definitions of metaphors, see Aristotle, *Poet.* 1457b; Quintilian, *Inst.* 8.6.8.

2. Soskice (1985, 15).

3. Lakoff and Johnson (2003, 145).

4. See further Heim (2017, 104–10).

5. For further methodological reflection on metaphors, see the contributions in Gibbs (2008).

6. E.g., Kieffer (1998).

early Christian conceptions of worship.[7] Paul's adoption metaphors have also been explored,[8] while the language of sonship has also been taken up and compared with similar Roman political language.[9] The function of apocalyptic imagery has likewise been usefully situated within its Jewish and Christian literary contexts and examined with a view to how it contributes to early Christian cosmologies.[10] These studies contribute to an increased awareness among students of Christian origins of the variety of ways in which early Christians employed language as well as the power of such imagistic language to frame not only a text but also readers' imaginations and senses of identity. The tower and household portrayals play a programmatic role in aiding readers of the *Shepherd* to understand how God is at work among the community of believers and what believers' corresponding identity and responsibilities are.

The Tower

The tower visions in Vis. 3 and Sim. 9 provide a rough framing device in the *Shepherd*. Both the woman and the shepherd show Hermas a vision of a tower that is under construction. Their visions occur relatively early (Vis. 3) and relatively late (Sim. 9) in the text. In both cases, the tower consists of the longest single point of focus that the woman or the shepherd puts before Hermas. This section explores the imagery of the tower and certain elements employed in the tower visions in order to reflect on both the symbolism of the metaphors and the way in which these pictures make meaning in the *Shepherd*. After briefly sketching the narratives around the tower visions, the significance of the tower is explored with regard to two factors: its depiction of unity in the community and its portrayal of holiness among its readers. This examination of the tower will then give way to a larger exploration of the symbols in Vis. 3 and Sim. 9 as well as an examination of how these symbols may be related to other early Christian imagery.

The woman shows Hermas a vision of a tower which he struggles to see without her aid (Vis. 3.2.4 [10.4]). Hermas is able, with the woman's help, to see a tower that is being built out of stones on top of a body of water (Vis. 3.2.5–9 [10.5–9]). The significance of the tower eludes him. When the woman wants to leave after showing him the tower, Hermas asks her what the purpose of him seeing the vision was if he is unable to understand it (Vis. 3.3.1 [11.1]). The woman gives

---

7. Legarth (1992); Kieffer (2000); Beale (2004); Hogeterp (2006); Attridge (2010); Gupta (2010); van Nes (2015); Brouwer (2018); Lookadoo (2018); Regev (2018; 2019). See also the older study of architectural metaphors in Paul in Howson (1868, 40–86). Insofar as these studies explore spatial concepts in the Pauline letter, they may be seen as part of what Maier (2015, 144) refers to as a "spatial turn" in New Testament scholarship.

8. E.g., Burke (2006); Heim (2017).

9. Peppard (2012).

10. Adams (2007); Newsom (2014, 208–9).

in and offers an extended interpretation of the tower, those who are involved in the tower's construction, and the stones that are utilized in the tower (Vis. 3.3.2–3.8.11 [11.2–16.11]). Her interpretation culminates with a series of instructions addressed to Hermas and his readers (Vis. 3.9.1–9 [17.1–9]) before the woman's identity and polymorphic appearances are explained to Hermas by a young man (Vis. 3.10.1–3.13.4 [18.1–21.4]).

The shepherd's interpretation of the second tower vision occurs in partial fulfillment of the shepherd's stated purpose for coming to Hermas in Vis. 5.5 (25.5): to show Hermas again all the things that he saw earlier. Whereas Hermas met the woman in a field near where he worked (Vis. 3.1.2–4 [9.2–4]), the shepherd takes Hermas to an otherworldly mountainous location in Arcadia (Sim. 9.1.4 [78.4]).[11] In addition to seeing a series of mountains surrounding him, Hermas finds a tall tower that has an enormous rock with a gate recently chiseled into it (Sim. 9.2.1–2 [79.1–2]). Those who are involved in the construction of the tower order that all stones that are to be used in the tower must enter into the tower by means of the gate (Sim. 9.3.4 [80.4]). The vision of the tower that Hermas receives from the shepherd takes more space to explain than the one that he received earlier. Indeed, it takes so much longer that there are two pauses in the construction, one before the lord of the tower comes to test the stones (Sim. 9.5.1–7 [82.1–7]) and another when the shepherd leaves at the end of the construction before interpreting the vision to him (Sim. 9.10.4–9.11.8 [87.4–88.8]). The shepherd's interpretation of the tower and its environs is likewise longer than the first explanation that Hermas received and stretches from Sim. 9.11.9–9.33.3 (88.9–110.3).

These lengthy visions form a memorable part of the *Shepherd* due to the detailed allegorical explanation of how the tower—which of course represents the community of believers—is in the process of being constructed.[12] Although there are a number of differences between the two visions that Hermas sees, the tower symbolizes unity in both visions. The woman tells Hermas that the tower represents the entire ἐκκλησία (Vis. 3.3.3 [11.3]). While the woman's identity is likewise tied to the tower, no attempt is made to distinguish between geographical locales or various groups of believers. All believers are depicted in the tower. Each part of the tower is also built on the same foundation. In Vis. 3, the tower is surreally constructed on water (Vis. 3.2.4 [10.4]; 3.3.5 [11.5]), while the tower is erected on top of the rock in Sim. 9 (Sim. 9.3.1 [80.1]; 9.4.2 [81.2]). The unity of the tower's construction is further highlighted in the vision that is mediated by the shepherd because the virgins who join the young men in building the tower must be the ones who set the stones in the tower (9.3.4 [80.4]; 9.4.3, 5–8 [81.3, 5–8]). Each of the stones that will be left in the tower must come by means of the virgins

---

11. Harris (1887; 1896, 1–20). For more on Arcadia in Sim. 9, see also the literature cited in Körtner and Leutzsch (1998, 301n.271).

12. On the use of tower imagery in early Christian art, see Brox (1991, 71–4); Osiek (1999, 7–8).

through the gate (9.3.4 [80.4]; 9.4.1 [81.1]). If they do not enter by such means, the stones turn a different color and must be thrown out (Sim. 9.4.6–8 [81.6–8]).

Thus another way in which unity is represented in the tower has to do with the outward appearance of the stones that comprise the tower. As Hermas sits next to the woman, he notices that the stones are placed in the tower "so that their joints are not visible" (ὥστε τὴν ἁρμογὴν αὐτῶν μὴ φαίνεσθαι).[13] "The construction of the tower looked like it was constructed from one stone" (ἐφαίνετο δὲ ἡ οἰκοδομὴ τοῦ πύργου ὡς ἐξ ἑνὸς λίθου ᾠκοδομημένη; Vis. 3.2.6 [10.6]).[14] Hermas likewise admires the tower at the end of the shepherd's vision "as if from one stone, not having one joint in it" (ὡσὰν ἐξ ἑνὸς λίθου μὴ ἔχων μίαν ἁρμογὴν ἐν ἑαυτῷ). The tower has a close connection to the rock on which it is founded because it appears to Hermas that it is hewn from the rock. The entire building appears to be μονόλιθος (Sim. 9.9.7 [86.7]). The union of the tower is likewise shown in the change that occurs in the stones upon entering into the tower. As both the woman and the shepherd make clear in their interpretations, the stones are of various colors and qualities. Yet in the second vision, they become white and lose their various colors upon entering into the tower (Sim. 9.4.5 [81.5]). As the building materials, which represent believers, are incorporated into this unique building, they take their place in something larger than any individual stone and join with the others who are in the process of being integrated. When the lord of the tower comes to test the stones, those who belong in the tower are implicitly assumed to remain intact. Other stones turn black, become rough, or crack when they are struck (Sim. 9.6.4–5 [83.4–5]), and these stones are cast out of the tower to make way for others.

While the tower clearly symbolizes unity as believers are brought into the tower, the tower visions also call the *Shepherd*'s readers to holiness.[15] The white color of the stones in the second vision recalls purity and cleanliness (Sim. 9.4.5 [81.5]).[16] The stones that are tested by the lord of the tower and do not withstand the strike from his rod are removed from the tower (Sim. 9.6.4–5 [83.4–5]). Removal from the tower is a result of not entering into the tower by the right means or of living in a way that does not coincide with the lifestyle that should

---

13. Tagliabue (2017, 234). Tagliabue's study of allegorical images in Vis. 1–4 is instructive throughout.

14. Similar language may be used to describe the way in which the virgins carry the stones into the tower. Ehrman (2003, 393) translates Sim. 9.3.5 (80.5) as "they were carrying them together like a single stone" (κατὰ ἕνα λίθον ἐβάσταζον ὁμοῦ). The prepositional phrase κατὰ ἕνα λίθον may also be understood distributively so that the virgins carry the stones "stone by stone" or "one at a time." Although I think that the distributive translation is preferable, the ambiguity is intriguing and the use of ὁμοῦ highlights the unity of the builders regardless of how one translates the prepositional phrase.

15. On the paraenetic function of Vis. 3, see Blomkvist (2011, 857–8); Tagliabue (2017, 236–7).

16. On the links between white and purity, see Blidstein (2017, 127n.70).

characterize the community.¹⁷ In the shepherd's vision, Hermas learns that all stones must enter the tower by being carried by the virgins through the gate (Sim. 9.4.8 [81.8]). The builders of the tower in Vis. 3 incorporate stones that come from the deep and some of those that come from dry land (Vis. 3.2.6–7 [10.6–7]). Other stones from the dry land or from nearby the tower are thrown away to various distances from the tower (Vis. 3.2.7–9 [10.7–9]). The stones that are thrown away from the tower represent lawless, hypocritical, and double-minded believers (Vis. 3.6.1–3.7.3 [14.1–15.3]). Those that remain in the tower live well and may even suffer for the Lord (Vis. 3.5.1–4 [13.1–4]). A similar phenomenon is found in Sim. 9. The lord of the tower instructs the shepherd to clean the stones in the tower but to throw away those that do not fit (Sim. 9.7.2 [84.2]).

All is not lost, however, for those who are thrown away or do not fit initially. When Hermas asks the shepherd how stones that are rejected can be put back into the tower, he learns that the shepherd will trim the stones himself (Sim. 9.7.4 [84.4]). Those that are smaller after being trimmed will be placed in the central portion of the tower, while those that are larger will support them in the outer walls of the tower (Sim. 9.7.5 [85.5]). The woman likewise retains hope for those stones that are thrown away from the tower. When Hermas asks her about the possibility of repentance for rejected stones, she tells him that there will be a place for such stones in the tower. Yet this place will be inferior and will only be granted after they repent and fulfill the time of their sin (Vis. 3.7.5–6 [15.5–6]).¹⁸ The hope for repentance is enhanced when one recalls the closing instructions given by the woman and the shepherd in each vision. The woman instructs her listeners to live peaceably with one another, not to overindulge or to be unfair to those who have less, and to cleanse their hearts by mixing wisdom into their heart (Vis. 3.9.1–10 [17.1–10]). The shepherd similarly tells Hermas and his readers to put themselves right "while the tower is still being built" (*dum adhuc turris aedificatur*; Sim. 9.32.1 [109.1]; see also Vis. 3.8.9 [16.9]).¹⁹ The shepherd leaves Hermas with a reminder that they had filled in certain marks on the stones. Hermas now finds that this process represents the wiping away of sins after repentance (Sim. 9.33.2–3 [110.2–3]). The tower is a place of holiness and stones are allowed to enter only if they repent and find their way into the tower by the means provided.

---

17. The testing of the stones is thus designed to keep the tower pure (Blidstein 2017, 144–5). There is a tension between the differentiation in the placement of the stones in the tower and the references to the unjointed and monolithic portrayals of the finished tower. This tension allows the *Shepherd* to recognize the individuality of particular believers while likewise giving full credence to depiction of the united people of God.

18. See also the reference to differentiated places within the tower in Sim. 8.2.5 (68.5); 8.6.6 (72.6); 8.7.3 (73.3); 8.8.3 (74.3).

19. Zahn (1868, 207–9).

Imagery and Interpretation within the Tower Visions

Thus far the analysis of the temple has interpreted the tower visions by paying attention to two chief ways in which the imagery contributes to the life of the community, namely, by encouraging unity and holiness among the readers. Three further lines of inquiry can be pressed regarding the tower as a whole before looking to other imagery within the tower visions. First, the preceding discussion of repentance leads into a long-standing discussion about the relationship between what is ideal and what is real in the tower visions. Second, one may also explore areas of overlap between the tower and temple imagery in early Christian literature. Finally, this section examines the multifaceted way in which the tower visions may have intersected with the lived experiences of Roman believers in the second century. Points of intersection include the likely living spaces of the *Shepherd*'s audience, the building materials mentioned by the woman and the shepherd, and the locations from which those materials originated.

The repetition of the tower visions in Vis. 3 and Sim. 9 has led interpreters to reflect on why two such similar visions occur in the *Shepherd*. Some interpreters have found the rationale in the contrast between an ideal church depicted in Vis. 3 and a real church portrayed in the tower of Sim. 9. Dibelius thinks that Vis 3 deals "von der idealen" while Sim. 9 considers "der sündigen und durch Buße zu reinigenden Kirche."[20] Zahn regards the woman's depiction of the tower as "die triumphirende Kirche" and the shepherd's tower vision as "die empirische Kirche."[21] Joly argues for a similar understanding using slightly different terms. For him, Vis. 3 represents "l'Église céleste" and Sim. 9 "l'Église terrestre."[22] However, there are signs in both visions that point both to the ideal of what the collective community ought to be like and to the reality that believers do not yet live in the way that the mediators instruct.[23] The incomplete nature of the tower and the continued calls to repentance in both Vis. 3 and Sim. 9 speak against such facile distinctions. The tower visions present a stunning picture of how believers are brought together through baptism and the Son, but neither vision shies away from noting that some stones in the tower require continued refining.

While the complicated picture of the tower that emerges from close study of Vis. 3 and Sim. 9 makes it difficult to set up simple distinctions between the two, the dual focus of the imagery on both unity and holiness fits with temple metaphors found elsewhere in early Christian literature. Since the tower is both the locus and the focus of God's work in Vis. 3 and Sim. 9, it is worth noting connections between temple metaphors elsewhere in early Christian literature. For example, Ephesians employs temple imagery to describe the unity that has

---

20. Dibelius (1923, 602).
21. Zahn (1868, 222). See also Vielhauer (1979, 149); Henne (1992c, 486–7).
22. Joly (1968, 288). For further references, see Brox (1991, 375–6).
23. Osiek (1999, 212). See similarly Walsh (2019b, 479n.45).

come about between Jews and Gentiles in Christ (Eph 2:19–21),[24] and Ignatius urges the Magnesians to run together to one temple at the close of a section that encourages unity with the bishop (Ign. *Magn.* 7.2; see also Ign. *Magn.* 6.1–7.2).[25] Other early Christian texts utilize temple metaphors to promote harmony among believers (e.g., 1 Cor 3:16–17; Ign. *Eph.* 9.1; 15.3; *Barn.* 4.11). The *Shepherd*'s tower visions are thus not alone in employing sacred building imagery to portray unity among believers. Nor is the *Shepherd* the only text to insist that such metaphorical language requires holiness of believers who are being incorporated into God's building. Paul employs a temple metaphor to insist on sexual purity (1 Cor 6:13–20). Likewise, although the imagery is employed for different ends within each text, *2 Clem.* 9.3, *Acts Paul* 3.5, and Ign. *Phld.* 7.2 link the purity of the flesh to God's temple.[26] Like the other texts, the *Shepherd*'s tower visions emphasize the unity and holiness of God's people. The *Shepherd*'s depiction of believers as a tower that is under construction by agents of God thus fits with the rhetorical aims of temple metaphors that are scattered across other early Christian texts during the first two centuries CE.

Although the tower is a literary creation and as such can be usefully read alongside metaphors elsewhere in early Christian literature, it is also a text that was likely read by believers living in and around Rome. While the archeological remains of senatorial homes on the hills may be memorable to the modern imagination, many early believers likely lived in crowded *insulae*.[27] Some apartments may have been for Rome's elites, but most buildings likely had a mixture of wealthy, subsistence, and impoverished residents.[28] Such evidence fits well with the socioeconomic mix described in the *Shepherd*. If Roman believers lived in the tenement houses of certain Roman mercantile neighborhoods,[29] then Andrew Wallace-Hadrill's encouragement to understand the archeological evidence pointing to a situation in which those with and without means lived side

---

24. Regev (2019, 61) points out that the Ephesian temple and building imagery also depicts the Ephesians as a model of holiness in which God dwells.

25. Legarth (1992, 218–31); Kieffer (2000, 298–9).

26. For readings of these statements in the context of other early Christian literature, see Lightfoot (1885–9, 1.2.230); Knopf (1920, 166); Ebner (2005, 68–9); Lookadoo (2018, 122–6).

27. I refer here to the domestic spaces as *insulae* and not to the blocks of land created by Roman streets.

28. For a study of housing remains in nearby Ostia, see DeLaine (2012). Horrell (2004; 2019, 27–48) explores domestic space in Corinth.

29. As described in Lampe (2003, 50–4). Even if one does not accept Lampe's precise analysis of the archeological evidence, the present description can be allowed to stand if a mix of people with different amounts of wealth lived nearby one another in first- and second-century Rome.

by side couples well with the *Shepherd*'s depiction of a community in which rich and poor believers must coexist and cooperate.[30]

Harry Maier, considering this evidence from the spaces that Roman believers are likely to have inhabited, proposes that the tower offers its audience a new way in which to imagine the spaces in which they lived.[31] By employing the concept of "thirdspace,"[32] Maier argues that the author of the *Shepherd* offers a new way of conceptualizing reality. No longer is the *insula* merely a cramped place in which to live. The author "takes the physical location and practices associated with the *insulae* of first and second century Rome and revisits those spaces with the help of an imagination steeped in apocalypse."[33] The apartments of Rome are precisely the locations in which God is at work incorporating believers into God's building. If Roman *insulae* had a role in the author's or readers' imaginations of the tower, it is notable that the towers in Vis. 3 and Sim. 9 are transferred from the likely living places of Hermas and his neighbors in Rome to surreal locations on the water or in Arcadia. In so doing, the author invites readers to see their humdrum spaces in a new light and to reconceive of the community with fresh eyes.

Another way in which readers are invited to rethink space when reading the tower visions can be found when the revealers describe the building materials to Hermas. While the people are depicted as stones in the tower, the pluriformity with which they appear reminds readers that believers have varied prior experiences and choices to make as they seek to be unified in the tower. If the tower presents believers as a collective body, stone imagery recognizes the individuality of each believer.[34]

The stones have different fates and are placed in distinct locations within the tower based on how they have lived. After Hermas's description of the building process (Vis. 3.2.4–9 [10.4–9]),[35] the woman's interpretation of the stones groups them into three broad categories. The first group is brought into the building and includes apostles, teachers, those who have suffered for the Lord's name, and those

---

30. Wallace-Hadrill (2003, 13–14); Maier (2015, 149–52). See also the floor plans that Wallace-Hadrill (2003, 16–17) has reconstructed for the first four floors of the Insula Aracoeli.

31. Maier (2015). For the use of thirdspace in relation to other early Christian literature, see also Maier (2013a, 103–4; 2013b; 2017).

32. Maier borrows this term from Edward Soja (1996, 10), who defines thirdspace as "an-Other way of understanding and acting to change the spatiality of human life, a distinct mode of critical spatial awareness."

33. Maier (2015, 156).

34. A similar phenomenon is found in Ign. *Eph.* 9.1, where the Ephesians are described as individual stones that are being incorporated into the Father's temple and God's building. On the use of construction imagery in Ign. *Eph.* 9.1 and building projects in second-century Antioch and Ephesus, see Corwin (1960, 37–8); Schoedel (1985, 67).

35. Harkins (2020, 63–5) rightly observes the kinesthetic quality of the narrator's description of the tower's construction.

whom the Lord has approved (Vis. 3.5.1-4 [13.1-4]). The woman also mentions stones that are not thrown far from the tower and that represent those who have sinned but desire to repent (Vis. 3.5.5 [13.5]). This group differs from the second major set, which are those who are broken and thrown far from the tower. These are not beneficial in the construction of the tower because they are wicked (Vis. 3.6.1-7 [14.1-7]). The final cluster of stones includes those that are thrown far from the tower and then make a secondary move, such as falling into the fire or rolling near the water. These stones stand for those who have rejected their place in the tower by thinking that there is a better way or by repenting to evil desires (Vis. 3.7.1-3 [15.1-3]). When Hermas asks about the possibility of repentance for stones that have been cast away from the building, the woman responds that those who repent will not be placed in the tower but will fit into an inferior place (Vis. 3.7.5-6 [15.5-6]).[36]

As with most of Sim. 9, the shepherd's description of the stones is more elaborate. The shepherd not only describes the stones in themselves but narrates two inspections of the stones in and around the tower. The first inspection is conducted by the lord of the tower (Sim. 9.6.1-8 [83.1-8]), while the second is overseen by the shepherd with Hermas's assistance (Sim. 9.8.1-9.9.7 [85.1-86.7]). The lord of the tower removes defective stones from the building, while the shepherd makes many of the stones around the tower suitable for placement in the tower. Those which the shepherd deems unsuitable must be cleared away from the tower. The stones that are initially rejected by the lord of the tower represent believers who have received the Son of God but who are ultimately led away by the vices that are depicted by the women in black (Sim. 9.13.6-9 [90.6-9]). The stones that are included in the tower after the shepherd trims them represent those who repent after straying (Sim. 9.14.1-2 [91.1-2]).[37] These stones are placed in varying places in the tower. For example, rough stones that are trimmed are placed in the middle of the building, while cracked stones that are trimmed are placed in the exterior because they are stronger (Sim. 9.8.2-3 [85.2-3]). Yet not all stones are included in the tower. As in Vis. 3, the stones have different fates and are placed in various locations within the tower.

Perhaps the most notable change in Sim. 9, however, comes in the connection of the Son of God with the stones. The Son of God is described as a rock (πέτρα) and provides the foundation upon which the tower is set (Sim. 9.2.1 [79.1]; 9.3.1

36. Brox (1989b) rightly emphasizes that the way in which the stones are differentiated should increase both the speed and the earnestness with which the audience acts to repent.

37. The shepherd's testing of the stones after a period during which the stones are left outside fits well with the description of stone quarrying in Vitruvius, *Architectura* 2.7.5; Pliny the Elder, *Nat.* 36.170. Pliny notes that a two-year preparatory period can provide a remedy for stones that are of doubtful quality, while Vitruvius's information may be of particular interest because of his location in Augustan Rome. If one follows Rüpke (1999, 155-8) in seeing the white stones in the tower visions with reference to salt, then images of salt mining may take the place of rock quarrying.

[80.1]; 9.12.1–2 [89.1–2]). Believers are then depicted as stones (λίθοι) of varying sizes and from different places throughout Sim. 9. Although the words are not etymologically linked, they are conceptually close to one another. The depiction of both the Son and believers as stones connects believers with the Son.[38] A similar use of stone imagery can be found in 1 Peter. The author refers to Jesus as the "living stone" (λίθον ζῶντα) and urges believers to come to him (1 Pet 2:4). Believers are then called "living stones" (λίθοι ζῶντες) that are in the process of becoming a spiritual house (1 Pet 2:5).[39] The connection between Jesus and believers is clearer in 1 Pet 2:4–5 because the author employs the same words as part of the same sentence. Yet the *Shepherd* employs similar imagery in Sim. 9 and ultimately ties the stone and rock together when Hermas notices that the stone tower appears to come out of the rock: "And the stone appeared to have been chiseled from the rock" (ἐφαίνετο δὲ ὁ λίθος ὡς ἐκ τῆς πέτρας ἐκκεκολαμμένος; Sim. 9.9.7 [86.7]).

The stones in Vis. 3 and Sim. 9 not only come to diverse ends but also have varied origins. Two areas from which stones originate are deserving of attention before turning to consider household language in the *Shepherd*. These can be loosely divided into stones from the water and stones from the land.

Water forms the foundation of the tower in Vis. 3 "because your life was saved and will be saved through water" (ὅτι ἡ ζωὴ ὑμῶν διὰ ὕδατος ἐσώθη καὶ σωθήσεται; Vis. 3.3.5 [11.5]). The water is thus representative of the baptism that initiates Hermas and his community into the tower.[40] Certain stones in the woman's vision come from the deep (ἐκ τοῦ βυθοῦ) and are placed in the tower without further modification (Vis. 3.2.5–6 [10.5–6]). The woman later explains to Hermas that these stones represent those who have suffered for the name of the Lord (Vis. 3.5.2 [13.2]). The water and the deep are thus distinguished in Vis. 3 with the water explicitly linked to baptism and the deep to the realm of the dead who have suffered. This distinction is not kept as tightly in Sim. 9.[41] The foundation of the tower has changed from water to the rock and the door (Sim. 9.2.1–2 [79.1–2]; 9.12.1–3 [89.1–3]). Stones from the deep (ἐκ τοῦ βυθοῦ) provide the next level of stones for the tower and depict the righteous who have died, prophets, apostles, and teachers (Sim. 9.15.4 [92.4]). After another question from Hermas, the shepherd goes on to explain that these stones must come through the water (δι' ὕδατος) in order to be made alive (Sim. 9.16.2 [93.2]). The water again appears to be connected to baptism,[42] but the shepherd conflates the water and

---

38. Such close connections are aided by elements of the story. For example, the stones must enter into the tower through the door, which likewise represents the Son (Sim. 9.2.2 [79.2]; 9.12.1, 3 [89.1, 3]).

39. See further Feldmeier (2008, 132, 135–6); Regev (2019, 62).

40. Dibelius (1923, 440–1); Blomkvist (2011, 859–60); Grundeken (2015a, 129). On the various ways in which water is utilized in the *Shepherd*, see Henne (1989, 131).

41. See further Walsh (2019b, 482–7).

42. For further discussion, see, e.g., Osiek (1999, 238); Ferguson (2009, 217–20); Blomkvist (2011, 864–5); Sandnes (2011, 1454); Grundeken (2015a, 131).

the deep in a way that the woman does not. While water is a place from which stones are raised into the tower in both of Hermas's visions, the woman maintains a distinction that the shepherd blurs in the latter telling.

Later, however, the shepherd clarifies something that is either implicit or incomplete in the woman's interpretation. When Hermas asks for an interpretation of the mountains, the shepherd links the twelve mountains to "the twelve tribes that inhabit the whole world" (δώδεκα φυλαί εἰσιν αἱ κατοικοῦσαι ὅλον τὸν κόσμον; Sim. 9.17.1 [94.1]).[43] The twelve tribes are described as twelve nations (δώδεκα ἔθνη) with diverse ways of thinking (Sim. 9.17.2 [94.2]).[44] The shepherd takes up language that is traditionally applied to Israel and reapplies it to the entire world. All of the rocks that are placed in the tower come from these mountains with the exception of the stones that come from the deep. The stones from the mountain are thus called by the name of God's Son and are unified in their thinking and faith (Sim. 9.17.4 [94.4]).[45] In the explanation that follows (Sim. 9.19.1–9.29.3 [96.1–106.3]), the mountains yield people who do evil and those who act righteously.[46] Not only is the shepherd's interpretation no longer bound by geography or cultural connections, the twelve tribes do not even signify the people of God. Rather, they are extended to the entire world. The shepherd's startling interpretation may stem, however, from the woman's explanation of the stones in Vis. 3.5.1–3.7.3 (13.1–15.3). In addition to the apostles, bishops, teachers, and deacons whose origins are not described (Vis. 3.5.1 [13.1]), the woman lists twelve total groups that are symbolized by the stones, eleven of which come from the land (Vis. 3.5.2–3.7.3 [13.2–15.3]).[47] The shepherd then completes this number by appealing to twelve mountains as a way of describing the cosmos.

While further distinctions can be found between the two visions, this study has shown that the elements within the tower visions contribute richly to the interpretations of Vis. 3 and Sim. 9. The woman and the shepherd mediate visions that call believers to unity but that acknowledge both the individuality of the community's members as well as flaws within the community as it is. Through these visions, the mediators are able to discuss additional topics of importance to

---

43. On the use of ὅλος and holistic phrases in the *Shepherd*, see Verheyden (2015, 590–3).
44. Bauckham (2017, 108–9).
45. Svigel (2016, 267).
46. Henne (1989, 131).
47. After the woman mentions the square white stones that fit precisely with one another (i.e., the apostles and others), she tells Hermas about (1) stones from the depths of the water that fit with one another; (2) stones carried from the dry land; (3) those who are still being placed in the building; (4) stones that are rejected and thrown away; (5) stones that are broken down and thrown far from the tower; (6) some that are lying around but not entering the building; (7) stones with cracks; (8) stones that are too short; (9) stones that are white and round; (10) stones that are thrown far from the tower and roll off the road; (11) stones that are thrown far from the tower and fall into the fire; and (12) stones that are thrown far from the tower and fall near the water without being able to enter the water.

the theological and social well-being of the community by repurposing everyday spaces and objects. Moreover, this way of speaking coincides nicely with some of the uses of household language in the *Shepherd*, and it is to this topic that the chapter turns next.

The House

The author of the *Shepherd* employs οἶκος-language often and in multiple ways. If the instances of *domus* are counted in the Latin translation of Sim. 10, the author employs the term nearly thirty times.[48] Mayo conveniently divides the various usages of this word into five senses.[49] The house can refer to one's place of residence and thus provides a location where revelation can take place (Vis. 2.4.2 [8.2]; Sim. 6.1.1 [61.1]). The house is also a place where hospitality should be extended to others (Sim. 8.10.3 [76.3]; 9.27.1–2 [104.1–2]). The author employs the house as a way to refer to Hermas's family, a phenomenon that is evident in Vis. 1.1.9 (1.9) and Sim. 10.1.2 (111.2). One may next understand household language with reference to the earthly city or kingdom in Sim. 1.4 (50.4). Finally, the author utilizes οἶκος-language in order to describe the community of believers. One of the clearest examples of this usage is found in the second tower vision (Sim. 9.13.9–9.14.1 [90.9–91.1]). While this division is convenient and enables one to grasp quickly the multifarious ways in which the term can be employed within the text, such a list risks missing how one sense shades into another. It is the third and fifth senses that take center stage in this section.

The *Shepherd*'s use of the term οἶκος blurs the lines between Hermas's immediate family and the community of Jesus-followers whom Hermas addresses. Hermas is assumed to be the leader of his family and can thus serve as a representative on behalf of the entire group. A key reason for Hermas's encounter with Rhoda and the woman is so that he can turn his household to the Lord (Vis. 1.3.1 [3.1]). His children's rejection of God and licentious lifestyle are closely connected to a betrayal of their parents (Vis. 2.2.2 [6.2]). The woman thus urges him to ask for righteousness so that he can take it to his house (Vis. 3.1.6 [9.6]), and the shepherd designates him more clearly as "the head of the house" (ἡ κεφαλὴ τοῦ οἴκου; Sim. 7.3 [66.3]).[50] Hermas is thus given the role of *paterfamilias* in the *Shepherd*.[51] In addition, Hermas plays this role to some degree with regard to the larger community of believers that he addresses. Hermas's revelations are mediated to

---

48. While the precise number is textually uncertain, the importance of οἶκος-terminology is enhanced when one notes that the related term οἰκοδομή is used more than seventy times in the *Shepherd*.

49. Mayo (2016, 122–56). For more on the house in the *Shepherd*, see Leutzsch (1989, 50–62).

50. Leutzsch (1989, 52).

51. Young (1994, 243–4); Mayo (2016, 163–6).

him by the woman and the shepherd, but he himself serves in the mediatory role between the community and God or God's revealers. Hermas takes a key role in speaking to the people of God and holding them to account in a way that he had previously failed to do with his own family.

One may press further, however, by exploring connections between Hermas's οἶκος and other believers. When Rhoda addresses Hermas's possibility of repentance, she mentions Hermas, his house, and all the saints (Vis. 1.1.9 [1.9]). Hermas's house is closely connected to other believers as sinners in need of repentance. This blurring of the lines between Hermas's family and other believers continues in the Mandates. The shepherd encourages Hermas to keep the commandment so that his repentance and that of his household may be single-minded (Mand. 2.7 [27.7]). The shepherd's exhortation to Hermas serves as a reminder to believers that they are responsible for family relationships in addition to themselves.[52] Since the Mandates are intended for all believers, however, the referent of the household should be understood in broader terms than Hermas's immediate family alone. The household stands for all believers.[53] The same is true of Mand. 5.1.7 (33.7), where Hermas and his house are warned against allowing angry tendencies to overcome them. The reference to Hermas and his household gives way to a promise for "all" (πάντες) who repent with their whole hearts. Just as the shepherd will be with Hermas, so also he promises to be with those who repent. The reference to the household in Mand. 12.3.6 (46.6) appears to play a similarly ambiguous role, describing both Hermas's family and all believers. The link between Hermas's children and household suggests that the household should be understood with reference to Hermas's family. Yet the shepherd's immediately preceding discussion in which he speaks of a "person" (ἄνθρωπος) being unable to keep the commandments extends this meaning to include other believers.

The lines between the *Shepherd*'s utilization of οἶκος with reference both to Hermas's immediate family and other believers is thus scattered throughout the *Shepherd* with sufficient regularity that one should not be surprised when coming across a clear reference to all believers as an οἶκος in Sim. 9.13.9–9.14.1 (90.9–91.1). The shepherd employs the term when telling Hermas why some stones were removed from the tower by the women who are dressed in black. Those who desire the qualities represented by the women are removed from God's house, while those who are not deceived remain in God's house (Sim. 9.13.9 [90.9]). When Hermas asks if it is possible to reenter God's house if they repent (Sim. 9.14.1 [91.1]), the shepherd holds out hope for their reentry if they take up the power of the virgins. He then explains, "For this is also why there was a delay of the construction" (διὰ τοῦτο γὰρ καὶ τῆς οἰκοδομῆς ἀνοχὴ ἐγένετο; Sim. 9.14.2 [91.2]). This will allow them to reenter "the construction of the tower" (ἡ οἰκοδομὴ τοῦ πύργου). The

---

52. Osiek (1999, 106).

53. Dibelius (1923, 501). One need not accept Dibelius's (1923, 445–6) arguments for a purely symbolic and unautobiographical understanding of Hermas's family in order to see the household as having some representative value.

term οἰκοδομή is used more often in the *Shepherd* and particularly in the tower visions.⁵⁴ The *Shepherd* links the building and the house in a way that goes beyond mere etymology (Sim. 9.13.9–9.14.2 [90.9–91.2]). The house, the building, and the tower can be used as synonyms that point to the same reality, namely, the people of God into which God is incorporating anyone who will enter through the Son and take up the virtues epitomized by the virgins.

The house thus takes on a significant place within the *Shepherd*. It employs an image from everyday life with which readers would of course be familiar. The author simultaneously makes use of a term that had multiple resonances. A house not only may refer to a residence in which one would be expected to welcome guests but can also denote both the people who dwell in the household and people who live together in a way that forms a new set of familial bonds. The *Shepherd* makes use of all of these meanings and, in so doing, offers a suggestive image that blurs the lines between the multiple senses that the word may connote. The household illustrates the present reality of the community. For the author of the *Shepherd*, the community is in need of repentance and purity. Yet the household is also set apart as a place where believers may belong, into which they are called, and in which they have responsibilities. Close-knit relationships are formed in the household. It is precisely these close-knit relationships that demand care for holiness from those who inhabit the household. When a life of holiness and repentance is not maintained, the relationships of believers with God and the relationships that believers have with one another suffer. The most prominent example of difficulties in interpersonal relationships concern discrepancies in wealth and commitment to the community among believers, but the *Shepherd* urges believers to look after their household in a variety of ways.

Because the lines that define the household are blurred in the *Shepherd*, Hermas is portrayed as the *paterfamilias* of both his immediate family and the audience that he addresses.⁵⁵ This is not to say that the *Shepherd* establishes Hermas as the exclusive leader of God's house that Roman readers may have known. Little is said in the *Shepherd* about precisely how the Roman community of believers was organized.⁵⁶ However, insofar as Hermas mediates the visions that he received in his house to the household of God, he plays a leading role as an interpreter and hermeneut of what God is doing, who the people of God are, and how they should act. As the leader of the household within this text, Hermas employs household imagery both to clarify the people's identity and to invite those who should repent to reenter their home. His responsibility as a leader is set out in his final conversation with the angel who handed him over to the shepherd. The angel

---

54. For οἰκοδομή in the tower visions, see, e.g., Vis. 3.2.6–8 (10.6–8); 3.4.1–2 (12.1–2); 3.5.1–5 (13.1–5); 3.6.5–6 (14.5–6); Sim. 9.1.2 (78.2); 9.3.3–4 (80.3–4); 9.7.4–7 (84.4–7); 9.9.2–4 (86.2–4); 9.15.4–6 (92.4–6); 9.17.3–4 (94.3–4).

55. Hermas thus has "as a primary task the intensification of group boundaries in order to effect a radical privatization of the οἶκος" (Young 1994, 245).

56. See the prosopographical study in Chapter 6 and the literature cited there.

promises that the virgins can stay in Hermas's house (Sim. 10.3.1 [113.1]), but Hermas must keep his house clean (*conmunda domum tuam*; Sim. 10.3.2 [113.2]). The virgins will gladly live in a clean house, but they will leave at the first sight of impurity. Hermas's charge is thus to keep his house clean or, as the angel says later in the dialogue, to "live courageously in this ministry" (*uiriliter in ministerio hoc conversare*; Sim. 10.4.1 [114.1]).[57] Yet the tower is never far from view. The angel reminds him that the work on the building has been suspended in order for people to act rightly (Sim. 10.4.4 [114.4]). The narrative then draws to a close with a promise from the angel to send the shepherd and the virgins back to Hermas to live "in my [Hermas's] house" (*in domum meam*; Sim. 10.4.5 [114.5]).

Conclusion

The tower and the household are multifaceted images that are employed in the *Shepherd* to portray believers in a variety of states. Both images allow the author to depict the community in its current flawed state and simultaneously to visualize a community in which all flaws have been removed. By using the tower, the house, and the various elements connected to these central images, the *Shepherd* draws readers into the story by employing objects from everyday life. The tower and household urge readers to think of their place in the tower and to respond in ways that are appropriate for stones in the tower and for members of the household. Yet the *Shepherd* transforms these ordinary objects in ways that enable believers to rethink both the spaces that they inhabit and the relationships that exist in the community. The tower and the household focus believers' attention on how God is at work in the audience of the *Shepherd*. Each of the images can be studied on its own, but collectively they work together to conceptualize the community with a view to both its relationship to God and believers' relationship to one another.

The *Shepherd* is a text that makes heavy use of imagery, parables, and metaphors as the woman and the shepherd educate Hermas about the community, its problems, its responsibilities, and God's activity in and for believers. This chapter hopes to have shown how two prominent images work together in order to depict the community as a place in which believers are called and in which they also have obligations for themselves and toward others. These pictures can be profitably studied on their own and in connection with one another in the *Shepherd*. Given the extensive use of other sets of imagery, such as the botanical and agrarian imagery employed in Sim. 2, 5, and 8, the examination of the *Shepherd*'s figurative way of speaking constitutes a potentially fascinating field of research. The *Shepherd*'s use of illustrations can also be explored alongside other instances of similar metaphorical language in early Christian documents. The study of imagery in the *Shepherd* can therefore be paired with metaphor studies

---

57. Young (1994).

in other early Christian literature in order to deepen our understanding of early Christian rhetoric.[58] This chapter has been more limited in its scope, but it has shown that the tower and household are central to the images employed in the *Shepherd* in order to teach Hermas and his community about the various ways in which members of the community relate to one another.

---

58. See, e.g., Soyars's (2019, 187–91) study of clothing metaphors in the Similitudes and the Pauline corpus.

Chapter 12

SPIRIT LANGUAGE IN MANDATES 5–11: FROM ANCIENT PHILOSOPHY TO CONTEMPORARY THEOLOGY

This book has attempted to be consistent in its focus on the text of the *Shepherd*. For those seeking to read the *Shepherd* well, the visions, stories, mandates, instructions, similitudes, and parables within the 114 chapters of this apocalypse must remain of foremost importance. Particular care for the *Shepherd* itself has been demonstrated in the structure of this book. Chapter 1 opened Part I by summarizing the *Shepherd*'s unwieldy narrative. Chapter 5 began Part II by placing the task of exegesis, that is, a careful interpretive reading of the *Shepherd*, at the forefront of the topical studies that have since followed. This chapter concludes the book with a similarly textual focus by offering exegetical comments on several of the Mandates. However, this chapter also illustrates how the task of exegesis may be undertaken with different emphases.[1]

In this chapter we will take up language pertaining to *spirit* in two ways. First, this chapter highlights the example of the *Shepherd*'s embeddedness within its complex Greco-Roman literary environment. In particular, it builds upon a study by Clare Rothschild in which she notes similarities between Galen's medical discussions of the spirit (πνεῦμα) and the *Shepherd*'s understanding of spirit in Mand. 5 (33.1–34.8).[2] The *Shepherd* employs similar language in Mand. 9–11 (39.1–43.21), and much of this chapter is dedicated to illustrating how the *Shepherd*'s discussion of the spirit contributes to the instructions that are given to Hermas. By devoting attention to how the *Shepherd* employs such language across several passages, one also notices structural elements in the Mandates that provide cohesion across this section of the *Shepherd*. By considering both how the *Shepherd* employs pneumatic terminology and its similarities to another author from around the same time, readers can thus observe key ways in which the *Shepherd* is organized and thereby instructs its Roman audience.

The second way in which this textually focused chapter emphasizes something different is by asking questions about the contemporary usefulness of the *Shepherd*'s

---

1. For a similar distinction between multiple ways of conducting close readings, see Fowl (2014, 60) as well as the fuller examples with respect to Ephesians in Fowl (2014, 45–75).
2. Rothschild (2017).

teaching. This follows from the recognition that contemporary scholars bring their own issues and questions to ancient texts. The chapter delves into references to the *Shepherd* found in the works of Sarah Coakley which suggest that the *Shepherd*'s spirit-language might be useful in contemporary Trinitarian theology. Moreover, although the *Shepherd* knows nothing of present-day analytical or behavioral psychology, the shepherd's instructions in these commandments continue to be potent in a world where people desire to look inward in order to know themselves better. The *Shepherd*'s words continue to have implications for present-day readers. By beginning with a closely textual focus and inquiring about the effects of this text, Chapter 12 highlights alternative means by which the *Shepherd* can be usefully studied and provides a closing to this book that suggests the *Shepherd*'s influence is far from dead.

The Spirit in Medical and Philosophical Writing

In a recent study of Mand. 5.1.3 (33.3), Clare Rothschild considers how the *Shepherd* employs a number of terms in the Mandates that are of interest to this chapter. In particular, she gives attention to spirit (πνεῦμα), irascibility (ὀξυχολία), pain (λύπη), and double-mindedness (διψυχία). She observes a number of similarities between the *Shepherd*'s language in Mand. 5 (33.1–34.8) and second-century medical literature. She then argues that "a popular second-century medical theory lies behind the presentation of ὀξυχολία" and considers the implications of this observations for how scholars should understand the background of the *Shepherd*.[3] Rothschild's essay outlines Galen of Pergamum's understanding of anger.[4] Working from a tripartite Platonic understanding of the soul, Galen considers anger as an ailment that originates in the heart.[5] Galen finds two categories of causes for a problematic pulse: things that dissolve and things that compress the vital faculty (*Puls.* 471). Among the things that dissolve the natural faculty, Galen lists "powerful affections of the soul," while bodily affections are thought to compress the soul (*Puls.* 471).[6] "Anger is one of the powerful affections of the soul that in excess becomes a non-natural cause altering the pulse and dissolving the vital faculty."[7] Where anger, pain, or fear is present for long periods of time, the pulse weakens and dissipates the animating force. This dissolution happens quickly when these emotions are severe or at a high level, while such a weakening occurs more slowly when the emotions are mild (*Puls.* 473–474).

---

3. Rothschild (2017, 228).

4. Peter Singer includes a helpful introduction of the main issues regarding Galen's life and works in his translation of Galen's works (1997, vii–xlii).

5. Von Staden (2012, 74).

6. Translation from Singer (1997, 334).

7. Rothschild (2017, 233).

The Mandates also give attention to another characteristic on which Galen reflected, namely, grief or distress. In a letter that Galen wrote following a fire in Rome that destroyed much of his library and medicine in 192, Galen discusses the avoidance of grief. If λύπη is translated as *grief, pain*, or *distress*, Galen takes up the topic of *ungrief, unpain*, or *undistress* (ἀλυπία or ἀλυπησία).[8] Although this makes for an ugly English translation, Galen's point is clear. His letter is a discussion of the opposite of grief, pain, and distress. He ostensibly writes the letter to a friend who wants to know the training, arguments, or teachings that prepared him to react to the destruction of his valued possessions without distress (*Adol.* 1). Galen highlights the value of what he lost in order to emphasize both the enormity of his loss and the strength of how he reacted (*Adol.* 4–5; 19–30). In Galen's treatise, one finds a good example of how λύπη can be defined. It is not only grief or sorrow, as one might think of in situations of bereavement. The lexeme can include such meanings, but it is not limited to them. Rather, the word can be used to describe pain and distress.[9] This will be important to recall when interpreting Mand. 10 (40.1–42.4).

Rothschild thus rightly observes that Galen's focus on the heart as the seat of anger should alert readers of the Mandates to medical texts as a source of interpretive knowledge. However, Galen's comments on avoiding distress following the loss of his books and medicines should also alert readers to Galen's interactions with the philosophy of his day. He urges his fellow doctors to "know all the parts of philosophy: the logical, the physical, and the ethical" (*Opt. Med.* 60).[10] Doctors' knowledge should envelop knowledge of how humans think, are composed, and should act. Galen's holistic approach to medicine is reminiscent of Cicero's belief that the study of physics and ethics cannot be separated (*Fin.* 3.72). When this observation is coupled with the *Shepherd*'s focus on spirit at this point in the Mandates and an awareness that spirit was a topic of philosophical discussion during the first two centuries, an additional background in light of which to read these Mandates opens up.

Although many in the Christian tradition would ultimately come to think of the spirit as immaterial and thus completely different from physical entities, many philosophers who discuss the spirit in the late Roman Republic and early Roman Empire describe the spirit in terms of a material. In addition to major elements like water, fire, earth, and air, spirit could be discussed as a different kind of substance. Moreover, it could be related to the ether, that is, the material that existed beyond

---

8. On the title of the work and the difficulty of capturing the nuance in English translation, see Rothschild and Thompson (2011, 110).

9. For more on the varied uses of λύπη, see LSJ, λυπέω; *PGL*, λύπη.

10. Translation from Singer (1997, 33). Later in the same work, Galen continues, "If, then, philosophy is necessary to doctors with regard both to preliminary learning and to subsequent training, clearly all true doctors must also be philosophers" (*Opt. Med.* 61; trans. Singer 1997, 33). Elsewhere he calls philosophy "that greatest of divine goods" (*Art.* 3; trans. Singer 1997, 35).

the earth's moon and permeates space, the stars, and other planetary bodies. Cicero describes the spirit as divine and continuous, ascribing to the spirit tidal changes, seasonal weather alterations, summer and winter solstices, and the maintenance of the stars in their respective courses (*Nat. d.* 2.7.19). Later in the same work, Cicero writes that there is nobody who has been great (*magnus*) without experiencing at least some divine inspiration (*adflatu divino*; *Nat. d.* 2.66.167).[11] For someone to become great, the spirit must enter them. Galen notes that the Stoics thought that the spirit was the essence of the soul (*SMT* 5.9).[12] In other words, the spirit is the material of which the soul is comprised. When Diogenes Laertius later offers an account of Zeno's philosophy, he describes a belief that nature is a workmanlike fire, which is itself a fiery and fashioning spirit (*Lives* 7.1 [Zeno] 156).[13] The spirit is not only able to effect change but also to have its temperature described. If the spirit can be sensed with the physical senses, it stands to reason that the spirit must have been material rather than immaterial, even if the physicality of the spirit must be described differently than the physicality of objects like water and air.

Nor is discussion of a material spirit limited only to non-Christian Greco-Roman philosophers.[14] Tatian recognizes two kinds of spirit and incorporates them into his own doctrine of creation (*Or.* 12.1). One form of spirit perdures only in God and can thus only be rightly spoken of in relation to God. However, Tatian also speaks of a "material spirit" (πνεῦμα ὑλικόν) that the Creator placed in the world (*Or.* 12.3).[15] Tertullian is also aware of Stoic teachings on the spirit and utilizes them in his own treatise on the soul. Noting that spirit and breath are closely related, Tertullian maintains that the spirit is a material substance (*An.* 5). Finally, although writing at a much later time, Nemesius likewise refers to the Stoics and their belief that the spirit is a hot substance (*SVF* 2.773). All of these statements suggest that the spirit is best described as a corporeal substance of some sort. This is not to say that all these figures would agree on precisely what kind of material the spirit is, but their statements suggest a general agreement that the spirit can be described in physical terms.

Starting from Rothschild's helpful observations about Galen's medical discussions of anger and irascibility, this section has added that Galen's *De adolore* enables readers of the *Shepherd* to understand the meaning of λύπη more

---

11. Engberg-Pedersen (2010, 20–1).

12. See also *SVF* 2.777.

13. See also *SVF* 2.774. Alexander of Aphrodisias also refers to the spirit as a fire, but he attributed a view to the Stoics that the soul was a combination of fire and air (*SVF* 2.786).

14. Joly notes the materiality of the spirit in portions of the *Shepherd*, but he risks missing an important interpretive context when he refers to *Shepherd*'s "gaucherie d'expression." In the additions to the second edition, he rightly observed that both early Jewish and early Christian texts sometimes refer to a spirit that is conceived of as material in some sense (Joly 1968, 191n.1; 431).

15. Strutwolf and Lakmann (2016, 230). Tatian also thinks that the demons have a material spirit (*Or.* 12.5), on which see Timotin (2016, 275–8).

clearly. It is not merely grief or pain, but also includes something like distress. Irascibility and distress will prove to be important concepts when reading the Mandates, particularly Mand. 5 and 10 (33.1–34.8; 40.1–42.4). Galen's comments on grief along with his encouragement elsewhere that doctors should know philosophy then led to a discussion of another important term in this section of the Mandates, namely, spirit. Having explored the materiality of spirit in at least some philosophical discussion during the Late Roman Republic and Early Roman Empire, the chapter can now turn its attention directly to the Mandates in the hopes that these observations from surrounding literature enable a clearer understanding of the *Shepherd*.

Mandates 5, 9–11 (33.1–34.8; 39.1–43.21)

Although Rothschild gives some exegetical attention to Mand. 10 (40.1–42.4), her primary focus is on Mand. 5 (33.1–34.8).[16] This section builds on her observations and adds further exegetical remarks on Mand. 9 and 11 (39.1–12; 43.1–21), in which similar terminology can be found. It pays particular attention to two matters. First, the shepherd offers Hermas paired elements in these commandments in which one element is not only good but usually is also sensitive and in need of defense from the evil element. Second, in light of the physicality of the spirit elsewhere in philosophical and early Christian texts, this section also considers the physical imagery that the *Shepherd* utilizes in order to make its point.

The shepherd instructs Hermas to be patient and discerning at the start of Mand. 5. If Hermas does these things, he will rule over any evil deeds and act in righteousness (Mand. 5.1.1 [33.1]). In the next sentence, the shepherd offers a rationale for acting in the way that he has commanded. If Hermas acts patiently, the holy spirit that dwells in him will not be obscured by another evil spirit (Mand. 5.1.2 [33.2]). The person is described as a vessel or place and can be inhabited by a holy or an evil spirit.[17] Patience is expansive, joyful, glorifies the Lord, and prospers in a spacious area (Mand. 5.2.3 [34.3]).[18] However, the holy spirit is sensitive and cannot coexist well with an evil spirit (Mand. 5.2.6 [34.6]).[19] If patience enables the holy spirit to flourish, the tendency to become angry easily causes distress for the holy spirit and is thus an attribute of the devil (Mand. 5.1.3 [33.3]).[20] Irascibility generates bitterness in a person regarding trivial matters (Mand. 5.2.2 [34.2]) and gives way to wrath and vengefulness (Mand. 5.2.4 [34.4]).[21] Patience and

---

16. See Rothschild (2017, 236–42).

17. Blidstein (2017, 145).

18. On the stabilizing role that patience can play in relation to irascibility, see Rothschild (2017, 239–40).

19. Hauck (1993, 192).

20. On the devil in the *Shepherd*, see Farrar (2018, 527–8, 535, 539).

21. See also Ps.-Phoc. 63–64. On the translation of the terms in Mand. 5.2.4 (34.4), see Joly (1968, 167n.1).

irascibility are thus set up as contrasting modes of living. Patience is a mark of the holy spirit, which is pure and sensitive. Irascibility is a mark of an evil spirit and can drive out patience and the holy spirit (Mand. 5.2.7 [34.7]). For this reason, it must be protected and cultivated (Mand. 5.1.7; 5.2.8 [33.7; 34.8]).

The *Shepherd* relies upon two different images in order to draw out this teaching. The first set of images utilizes space and light. When patience is allowed to rule Hermas's life, the holy spirit is not obscured or eclipsed by an evil spirit.[22] In other words, light shines upon the holy spirit so that it is clear to see. Patience also enables the holy spirit to live in a spacious room. When not obstructed by an evil spirit, the holy spirit fills this room with joy and dwells in light by which it can be clearly seen (Mand. 5.1.2 [33.2]). If the evil spirit dwells alongside the holy spirit, however, the evil spirit chokes the holy spirit (Mand. 5.1.3 [33.3]). Because the holy spirit is sensitive, it becomes distressed and does not have the space to serve the Lord as it would like. Rather, this conflict in a person becomes evil for that person (Mand. 5.1.4 [33.4]). After employing spatial imagery, the shepherd then utilizes an additional analogy. If one places a small amount of wormwood into a jar of honey, the honey is spoiled because the bitter taste of the wormwood disseminates throughout the honey (Mand. 5.1.5 [33.5]).[23] The honey's taste has been changed, and the owner no longer enjoys it because it has become useless. The shepherd tells Hermas that patience is sweeter than honey and is useful to the Lord. On the other hand, irascibility is useless. When the two are mixed within a person, patience is polluted and the person's intercession is no longer useful to God (Mand. 5.1.6 [33.6]).

Mand. 5 (33.1–34.8) contrasts patience and irascibility. The *Shepherd* employs the images of a well-lit, spacious room as well as honey and wormwood in order to develop the contrast. Mand. 9 (39.1–12) warns against double-mindedness (διψυχία). The *Shepherd* is particularly concerned with the topic of prayer at this point. Debate (διαλόγισμος) is related to double-mindedness. On the opposite side of these, the *Shepherd* places faith (πίστις) and the adverb "without doubt" (ἀδιστάκτως).[24] Hermas should put away double-mindedness and should never

---

22. The *Shepherd* uses a passive form of the verb ἐπισκοτέω (*episkoteō*), which means "to put someth. in the way so that an object cannot be clearly discerned" (BDAG, s.v., 2). Diogenes Laertius introduces his biography of Demetrius by noting his popularity with the Athenians that was eclipsed (ἐπεσκοτήθη) "by all-devouring jealousy" (*Lives* 5 [Demetrius]) 76. Jealousy obscures Diogenes's fame, just as the *Shepherd* warns that an evil spirit obscures the holy spirit.

23. Similar imagery of honey being mixed with other substances can be found in the Muratorian fragment, l. 67. For references to similar imagery, see Dibelius (1923, 515); Körtner and Leutzsch (1998, 451n.104).

24. "The idea of purity may be compared to the pure, single heart, which many first- and early-second-century sources opposed to a double or defiled heart" (Blidstein 2017, 127). Although Mand. 9 juxtaposes double-mindedness and faith, the *Shepherd* elsewhere discusses single-mindedness (ἁπλότης; e.g., Vis. 1.2.4 [2.4]; 3.9.1 [17.1]; Mand. 2.1 [27.1]; Sim. 9.24.2 [101.2]). See the discussion in Chapter 10 of this book.

ask something of the Lord while being double-minded (Mand. 9.1 [39.1]). Those who are double-minded doubt God and do not receive their requests (Mand. 9.5 [39.5]). Even worse, double-mindedness has the capacity to uproot people from faith (Mand. 9.9 [39.9]). For this reason, the shepherd tells Hermas that double-mindedness is the daughter of the devil. Rather than debating his sinfulness, Hermas should pray without doubt because God is compassionate and does not hold grudges (Mand. 9.2-3 [39.2-3]). The shepherd tells Hermas that he will not lack anything if he asks without doubting (Mand. 9.4 [39.4]). Those who are complete in their faith ask for all things confidently from the Lord, and they receive because they ask without doubting (Mand. 9.6 [39.6]). Hermas is then charged to cleanse his heart from double-mindedness and to put on faith instead (Mand. 9.7 [39.7]). Faith is strong, and Hermas should believe that he will receive whatever he asks from God in faith. Hermas must trust that his request will be answered even when fulfillment takes a long time.

The *Shepherd* uses cleansing and clothing metaphors in Mand. 9.4, 7, 10 (39.4, 7, 10). Hermas is instructed to cleanse his heart from the empty things found in this age in order to stay away from double-mindedness. Likewise, he should steer clear of the things that the shepherd has already told him (Mand. 9.4 [39.4]).[25] Hermas is told much the same thing a few verses later, namely, that he should cleanse his heart from double-mindedness. However, the shepherd immediately adds that Hermas should clothe himself instead with faith.[26] Faith and double-mindedness are not only defined in opposing terms and with contrasting consequences. They also appear as opposites in the imagery. Double-mindedness must be cleansed away. Faith must be worn like clean clothes. In Mand. 9.10 (39.10), Hermas is again urged to clothe himself in faith, "which is strong and powerful" (τὴν ἰσχυρὰν καὶ δυνατήν). However, cleansing and clothing are not the only images that the shepherd employs. He also appeals to spatial imagery to explain the power of faith and corresponding weakness of double-mindedness (Mand. 9.11-12 [39.11-12]). Faith comes from above and is from the Lord. On the other hand, double-mindedness is an earthly spirit that comes from the devil.[27] Since faith has power, the shepherd concludes by urging Hermas to serve faith. By doing this, he will live to God.

---

25. It is difficult to determine exactly what the shepherd has in mind when speaking of "the words that I have already spoken to you" (Mand. 9.4 [39.4]). L¹ understands these as "the words which were already given to you by God" (*praedicta tibi uerba a deo*), suggesting everything that the *Shepherd* has said before is in view. Dibelius also follows this interpretation (1923, 530). L² understands the shepherd to refer to the vice list in "the previous Mandate" (*ante praecepta*). See also Mand. 8.3-6 (38.3-6). Brox follows a similar interpretation (1991, 238). I am tentatively in favor of the tradition reflected in L¹, but the evidence upon which to base one's judgment is slight.

26. Soyars (2019, 187-91).

27. Hauck (1993, 192).

Mandates 10 and 11 (40.1–43.21) continue to use paired characteristics and images to illustrate the patterns of each virtue or vice. The shepherd begins Mand. 10.1 (40.1) in the same way as Mand. 9.1 (39.1), namely, by commanding Hermas to put away from himself (ἆρον ἀπὸ σεαυτοῦ).[28] Hermas is now instructed to put away distress (λύπη). The shepherd links distress with irascibility and double-mindedness from Mand. 5 and 9 (33.1–34.8; 39.1–12), referring to distress as their sister (Mand. 10.1.1 [40.1]). After Hermas asks for an explanation of this relationship (Mand. 10.1.2 [40.2]), the shepherd eventually maintains that distress crushes the holy spirit but also saves again (Mand. 10.2.1 [41.1]). The shepherd's claim is explained in terms of both double-mindedness and irascibility (Mand. 10.2.2–3 [41.2–3]). Both double-mindedness and anger allow distress to enter a person after they have failed at their endeavors. This supports the sororal depiction of the three at the beginning of Mand. 10. However, in the case of irascibility, distress may lead to repentance when they are grieved by what they have done. "Therefore, this distress seems to have salvation" (αὕτη οὖν ἡ λύπη δοκεῖ σωτηρίαν ἔχειν; Mand. 10.2.4 [41.4]).[29] Yet both distress the spirit, and Hermas should put all of these things away from him (Mand. 10.2.5–6). Rather than allowing distress to play such a prominent role, Hermas's life should instead be characterized by cheerfulness (ἱλαρότης; Mand. 10.3.1 [42.1]). Cheerfulness is pleasing to God, and cheerful people do and think good things while despising distress. However, distressed people act in evil ways by grieving the holy spirit, acting lawlessly, and failing to pray (Mand. 10.3.2 [42.2]).[30]

The shepherd again employs imagery to explain distress. He maintains continuity with his comments regarding double-mindedness by employing cleansing and clothing images. Hermas should be clothed with cheerfulness (Mand. 10.3.1 [42.1]), and he should cleanse himself from evil distress (Mand. 10.3.4 [42.4]). The shepherd also utilizes a vineyard metaphor when explaining how those in the community who are heavily engaged in business affairs and friendships with those outside of the community fail to understand what God has said. They are like vineyards that have become barren because of thorns and weeds (Mand. 10.1.5 [40.5]).[31] The most developed imagery, however, enhances the contrast between distress and cheerfulness. Distress is discussed in weighty terms. It inhibits prayers from rising to God's altar (Mand. 10.3.2 [42.2]). Because distress takes root deep in the heart, prayer is simply unable to rise (Mand. 10.3.3 [42.3]). The shepherd follows this image with another. Distress is compared to vinegar, and the holy spirit is compared to wine. When vinegar and wine are mixed, they do not bring

---

28. On the implications of the identical openings of Mand. 9.1 (39.1); 10.1 (40.1); 12.1 (44.1), see Bandini (2001, 130).

29. Hermas's distress upon seeing the shepherd's change in form in Vis. 5.4 may provide a different example of how λύπη can function positively within the world of the *Shepherd*.

30. Blidstein (2017, 145–6).

31. See the similar imagery of barrenness in Dio Chrysostom, *Ven.* 34 (*Or.* 7.34).

the same enjoyment as wine alone. Likewise, grief mixed with the holy spirit does not allow prayer to work in the same way (Mand. 10.3.3 [42.3]).

These images then give way to the *Shepherd*'s extensive comments on true and false prophets (Mand. 11 [43.1–21]).[32] Unlike in the other three mandates discussed thus far, the shepherd opens this commandment with a vision. Hermas sees some people who are seated on a bench and another person who is seated on a chair. Those on the bench are described as faithful, while the person in the chair is referred to as a false prophet (Mand. 11.1 [43.1]). False prophets serve the double-minded and have no power from the divine spirit (Mand. 11.2 [43.2]). False prophets exalt themselves and desire positions of honor (Mand. 11.12 [43.12]). They desire money and luxurious treatment as payment for their prophecy, and they avoid righteous people. Instead, they spend their time with double-minded and empty people (Mand. 11.13 [43.13]). They themselves are empty and thus offer empty answers (Mand. 11.3 [43.3]). The image of emptiness is enhanced in Mand. 11.13–15 (43.13–15).[33] False prophets are empty vessels and, just as empty vessels are often placed side by side in a store room, so also false prophets speak to other empty vessels in the community. When they meet faithful people, the earthly spirit is silenced and flees from the false prophet in fear. Empty jars remain empty until filled with something else.

While empty people approach false prophets for answers, prophets that come from God do not need to be consulted. Rather, they speak the words of God at God's behest (Mand. 11.5, 8 [43.5, 8]). They are gentle, quiet, and humble (Mand. 11.8 [43.8]). When prophets enter into a righteous assembly, the righteous in that assembly pray for the prophet. At this point, "the angel of the prophetic spirit" (ὁ ἄγγελος τοῦ πνεύματος τοῦ προφητικοῦ) fills the prophet so that the prophet can speak what the Lord desires to say (Mand. 11.9 [43.9]).[34] The contrast between true and false prophets is further enhanced by another set of images near the end of the shepherd's instructions. The shepherd refers to this final imagery as a parable (παραβολή; Mand. 11.18 [43.18]).[35] The shepherd challenges Hermas to take a stone and throw it to the sky to see if he can reach the sky. Alternatively, one might try to pump water into the sky to pierce it (Mand. 11.18 [43.18]). Hermas says that these things are impossible. The shepherd notes that earthly spirits are similarly powerless (Mand. 11.19 [43.19]). The shepherd then appeals to hailstones

---

32. The *Shepherd* appears to follow septuagintal practice of specifying false prophets but not using an adjective or compound to refer to true prophets. On true and false prophecy in early Judaism, see Reiling (1971).

33. Jefford (2010, 311–12).

34. For a useful overview of the filling of prophets with a spirit in the Greco-Roman world, see Reiling (1973, 113–20).

35. Mand. 11 thus provides a helpful warning against using the terms Visions, Mandates, and Similitudes (or Parables) as genre markers in the *Shepherd*. This mandate begins with a vision, contains a parable, and is located in the section that has come to be known as the Mandates.

and raindrops (Mand. 11.20 [43.20]). Both are extremely powerful. Although hailstones are small, they cause significant pain when they strike a person on the head. Likewise, rain that falls from a roof has the power to bore a hole into a rock. The shepherd concludes: "You see then that the smallest things from above have great power when they fall to the earth. So also the divine spirit is powerful when it comes from above" (Mand. 11.21 [43.21]).[36]

In Mand. 5; 9–11 (33.1–34.8; 39.1–43.21), the *Shepherd* employs opposing characteristics.[37] The *Shepherd* divides the world sharply into those who are characterized by irascibility or patience, double-mindedness or faith, distress or cheerfulness, and prophets or false prophets. This world is inhabited by spirits that affect and are affected by human action. In each of the Mandates, the *Shepherd* utilizes additional imagery in order to highlight his point. Although the spirits are sharply divided, the imagery suggests that some mixture is possible but harmful. For example, a little wormwood changes the flavor of honey, and a little vinegar changes the quality of wine. The physicality of the images also suggests physicality in the spirits that are in view. While the similar features in these Mandates suggest that these connections should be made by readers, two related questions may now be asked. First, how are Mand. 5; 9–11 (33.1–34.8; 39.1–43.21) structured within the *Shepherd*? Second, how does the intervening material in Mand. 6–8 (35.1–38.12) function?

The Structure and Function of Mand. 5–11 (33.1–43.21)

In order to answer the first question, it will be helpful to start with the second. The similarities between Mand. 5; 9–11 (33.1–34.8; 39.1–43.21) are mirrored in some ways by connections that bind Mand. 6–8 (35.1–38.12) together. In Mand. 6.1.1 (35.1), the shepherd tells Hermas that he will clarify the powers of faith, fear, and self-control. The shepherd proceeds to discuss faith as part of a two-ways tradition in Mand. 6 (35.1–36.10),[38] to outline how fear works in Mand. 7 (37.1–5), and to teach Hermas about self-control in Mand. 8 (38.1–12). The shepherd also notes that his instructions to Hermas link back to Mand. 1.2 (26.2). The shepherd's initial mandate immediately follows his meeting with Hermas in Vis. 5 (25.1–7). After telling Hermas to believe in God and encapsulating something of who God is, the shepherd urges Hermas, "Believe, therefore, in him, and fear him, and be self-controlled because you fear him" (Mand. 1.2 [26.2]).[39] The shepherd suggests that there are connections between these three imperatives by linking

---

36. On the images in Mand. 11.18–21 (43.18–21), see Brox (1989a, 275–6).

37. Joly (1968, 187n.2) also finds connections between Mand. 5; 9–10 (33.1–34.8; 39.1–42.4).

38. See further Osiek (1999, 122–5).

39. Bandini (2001, 129).

fear and self-control in the final instruction.[40] Yet these interrelationships are not pursued until Mand. 6–8 (35.1–38.12). Why does the author of the *Shepherd* place this exposition of faith, fear, and self-control between the conversations about irascibility, double-mindedness, distress, and false prophets?

One possible answer is that these sections were written by separate authors or at different times. If so, these passages may have been compiled in their current order with more or less consideration. For example, Dibelius proposes that Mand. 6–8 represents a reworking of originally Jewish ethical teaching.[41] As was discussed in Chapter 7, the *Shepherd* shares similarities with various elements of early Jewish literature. Yet a literary reworking of either Mand. 6–8 or Mand. 5–11 from a Jewish source by the author of the *Shepherd*, though not impossible, is an unsatisfactory explanation for two reasons. First, the answer is based on speculation. The manuscripts that contain extended portions of the Mandates place the text in the same order, and it is unclear how one would establish that these passages were written by different hands or at separate times. Second, the answer risks engaging in chronological snobbery.[42] Interpreters who too quickly suggest multiple authors simply because a text does not appear in the form that they expect may be in danger of asserting themselves over the text.[43] Moreover, even if various authors were involved in compiling this text, the Mandates have been received in this order. One is thus encouraged to consider another answer.

The placement of Mand. 5 (33.1–34.8) and Mand. 9–11 (39.1–43.21) on either side of Mand. 6–8 (35.1–38.12) suggests a loosely chiastic structure in this portion of the Mandates. However, problems arise with this proposal. If this section is designated a chiasm, it is unbalanced. The first part of the chiasm, Mand. 5 (33.1–34.8), is dwarfed by its counterpart in Mand. 9–11 (39.1–43.21). Moreover, it is not clear what is gained for the interpreter by referring to this section of the Mandates as a chiasm. The links do not appear in a way that suggests a particularly chiastic structure. One may thus consider alternatives to a strict chiasm. It is better to think of the twofold spirits that appear throughout Mand. 5–11 (33.1–43.21) as

---

40. The Ethiopic translation adds a similar link between faith and fear that would intensify the relationships between these three. However, this variant is not attested elsewhere in the manuscript tradition. See the list of witnesses in Körtner and Leutzch (1998, 191).

41. Dibelius (1923, 520).

42. On chronological snobbery and the objections that Owen Barfield and C. S. Lewis developed to this attitude, see McGrath (2014, 42–3). Barfield seems to have played the leading role in their conversations. Before meeting Barfield, Lewis wrote to Arthur Greeves about "the recognised scientific account of the growth of religions" and considered religion to have developed when "primitive man found himself surrounded by all sorts of terrible things that he didn't understand" (October 12, 1916; Hooper 2004–7, 1.231).

43. Rowan Williams helpfully writes about the need to learn to critique the present and the responses common to that time in order to learn more accurately from the past (2005, 4–31).

the unifying element that provides cohesion to this section. However, the way in which the two spirits are revealed in the respective Mandates differs somewhat.

As the shepherd resumes talking to Hermas in Mand. 6.1.1 (35.1), he wants to explain the power of the three characteristics from Mand. 1.2 (26.2), "for their effects are twofold" (διπλαῖ γάρ εἰσιν αἱ ἐνέργειαι αὐτῶν).[44] The twofold nature of the effects provides the distinguishing mark of the shepherd's teaching for the following three mandates,[45] and the shepherd clarifies that the two elements of each characteristic pertains "to what is righteous and unrighteous" (Mand. 6.1.1 [35.1]). Little is said about the twofold nature of faith. Rather, the shepherd instructs Hermas primarily about the two ways of the righteous and unrighteous (Mand. 6.1.2–5 [35.2–5]) and the two angels, one of whom is righteous while the other is unrighteous (Mand. 6.2.1–10 [36.1–10]). Hermas is instructed to believe, that is, to be faithful to, the angel of righteousness (Mand. 6.2.3, 6 [36.3, 6]). At the conclusion of the shepherd's discussion, Hermas is again taught to believe the works of the righteous angel. Moreover, he should also believe that the works of the evil angel are grievous. Faith is thus to be exercised in alternating ways when encountering the righteous and unrighteous angels, but faith is nevertheless to be applied.

The shepherd's focus on the twofold nature of the characteristics from Mand. 1.2 (26.2) continues as he discusses fear and self-control. Hermas should "fear the Lord and keep his commandments" (φοβήθητι, φησί, τὸν κύριον καὶ φύλασσε τὰς ἐντολάς; Mand. 7.1 [37.1]).[46] Fear of the Lord enables one to work in a way that is beyond criticism, because fear of the Lord is associated with doing all things well. The devil should not be feared, since his works are powerless (Mand. 7.2 [37.2]). Yet while the devil himself should not be feared, his works may be feared (Mand. 7.3 [37.3]). When someone fears the Lord, they also fear the devil's works and do not do them. "Therefore, fears are of two kinds" (δισσοὶ οὖν εἰσιν οἱ φόβοι; Mand. 7.4 [37.4]). Fear of the Lord keeps one from acting wickedly, while the fear of the Lord also leads one to do good. Although the application of the twofold work of fear shifts somewhat, the two ways in which fear functions provides the organizing theme of Mand. 7. The explanation of the twofold nature of self-control appears early in Mand. 8. Self-control is necessary in certain situations but is not needed in others (Mand. 8.1 [38.1]). When Hermas asks to hear more about the respective situations, the shepherd says that he should be self-controlled regarding evil but without self-control with respect to good things (Mand. 8.2 [38.2]). Although self-control regarding good things results in evil, self-control when dealing with what is evil allows one to do what is good. By examining self-control in these two ways, Hermas can live to God (Mand. 8.12 [38.12]).

---

44. The twofold nature of creation can be found elsewhere in Jewish wisdom and testamental literature. E.g., Sir 33:14; 42:24; *Ps.-Phoc.* 65–67; *T. Jud.* 20.1; *T. Ash.* 1.3–4.

45. Dibelius (1923, 520); Brox (1991, 223–4).

46. See the similar language in Eccl 12:13 (LXX): τὸν θεὸν φοβοῦ καὶ τὰς ἐντολὰς αὐτοῦ φύλασσε.

The twofold function of faith, fear, and self-control provides Mand. 6–8 (35.1–38.12) with their cohesion and contributes to the bifurcation found throughout Mand. 5; 9–11 (33.1–34.8; 39.1–43.21). In each of these commandments, the shepherd instructs Hermas to take up one sort of activity and to avoid another action. However, Mand. 5; 9–11 (33.1–34.8; 39.1–43.21) and Mand. 6–8 (35.1–38.12) articulate the shepherd's aims differently. In the former, the paths of righteousness and unrighteousness are set out clearly in the virtues and vices around which Mand. 5; 9–11 (33.1–34.8; 39.1–43.21) are organized. The shepherd tells Hermas to avoid irascibility, double-mindedness, distress, and false prophets. Rather, Hermas should be patient, faithful, and cheerful while giving attention to how God speaks through true prophets. On the other hand, Mand. 6–8 (35.1–38.12) recommend only faith, fear, and self-control. No corresponding vice is offered as a contrast. The shepherd instead tells Hermas to practice these virtues in different ways regarding righteousness and unrighteousness. Faith should follow the path of righteousness by trusting the works of the righteous angels and believing that what the angel of unrighteousness does is dangerous. Fear should be directed toward God so that Hermas acts rightly, but fear may also be evident when looking at the devil's works so that he does not do what is wrong. Self-control should be exercised over evil, but good things can be indulged freely. The *Shepherd*'s binary division of the world thus provides cohesion throughout Mand. 5–11 (33.1–43.21).

Reflecting on the Shepherd *for the Present*

Most readers of this book are likely to be engaged in some sort of historical or theological studies—whether the primary object of study involves the New Testament, Apostolic Fathers, early Jewish writings, or Greco-Roman texts. It may seem surprising, then, to end with reflections on the *Shepherd*'s importance for the present. Historians have rightly become quick to recognize that each researcher brings something of their own experience and own biases to their study. Moreover, each generation of scholars asks different questions. As important as the studies of Rudolf Anger, Wilhelm Dindorf, and Theodor Zahn remain,[47] those who explore the *Shepherd* today not only have additional evidence to evaluate but also alternative questions to examine. From these observations, one might make a further leap to inquire about the significance of the *Shepherd* in the present. The *Shepherd* has been referred to in recent discussions of Trinitarian theology, and it is also intriguing to read this section of the Mandates alongside popular discussions of anger, distress, and depression.

One of the most interesting allusions to the *Shepherd* in recent discourse about Trinitarian theology comes in Sarah Coakley's *God, Sexuality, and the Self*, where she lists the *Shepherd* along with other texts from the second century that, according to Coakley, develop a prayer-based model of the Trinity.

---

47. Anger and Dindorfius (1856); Zahn (1868); Gebhardt, Harnack, and Zahn (1906).

> The highly popular *Shepherd of Hermas*, for instance, is rife with these prophetic and visionary claims, and also contains an extended and profound reflection on the transformative potential of the indwelling Spirit.[48]

This remark is enticing but is left undeveloped. Coakley illustrates her points in more detail with attention to Paul, Origen, Gregory of Nyssa, and Augustine.[49] Although Chapter 9 showed that more is said about the spirit than what appears in Mand. 5; 9–11 (33.1–34.8; 39.1–43.21), the exegesis of this portion of the Mandates largely supports Coakley's analysis.

Coakley begins her discussion with Paul's description of the spirit's activity in Rom 8.[50] The spirit is the initial point of contact for believers in Rom 8 as the spirit joins believers in crying out to the Father (Rom 8:15–16). The spirit even intercedes alongside the Romans when they do not know what to pray, since God knows the mind of the spirit because the spirit intercedes for believers according to God's will (Rom 8:26–27). The experience of the spirit is thus a primary way in which believers know God in Rom 8, and this knowledge is gained through the practice of prayer.[51] Coakley traces other experiential models of the Trinity through the second and third centuries in texts like the *Didache*, the *Shepherd*, Irenaeus, and Tertullian.[52] Yet it is Origen's *de Oratione* that receives the most attention.[53] Coakley notes that the spirit is given priority in Origen's treatise just as in Rom 8. Indeed, Rom 8 receives explicit attention in Origen's commentary (*Or.* 2.1, 3; 10.5; 14.5).[54] Throughout the argument, Coakley also notes points in the language of Paul and Origen where the spirit's role in prayer is described with a view to gendered language. Both Paul and Origen employ the image of a woman in labor when considering the spirit's role in prayer (Rom 8:26; Origen, *Or.* 8.1).

The portrayal of the spirit in the *Shepherd* generally fits well with the overarching concerns that Coakley outlines in Paul and Origen. The *Shepherd* likewise places the spirit in an experiential relationship to the Roman believers who were its first audience. According to Mand. 5; 9–11 (33.1–34.8; 39.1–43.21), the spirit is experienced when patience, faith, cheerfulness, and true prophecy are present in a believer's life. All of these come from God, although prophecy may be the experience in which this is most clearly outlined within the Mandates examined in this chapter. True prophets speak the word of God only when they are divinely urged to do so (Mand. 11.5, 8 [43.5, 8]). They cannot be bribed or otherwise

---

48. Coakley (2013a, 120).

49. See further Coakley (2003; 2013a, 100–45; 2013b, 379–88).

50. Despite mentioning different authors, I will continue the practice used throughout this book of not capitalizing *spirit* or *holy spirit*.

51. Coakley (2003, 260–1; 2013a, 111–15; 2013b, 382–4).

52. Coakley (2013a, 120–6; 2013b, 383).

53. Coakley (2003, 262–4; 2013a, 126–32; 2013b, 384–8). For concise introductions to Origen's treatise, see Trigg (1998, 41–2); Stewart-Sykes (2004, 95–107).

54. For more on Rom 8 in Origen's treatise, see Perrone (2011, 469–72).

motivated to speak as true prophets apart from the spirit's divinely received sanction. The spirit's power is likewise evident in the imagery that the shepherd describes to Hermas. The holy spirit can fill a room with joy and light (Mand. 5.1.2 [33.2]). It is light enough if uninhibited to allow prayers to rise to God's altar (Mand. 10.3.2 [42.2]). Finally, the spirit comes from above and overwhelms the power of earthly spirits (Mand. 9.11 [39.11]; 11.18–21 [43.18–21]). Although the holy spirit is portrayed in multiple ways throughout the *Shepherd*, the description of the spirit's actions in Mand. 5; 9–11 (33.1–34.8; 39.1–43.21) largely coheres with Coakley's analysis of the experiential and prayer-based model of the Trinity insofar as the primary experience of believers is with the spirit and these interactions are potent.

Yet these Mandates also stretch Coakley's analysis in two key ways. First, more attention is given to believers in their interactions with the spirit. "The holy spirit that dwells in you" (τὸ πνεῦμα τὸ ἅγιον τὸ κατοικοῦν ἐν σοί; Mand. 5.1.1 [33.1]) is depicted in terms that emphasize the believer as an active dwelling place. Human actions thus have enormous impact on the holy spirit. Although the spirit remains potent as long as it dwells within the person, its potency is closely tied to its location within the believer. However, the holy spirit can also be crushed and driven away, leading to the second way in which these Mandates might be used to build upon Coakley's theological arguments. The experience of believers with the holy spirit may well be one in which they perceive their interactions with the spirit as delicate.[55] A person's encounter with the spirit can end suddenly if irascibility, double-mindedness, distress, and false prophecy are granted a place. The *Shepherd* can thus be helpfully read alongside Coakley's suggestion that it "contains an extended and profound reflection on the transformative potential of the indwelling Spirit."[56] Yet these Mandates may also shed further light on how believers experience their interactions with the spirit, not only in prayer but also in times of distress and upheaval.

The human experience of the spirit in these Mandates leads on to the next topic, namely, some possible points of connection between the *Shepherd*'s discussion of irascibility and distress and current, popular understandings of anger, grief, and depression. It is particularly appropriate to draw on nontechnical works in light of the *Shepherd*'s nontechnical or popular use of medical and philosophical terminology in Mand. 5; 9–11. Although there may be differences in how current and ancient readers of the *Shepherd* conceive of anger, distress, patience, and joyfulness, the shepherd's instructions to Hermas about these particular virtues and vices may have life in them yet.

The shepherd warns Hermas not to allow anger a place in his life for fear that the spirit of irascibility will choke the holy spirit and pollute Hermas (Mand. 5.1.3 [33.3]). This portion of the *Shepherd* is intriguing to read in a time when everything from driving a car to participating in politics bears the marks of anger.

---

55. Morgan-Wynne (1989).
56. Coakley (2013a, 120).

On crowded roads with distracted drivers, it is easy to become acutely angry. Road rage is a feeling that many have experienced, and those who have found a surge in anger within themselves while driving have probably experienced this multiple times.[57] Likewise, political commentators and psychologists have in recent years referred to the "politics of anger."[58] As Galen already did in the second century, psychologists have also noted the effects of anger.[59] Complaints about physical pain and sickness in children can be a sign of anger, and one study of children with special education needs suggests that adaptive anger techniques may be important starting points in avoiding "the widespread problem of school-related somatic complaints."[60] Another study suggests that family cohesion can moderate physical complaints that are linked with anger,[61] but this does not undue the link between complaints of bodily hurts and anger. The shepherd instructs Hermas to consider the power of anger in Mand. 5, and the physicality of the imagery and discussion of spirits suggest that anger has corporeal consequences.[62]

One may say similar things about the impact of grief, distress, and depression, which tends to demonstrate itself in the decline of one's health and decision-making processes.[63] Self-blame can also arise during times of grief, and "for many men who have adopted the traditional male gender role, grief is extremely uncomfortable."[64] Although λύπη may be used more broadly than for grief alone, the shepherd instructs Hermas about the power of this spirit in Mand. 10 (40.1–42.4). Distress crushes the holy spirit and is exacerbated by the presence of anger in one's heart (Mand. 10.2.1–3 [41.1–3]). Such distress can lead one to change one's behavior and bring about salvation after acting in ways that cause regret (Mand. 10.2.4 [41.4]), but this is not always the case and believers are instructed to remove distress (Mand. 10.2.5 [41.5]). We may wish to augment some of what the *Shepherd* says on the topic to allow a fuller place for grieving loss in ways that are palliative and health promoting. Nevertheless, the *Shepherd* continues to have things that can be valuable for present-day readers and, as long as one is sensitive to the historical peculiarities of the text, may be read with this in mind.

---

57. Lawrence (2003).

58. Rodrik (2016); Verano (2018). See also Mishra (2016), who refers to "the age of anger" in a discussion of twenty-first-century politics in the *Guardian*.

59. Von Staden (2012); Rothschild (2017).

60. Otterpohl et al. (2017, 67).

61. Liu, Liu, and Zhao (2017).

62. Rothschild (2017). For further studies of the somatic effects of anger, see Meier et al. (2013); May et al. (2014).

63. One interesting area of study includes the somatic effects of depression among the elderly. See, e.g., Verhaak et al. (2014); Hegeman et al. (2017). These studies may be particularly intriguing in light of the depiction of Hermas—via the woman, who serves as a mirror of Hermas's soul—as elderly prior to his repentance (Vis. 3.10.1–3.13.4 [18.1–21.4]).

64. Cochran and Rabinowitz (2000, 68).

The *Shepherd* thus has useful things to say about prolonged tendencies to be angry as well as about grief and distress. When speaking to Hermas, the shepherd acknowledges the power of these emotions to wreak havoc on the lives of those in whom these practices are allowed to settle. This is not to say that the *Shepherd* offers a comprehensive picture of how one should think. It clearly does not. For example, there is no mention of a right place for anger when injustice occurs or the proper role of grief when losing a loved one. However, the *Shepherd* discusses these practices in alignment with some of the ways in which contemporary psychologists talk about anger and grief. The *Shepherd* admits the capacity that these feelings have to ruin one's inner disposition and potentially one's whole life. In addition, the language of two spirits, although contemporary medical professionals would of course use other language, offers a useful image with which to imagine how anger and distress work in human beings. Anger and distress sometimes fall upon people without the conscious awareness of their victims. If the diagnosis of the problem has some utility, what can be said of the *Shepherd*'s solutions?

Let us turn first to the *Shepherd*'s recommendation of patience as an antidote to anger. When anger arises in response to a world or a self that is hurried, patience remains a useful prescription for contemporary readers of the *Shepherd*. As the pressures of life mount to respond to the latest text message, to answer the most recent e-mail, or to return the call that was missed earlier in the day, the shepherd's instruction is to "be patient and understanding" (Mand. 5.1.1 [33.1]). The claim that patience allows the holy spirit "not to be overshadowed by another evil spirit" (Mand. 5.1.2 [33.2]) remains similarly important to heed. Admittedly, the shepherd's instructions may need some updating and additional explanation to be heard by most in the twenty-first century. However, readers of the *Shepherd* who focus on the historical significance of the text may find that the *Shepherd* has the power to influence contemporary readers as well. The same is true for those who experience anger, irritability, or irascibility because of frustrations in their career or personal life. Although one may want to temper the shepherd's language in Mand. 5.2.2 (34.2) to include an acknowledgment that these frustrations are not unusual, his warning to Hermas about the way in which embitterment can set into one's life "out of nothing" or "for no reason" (ἐκ τοῦ μηδενός; Mand. 5.2.2 [34.2]) remains instructive. Such anger is often insidious, and patience is at least part of a useful response.[65]

The same can be said of cheerfulness as a response to distress and grief. One could, of course, misuse the *Shepherd*'s advice to catastrophic ends if they do not allow some place for grief in circumstances such as death or the breakdown of a relationship. However, if one understands λύπη in a larger sense or as part of

---

65. It is also worth noting that patience is an active disposition in the *Shepherd*. See especially the command to put on patience in Mand. 5.2.8 (34.8). This may be situated alongside David Brooks's (2015, 53–6, here at 56) advice that sins like anger must "be fought through habits of restraint." Brooks depicts these habits of restraint as habits that must be actively taken up in the struggle against anger.

a larger lifestyle that is constantly distressed, the shepherd's teaching is again insightful. Those who are characterized by joy may indeed find it easier to do and think good things (Mand. 10.3.1 [42.1]). More importantly, however, the image of distress as heavier than cheerfulness hints at the power that distress can wield once it is given a regular place in one's life (Mand. 10.3.2–3 [42.2–3]). This language has the capacity to speak to the experience of readers even today, since part of the response to a lifestyle encumbered by distress may well include actively engaging in practices that cultivate joy and cheerfulness. The images of vinegar and wine likewise suggest the power of distress to ruin any sense of joy in a person's life (Mand. 10.3.4–5 [42.4–5]).[66]

The *Shepherd*'s instructions in Mand. 5; 9–10 (33.1–34.8; 39.1–42.4) may thus continue to be relevant in the twenty-first century. The imagery and discussions of anger and distress are particularly pertinent for present-day readers because they offer a unique way of considering the power of these emotions. The solutions that the *Shepherd* offers are likewise worthy of consideration in the present. The *Shepherd*'s thought at various points is incomplete or in need of further clarification. Yet the underdeveloped elements of what is revealed to Hermas along with those portions that are so far removed from the twenty-first century as to be nearly impossible to take up should not push readers away from considering the significance of this text for the present. The shepherd's instructions to Hermas deserve close attention. If this advice is to be taken seriously in the present, readers should press further into the *Shepherd*'s instructions to consider what implications these teachings might have and how they might continue to help those who seek to live in a way that is characteristically marked by patience, single-mindedness, and joy. Like Hermas, such readers may enable others to avoid distress and thereby "acquire great joy for themselves" (*magnum gaudium sibi adquirit*; Sim. 10.4.3 [114.3]). In order to do this, it may be necessary to recognize the multiple roles that the holy spirit plays in prayer, education, training, and revelation within the textual world of the *Shepherd* and the development of early Christian theology more broadly.

Conclusion

This book has ended with a brief look to the present, but the findings of the final section only become useful alongside historical study. The *Shepherd* is a historical text, one that originated around the city of Rome when the Roman Empire was

---

66. Perhaps a similar thing can be said about the power of single-mindedness to speak to "an age of distraction." I borrow this language from the title of Jacobs (2011), but see also Jacobs (2016) and the recommendations made in Jacobs (2017). If double-mindedness in the *Shepherd* refers to distractions that draw people away from what is most important, single-mindedness may enable one to place their focus on those things that are central in one's life. For those who are sympathetic to the *Shepherd*, there is a need to consider how single-mindedness might function in the affairs of daily life.

at its pinnacle. This book has been written as a guide whose aim is to enable and to encourage readers to engage the *Shepherd* in a more detailed way. With this in mind, the book began in Part I by offering an overview of the entire text, exploring the manuscripts and reception history from which we know the *Shepherd*, and studying critical issues like authorship and place of composition. Although Part I dealt with a number of issues, the focus was consistently placed on the text of the *Shepherd* with the goal of reading the text well.

Part II continued this textual focus by beginning and ending with exegetical considerations of select passages. Chapter 5 took up Sim. 5 (54.1–60.4), while this final chapter has concluded the book by exploring textual features and structural elements in Mand. 5–11 (33.1–43.21) with a particular focus on Mand. 5; 9–11 (33.1–34.8; 39.1–43.21). Chapters 6 and 11 buffered the exegetical chapters at the beginning and end of Part II with broader literary studies that concentrated on the text of the *Shepherd*. To study the *Shepherd* well requires readers to know the text well, and this book has attempted to model how such studies might be undertaken. Researchers who examine the *Shepherd* must also know the historical environment in which the text was written, and Chapters 7 and 8 outlined elements of the Greco-Roman, early Jewish, and early Christian literary environments that are useful to know in studying the *Shepherd*. Likewise, readers of the *Shepherd* should also seek to be empathetic with the *Shepherd*'s theological views, even if they may not personally share the views that the *Shepherd* expresses. Chapters 9 and 10 thus explored theological discussions that take place in the text with a focus on repentance and the language used for Jesus and the holy spirit.

Historical study requires one to examine their own biases and to know their own times. In recognizing the way in which our views affect our understanding of the *Shepherd* and the questions that we put to the text, one may also recognize that the *Shepherd* contains words that may continue to be of use in the present. Visions and parables provide materials that have the power to continue to shape our imaginations. The development of Hermas's character provides literary formation to the text, while historical details sprinkled into the descriptions offer suggestive insights about the lived experiences of Roman believers. The understanding of repentance as a way of knowing is suggestive as twenty-first-century readers continue to reconceive both what we know and how we know it. Finally, the portions of the Mandates that have been explored in this chapter recognize both the potency of negative emotions and the importance of developing divinely implanted, pneumatically inspired practices to oppose them. This book, like the angel, shepherd, and virgins who left Hermas (Sim. 10.4.5 [114.5]), must draw to a close. Yet by reflecting further on the text, the *Shepherd* may remain and reveal new things to those who study it today.

BIBLIOGRAPHY

Primary Sources

Acts of Paul

Barrier, Jeremy W. 2009. *The Acts of Paul and Thecla: A Critical Introduction and Commentary*. WUNT 2.270. Tübingen: Mohr Siebeck.

Pervo, Richard I. 2014. *The Acts of Paul: A New Translation with Introduction and Commentary*. Eugene: Cascade.

Acts of Thomas

Klijn, A. F. J. 2003. *The Acts of Thomas: Introduction, Text, and Commentary*, 2nd. ed. NovTSup108. Leiden: Brill.

Alexander of Aphrodisias

de Mixtione

Bruns, Ivo. 1892. *Alexandri Aphrodisiensis, Scripta Minora: Quaestiones, De fato, De mixtione*. Berlin: Reimer.

Todd, Robert B. 1976. *Alexander of Aphrodisias on Stoic Physics: A Study of the De Mixtione with Preliminary Essays, Text, Translation, and Commentary*. PhA 28. Leiden: Brill.

Ambrose of Milan

Hexaemeron libri sex

Savage, John J. 1961. *Saint Ambrose: Hexameron, Paradise, and Cain and Abel*. FC 42. New York: Fathers of the Church.

Schenkl, Karl. 1896. *S. Ambrosii Opera: Pars I*. CSEL 32. Prague: Tempsky.

Antiochus the Monk

Pandectes

PG 89.1421–1849 in *Patrologia Graeca*. Edited by Jacques-Paul Migne. 162 vols. Paris, 1857–86.

Apocalypse of Peter (Coptic)

Desjardins, Michel, and James Brashler. 2000. "NHC VII,3: *Apocalypse of Peter.*" Pages 201–47 in *The Coptic Gnostic Library: A Complete Edition of the Nag Hammadi Codices*. Edited by James M. Robinson. Vol. 4. Leiden: Brill.

Havelaar, Henriette W. 1999. *The Coptic Apocalypse of Peter (Nag Hammadi Codex VII, 3)*. TUGAL 144. Berlin: Akademie Verlag.

Apocalypse of Abraham

Rubinkiewicz, R. 1983–5. "Apocalypse of Abraham." Pages 681–705 in *The Old Testament Pseudepigrapha*. Edited by James H. Charlesworth. 2 vols. New York: Doubleday.

Apostolic Constitutions

Metzger, Marcel. 1985. *Les constitutions apostoliques: Tome I (Livres I–II)*. SC 320. Paris: Cerf.

Metzger, Marcel. 1986. *Les constitutions apostoliques: Tome II (Livres III–V)*. SC 329. Paris: Cerf.

Metzger, Marcel. 1987. *Les constitutions apostoliques: Tome III (Livres VI–VII)*. SC 336. Paris: Cerf.

Apostolic Fathers

Ehrman, Bart D. 2003. *The Apostolic Fathers*. 2 vols. LCL 24–5. Cambridge: Harvard University Press.

Fischer, Joseph A. 1981. *Die apostolischen Väter*. 8th ed. SUC 1. Munich: Kösel.

Gebhardt, Oscar von, Adolf von Harnack, and Theodor Zahn. 1906. *Patrum apostolicorum opera*. 5th ed. Leipzig: Hinrichs.

Holmes, Michael W. 2007. *The Apostolic Fathers: Greek Texts and English Translations*. 3rd ed. Grand Rapids: Baker Academic.

Lake, Kirsopp. 1912–13. *The Apostolic Fathers*. 2 vols. LCL 24–5. Cambridge: Harvard University Press.

Lefort, Louis-Théophile. 1952a. *Les Pères apostoliques en copte*. CSCO 135. Scriptores coptici 17. Louvain: Durbecq.

Lefort, Louis-Théophile. 1952b. *Les Pères apostoliques en copte*. CSCO 136. Scriptores coptici 18. Louvain: Durbecq.

Lindemann, Andreas, and Henning Paulsen. 1992. *Die apostolischen Väter*. Tübingen: Mohr Siebeck.

Lucchesi, Enzo. 1981. "Compléments aux Pères apostoliques en copte." *Analecta Bollandiana* 99: 395–408.

Prinzivalli, Emanuela, and Manlio Simonetti. 2010–15. *Seguendo Gesù: Testi cristiani delle origini*. 2 vols. Milan: Mondadori.

Wengst, Klaus. 1984. *Didache (Apostellehre), Barnabasbrief, Zweiter Klemensbrief, Schrift an Diognet*. SUC 2. Darmstadt: Wissenschaftliche Buchgesellschaft.

Apuleius

Metamorphoses

Gaselee, Stephen. 1915. *Apuleius: The Golden Ass, Being the Metamorphoses of Lucius Apuleius*. LCL. Cambridge: Harvard University Press.

Aristides

Apologia

Pouderon, Bernard, and Marie-Joseph Pierre. 2003. *Aristide: Apologie*. SC 470. Paris: Cerf.
Robinson, J. Armitage. 1891. *The Apology of Aristides*. TS 1. Cambridge: Cambridge University Press.

Aristotle

De generatione et corruptione

Rashed, Marwen. 2005. *Aristote: De la génération et la corruption*. Budé. Paris: Les belles lettres.

Poetica

Kassel, Rudolf. 1966. *De arte poetica liber*. Scriptorum classicorum bibliotheca Oxoniensis. Oxford: Clarendon.

Athanasius of Alexandria

De decretis

Opitz, Hans-Georg. 1935. *De decretis Nicaenae synodi*. Athanasius Werke 2.1. Berlin: De Gruyter.

De incarnatione

Kannengiesser, Charles. 1973. *Sur l'incarnation du Verbe*. SC 199. Paris: Cerf.
Thomson, Robert W. 1971. *Athanasius: Contra Gentes and De Incarnatione*. OECT. Oxford: Oxford University Press.

ad Afros episcopos

von Stockhausen, Annette. 2002. *Athanasius von Alexandrien, Epistula ad Afros*. PTS 56. Berlin: De Gruyter.

Epistulae festales

Martin, Annik, and Albert Michelin. 1985. *Histoire (Acephale): Et index syriage des lettres festales d'Athanase d'Alexandria*. SC 317. Paris: Cerf.

Athenagoras

Legatio

Schoedel, William R. 1972. *Athenagoras:* Legatio *and* De Resurrectione. OECT. Oxford: Clarendon.

3 Baruch

Gaylord, H. E. 1983–5. 3 (Greek Apocalypse of) Baruch. Pages 653–79 in *The Old Testament Pseudepigrapha*. Edited by James H. Charlesworth. 2 vols. New York: Doubleday.

Caesarius of Arles

Sermones

Delage, Marie-José. 1978. *Césaire d'Arles: Sermons au peuple*. Vol. 2. SC 243. Paris: Cerf.

Catullus

Poems

Thomson, D. F. S. 1978. *Catullus: A Critical Edition*. Chapel Hill: University of North Carolina Press.

Cicero

De finibus

Rackham, Harris. 1914. *Cicero: On Ends*. LCL 40. Cambridge: Harvard University Press.

De natura deorum

Rackham, Harris. 1933. *Cicero: De natura deorum; Academia*. LCL 268. Cambridge: Harvard University Press.

Clement of Alexandria

Excerpta ex Theodoto

Stählin, Otto. 1909. *Clemens Alexandrinus: Stromata Buch VII–VIII, Excerpta ex Theodoto, Eclogae propheticae, Quis dives salvetur, Fragmente.* GCS 17. Leipzig: Hinrichs.

Stromateis

Stählin, Otto. 1906. *Clemens Alexandrinus: Stromata Buch I–VI.* GCS 15. Leipzig: Hinrichs.

Codex Claromontanus

Tischendorff, Constantine. 1852. *Codex Claromontanus.* Leipzig: Brockhaus.

Codex Visionum

Hurst, André, and Jean Rudhardt. 1999. *Papyri Bodmer XXX–XXXVII: "Codex des Visions."* Publications de la Bibliotheca Bodmeriana. Munich: Saur.

Hurst, André, Olivier Reverdin, and Jean Rudhardt. 1984. *Papyrus Bodmer XXIX: Vision de Dorothéos.* Publications de la Bibliotheca Bodmeriana. Geneva: Fondation Martin Bodmer.

Columella

De Arboribus

Forster, E. S., and Edward H. Heffner. 1955. *Columella: On Agriculture, Books 10–12: On Trees.* LCL 408. Cambridge: Harvard University Press.

Commodian

Instructiones

Poinsotte, Jean-Michel. 2009. *Commodien: Instructions.* Collection des universités de France, Série latine 392. Paris: Belles lettres.

Didache

Rordorff, Willy, and Andre Tuilier. 1978. *La doctrine des douze apôtres (Didachè).* SC 248. Paris: Cerf.

Didascalia apostolorum

Vööbus, Arthur. 1979. *The Didascalia Apostolorum in Syriac.* Volume 2. CSCO 408. Leuven: Peeters.

Didymus the Blind

Commentarii in Job

Hagedorn, Ursula. 1968. *Kommentar zu Hiob: Kapiteln 7,20c-11*. Papyrologische Texte und Abhandlungen 3. Bonn: Habelt.

Henrichs, Albert. 1968. *Kommentar zu Hiob: Kapiteln 5,1-6,29*. Papyrologische Texte und Abhandlungen 2. Bonn: Habelt.

Commentarii in Zachariam

Doutrelaeus, Louis. 1962. *Didyme l'Aveugle: Sur Zacharie*. Vol 1. SC 83. Paris: Cerf.
Doutrelaeus, Louis. 1962. *Didyme l'Aveugle: Sur Zacharie*. Vol 2. SC 84. Paris: Cerf.
Doutrelaeus, Louis. 1962. *Didyme l'Aveugle: Sur Zacharie*. Vol 3. SC 85. Paris: Cerf.

Dio Chrysostom

Orationes

Cohoon, J. W. 1949. *Dio Chrysostom in Five Volumes*. Vol. 1. LCL 257. Cambridge: Harvard University Press.

Diogenes Laertius

Lives of the Eminent Philosophers

Hicks, Robert Drew. 1925. *Diogenes Laertius: Lives of Eminent Philosophers*. 2 vols. LCL 184-5. Cambridge: Harvard University Press.

Dionysius of Halicarnassus

Antiquitates romanae

Jacoby, Karl. 1885. *Dionysii Halicarnasei Antiquitatum Romanarum*. 4 vols. Leipzig: Teubner.

1 Enoch

Isaac, E. 1983-5. "1 (Ethiopic Apocalypse of) Enoch." Pages 5-89 in *The Old Testament Pseudepigrapha*. Edited by James H. Charlesworth. 2 vols. New York: Doubleday.

2 Enoch

Andersen, F. I. 1983-5. "2 (Slavonic Apocalypse of) Enoch." Pages 91-221 in *The Old Testament Pseudepigrapha*. Edited by James H. Charlesworth. 2 vols. New York: Doubleday.

Epiphanius

Panarion

Williams, Frank. 2009. *The* Panarion *of Epiphanius of Salamis: Book 1 (Sects 1–46)*. 2nd ed. NHMS 63. Leiden: Brill.

Epistle of Aristeas

Pelletier, André. 1962. *Lettre d'Aristée à Philocrate*. SC 89. Paris: Cerf.
Schutt, R. J. H. 1983–5. "Letter of Aristeas." Pages 2.7–34 in *The Old Testament Pseudepigrapha*. Edited by James H. Charlesworth. 2 vols. New York: Doubleday.
Thackeray, Henry St. John. 1914. "Appendix: The Letter of Aristeas." Pages 531–606 in *An Introduction to the Old Testament in Greek*. By H. B. Swete. 2nd ed. Cambridge: Cambridge University Press.

Eusebius

Historia ecclesiastica

Bardy, Gustav. 1952. *Eusèbe de Césarée: Histoire ecclésiastique, Livres 1–4*. SC 31. Paris: Cerf.
Bardy, Gustav. 1955. *Eusèbe de Césarée: Histoire ecclésiastique, Livres 5–7*. SC 41. Paris: Cerf.

4 Ezra

Metzger, Bruce M. 1983–5. "The Fourth Book of Ezra." Pages 1.516–59 in *The Old Testament Pseudepigrapha*. Edited by James H. Charlesworth. 2 vols. New York: Doubleday.

Galen

De adolore

Rothschild, Clare K., and Trevor W. Thompson. 2011. "Galen: 'On the Avoidance of Grief.'" *EC* 2: 110–29.

De pulsibus libellus ad Tyrones

Singer, Peter N. 1997. *Galen: Selected Works*. Oxford World's Classics. Oxford: Oxford University Press.

Si quis optimus medicus est, eundum esse philosophum

Singer, Peter N. 1997. *Galen: Selected Works*. Oxford World's Classics. Oxford: Oxford University Press.

Gospel of Pseudo-Matthew

Ehrman, Bart D., and Zlatko Pleše. 2011. "The Gospel of Pseudo-Matthew." Pages 73–113 in *The Apocryphal Gospels: Texts and Translations*. Oxford: Oxford University Press.

Gospel of Thomas

Gathercole, Simon. 2014. *The Gospel of Thomas: Introduction and Commentary*. TENTS 11. Leiden: Brill.

Hildegard of Bingen

Scivias

Migne, Jacques-Paul. 1855. *Patrologia Curus Completus: Series Latina*. Vol. 197. Paris: Migne.

Hippolytus

Refutatio omnium haeresium

Litwa, M. David. 2016. *Refutation of All Heresies*. WGRW 40. Atlanta: Society of Biblical Literature.

Ignatius of Antioch

Letters

Camelot, Pierre. 1969. *Ignace d'Antioche, Polycarpe de Smyrne: Lettres: Martyre de Polycarpe*. 4th ed. SC 10. Paris: Cerf.

Irenaeus

Epideixis

Behr, John. 1997. *St. Irenaeus of Lyons: On the Apostolic Preaching*. PPS 17. Crestwood: St. Vladimir's Seminary Press.
Rousseau, Adelin. 1995. *Démonstration de la prédication apostolique*. SC 406. Paris: Cerf.

Adversus Haereses

Rousseau, Adelin, and Louis Doutreleau. 1965. *Contre les hérésies (Livre IV)*. 2 vols. SC 100. Paris: Cerf.

Rousseau, Adelin, and Louis Doutreleau. 1969. *Contre les hérésies (Livre V)*. 2 vols. SC 152–3. Paris: Cerf.
Rousseau, Adelin, and Louis Doutreleau. 1974. *Contre les hérésies (Livre III)*. 2 vols. SC 210–11. Paris. Cerf.
Rousseau, Adelin, and Louis Doutreleau. 1979. *Contre les hérésies (Livre I)*. 2 vols. SC 263–4. Paris. Cerf.
Rousseau, Adelin, and Louis Doutreleau. 1982. *Contre les hérésies (Livre II)*. 2 vols. SC 293–4. Paris. Cerf.

Jerome

De uiris illustribus

Richardson, Ernest Cushing. 1896. *Hieronymus: De uiris illustribus. Gennadius: De uiris illustribus*. TUGAL 14. Leipzig: Hinrichs.

Josephus

Antiquitates judaicae

Niese, Benedikt. 1885–95. *Flavii Iosephi opera*. 7 vols. Berlin: Weidmann.
Thackeray, Henry St. John, and Ralph Marcus. 1930–65. *Josephus: Jewish Antiquities*. 9 vols. LCL. Cambridge: Harvard University Press.

Jubilees

VanderKam, James C. 1989. *The Book of Jubilees: A Critical Text*. CSCO 510. Leuven: Peeters.

Justin

Apologiae I–II

Minns, Denis, and Paul Parvis. 2009. *Justin, Philosopher and Martyr: Apologies*. OECT. Oxford: Oxford University Press.

Dialogus cum Tryphone

Marcovich, Miroslav. 2005. *Iustini Martyris: Apologiae pro christianis; Dialogus cum Tryphone*. PTS 38/47. Berlin: De Gruyter.

Kerygma Petri

Dobschütz, Ernst von. 1893. *Das Kerygma Petri: Kritisch untersucht*. TUGAL 11.1 Leipzig: Hinrichs.

Latin Infancy Gospels (Arundel Form)

Ehrman, Bart D., and Zlatko Pleše. 2011. "The Latin Infancy Gospels (J Composition)." Pages 115–55 in *The Apocryphal Gospels: Texts and Translations*. Oxford: Oxford University Press.

Lucian

De morte Peregrini

Harmon, A. M. 1936. *Lucian in Eight Volumes*. Vol. 5. LCL 302. Cambridge: Harvard University Press.

Philopseudes

Harmon, A. M. 1921. *Lucian in Eight Volumes*. Vol. 3. LCL 130. Cambridge: Harvard University Press.

Muratorian Fragment

Lietzmann, Hans. 1902. *Das muratorische Fragment und die monarchianischen Prologe zu den Evangelien*. KTTVÜ. Bonn: Marcus & Weber.

Origen

Commentarium in evangelium Joannis

Preuschen, Erwin. 1903. *Der Johanneskommentar*. GCS 10. Origenes Werke 4. Leipzig: Hinrichs.

Commentarium in evangelium Matthaei

Klostermann, Erich. 1935. *Origenes Matthäuserklärung*. GCS 40. Origenes Werke 10. Leipzig: Hinrichs.

Commentarii in Romanos

Hammond Bammel, Caroline P. 1985. *Der Römerbrieftext des Rufin und seine Origenes-Übersetzung*. AGLB 10. Freiburg: Herder.
Scheck, Thomas P. 2001. *Origen: Commentary on the Epistle to the Romans, Books 1–5*. FC 103. Washington, DC: Catholic University of America Press.
Scheck, Thomas P. 2002. *Origen: Commentary on the Epistle to the Romans, Books 6–10*. FC 104. Washington, DC: Catholic University of America Press.

Contra Celsum

Borret, Marcel. 1967–76. *Origène: Contre Celse*. 5 vols. SC 132, 136, 147, 150, 227. Paris: Cerf.

De Oratione

Koetschau, Paul. 1899. *Origenes Buch V–VIII Gegen Celsus, Die Schrift vom Gebet*. GCS 3. Origenes Werke 2. Leipzig: Hinrichs.

Stewart-Sykes, Alistair. 2004. *Tertullian, Cyprian, Origen: On the Lord's Prayer*. PPS 29. Crestwood: St. Vladimir's Seminary Press.

De Principiis

Crouzel, Henri, and Manlio Simonetti. 1978–80. *Origène: Traité des principes*. 4 vols. SC 252-3, 268-9. Paris: Cerf.

Homiliae in Genesim

Baehrens, W. A. 1920. *Homilien zum Hexateuch in Rufins Übersetzung*. GCS 29. Origenes Werke 6. Leipzig: Hinrichs.

Ovid

Amores

Showerman, Grant. 1914. *Ovid: Heroides, Amores*. Revised by G. P. Goold. LCL 41. Cambridge: Harvard University Press.

Metamorphoses

Miller, Frank Justus. 1916. *Ovid: Metamorphoses*. 2 vols. LCL 42-3. Cambridge: Harvard University Press.

Philo of Alexandria

De migratione Abrahami

Colson, F. H., and G. H. Whitaker. 1932. *Philo: On the Confusion of Tongues*. LCL 261. Cambridge: Harvard University Press.

Legum allegoriae

Colson, F. H., and G. H. Whitaker. 1929. *Philo: On the Creation, Allegorical Interpretation of Genesis 2 and 3*. LCL 226. Cambridge: Harvard University Press.

Pliny the Elder

Naturalis historia

Jones, W. H. S., and H. Rackham. 1938–62. *Pliny: Natural History*. 10 vols. LCL. Cambridge: Harvard University Press.

Rauveret, Agnès. 1981. *Pline l'ancien: Histoire naturelle livre xxxvi*. Budé. Paris: Société d'édition "Les Belles Lettres."

Pliny the Younger

Epistulae

Radice, Betty. 1969. *Pliny the Younger: Letters, Panegyricus*. 2 vols. LCL 55, 59. Cambridge: Harvard University Press.

Plutarch

De defectu oraculorum

Babbit, Frank Cole. 1936. *Plutarch: Moralia*. Vol. 5. LCL 306. Cambridge: Harvard University Press.

Protevangelium Jacobi

Ehrman, Bart D., and Zlatko Pleše. 2011. "The Proto-Gospel of James." Pages 31–71 in *The Apocryphal Gospels: Texts and Translations*. Oxford: Oxford University Press.

Pseudo-Athanasius

Praecepta ad Antiochum

Dindorfius, Guilielmus. 1857. *Athanasii Alexandrini Praecepta ad Antiochum: Ad codices duos recensuit*. Leipzig: Weigel.

Pseudo-Clementine Homilia

Rehm, Bernhard, and Georg Strecker. 1992. *Die Pseudoklementinen: Homilien*. 3rd ed. GCS 42. Berlin: Akademie.

Pseudo-Cyprian

De aleatoribus

Harnack, Adolf von. 1888. "Der pseudocyprianische Traktat de aleatoribus, die älteste lateinische christliche Schrift, ein Werk des römischen Bischofs Victor I." TUGAL 5: 1–135.

Pseudo-Phocylides

Sentences

Horst, Pieter W. van der. 1978. *The Sentences of Pseudo-Phocylides*. SVTP 4. Leiden: Brill.
Horst, Pieter W. van der. 1983–5. "Pseudo-Phocylides." Pages 2.565–582 in *The Old Testament Pseudepigrapha*. Edited by James H. Charlesworth. 2 vols. New York: Doubleday.

Pseudo-Tertullian

Carmen adversus Marcionitas

Pollmann, Karla. 1991. *Das Carmen adversus Marcionitas: Einleitung, Text, Übersetzung und Kommentar*. Göttingen: Vandenhoeck & Ruprecht.

Quintilian

Institutio oratoria

Russell, Donald A. 2002. *Quintillian: The Orator's Education*. 5 vols. LCL 124–7, 494. Cambridge: Harvard University Press.

Rufinus

Commentarius in symbolum apostolorum

Simonetti, Manlius. 1961. Pages 125–82 in *Tyrannius Rufinus: Opera*. CCSL 20. Turnhout: Brepols.

Shepherd of Hermas

d'Abbadie, Antoine. 1860. *Hermae Pastor: Aethiopice primum edidit et aethiopica latine vertit*. Leipzig: Brockhaus.
Anger, Rudolfus, and Guilielmus Dindorfius. 1856. *Hermae Pastor: Graece*. Leipzig: Weigel.
Bandini, Michele. 2000. "Un nuovo frammento greco del *Pastore* di Erma." *RHT* 30: 109–22.
Bandini, Michele. 2001. "Il *Pastore* di Erma: Datazione e struttura." Pages 123–35 in *Il cristianesimo delle origini: I Padri apostolici*. Edited by Anna Lenzuni. Bologna: EDB.
Bonner, Campbell. 1925. "A Papyrus Codex of the Shepherd of Hermas." *HTR* 18: 115–27.
Bonner, Campbell. 1927. "A New Fragment of the Shepherd of Hermas (Michigan Papyrus 44-H)." *HTR* 20: 105–16.
Bonner, Campbell. 1934. *A Papyrus Codex of the Shepherd of Hermas*. Ann Arbor: University of Michigan Press.
Carlini, Antonio, and Luigi Giaccone. 1991. *Papyrus Bodmer XXXVIII: Erma: Il Pastore*. Cologny: Bibliotheca Bodmeriana.

Carlini, Antonio, and Michele Bandini. 2011. "Il Pastore di Erma: Nuove testimonianze e vecchi problemi." Pages 91–105 in *I papiri letterari cristiani: Atti del Convegno internaz*. Edited by Guido Bastianini and Angelo Casanova. Testi di Papirologia 13. Florence: Istituto Papirologico G. Vitelli.

Cecconi, Paolo. 2010–11. "Il *Pastore* di Erma e i nuovi fogli del *Codex Sinaiticus*." Res Publica Litterarum 33–4: 112–43.

Coneybeare, F. C. 1898. "A Quotation from 'The Shepherd of Hermas.'" *Athenaeum* 3689: 65–6.

Diels, Hermann, and Adolf von Harnack. 1891. "Über einen Berliner Papyrus des Pastor Hermae." *SPAW* 427–31.

Erho, Ted. 2012. "A Third Ethiopic Witness to the *Shepherd of Hermas*." *La Parola del Passato* 67: 363–70.

Erho, Ted. 2020. "A Fourth Ethiopic Witness to the *Shepherd of Hermas*." Pages 241–66 in *Caught in Translation: Studies on Versions of Late-Antique Christian Literature*. Edited by Madalina Toca and Dan Batovici. TSEC 17. Leiden: Brill.

d'Etaples, Jacques Le Fèvre. 1513. *Liber trium vivorum et trium spiritualium virginum*. Paris: Estienne.

Gebhardt, Oscar von, and Adolf von Harnack. 1877. *Hermae Pastor Graece*. Leipzig: Hinrichs.

Grenfell, Bernard P., and Arthur S. Hunt. 1901. *The Amherst Papyri*. Vol. 2. London: Oxford University Press.

Gronewald, Michael. 1974. "Ein liturgischer Papyrus: Gebet und Ode 8: P. Mich. Inv. 6427." *ZPE* 14: 193–200.

Gronewald, Michael. 1980. "Ein verkannter Hermas-Papyrus (P. Iand. I 4 = Hermae Pastor, Mand. XI 19–21; XII 1, 2–3." *ZPE* 40: 53–54.

Harnack, Adolf von. 1898. "Über zwei von Grenfell und Hunt entdeckte und publicirte altchristliche Fragmente." *SPAW* 516–20.

Hilgenfeld, Adolf. 1873. *Hermae Pastor: Veterem latinam interpretationem e codicibus edidit*. Leipzig: Reisland.

Hilgenfeld, Adolf. 1881. *Hermae Pastor: Graece*. 2nd ed. Leipzig: Weigel.

Joly, Robert. 1968. *Hermas le Pasteur*. 2nd ed. SC 53. Paris: Cerf.

Kilpatrick, G. D. 1947. "A New Papyrus of the Shepherd of Hermas." *JTS* 191: 204–5.

Körtner, Ulrich H. J., and Martin Leutzsch. 1998. *Papiasfragmente, Hirt des Hermas*. SUC 3. Darmstadt: Wissenschaftliche Buchgesellschaft.

Lake, Kirsopp. 1907. *Facsimiles of the Athos Fragments of the Shepherd of Hermas*. Oxford: Clarendon.

Lambros, Spyr. P. 1888. *A Collation of the Athous Codex of the Shepherd of Hermas*. Translated by J. Armitage Robinson. Cambridge: Cambridge University Press.

van Lantschoot, Arnold. 1962. "Un second témoin éthiopien du Pasteur d'Hermas." *Byzantion* 32: 93–5.

Lappa-Zizicas, Eurydice. 1965. "Cinq fragments du *Pasteur* d'Hermas dans un manuscrit de la Bibliothèque Nationale de Paris." *RSR* 53: 251–6.

Leipoldt, Johannes. 1909–10. "Ein neues saidisches Bruchstück des Hermasbuches." *ZÄS* 46: 137–9.

Lenaerts, Jean. 1979. "Un papyrus du *Pasteur* d'Hermas: P. Iand, 1,4." *CdE* 54: 356–8.

Mazzini, Innocenzo. 1980. "Il codice urbinate 486 e la versione palatina del Pastore di Erma." *Prometheus* 6: 181–8.

Mercati, Silvo Giuseppe. 1925. "Passo del Pastore di Erma riconosciuto nel Pap. Oxy. 1828." *Bib* 6: 336–8.
Müller, F. W. K. 1905. "Eine Hermas-Stelle in manischäischer Version." *SPAW* 1077–83.
Outtier, Bernard. 1990–1. "La version géorgienne de la *Pasteur* d'Hermas." *Revue des études géorgiennes et caucasiennes* 6–7: 211–16.
Pintaudi, Rosario, Růžena Dostálová, and Ladislav Vidman, eds. 1988. *Papyri Graecae Wessely Pragenses (P.Prag. 1)*. Papyrologica Florentina 16. Florence: Gonelli.
Powell, J. Enoch. 1936. *The Rendel Harris Papyri of Woodbrooke College, Birmingham*. Cambridge: Cambridge University Press.
Schmidt, Karl, and Wilhelm Schubart. 1909. "Ein Fragment des Pastor Hermae aus der Hamburger Stadtbibliothek." *SPAW* 1076–81.
Stegmüller, Otto. 1937. "Christlichte Texte aus der Berliner Papyrussammlung." *Aeg* 17: 452–62.
Tornau, Christian, and Paolo Cecconi. 2014. *The Shepherd of Hermas in Latin: Critical Edition of the Oldest Translation* Vulgata. TUGAL 173. Berlin: De Gruyter.
Treu, Kurt. 1970. "Ein neuer Hermas-Papyrus." *VC* 24: 34–9.
Vezzoni, Anna. 1988. "Un testimone inedito della versione palatina del *Pastore* di Erma." *SCO* 37: 241–65.
Vezzoni, Anna. 1994. *Il Pastore di Erma: Versione palatina, con testo a fronte*. Nuovo melograno 13. Florence: Casa editrice Le lettere.
Weinel, Heinrich. 1904. "Der Hirt des Hermas." Pages 217–92 in *Neutestamentliche Apokryphen in deutscher Übersetzung und mit Einleitungen*. Edited by Edgar Hennecke. Tübingen: Mohr.
Whittaker, Molly. 1956. *Der Hirt des Hermas*. GCS 48. Berlin: Akademie.
Whittaker, Molly. 1967. *Der Hirt des Hermas*. 2nd ed. GCS 48. Berlin: Akademie.

Sibylline Oracles

Collins, John J. 1983–5. "Sibylline Oracles." Pages 1.335–472 in *The Old Testament Pseudepigrapha*. Edited by James H. Charlesworth. 2 vols. New York: Doubleday.
Geffcken, Johannes. 1902. *Die Oracula Sibyllina*. GCS 8. Leipzig: Hinrichs.

Stoicorum Veterum Fragmenta (SVF)

Arnim, Hans Friedrich August. 1903–24. *Stoicorum Veterum Fragmenta*. Leipzig: Teubner.

Tabula Cebetis

Fitzgerald, John T., and L. Michael White. 1983. *The Tabula of Cebes*. SBLTT 24. Chico, CA: Scholars.
Hirsch-Luipold, Rainer, Reinhard Feldmeier, Barbara Hirsch, Lutz Koch, and Heinz-Günther Nesselrath. 2005. *Die Bildtafel des Kebes: Allegorie des Lebens*. SAPERE 8. Darmstadt: Wissenschaftliche Buchgesellschaft.
Praechter, Karl. 1893. ΚΕΒΗΤΟΣ ΠΙΝΑΞ: *Cebetis Tabula*. Leipzig: Teubner.

Tatian

Oratio ad Graecos

Nesselrath, Heinz-Günther. 2016. *Gegen falsche Götter und falsche Bildung: Tatian, Rede an die Griechen*. SAPERE 28. Tübingen: Mohr Siebeck.

Tertullian

De anima

Waszink, Jan Hendrick. 1954. *Tertullianus: De Anima*. CCSL 2. Turnhout: Brepols.

De oratione

Evans, Ernest. 1953. *Tertullian's Tract on the Prayer: Latin Text with Critical Notes, and English Translation, an Introduction, and Explanatory Observations*. London: SPCK.

De praescriptione haereticorum

Refoulé, R. François. 1957. *Tertullien: Traité de la prescription contre les hérétiques*. SC 46. Paris: Cerf.

Adversus Praxean

Evans, Ernest. 1948. *Adversus Praxean Liber: Tertullian's Treatise against Praxeas*. London: SPCK.

Theophilus of Antioch

Ad Autolycum

Grant, Robert M. 1970. *Theophilus of Antioch: Ad Autolycum*. OECT. Oxford: Clarendon.

Vergil

Aeneid

Fairclough, H. Rushton. 1916. *Virgil: Eclogues, Georgics, Aeneid I–VI*. LCL 63. Cambridge: Harvard University Press.
Fairclough, H. Rushton. 1918. *Virgil: Aeneid VII–XII, the Minor Poems*. LCL 64. Cambridge: Harvard University Press.

Eclogues

Fairclough, H. Rushton. 1916. *Virgil: Eclogues, Georgics, Aeneid I–VI.* LCL 63. Cambridge: Harvard University Press.

Georgics

Fairclough, H. Rushton. 1916. *Virgil: Eclogues, Georgics, Aeneid I–VI.* LCL 63. Cambridge: Harvard University Press.

Vitruvius

de Architectura

Granger, Frank. 1933–5. *Vitruvius: On Architecture.* 2 vols. LCL 251, 280. Cambridge: Harvard University Press.

Secondary Sources

Abramowski, Luise. 1984. "Die Entstehung der dreigliedrigen Taufformel—Ein Versuch." *ZTK* 81: 417–46.

Adam, Karl. 1906. "Die Lehre von dem heiligen Geiste bei Hermas und Tertullian." *TQ* 88: 36–61.

Adams, Edward. 2007. *The Stars Will Fall from Heaven: Cosmic Catastrophe in the New Testament and Its World.* London: T&T Clark Continuum.

Aland, Kurt, Christian Hannick, and Klaus Junack. 1980. "Bibelhandschriften II: Neues Testament." *TRE* 6: 114–31.

Aldridge, Robert E. 1999. "Peter and the 'Two Ways.'" *VC* 53: 233–64.

Alexander, Loveday. 2009. "Prophets and Martyrs as Exemplars of Faith." Pages 405–21 in *The Epistle to the Hebrews and Christian Theology.* Edited by Richard Bauckham, Daniel R. Driver, Trevor A. Hart, and Nathan MacDonald. Grand Rapids: Eerdmans.

Alikin, Valeriy A. 2010. *The Earliest History of the Christian Gathering: Origin, Development and Content of the Christian Gathering in the First to Third Centuries.* VCSup 102. Leiden: Brill.

Allison, Dale C. 2011. "Eldad and Modad." *JSP* 21: 99–131.

Arbesmann, Rudolph. 1949–51. "Fasting and Prophecy in Pagan and Christian Antiquity." *Traditio* 7: 1–71.

Armstrong, Jonathan J. 2008. "Victorinus of Pettau as the Author of the Canon Muratori." *VC* 62: 1–34.

Attridge, Harold W. 1989. *The Epistle to the Hebrews.* Hermeneia. Minneapolis: Fortress.

Attridge, Harold W. 2010. "Temple, Tabernacle, Time, and Space in John and Hebrews." *EC* 1: 261–74.

Aune, David E. 1978. "*Herm. Man.* 11.2: Christian False Prophets Who Say What People Wish to Hear." *JBL* 97: 103–4.

Aune, David E. 1983. *Prophecy in Early Christianity and the Ancient Mediterranean World.* Grand Rapids: Eerdmans.

Bammel, Caroline P. Hammond. 1981. "Philocalia IX, Jerome, Epistle 121, and Origen's Exposition of Romans VII." *JTS* 32: 50–81.

Bammel, Caroline P. Hammond. 1996. "Patristic Exegesis of Romans 5:7." *JTS* 47: 532–42.

Bandini, Michele, and Gianfrancesco Lusini. 1998. "Nuove acquisizioni intorno alla tradizione testuale del '*Pastore*' di Erma in greco e in etiopico." *SCO* 46: 625–35.

Barclay, John M. G. 1987. "Mirror-Reading a Polemical Letter: Galatians as a Test Case." *JSNT* 31: 73–93.

Barclay, John M. G. 2004. "Poverty in Pauline Studies: A Response to Steven Friesen." *JSNT* 26: 363–6.

Barclay, John M. G. 2014. "Pure Grace?" *ST* 68: 4–20.

Barclay, John M. G. 2015. *Paul and the Gift*. Grand Rapids: Eerdmans.

Barclay, John M. G. 2018. "La gracia y la forma de la salvación en Pablo." *RevistB* 80: 241–59.

Barnard, Leslie W. 1964. Review of *Die Apostolischen Vater I: Der Hirt des Hermas*. Edited by Molly Whittaker. GCS 48. Berlin: Akademie, 1956 and *Hermas et les Pasteurs: Les trois auteurs du Pasteur d'Hermas*, by Stanislas Giet, Paris: Presses Universitaires de France, 1963. *VC* 18: 183–6.

Barnard, Leslie W. 1966. *Studies in the Apostolic Fathers and Their Backgrounds*. New York: Shocken.

Barnard, Leslie W. 1968. "The Shepherd of Hermas in Recent Study." *HeyJ* 9: 29–36.

Barnes, Michele Rene. 2001. "Early Christian Binitarianism: The Father and the Holy Spirit." A Paper Presented to the Annual Meeting of the North American Patristics Society.

Batovici, Dan. 2011. "Contrasting Ecclesiastical Functions in the Second Century: 'Diakonia,' 'Diakonoi,' 'Episkopoi,' and 'Presbyteroi' in the *Shepherd of Hermas* and Ignatius of Antioch's *Letters*." *Aug* 51: 303–14.

Batovici, Dan. 2013. "Hermas in Clement of Alexandria." Pages 41–51 in *Studia Patristica LXVI*. Edited by Markus Vinzent. Leuven: Peeters.

Batovici, Dan. 2014. "Textual Revisions of the *Shepherd of Hermas* in Codex Sinaiticus." *ZAC* 18: 443–70.

Batovici, Dan. 2015a. "The Appearance of Hermas's Text in Codex Sinaiticus." Pages 149–59 in *Codex Sinaiticus: New Perspectives on the Ancient Biblical Manuscript*. Edited by Scott McKendrick, David Parker, Amy Myshrall, and Cillian O'Hogan. London: British Library.

Batovici, Dan. 2015b. "*Hermas*' Authority in Irenaeus' Works: A Reassessment." *Augustinianum* 55: 5–31.

Batovici, Dan. 2015c. "The Less-Expected Books in *Codex Sinaiticus* and *Alexandrinus*: Codicological and Palaeographical Considerations." Pages 39–50 in *Comment le Livre s'est fait livre: La fabrication des manuscrits bibliques (IVe–XVe siècle): Bilan, résultats, perspectives de recherche*. Edited by Chiara Ruzzier and Xavier Hermand. Turnhout: Brepols.

Batovici, Dan. 2015d. "Apocalyptic and Metanoia in the *Shepherd of Hermas*." *Apocrypha* 26: 151–70.

Batovici, Dan. 2016a. "The Apostolic Fathers in Codex Sinaiticus and Codex Alexandrinus." *Bib* 97: 581–605.

Batovici, Dan. 2016b. "A New Hermas Papyrus Fragment in Paris." *APF* 62: 20–36.

Batovici, Dan. 2016c. "Two Notes on the Papyri of the *Shepherd of Hermas*." *APF* 62: 384–95.

Batovici, Dan. 2017a. "The *Shepherd of Hermas* in Recent Scholarship on the Canon: A Review Article." *ASE* 34: 89–105.

Batovici, Dan. 2017b. "Two Lost Lines of the Coptic Hermas in BnF Copte 130 (2) F. 127." *JTS* 68: 572–5.

Batovici, Dan. 2018. "Hermas in Latin: Notes on a Recent Edition." *ETL* 94: 151–7.

Bauckham, Richard. 1974. "The Great Tribulation in the Shepherd of Hermas." *JTS* 25: 27–40.

Bauckham, Richard. 1993a. *The Climax of Prophecy: Studies on the Book of Revelation*. Edinburgh: T&T Clark.

Bauckham, Richard. 1993b. *The Theology of the Book of Revelation*. Cambridge: Cambridge University Press.

Bauckham, Richard. 1998. *God Crucified: Monotheism and Christology in the New Testament*. Milton Keynes: Paternoster.

Bauckham, Richard. [2004] 2008. "The Spirit of God in Us Loathes Envy: James 4:5." Pages 270–81 in *The Holy Spirit and Christian Origins: Essays in Honor of James D. G. Dunn*. Edited by Graham N. Stanton, Bruce W. Longenecker, and Stephen C. Barton. Grand Rapids: Eerdmans. Reprinted in *The Jewish World around the New Testament*. Edited by Richard Bauckham. WUNT 233. Tübingen: Mohr Siebeck.

Bauckham, Richard. 2008. *Jesus and the God of Israel: God Crucified and Other Studies in the New Testament's Christology of Divine Identity*. Grand Rapids: Eerdmans.

Bauckham, Richard. 2013. "Eldad and Modad." Pages 244–56 in *Old Testament Pseudepigrapha: More Noncanonical Scriptures*. Edited by Richard Bauckham, James R. Davila, and Alexander Panayotov. Vol. 1. Grand Rapids: Eerdmans.

Bauckham, Richard. 2017. "Messianic Jewish Identity in James." Pages 101–20 in *Muted Voices of the New Testament: Readings in the Catholic Epistles and Hebrews*. Edited by Katherine M. Hockey, Madison N. Pierce, and Francis Watson. LNTS 565. London: Bloomsbury T&T Clark.

Bauer, Walter. 1909. *Das Leben Jesu im Zeitalter der neutestamentlichen Apokryphen*. Tübingen: Mohr Siebeck.

Bautista, Ramon L. 2014. "Discernment of Spirits in *The Shepherd of Hermas* and Origen." *Landas* 28.2: 1–43.

Baynes, Leslie. 2012. *The Heavenly Book Motif in Judeo-Christian Apocalypses, 200 B.C.E.–200 C.E.* JSJSup 152. Leiden: Brill.

Beale, Gregory K. 2004. *The Temple and the Church's Mission: A Biblical Theology of the Dwelling Place of God*. Downers Grove: IVP Academic.

Beasley-Murray, George R. 1999. *John*. 2nd ed. WBC 36. Nashville: Thomas Nelson.

Beavis, Mary Ann. 2018. "The Parable of the Slave, Son, and Vineyard: An Early Christian Freedman's Narrative (Hermas, *Similitudes* 5.2–11)." *CBQ* 80: 655–69.

Bebbington, David W. 1989. *Evangelicalism in Modern Britain: A History from the 1730s to the 1980s*. London: Unwin Hyman.

Bennema, Corenlius. 2014. "Mimesis in John 13: Cloning or Creative Articulation." *NovT* 56: 261–74.

Berger, Klaus. 1992. *Synopse des Vierten Buch Esra und der Syrischen Baruch-Apokalypse*. Tübingen: Francke.

Berger, Klaus. 2018. *Leih mir deine Flügel, Engel: Die Apokalypse des Johannes im Leben der Kirche*. Freiburg: Herder.

Black, Max. 1962. *Models and Metaphors: Studies in Language and Philosophy*. Ithaca: Cornell University Press.

Blenkinsopp, Joseph. 1990. *Ezekiel*. IBC. Louisville: Westminster John Knox.

Blidstein, Moshe. 2017. *Purity, Community, and Ritual in Early Christian Literature*. SAR. Oxford: Oxford University Press.

Blischke, Mareike Verena. 2007. *Die Eschatologie in der Sapientia Salomonis*. FAT 2.26. Tübingen: Mohr Siebeck.

Blomkvist, Vemund. 2011. "The Teaching on Baptism in the Shepherd of Hermas." Pages 849–70 in *Ablution, Initiation, and Baptism: Late Antiquity, Early Judaism, and Early Christianity*. Edited by David Hellholm, Tor Vegge, Øyvind Norderval, and Christer Hellholm. 3 vols. BZNW 176. Berlin: De Gruyter.

Blumell, Lincoln H., and Thomas A. Wayment, eds. 2015. *Christian Oxyrhynchus: Texts, Documents, and Sources*. Waco: Baylor University Press.

Bogdanos, Theodore. 1977. "The 'Shepherd of Hermas' and the Development of Medieval Visionary Allegory." *Viator* 8: 33–46.

Booth, Wayne C. 1979. "Metaphor as Rhetoric: The Problem of Evaluation." Pages 47–70 in *On Metaphor*. Edited by Sheldon Sacks. Chicago: University of Chicago Press.

Bovon, François. 2009. "Canonical, Rejected, and Useful Books." Pages 318–22 in *New Testament and Christian Apocrypha: Collected Studies II*. Edited by Glenn E. Snyder. WUNT 237. Tübingen: Mohr Siebeck.

Bovon, François. 2012. "Beyond the Canonical and Apocryphal Books, the Presence of a Third Category: The Books Useful for the Soul." *HTR* 105: 125–37.

Bovon, François. 2015. "'Useful for the Soul': Christian Apocrypha and Christian Spirituality." Pages 185–95 in *The Oxford Handbook of Early Christian Apocrypha*. Edited by Andrew F. Gregory and Christopher M. Tuckett. Oxford: Oxford University Press.

Brakke, David. 1994. "Canon Formation and Social Conflict in Fourth-Century Egypt: Athanasius of Alexandria's Thirty-Ninth *Festal Letter*." *HTR* 87: 395–419.

Bremmer, Jan N. 2017. "Lucian on Peregrinus and Alexander of Abonuteichos: A Sceptical View of Two Religious Entrepreneurs." Pages 49–78 in *Beyond Priesthood: Religious Entrepreneurs and Innovators in the Roman Empire*. Edited by Richard L. Gordon, Georgia Petridou, and Jörg Rüpke. RVV 66. Berlin: De Gruyter.

Bremmer, Jan N., Wout J. van Bekkum, and Arie L. Molendijk. 2006. *Paradigms, Poetics, and Politics of Conversion*. Groningen Studies in Cultural Change 18. Leuven: Peeters.

Breytenbach, Cilliers. 1999. "Gnädigstimmen und opferkultische Stühne im Urchristentum und seiner Umwelt." Pages 419–42 in *Das Urchristentum in seiner literarischen Geschicht: Festschrift für Jürgen Becker zum 65. Geburtstag*. Edited by Ulrich Mell and Ulrich B. Müller. BZNW 100. Berlin: De Gruyter.

Breytenbach, Cilliers. 2003. "'Christus starb für uns': Zur Tradition und paulinischen Rezeption der sogenannten 'Sterbeformeln.'" *NTS* 49: 447–75.

Breytenbach, Cilliers. 2010a. "'Christus starb für uns': Zur Tradition und paulinischen Rezeption der sogenannten 'Sterbeformeln.'" Pages 95–126 in *Grace, Reconciliation and Concord: The Death of Christ in Graeco-Roman Metaphors*. NovTSup 135. Leiden: Brill.

Breytenbach, Cilliers. 2010b. "Gnädigstimmen und Gnädigsein in urchristlichen Texten." Pages 35–58 in *Grace, Reconciliation and Concord: The Death of Christ in Graeco-Roman Metaphors*. NovTSup 135. Leiden: Brill.

Bricker, Daniel P. 1995. "The Doctrine of the 'Two Ways' in Proverbs." *JETS* 38: 501–17.

Briggman, Anthony. 2015. "Literary and Rhetorical Theory in Irenaeus, Part 1." *VC* 69: 500–27.

Briggman, Anthony. 2019. *God and Christ in Irenaeus*. OECS. Oxford: Oxford University Press.

Brookins, Timothy A. 2013. "The (In)frequency of the Name 'Erastus' in Antiquity: A Literary, Papyrological, and Epigraphical Catalog." *NTS* 59: 496–516.

Brooks, David. 2015. *The Road to Character*. New York: Random House.

Brooks, James A. 1992. "Clement of Alexandria as a Witness to the Development of the New Testament Canon." *SecCent* 9: 41–55.

Brouwer, Leendert. 2018. "Temple Symbolism and Mission in the Pauline Churches." *Missionalia* 46: 85–108.

Brox, Norbert. 1989a. "Die kleinen Gleichnisse im Pastor Hermae." *MTZ* 40: 263–278.

Brox, Norbert. 1989b. "Die weggeworfenen Steine im Pastor Hermae Vis III,7,5." *ZNW* 80: 130–3.

Brox, Norbert. 1991. *Der Hirt des Hermas*. KAV 7. Göttingen: Vandenhoeck & Ruprecht.

Buch-Hansen, Gitte. 2010. *"It Is the Spirit That Gives Life:" A Stoic Understanding of Pneuma in John's Gospel*. BZNW 173. Berlin: De Gruyter.

Bucur, Bogdan G. 2006. "Observations on the Ascetic Doctrine of the *Shepherd of Hermas*." *StudMon* 48: 7–23.

Bucur, Bogdan G. 2007. "The Son of God and the Angelomorphic Holy Spirit: A Rereading of the Shepherd's Christology." *ZNW* 98: 120–42.

Bucur, Bogdan G. 2009. *Angelomorphic Pneumatology: Clement of Alexandria and Other Early Christian Witnesses*. VCSup 95. Leiden: Brill.

Burke, Trevor J. 2006. *Adopted into God's Family: Exploring a Pauline Metaphor*. Downers Grove: IVP Academic.

Cameron, Averil. 2003. *Fifty Years of Prosopography: The Later Roman Empire, Byzantium and Beyond*. Oxford: Oxford University Press.

Campenhausen, Hans Freiherr von. 1972. *The Formation of the Christian Bible*. Translated by John A. Baker. Philadelphia: Fortress.

Cantalamessa, Raniero. 1962. *La cristologia di Tertulliano*. Paradosis 18. Freiburg: Edizioni Universitarie Friburgo Svizzera.

Carlini, Antonio. 1985. "Le passegiate di Erma verso Cuma (su due luoghi controversi del *Pastore*)." Pages 105–9 in *Studi in onore di Edda Bresciani*. Edited by S. F. Bondi, S. Pernigotti, F. Serra, and A. Vivian. Pisa: Giardini.

Carlini, Antonio. 1987. "La tradizione testuale del Pastore di Erma e i nuovi papiri." Pages 23–43 in *Le Strade del testo*. Edited by Guglielmo Cavallo. Studi e commenti 5. Lecce: Adriatica Editrice.

Carlini, Antonio. 1988. "Erma (*Vis*. II 3,1) testimone testuale di Paolo?" *SCO* 37: 235–9.

Carmignac, Jean. 1979. "Qu'est-ce que l'apocalyptique? Son emploi à Qumrân." *RevQ* 10: 3–33.

Carroll, Scott T. 1991. "An Early Church Sermon against Gambling (CPL 60)." *SecCent* 8: 83–95.

Cecil, David. 1949. *Reading as One of the Fine Arts: An Inaugural Lecture Delivered Before the University of Oxford on 28 May 1949*. Oxford: Clarendon.

Cecconi, Paolo. 2012. "The *Vulgata* Translation of *Hermae Pastor*: New Unknown Sources." *Res Publica Literrarum* 35: 35–49.

Cecconi, Paolo. 2018. "The Codex Sinaiticus and Hermas: The Ways of a Crossed Textual Transmission." *ZAC* 22: 278–95.

Chadwick, Henry. 1957. "The New Edition of Hermas." *JTS* 8: 274–80.

Choat, Malcolm, and Rachel Yuen-Collingridge. 2010. "The Egyptian Hermas: The Shepherd in Egypt before Constantine." Pages 191–212 in *Early Christian Manuscripts: Examples of Applied Method and Approach*. Edited by Thomas J. Kraus and Tobias Nicklas. TENT 5. Leiden: Brill.

Cirillo, Luigi. 1973. "La christologie pneumatique de la cinquième parabole du 'Pasteur' d'Hermas." *RHR* 184: 25–48.

Coakley, Sarah. 2003. "The Trinity, Prayer and Sexuality." Pages 258–67 in *Feminism and Theology*. Edited by Janet Martin Soskice and Diana Lipton. Oxford Readings in Feminism. Oxford: Oxford University Press.

Coakley, Sarah. 2013a. *God, Sexuality, and the Self: An Essay "On the Trinity."* Cambridge: Cambridge University Press.

Coakley, Sarah. 2013b. "Prayer, Politics and the Trinity: Vying Models of the Trinity in the Third–Fourth Century Debates on Prayer and 'Orthodoxy.'" *SJT* 66: 379–99.

Cochran, Sam V., and Fredric E. Rabinowitz. 2000. *Men and Depression: Clinical and Empirical Perspectives*. San Diego: Academic Press.

Coleborne, William. 1969. "A Linguistic Approach to the Problem of Structure and Composition of the *Shepherd of Hermas*." *Colloquium* 3: 133–42.

Coleborne, William. 1970. "The Shepherd of Hermas: A Case for Multiple Authorship and Some Implications." *StPatr* 10: 65–70.

Collins, John J. 1979. "Introduction: Towards the Morphology of a Genre." *Semeia* 14: 1–20.

Collins, John J. 1983–5. "Introduction to the Sibylline Oracles." Pages 1.317–26 in *The Old Testament Pseudepigrapha*. Edited by James H. Charlesworth. 2 vols. New York: Doubleday.

Collins, John J. 1998. *The Apocalyptic Imagination: An Introduction to Jewish Apocalyptic Literature*. 2nd ed. Grand Rapids: Eerdmans.

Collins, John J. 2014. "What is Apocalyptic Literature?" Pages 1–16 in *The Oxford Handbook of Apocalyptic Literature*. Edited by John J. Collins. Oxford: Oxford University Press.

Collins, John J. 2016. "The Genre Apocalypse Reconsidered." *ZAC* 20: 21–40.

Collins, Paul M. 2008. *The Trinity: A Guide for the Perplexed*. London: T&T Clark Continuum.

Corwin, Virginia. 1960. *St. Ignatius and Christianity in Antioch*. YPR 1. New Haven: Yale University Press.

Cosaert, Carl P. 2008. *The Text of the Gospels in Clement of Alexandria*. NTGF 9. Atlanta: Society of Biblical Literature.

Cotterill, J. M., and Charles Taylor. 1910. "Plutarch, Cebes, and Hermas." *JP* 31: 14–41.

Cox Miller, Patricia. 1988. "'All the Words Were Frightful': Salvation by Dreams in the Shepherd of Hermas." *VC* 42: 327–38.

D'Alès, Athémar. 1905. *La théologie de Tertullien*. 3rd ed. BTH. Paris: Beauchesne.

D'Alès, Athémar. 1914. *L'édit de Calliste: Études sur l'origine de la penitence chrétienne*. BTH. Paris: Beauchesne.

Daniélou, Jean. 1964. *The Theology of Jewish Christianity*. Translated by John A. Barker. London: Darton, Longman & Todd.

Deissmann, Adolf. 1925. *St. Paul: A Study in Social and Religious History*. Translated by Lionel R. M. Strachan. New York: Hodder & Stoughton.

DeLaine, Janet. 2012. "Housing Roman Ostia." Pages 327–51 in *Contested Spaces: Houses and Temples in Roman Antiquity and the New Testament*. Edited by David L. Balch and Annette Weissenrieder. WUNT 285. Tübingen: Mohr Siebeck.

Delkurt, Holger. 1999. "Die Engelwesen in Sach 1,8-15." *BN* 99: 20–41.

Dibelius, Martin. 1921. "Der Offenbarungsträger im 'Hirten' des Hermas." Pages 105–18 in *Harnack-Ehrung: Beiträge zur Kirchengeschichte ihrem Lehrer Adolf von Harnack zu seinem siebzigsten Geburtstage (7. Mai 1921)*. Leipzig: Hinrichs.

Dibelius, Martin. 1923. *Der Hirt des Hermas*. Die apostolischen Väter 4. HNT Ergänzungsband. Tübingen: Mohr Siebeck.

Docherty, Susan E. 2009. *The Use of the Old Testament in Hebrews: A Case Study in Early Jewish Bible Interpretation*. WUNT 2.238. Tübingen: Mohr Siebeck.

Dorival, Gilles. 2013. "Origen." Pages 605–28 in *The New Cambridge History of the Bible: From the Beginnings to 600*. Edited by James Carleton Paget and Joachim Schaper. Vol. 1. Cambridge: Cambridge University Press.

Downs, David J. 2016. *Alms: Charity, Reward, and Atonement in Early Christianity*. Waco: Baylor University Press.

Downs, David J. 2019. "Physical Weakness, Illness and Death in 1 Corinthians 11.30: Deprivation and Overconsumption in Pauline and Early Christianity." *NTS* 65: 572–88.

Doyle, Arthur Conan. 1891. "A Scandal in Bohemia." *The Strand* 2 (July–December): 61–75.

Doyle, Arthur Conan. 1892. *The Adventures of Sherlock Holmes*. London: Harper.

Drummond, James. 1905. "Shepherd of Hermas." Pages 105–23 in *The New Testament in the Apostolic Fathers*. Edited by A Committee of the Oxford Society of Historical Theology. Oxford: Clarendon.

Dunderberg, Ismo. 2005. "The School of Valentinus." Pages 64–99 in *A Companion to Second-Century "Heretics"*. Edited by Antti Marjanen and Petri Luomanen. VCSup 76. Leiden: Brill.

Dunderberg, Ismo. 2010. "Stoic Traditions in the School of Valentinus." Pages 220–38 in *Stoicism in Early Christianity*. Edited by Tuomas Rasimus, Troels Engberg-Pedersen, and Ismo Dunderberg. Peabody: Hendrickson.

Dunn, James D. G. 1974. "Paul's Understanding of the Death of Jesus." Pages 125–41 in *Reconciliation and Hope: New Testament Essays on Atonement and Eschatology Presented to L. L. Morris on His 60th Birthday*. Edited by Robert Banks. Carlisle: Paternoster.

Dunn, Peter W. 1996. "The *Acts of Paul* and the Pauline Legacy in the Second Century." Ph.D. diss., University of Cambridge.

Dyer, Bryan R. 2017. *Suffering in the Face of Death: The Epistle to the Hebrews and Its Context of Situation*. LNTS 568. London: Bloomsbury T&T Clark.

Ebner, Martin. 2005. "Paulinische Seligpreisungen à la Thekla: Narrative Relecture der Maarismenreihe in ActThecl 5f." Pages 64–79 in *Aus Liebe zu Paulus? Die Akte Thekla neu aufgerollt*. Edited by Martin Ebner. SBS 206. Stuttgart: Katholisches Bibelwerk.

Eck, Werner. 2010. "Prosopography." Pages 146–59 in the *Oxford Handbook of Roman Studies*. Oxford: Oxford University Press.

Ehrman, Bart D. 1983. "The New Testament Canon of Didymus the Blind." *VC* 37: 1–21.

Ehrman, Bart D., and Zlatko Pleše. 2011. *The Apocryphal Gospels: Texts and Translations*. Oxford: Oxford University Press.

Elliott, J. K. 1996. "Manuscripts, the Codex, and the Canon." *JSNT* 63: 105–23.

Engberg-Pedersen, Troels. 2010. *Cosmology and Self in the Apostle Paul*. Oxford: Oxford University Press.

Erho, Ted. 2015. "The Shepherd of Hermas in Ethiopia." Pages 97–117 in *L'Africa, L'Oriente Mediterraneo e l'Europa: Tradizioni e Culture a Confronto*. Edited by Paolo Nicelli. Africana Ambrosiana 1. Rome: Bulzoni Editore.

Farrar, Thomas J. 2018. "The Intimate and Ultimate Adversary: Satanology in Early Second-Century Christian Literature." *JECS* 26: 517–46.

Feldmeier, Reinhard. 2005. "*Padeia salvatrix*: Zur Anthropologie und Soteriologie der *Tabula Cebetis*." Pages 149–63 in *Die Bildtafel des Kebes: Allegorie des Lebens*. Edited by Rainer Hirsch-Luipold, Reinhard Feldmeier, Barbara Hirsch, Lutz Koch, and Heinz-Günther Nesselrath. SAPERE 8. Darmstadt: Wissenschaftliche Buchgesellschaft.

Feldmeier, Reinhard. 2008. *The First Letter of Peter: A Commentary on the Greek Text*. Translated by Peter H. Davids. Waco: Baylor University Press.

Ferguson, Everett. 1982. "Canon Muratori: Date and Provenance." Pages 677–83 in *Studia Patristica* XVII. Edited by Elizabeth A. Livingstone. Oxford: Pergamon.

Ferguson, Everett. 2009. *Baptism in the Early Church: History, Theology, and Liturgy in the First Five Centuries*. Grand Rapids: Eerdmans.

Fletcher-Louis, Crispin. 1997. *Luke-Acts: Angels, Christology and Soteriology*. WUNT 2.94. Tübingen: Mohr Siebeck.

Fletcher-Louis, Crispin. 2011. "Jewish Apocalyptic and Apocalypticism." Pages 1569–607 in *The Study of Jesus*. Vol. 2 of *Handbook for the Study of the Historical Jesus*. Leiden: Brill.

Förster, Niclas. 1999. *Marcus Magus: Kult, Lehre und Gemeindeleben einer valentinianischen Gnostikergruppe: Sammlung der Quellen und Kommentar*. WUNT 114. Tübingen: Mohr Siebeck.

Foster, Paul. 2012. "Irenaeus and the Noncanonical Gospels." Pages 105–17 in *Irenaeus: Life, Scripture, Legacy*. Edited by Paul Foster and Sara Parvis. Minneapolis: Fortress.

Foster, Paul. 2016. *Colossians*. BNTC. London: Bloomsbury T&T Clark.

Fowl, Stephen E. 2014. *Ephesians: Being a Christian, at Home and in the Cosmos*. T&T Clark Study Guides to the New Testament. London: Bloomsbury T&T Clark.

Frey, Jörg. 2013. *Die Herrlichkeit des Gekreuzigten*. WUNT 307. Tübingen: Mohr Siebeck.

Frey, Jörg. 2018. *The Letter of Jude and the Second Letter of Peter: A Theological Commentary*. Translated by Kathleen Ess. Waco: Baylor University Press.

Friesen, Steven J. 2004. "Poverty in Pauline Studies: Beyond the So-Called New Consensus." *JSNT* 26: 323–61.

Friesen, Steven J. 2010. "The Wrong Erastus: Ideology, Archaeology, and Exegesis." Pages 231–56 in *Corinth in Context: Comparative Studies on Religion and Society*. Edited by Steven J. Friesen, Daniel N. Schowalter, and James C. Walters. NovTSup 134. Leiden: Brill.

Friesen, Steven J. 2014. "Apocalypse and Empire." Pages 163–79 in *The Oxford Handbook of Apocalyptic Literature*. Edited by John J. Collins. Oxford: Oxford University Press.

Fuentes-Utrilla, Pablo, Rosana López-Rodríguez, and Luis Gil. 2004. "The Historical Relationship of Elms and Vines." *IASRF* 13: 7–15.

Gavaler, Chris. 2015. "Genre Apocalypse." *Chronicle of Higher Education* 61.20 (January 30): 13–15.

Gerardo Americano, Sergio. 2017a. "Ignazio d'Antiochia nel '*Pandette della Sacra Scrittura*' di Antioco di San Saba (CPG 7842–7844): Tradizione manoscritta." *Aug* 57: 191–208.

Gerardo Americano, Sergio. 2017b. "Ignazio d'Antiochia nel '*Pandette della Sacra Scrittura*' di Antioco di San Saba (CPG 7842–7844): Testo critico e commento." *Aug* 57: 541–67.

Gibbs, Raymond W. 2008. *The Cambridge Handbook of Metaphor and Thought*. Cambridge: Cambridge University Press.

Gieschen, Charles. 1998. *Angelomorphic Christology: Antecedents and Early Evidence*. AGJU 42. Leiden: Brill.

Giet, Stanislas. 1961. "L'Apocalypse d'Hermas et la Pénitence." *StPatr* 3: 214–18.
Giet, Stanislas. 1963. *Hermas et les Pasteurs: Les trois auteurs du Pasteur d'Hermas.* Paris: Presses universitaires de France.
Giet, Stanislas. 1966. "Les trois auteurs du Pastor d'Hermas." *StPatr* 8: 10–23.
Glancy, Jennifer A. 2002. *Slavery in Early Christianity.* Oxford: Oxford University Press.
Gleede, Benjamin. 2016. *Parabiblica Latina: Studien zu den griechisch-lateinischen Übersetzungen parabiblischer Literatur unter besonderer Berücksichtigung der apostolischen Väter.* VCSup 137. Leiden: Brill.
Goff, Matthew. 2014. "Wisdom and Apocalypticism." Pages 52–68 in *The Oxford Handbook of Apocalyptic Literature.* Edited by John J. Collins. Oxford: Oxford University Press.
Gonzalez, Justo L. 1984. *The Story of Christianity.* 2 vols. San Francisco: Harper & Row.
Goodrich, John K. 2010. "Erastus, *Quaestor* of Corinth: The Administrative Rank of ὁ οἰκονόμος τῆς πόλεως (Rom 16.23) in an Achaean Colony." *NTS* 56: 90–115.
Goodrich, John K. 2011. "Erastus of Corinth (Romans 16.23): Responding to Recent Proposals on His Rank, Status, and Faith." *NTS* 57: 583–93.
Goodspeed, Edgar J. 1946. "The Date of Commodian." *CP* 41: 46–7.
Grant, Robert M. 1962. "The Apostolic Fathers' First Thousand Years." *CH* 31: 421–29.
Grant, Robert M. 1964. Review of *Hermas et les Pasteurs: Les trois auteurs du Pasteur d'Hermas*, by Stanislas Giet. Paris: Presses universitaires de France, 1963. *Gnomon* 36: 357–9.
Grillmeier, Aloys. 1975. *Christ in Christian Tradition: From the Apostolic Age to Chalcedon (451).* 2nd ed. Translated by John Bowden. Vol. 1. Atlanta: John Knox.
Grundeken, Mark. 2015a. *Community Building in the Shepherd of Hermas: A Critical Study of Some Key Aspects.* VCSup 131. Leiden: Brill.
Grundeken, Mark. 2015b. "The Shepherd of Hermas and the Roman Empire." Pages 187–204 in *People under Power: Early Jewish and Christian Responses to the Roman Power Empire.* Amsterdam: Amsterdam University Press.
Grundeken, Mark. 2018. "Diakone in Rom? Das Zeugnis des Hirten des Hermas." *VC* 72: 93–101.
Grünstäudl, Wolfgang. 2013. *Petrus Alexandrinus: Studien zum historischen und theologischen Ort des zweiten Petrusbriefes.* WUNT 2.353. Tübingen: Mohr Siebeck.
Guignard, Christophe. 2019. "The Muratorian Fragment as a Late Antique Fake?" *RevScRel* 93: 73–90.
Gupta, Nijay K. 2010. *Worship that Makes Sense to Paul: A New Approach to the Theology and Ethics of Paul's Cultic Metaphors.* BZNW 175. Berlin: De Gruyter.
Gupta, Nijay K. 2012. "Mirror-Reading Moral Issues in Paul's Letters." *JSNT* 34: 361–81.
Haas, C. 1993. "Die Pneumatologie des 'Hirten des Hermas.'" *ANRW* 27.1: 552–86. Part 2, *Principat*, 27.1 Edited by Wolfgang Haase. Berlin: De Gruyter.
Hahneman, Geoffrey M. 1992. *The Muratorian Fragment and the Development of the Canon.* Oxford Theological Monographs. Oxford: Oxford University Press.
Hahneman, Geoffrey M. 2002. "The Muratorian Fragment and the Origins of the NT Canon." Pages 405–15 in *The Canon Debate.* Edited by Lee M. McDonald and James A. Sanders. Peabody: Hendrickson.
Hallaschka, Martin. 2010. "Zechariah's Angels: Their Role in the Night Visions and in the Redaction History of Zec 1,7-6,8." *SJOT* 24: 13–27.
Hannah, Darrel D. 1999. *Michael and Christ: Michael Traditions and Angel Christology in Early Christianity.* WUNT 2.109. Tübingen: Mohr Siebeck.

Hanson, Paul D. 1976a. "Apocalypse, Genre." Pages 27–8 in *Interpreter's Dictionary of the Bible: Supplementary Volume*. Edited by Keith R. Crim. Nashville: Abingdon.

Hanson, Paul D. 1976b. "Apocalypticism." Pages 28–34 in *Interpreter's Dictionary of the Bible: Supplementary Volume*. Edited by Keith R. Crim. Nashville: Abingdon.

Harkins, Angela Kim. 2020. "Looking at the *Shepherd of Hermas* through the Experience of Lived Religion." Pages 49–70 in *Lived Religion in the Ancient Mediteranean World: Approaching Religious Transformations from Archaeology, History and Classics*. Edited by Valentino Gasparini, Maik Patzelt, Rubina Raja, Anna-Katharina Rieger, Jörg Rüpke, and Emiliano Urciuoli. Berlin: De Gruyter.

Harnack, Adolf von. 1888. *Lehrbuch der Dogmengeschichte*. 2nd ed. Vol. 1. Freiburg: Mohr.

Harnack, Adolf von. 1891. "Geschichte der Lehre von der Seligkeit allein durch den Glauben in der alten Kirche." *ZTK* 1: 82–178.

Harnack, Adolf von. 1919. *Der kirchengeschichtliche Ertrag der exegetischen Arbeiten des Origenes, II. Teil: Die beiden Testamente mit Ausschluss des Hexateuchs und des Richterbuches*. TUGAL 42.4. Leipzig: Hinrichs.

Harris, J. Rendel. 1887. "Hermas in Arcadia." *JBL* 7: 69–83.

Harris, J. Rendel. 1896. *Hermas in Arcadia and Other Essays*. Cambridge: Cambridge University Press.

Harrison, Stephen. 2015. "Lucius in *Metamorphoses* Books 1–3." Pages 3–14 in *Characterisation in Apuleius'* Metamorphoses. Edited by Stephen Harrison. Pierides 5. Newcastle upon Tyne: Cambridge Scholars.

Hartley, L. P. [1953] 2002. *The Go-Between*. New York: New York Review of Books.

Hauck, Robert J. 1993. "The Great Fast: Christology in the *Shepherd* of Hermas." *ATR* 75: 187–98.

Hefele, Karl Josef von. 1839. Review of *Der Hirte des Hermas: Ein Beitrag zur Patristik*, by Karl Reinhold Jachmann, Königsberg: Bon, 1838. *TQ* 20: 169–84.

Hegeman, Johanna M., Esther M. van Fenema, Hannie C. Comijs, Rob M. Kok, Roos C. van der Mast, and Margot W. M. de Waal. 2017. "Effect of Chronic Somatic Diseases on the Course of Late-Life Depression." *International Journal of Geriatric Psychiatry* 32: 779–87.

Heim, Erin. 2017. *Adoption in Galatians and Romans: Contemporary Metaphor Theories and the Pauline* Huiothesia *Metaphors*. BibInt 153. Leiden: Brill.

Heine, Ronald E. 1989. "The Gospel of John and the Montanist Debate at Rome." *StPatr* 21: 95–100.

Heine, Ronald E. 2000. "Recovering Origen's Commentary on Ephesians from Jerome." *JTS* 51: 478–514.

Hellholm, David. 1986. "The Problem of Apocalyptic Genre and the Apocalypse of John." *Semeia* 36: 13–64.

Hellholm, David. 2009. "Der Hirt des Hermas." Pages 226–53 in *Die Apostolischen Väter: Eine Einleitung*. Edited by Wilhelm Pratscher. Göttingen: Vandenhoek & Ruprecht.

Hellholm, David. 2010. "The Shepherd of Hermas." Pages 215–42 in *The Apostolic Fathers: An Introduction*. Edited by Wilhelm Pratscher. Translated by Elisabeth G. Wolfe. Waco: Baylor University Press.

Hemmerdinger, Bertrand. 1966. "Observations critiques sur Irénée, IV (*Sources chrétiennes* 100) ou les mésaventures d'un philologue." *JTS* 17: 308–26.

Hengel, Martin. 1973. *Judentum und Hellenismus: Studien zu ihrer Begegnung unter besonderer Berücksichtigung Palästinas bis zur Mitte des 2.Jh.s v.Chr.* 2nd. ed. WUNT 10. Tübingen: Mohr Siebeck.

Hengel, Martin. 1974. *Judaism and Hellenism: Studies in Their Encounter during the Early Hellenistic Period*. Translated by John Bowden. Philadelphia: Fortress.

Hengel, Martin. 1995. *Studies in Early Christology*. Edinburgh: T&T Clark.

Hengel, Martin, and Anna Maria Schwemer. 2007. *Jesus und das Judentum*. Geschichte des frühen Christentums 1. Tübingen: Mohr Siebeck.

Hengel, Martin, and Anna Maria Schwemer. 2019. *Jesus and Judaism*. BMSSEC 7. Translated by Wayne Coppins. Waco: Baylor University Press.

Henne, Philippe. 1988. "A propos de la christologie du Pasteur d'Hermas: La cohérence interne des niveaux d'explications dans la *Cinquième Similitude*." *RSPT* 72: 569–78.

Henne, Philippe. 1989. "La polysémie allégorique dans le *Pasteur* d'Hermas." *ETL* 65: 131–5.

Henne, Philippe. 1990. "La véritable christologie de la *Cinquième Similitude*." *RSPT* 74: 182–204.

Henne, Philippe. 1992a. "Athanase avait-il une version complète du *Pasteur* d'Hermas?" *RevScRel* 66: 69–76.

Henne, Philippe. 1992b. *La christologie chez Clément de Rome et dans le Pasteur d'Hermas*. Paradosis 33. Fribourg: Éditions Universitaires Fribourg Suisse.

Henne, Philippe. 1992c. "Un seul 'Pasteur', un seul Hermas." *RTL* 23: 482–8.

Henne, Philippe. 1992d. *L'unité du Pasteur d'Hermas: Tradition et redaction*. CahRB 31. Paris: Gabalda.

Henne, Philippe. 1993. "La datation du canon de Muratori." *RB* 100: 54–75.

Hill, Charles E. 2004. *The Johannine Corpus in the Early Church*. Oxford: Oxford University Press.

Hill, Charles E. 2013. "'The Writing Which Says'... The *Shepherd* of Hermas in the Writings of Irenaeus." Pages 127–38 in *Studia Patristica LXV*. Edited by Markus Vinzent. Leuven: Peeters.

Hillhorst, Antonius. 1976. *Semitismes et latinismes dans le Pasteur d'Hermas*. GCP 5. Nijmegen: Dekker & Van de Vegt.

Hirsch-Luipold, Rainer. 2005a. "Einleitung." Pages 11–37 in *Die Bildtafel des Kebes: Allegorie des Lebens*. Edited by Rainer Hirsch-Luipold, Reinhard Feldmeier, Barbara Hirsch, Lutz Koch, Heinz-Günther Nesselrath. SAPERE 8. Darmstadt: Wissenschaftliche Buchgesellschaft.

Hirsch-Luipold, Rainer. 2005b. "Text und Übersetzung." Pages 67–145 in *Die Bildtafel des Kebes: Allegorie des Lebens*. Edited by Rainer Hirsch-Luipold, Reinhard Feldmeier, Barbara Hirsch, Lutz Koch, and Heinz-Günther Nesselrath. SAPERE 8. Darmstadt: Wissenschaftliche Buchgesellschaft.

van den Hoek, Annewies. 1996. "Techniques of Quotation in Clement of Alexandria: A View of Ancient Literary Working Methods." *VC* 50: 223–43.

Hogeterp, Albert L. A. 2006. *Paul and God's Temple: A Historical Interpretation of Cultic Imagery in the Corinthian Correspondence*. BTS 2. Leuven: Peeters.

Hooper, Walter, ed. 2004–7. *The Collected Letters of C. S. Lewis*. 3 vols. San Francisco: HarperCollins.

Horrell, David G. 2004. "Domestic Space and Christian Meetings at Corinth: Imagining New Contexts and the Buildings East of the Theatre." *NTS* 50: 349–69.

Horrell, David G. 2019. *The Making of a Christian Morality: Reading Paul in Ancient and Modern Contexts*. Grand Rapids: Eerdmans.

Horsley, G. H. R., and S. R. Llewelyn, eds. 1982. *New Documents Illustrating Early Christianity*. Vol. 2. Sydney: Macquarie University Press.

Houghton, H. A. G. 2016. *The Latin New Testament: A Guide to Its Early History, Texts, and Manuscripts.* Oxford: Oxford University Press.

Howson, John S. 1868. *The Metaphors of St. Paul.* London: Strahan.

Huber, Lynn R. 2007. *Like a Bride Adorned: Reading Metaphor in John's Apocalypse.* ESEC 10. New York: T&T Clark International.

Huber, Lynn R. 2013. *Thinking and Seeing with Women in Revelation.* LNTS 475. London: Bloomsbury T&T Clark.

Humphrey, Edith McEwan. 1995. *Transformation and Apocalyptic Identity in Joseph and Aseneth, 4 Ezra, the Apocalypse, and the Shepherd of Hermas.* JSPSup 17. Sheffield: Sheffield Academic Press.

Humphries, Mark. 2008. "Rufinus's Eusebius: Translation, Continuation, and Edition in the Latin *Ecclesiastical History.*" *JECS* 16: 143–64.

Hurtado, Larry W. 2003. *Lord Jesus Christ: Devotion to Jesus in Earliest Christianity.* Grand Rapids: Eerdmans.

Hurtado, Larry W. 2016a. *Destroyer of the Gods: Early Christian Distinctiveness in the Greco-Roman World.* Waco: Baylor University Press.

Hurtado, Larry W. 2016b. *Why on Earth Did Anyone Become a Christian in the First Three Centuries?* Milwaukee: Marquette University Press.

Hvalvik, Reidar. 2006. "Christ Proclaiming His Law to the Apostles: The *Traditio Legis*-Motif in Early Christian Art and Literature." Pages 405–37 in *The New Testament and Early Christian Literature in Greco-Roman Literature: Studies in Honor of David E. Aune.* Edited by John Fotopoulos. NovTSup 122. Leiden: Brill.

Hvalvik, Reidar. 2007. "Jewish Believers and Jewish Influence in the Roman Church until the Early Second Century." Pages 179–216 in *Jewish Believers in Jesus.* Edited by Oskar Skarsaune and Reidar Hvalvik. Peabody: Hendrickson.

Hwang, Alexander Y. 2010. "Manifold Grace in John Cassian and Prosper of Aquitaine." *SJT* 63: 93–108.

Ioannidou, Grace. 1996. *Catalogue of Greek and Latin Literary Papyri in Berlin (P.Berol.inv. 21101–21299, 21911).* Mainz: P. von Zabern.

Jachmann, Karl Reinhold. 1838. *Der Hirte des Hermas: Ein Beitrag zur Patristik.* Königberg: Bon.

Jacobs, Alan. 2011. *The Pleasures of Reading in an Age of Distraction.* New York: Oxford University Press.

Jacobs, Alan. 2016. "Habits of Mind in an Age of Distraction." *Comment.* Available at https://www.cardus.ca/comment/article/4868/habits-of-mind-in-an-age-of-distraction.

Jacobs, Alan. 2017. *How to Think: A Survival Guide for a World at Odds.* New York: Currency.

Jeffers, James S. 1991. *Conflict at Rome: Social Order and Hierarchy in Early Christianity.* Minneapolis: Fortress.

Jefford, Clayton N. 2006. *The Apostolic Fathers and the New Testament.* Grand Rapids: Baker Academic.

Jefford, Clayton N. 2010. "Prophecy and Prophetism in the Apostolic Fathers." Pages 295–316 in *Prophets and Prophecy in Jewish and Early Christian Literature.* Edited by Joseph Verheyden, Korinna Zamfir, and Tobias Nicklas. WUNT 2.286. Tübingen: Mohr Siebeck.

Jefford, Clayton N. 2017. "Missing Pauline Tradition in the Apostolic Fathers? *Didache, Shepherd of Hermas,* Papias, the *Martyrdom of Polycarp,* and the *Epistle to Diognetus.*" Pages 41–60 in *The Apostolic Fathers and Paul.* Edited by Todd D. Still and David E. Wilhite. PPSD 2. London: Bloomsbury T&T Clark.

Jensen, Robin M., Peter Lampe, William Tabbernee, and D. H. Williams. 2014. "Italy and Environs." Pages 379–431 in *Early Christianity in Contexts: An Exploration across Cultures and Continents*. Edited by William Tabbernee. Grand Rapids: Baker Academic.

Johnson, Luke Timothy. 2006. *Hebrews: A Commentary*. NTL. Louisville: Westminster John Knox.

Joly, Robert. 1963. *Le tableau de Cébes et la philosophie religieuse*. CL 61. Brussels: Revue d'Études Latines.

Joly, Robert. 1967. "Hermas et le Pasteur." *VC* 21: 201–18.

Joly, Robert. 1993. "Le milieu complexe du 'Pasteur d'Hermas.'" *ANRW* 27.1: 524–551. Part 2, *Principat*, 27.1. Edited by Wolfgang Haase. Berlin: De Gruyter.

Jongkind, Dirk. 2007. *Scribal Habits of Codex Sinaiticus*. TS 5. Piscataway: Gorgias.

Joyce, Paul. 2007. *Ezekiel: A Commentary*. LHBOTS 482. London: T&T Clark Continuum.

Kelly, J. N. D. 1968. *Early Christian Doctrines*. 4th ed. London: Black.

Kieffer, René. 1998. "From Linguistic Methodology to the Discovery of a World of Metaphors." *Semeia* 81: 77–93.

Kieffer, René. 2000. "La demeure divine dans le temple et sur l'autel chez Ignace d'Antioche." Pages 287–301 in *La cité de Dieu: Die Stadt Gottes: 3. Symposium Strasbourg, Tübingen, Uppsala 19.–23. September 1998 in Tübingen*. Edited by Martin Hengel, Siegfried Mittmann, and Anna Maria Schwemer. WUNT 129. Tübingen: Mohr Siebeck.

Kirkland, Alastair. 1990. "The Transmission of the Shepherd of Hermas." *Acta Patristica et Byzantina* 1: 134–43.

Koch, Klaus. 1972. *The Rediscovery of Apocalyptic*. SBT 2.22. Naperville: Allenson.

Koester, Craig R. 2008. *The Word of Life: A Theology of John's Gospel*. Grand Rapids: Eerdmans.

Koester, Craig R. 2014. *Revelation*. 2 vols. AYB 38. New Haven: Yale University Press.

Koester, Craig R. 2018. *Revelation and the End of All Things*. 2nd ed. Grand Rapids: Eerdmans.

Koschorke, Klaus. 1978. *Die Polemik der Gnostiker gegen das kirchliche Christentum: Unter besonderer Berücksichtigung der Nag-Hammadi-Traktate "Apokalypse des Petrus" (NHC VIII, 3) und "Testimonium Veritatis" (NHC IX, 3)*. NHS 12. Leiden: Brill.

Köster, Helmut. 1957. *Synoptische Überlieferungen bei den apostolischen Vätern*. TUGAL 65. Berlin: Akademie.

Knopf, Rudolf. 1920. *Die Lehre der zwölf Apostel, Die zwei Clemensbriefe*. HNT Ergänzungsband. Die apostolischen Väter 1. Tübingen: Mohr Siebeck.

Kraft, Heinrich. 1964. *Clavis patrum apostolicorum*. Darmstadt: Wissenschaftliche Buchgesellschaft.

Kruger, Michael J. 2012. "The Definition of the Term 'Canon': Exclusive or Multi-Dimensional." *TynBul* 63: 1–20.

Kulik, Alexander. 2010. *3 Baruch: Greek-Slavonic Apocalypse of Baruch*. CEJL. Berlin: De Gruyter.

Kuruvilla, Abraham. 2013. *Privilege the Text: A Theological Hermeneutic for Preaching*. Chicago: Moody.

Lake, Kirsopp. 1911. "The Shepherd of Hermas and Christian Life in Rome in the Second Century." *HTR* 4: 25–46.

Lake, Kirsopp. 1920. *Landmarks in the History of Early Christianity*. London: Macmillan.

Lake, Kirsopp. 1925. "The Shepherd of Hermas." *HTR* 18: 279–80.

Lakoff, George, and Mark Johnson. 2003. *Metaphors We Live By*. 2nd ed. Chicago: University of Chicago Press.

Lampe, Peter. 1989. *Die stadtrömischen Christen in den ersten beiden Jahrhunderten: Untersuchungen zur Sozialgeschichte*. WUNT 2.18. Tübingen: Mohr Siebeck.

Lampe, Peter. 2003. *From Paul to Valentinus: Christians at Rome in the First Two Centuries*. Translated by Michael Steinhauser. Minneapolis: Fortress.

Lawrence, Jean. 2003. "The Root Cause of Road Rage." *WebMD*. Available at https://www.webmd.com/women/features/root-cause-of-road-rage#1

Layton, Bentley. 1968. "The Sources, Date, and Transmission of *Didache* 1.3b–2.1." *HTR* 61: 343–83.

Lebram, Jürgen. 1978. "Apokalyptic/Apokalypsen II." Pages 192–202 in *Theologische Realenzyklopädie*. Edited by Gerhard Müller. Vol. 3. Berlin: De Gruyter.

Legarth, Peter V. 1992. *Guds tempel: Tempelsymbolisme og kristologi hos Ignatius af Antiokia*. MVS 3. Århus: Kolon.

Lehtipuu, Outi. 2015. *Debates over the Resurrection of the Dead: Constructing Early Christian Identity*. OECS. Oxford: Oxford University Press.

Leiman, Sid. Z. 1974. "The Inverted *Nuns* at Numbers 10:35–36 and the Book of Eldad and Medad." *JBL* 93: 348–55.

Leutzsch, Martin. 1989. *Die Wahrnehumng sozialer Wirklichkeit im "Hirten des Hermas."* FRLANT 150. Göttingen: Vandenhoeck & Ruprecht.

Levine, Baruch A. 1976. "More on the Inverted *Nuns* of Num 10:35–36." *JBL* 95: 122–4.

Levison, John R. 1995a. "The Angelic Spirit in Early Judaism." *SBLSP* 34: 464–93.

Levison, John R. 1995b. "The Prophetic Spirit as an Angel according to Philo." *HTR* 88: 189–207.

Levison, John R. 1997. *The Spirit in First Century Judaism*. AGJU 29. Leiden: Brill.

Lightfoot, J. B. 1889–91. *The Apostolic Fathers: Clement, Ignatius, and Polycarp: Revised Texts with Introductions, Notes, Dissertations, and Translations*. 2nd ed. 2 parts in 5 vols. London: Macmillan.

Link, Adolf. 1888. *Die Einheit des Pastor Hermae*. Marburg: Elwert.

Lipsett, Diane B. 2011. *Desiring Conversion: Hermas, Thecla, Aseneth*. Oxford: Oxford University Press.

Liu, Liang, Cuilian Liu, and Xudong Zhao. 2017. "Linking Anger Trait with Somatization in Low-Grade College Students: Moderating Roles of Family Cohesion and Adaptability." *Shanghai Archives of Psychiatry* 29: 30–40.

Longenecker, Bruce. 2009. "Exposing the Economic Middle: A Revised Economy Scale for the Study of Early Urban Christianity." *JSNT* 31: 243–78.

Lookadoo, Jonathon. 2017a. "Polycarp, Paul, and the Letters to Timothy." *NovT* 59: 366–83.

Lookadoo, Jonathon. 2017b. "The Role of the Star in *Ephesians* 18–20: Ignatius of Antioch, Polymorphic Christology, and Second Temple Stars." *JECH* 7: 62–88.

Lookadoo, Jonathon. 2018. *The High Priest and the Temple: Metaphorical Depictions of Jesus in the Letters of Ignatius of Antioch*. WUNT 2.473. Tübingen: Mohr Siebeck.

Lookadoo, Jonathon. Forthcoming. "Imagery and Biblical Interpretation: Considering the Use of Feminine Imagery in Revelation and the *Shepherd of Hermas*." *RB*.

Lucchesi, Enzo. 1989. "Le *Pasteur* d'Hermas en copte: Perspective nouvelle." *VC* 43: 393–6.

Lusini, Gianfrancesco. 2001. "Nouvelles recherches sur le texte du Pasteur d'Hermas." *Apocrypha* 12: 79–97.

Lust, Johan, Erik Eynikel, and Katrin Hauspie, eds. 2003. *A Greek-English Lexicon of the Septuagint*. Rev. ed. Stuttgart: Deutschebibelgesellschaft.

Maier, Harry O. 1992. *The Social Setting of the Ministry as Reflected in the Writings of Hermas, Clement, and Ignatius*. SR 1. Waterloo: Wilfrid Laurier University Press.

Maier, Harry O. 1993. "Purity and Danger in Polycarp's Epistle to the Philippians: The Sin of Valens in Social Perspective." *JECS* 1: 229–47.

Maier, Harry O. 1997. "Staging the Gaze: Early Christian Apocalypses and Narrative Self-Representation." *HTR* 90: 131–54.

Maier, Harry O. 2005. "The Politics and Rhetoric of Discord and Concord in Paul and Ignatius." Pages 307–24 in *Trajectories through the New Testament and the Apostolic Fathers*. Edited by Andrew F. Gregory and Christopher M. Tuckett. Oxford: Oxford University Press.

Maier, Harry O. 2013a. *Picturing Paul in Empire: Imperial Image, Text and Persuasion in Colossians, Ephesians and the Pastoral Epistles*. London: Bloomsbury T&T Clark.

Maier, Harry O. 2013b. "Soja's Thirdspace, Foucault's Heterotopia and de Certeau's Practice: Time-Space and Social Geography in Emergent Christianity." *HSR* 38.3: 76–92.

Maier, Harry O. 2015. "From Material Place to Imagined Space: Emergent Christian Community as Thirdspace in the *Shepherd of Hermas*." Pages 143–60 in *Early Christian Communities between Ideal and Reality*. Edited by Mark Grundeken and Joseph Verheyden. WUNT 342. Tübingen: Mohr Siebeck.

Maier, Harry O. 2017. "Paul, Ignatius and Thirdspace: A Socio-Geographic Exploration." Pages 162–80 in *The Apostolic Fathers and Paul*. Edited by Todd D. Still and David E. Wilhite. PPSD 2. London: Bloomsbury T&T Clark.

Marjanen, Antti. 2005. "Montanism: Egalitarian Ecstatic 'New Prophecy.'" Pages 185–212 in *A Companion to Second-Century Christian "Heretics."* VCSup 76. Leiden: Brill.

Markschies, Christoph. 2015. *Christian Theology and Its Institutions in the Early Roman Empire: Prolegomena to a History of Early Christian Theology*. Translated by Wayne Coppins. BMSSEC 3. Waco: Baylor University Press.

Marshall, John W. 2005. "Objects of Ignatius' Wrath and Jewish Angelic Mediators." *JEH* 56: 1–23.

Martin, Dale B. 1990. *Slavery as Salvation: The Metaphor of Slavery in Pauline Christianity*. New Haven: Yale University Press.

Martin, E. G. 1983–5. "Eldad and Monad." Pages 463–5 in *The Old Testament Pseudepigrapha*. Edited by James H. Charlesworth. 2 vols. New York: Doubleday.

Martín, Juan Pablo. 1978. "Espíritu y dualismo de espíritus en el Pastor de Hermas y su relación con el judaísmo." *VetChr* 15: 295–345.

Massaux, Édouard. 1986. *Influence de l'Évangile de saint Matthieu sur la littérature chrétienne avant saint Irénée*. BETL 75. Leuven: Peeters.

May, Ross W., Marcos A. Sanchez-Gonzalez, Kirsten A. Hawkins, Wayne B. Batchelor, and Frank D. Fincham. 2014. "Effect of Anger and Trait Forgiveness on Cardiovascular Risk in Young Adult Females." *American Journal of Cardiology* 114: 47–52.

Mayo, José Eusebio Pérez. 2016. *Hausgemeinden and kirchliche Ämter im Hirten des Hermas*. Dissertationen der LMU München 6. Munich: Universitätsbibliothek Ludwig-Maximilians-Universität München.

McDonald, Lee Martin. 2009. *Forgotten Scriptures: The Selection and Rejection of Early Religious Writings*. Louisville: Westminster John Knox.

McFarland, Orrey. 2013. "'The One Who Calls in Grace': Paul's Rhetorical and Theological Identification with the Galatians." *HBT* 35: 151–65.

McFarland, Orrey. 2016. *God and Grace in Philo and Paul*. NovTSup 164. Leiden: Brill.
McGrath, Alister E. 2014. *The Intellectual World of C. S. Lewis*. Chichester: Wiley Blackwell.
Meggitt, Justin J. 1996. "The Social Status of Erastus (Rom. 16:23)." *NovT* 38: 218–23.
Meier, Laurenz L., Sven Gross, Paul E. Spector, and Norbert K. Semmer. 2013. "Relationship and Task Conflict at Work: Interactive Short-Term Effects on Angry Mood and Somatic Complaints." *Journal of Occupational Health Psychology* 18: 144–56.
Mews, Constant J. 2000. "From *Scivias* to the *Liber Divinorum Operum*: Hildegard's Apocalyptic Imagination and the Call to Reform." *JRH* 24: 44–56.
Michaels, J. Ramsey. 2010. *The Gospel of John*. NICNT. Grand Rapids: Eerdmans.
Mishra, Pankaj. 2016 (8 December). "Welcome to the Age of Anger." *Guardian*. Available at https://www.theguardian.com/politics/2016/dec/08/welcome-age-anger-brexit-trump.
Mohrmann, Christine. 1949. "Les origines de la latinité chrétienne à Rome." *VC* 3: 67–106.
Mohrmann, Christine. 1953. "Statio." *VC* 7: 221–45.
Moo, Jonathan A. 2011. *Creation, Nature and Hope in 4 Ezra*. FRLANT 237. Göttingen: Vandenhoeck & Ruprecht.
Morgan-Wynne, John Eifion. 1989. "The Delicacy of the Spirit in the Shepherd of Hermas and in Tertullian." *StPatr* 21: 154–7.
Moxnes, Halvor. 1974. "God and His Angel in the Shepherd of Hermas." *ST* 28: 49–56.
Muddiman, John. 2005. "The Church in Ephesians, *2 Clement*, and the *Shepherd of Hermas*." Pages 107–21 in *Trajectories through the New Testament and the Apostolic Fathers*. Edited by Andrew F. Gregory and Christopher M. Tuckett. Oxford: Oxford University Press.
Müller, Ulrich B. 1989. "Literarische und formgeschichtliche Bestimmung der Apokalypse des Johannes als einem Zeugnis frühchristlicher Apokalyptik." Pages 599–619 in *Apocalypticism in the Mediterranean World and the Near East*. Edited by David Hellholm. 2nd ed. Tübingen: Mohr Siebeck.
Muraoka, Takamitsu. 2009. *A Greek-English Lexicon of the Septuagint*. Rev. ed. Leuven: Peeters.
Musurillo, Herbert A. 1951. "The Need of a New Edition of Hermas." *TS* 12: 382–7.
Nagel, Titus. 2000. *Die Rezeption des Johannesevangeliums im 2. Jahrhundert: Studien zur vorirenäischen Aneignung und Auslegung des vierten Evangeliums in christlicher und christlich-gnostischer Literatur*. ABG 2. Leipzig: Evangelische Verlagsanstalt.
Najman, Hindy. 2014. "The Inheritance of Prophecy in Apocalypse." Pages 36–51 in *The Oxford Handbook of Apocalyptic Literature*. Edited by John J. Collins. Oxford: Oxford University Press.
Newman, Barbara J. 1990. "Introduction." Pages 9–53 in *Hildegard of Bingen: Scivias*. The Classics of Western Spirituality. Edited by Columba Hart, and Jane Bishop. New York: Paulist.
Newsom, Carol. 2005. "Spying Out the Land: A Report from Genology." Pages 437–50 in *Seeking Out the Wisdom of the Ancients*. Edited by Ronald L. Troxel, Kelvin G. Friebel, and Dennis R. Magary. Winona Lake: Eisenbrauns.
Newsom, Carol. 2014. "The Rhetoric of Jewish Apocalyptic Literature." Pages 201–17 in *The Oxford Handbook of Apocalyptic Literature*. Edited by John J. Collins. Oxford: Oxford University Press.
Nickelsburg, George W. E. 2001. *1 Enoch 1*. Hermeneia. Minneapolis: Fortress.

Niederwimmer, Kurt. 1975. *Askese und Mysterium: Über Ehe, Ehescheidung und Eheverzicht in den Anfängen des christlichen Glaubens*. FRLANT 113. Göttingen: Vandenhoeck & Ruprecht.

Niederwimmer, Kurt. 1993. *Die Didache*. 2nd ed. KAV 1. Göttingen: Vandenhoeck & Ruprecht.

Niederwimmer, Kurt. 1998. *The Didache: A Commentary*. Hermeneia. Minneapolis: Fortress.

Noll, Mark A. 2003. *The Rise of Evangelicalism: The Age of Edwards, Whitefield and the Wesleys*. A History of Evangelicalism 1. Downers Grove: IVP Academic.

Oakes, Peter. 2004. "Constructing Poverty Scales for Graeco-Roman Society: A Response to Steven Friesen's 'Poverty in Pauline Studies.'" *JSNT* 26: 367–71.

Oakes, Peter. 2009. "Methodological Issues in Using Economic Evidence in Interpretation of Early Christian Texts." Pages 9–34 in *Engaging Economics: New Testament Scenarios and Early Christian Reception*. Edited by Bruce Longenecker and Kelly Liebengood. Grand Rapids: Eerdmans.

O'Brien, D. P. 1997. "The Cumaean Sibyl as the Revelation-Bearer in the *Shepherd of Hermas*." *JECS* 5: 473–96.

Osborn, Eric. 1997. *Tertullian: First Theologian of the West*. Cambridge: Cambridge University Press.

Osiek, Carolyn. 1983. *Rich and Poor in the Shepherd of Hermas: An Exegetical-Social Investigation*. CBQMS 15. Washington, DC: Catholic Biblical Association.

Osiek, Carolyn. 1986. "The Genre and Function of the *Shepherd of Hermas*." *Semeia* 36: 113–21.

Osiek, Carolyn. 1999. *Shepherd of Hermas: A Commentary*. Hermeneia. Minneapolis: Fortress.

Osiek, Carolyn, Margaret Y. MacDonald, and Janet H. Tulloch. 2006. *A Woman's Place: House Churches in Earliest Christianity*. Minneapolis: Fortress.

Otterpohl, Nantje, Daniela Stranghoener, Marc Vierhaus, and Malte Schwinger. 2017. "Anger Regulation and School-Related Somatic Complaints in Children with Special Educational Needs: A Longitudinal Study." *Learning and Individual Differences* 56: 59–67.

Otranto, Rosa. 1997. "Alia tempora, alii libri: Notizie ed elenchi di libri cristiani su papiro." *Aeg* 77: 101–24.

Outtier, Bernard. 2004–11. "Traductions du Grec en Georgien." Pages 2.1186–9 in *Übersetzung—Translation—Traduction*. Edited by Harald Kittel, Armin Paul Frank, Norbert Greiner, Theo Hermans, Werner Koller, José Lambert, and Fritz Paul. 3 vols. Berlin: De Gruyter Mouton.

Papandrea, James L. 2012. *Reading the Early Church Fathers: From the Didache to Nicaea*. Mahwah: Paulist.

Papandrea, James L. 2016. *The Earliest Christologies: Five Images of Christ in the Postapostolic Age*. Downers Grove: IVP Academic.

Parker, David C. 2008. *An Introduction to the New Testament Manuscripts and Their Texts*. Cambridge: Cambridge University Press.

Parker, David C. 2010. *Codex Sinaiticus: The Story of the World's Oldest Bible*. London: British Library.

Peppard, Michael. 2012. *The Son of God in the Roman World: Divine Sonship in Its Social and Political Context*. Oxford: Oxford University Press.

Perrone, Lorenzo. 2011. *La preghiera secondo Origene: L'impossibilità donata*. LCA 24. Brescia: Morcelliana.

Phan, Peter C. 2011. "Developments of the Doctrine of the Trinity." Pages 3–13 in *The Cambridge Companion to the Trinity*. Edited by Peter C. Phan. Cambridge: Cambridge University Press.

Porter, Stanley E. 1990. "Is *dipsychos* (James 1,8; 4,8) a 'Christian' Word?" *Bib* 71: 469–98.

Porter, Stanley E. 2015. *Constantine Tischendorf: The Life and Work of a 19th Century Bible Hunter*. London: Bloomsbury T&T Clark.

Poschmann, Bernhard. 1940. *Paenitentia secunda: Die kirchliche Buße im ältesten Christentum bis Cyprian und Origenes*. Bonn: Hanstein.

Pratscher, Wilhelm. 2018. "Die Rede von Gott im Kerygma Petri und in den Ignatiusbriefen." Pages 229–47 in *Die Briefe des Ignatios von Antiochia: Motive, Strategien, Kontexte*. Millennium Studies 72. Berlin: De Gruyter.

Prostmeier, Ferdinand R. 1999. *Der Barnabasbrief*. KAV 8. Göttingen: Vandenhoeck & Ruprecht.

Puech, Aimé. 1928. *Histoire de la littérature grecque chrétienne depuis les origines jusqu'à la fin de la IVe siècle*. Vol. 2. Paris: Société d'edition Les Belles Lettres.

Rahner, Karl. 1983. *Theological Investigations*. Vol. 15. London: Darton, Longman and Todd.

Regev, Eyal. 2018. "Community as Temple: Revisiting Cultic Metaphors in Qumran and the New Testament." *BBR* 28: 604–31.

Regev, Eyal. 2019. *The Temple in Early Christianity: Experiencing the Sacred*. AYBRL. New Haven: Yale University Press.

Reiling, Jannes. 1971. "The Use of ΨΕΥΔΟΠΡΟΦΗΤΗΣ in the Septuagint, Philo and Josephus." *NovT* 13: 147–56.

Reiling, Jannes. 1973. *Hermas and Christian Prophecy: A Study of the Eleventh Mandate*. NovTSup 37. Leiden: Brill.

Reiterer, Friedrich V. 2015. "Die *Sapientia Salomonis* im Kontext der frühjüdischen Weisheitsliteratur." Pages 175–89 in *Sapientia Salmonis (Weisheits Salomos)*. Edited by Karl-Wilhelm Niebuhr. Tübingen: Mohr Siebeck.

Reynolds, Benjamin E. 2013. "The Otherworldly Mediators in *4 Ezra* and *2 Baruch*: A Comparison with Angelic Mediators in Ascent Apocalypses and in Daniel, Ezekiel, and Zechariah." Pages 175–93 in *Fourth Ezra and Second Baruch: Reconstruction after the Fall*. Edited by Matthias Henze and Gabriele Boccaccini. JSJ Sup 164. Leiden: Brill.

Rhodes, James N. 2011. "The Two Ways Tradition in the *Epistle of Barnabas*: Revisiting an Old Question." *CBQ* 73: 797–816.

Richardson, I. A. 1936. *The Philosophy of Rhetoric*. New York: Oxford University Press.

Ricoeur, Paul. 1978. *The Rule of Metaphor: Multi-Disciplinary Studies of the Creation of Meaning in Language*. Translated by Robert Czerny. London: Routledge.

Robinson, J. Armitage. 1920. *Barnabas, Hermas, and the Didache*. London: SPCK.

Robinson, James M. 2011. *The Story of the Bodmer Papyri: From the First Monastery's Library in Upper Egypt to Geneva and Dublin*. Eugene: Cascade.

Rodrik, Dani. 2016. "The Politics of Anger." *Project Syndicate*. Available at https://www.project-syndicate.org/commentary/the-politics-of-anger-by-dani-rodrik-2016-03.

Rordorff, Willy. 1986. "Un chapitre d'éthique judéo-chrétienne. les Deux Voies." Pages 155–74 in *Liturgie, foi, et vie des premiers chrétiens: Études patristiques*. Edited by Willy Rordorf. ThH 75. Paris: Beauchesne. First published in *RSR* 60 (1972): 109–28.

Rothschild, Clare K. 2017. "Somatic Effects of Irascibility in Hermas, Mandates 5.1.3 (33.3)." Pages 227–44 in *New Essays on the Apostolic Fathers*. Edited by Clare K. Rothschild. WUNT 375. Tübingen: Mohr Siebeck.

Rothschild, Clare K. 2018. "The Muratorian Fragment as Roman Fake." *NovT* 60: 55–82.

Rothschild, Clare K. 2019. "Ethiopianising the Devil: ὁ μέλας in Barnabas 4." *NTS* 65: 223–45.
Rowland, Christopher. 1982. *The Open Heaven: A Study of Apocalyptic in Judaism and Early Christianity*. London: SPCK.
Rüpke, Jörg. 1999. "Apokalyptische Salzberge: Zum sozialen Ort und zur literarischen Strategie des 'Hirten des Hermas.'" *ARG* 1: 148–60.
Rüpke, Jörg. 2005. "Der Hirt des Hermas: Plausibilisierungs- und Legitimierungsstrategien im Übergang von Antike und Christentum." *ZAC* 8: 276–98.
Rüpke, Jörg. 2016. *On Roman Religion: Lived Religion and the Individual in Ancient Rome*. Townsend Lectures. Ithaca: Cornell University Press.
Ruwet, Jean. 1942–3. "Les 'antilegomena' dans les oeuvres d'Origène." *Bib* 23: 18–42; 24: 18–58.
Ruwet, Jean. 1944. "Les apocryphes dans les oeuvres d'Origène." *Bib* 25: 143–66, 311–34.
Sambursky, Samuel. 1959. *Physics of the Stoics*. London: Routledge & Kegan Paul.
Sambursky, Samuel. 1962. *The Physical World of Late Antiquity*. Princeton: Princeton University Press.
Sanders, E. P. 1989. "The Genre of Palestinian Jewish Apocalypses." Pages 447–59 in *Apocalypticism in the Mediterranean World and the Near East*. Edited by David Hellholm. 2nd ed. Tübingen: Mohr Siebeck.
Sanders, James A. 1972. *Torah and Canon*. Philadelphia: Fortress.
Sandnes, Karl Olav. 2011. "Seal and Baptism in Early Christianity." Pages 1441–81 in *Ablution, Initiation, and Baptism: Late Antiquity, Early Judaism, and Early Christianity*. Edited by David Hellholm, Tor Vegge, Øyvind Norderval, Christer Hellholm. 3 vols. BZNW 176. Berlin: De Gruyter.
Sandt, Huub van de, and David Flusser. 2002. *The Didache: Its Jewish Sources and Its Place in Early Judaism and Christianity*. CRINT 3.5. Assen: Van Gorcum.
Sauer, Georg. 2000. *Jesus Sirach*. ATD Apokryphen 1. Göttingen: Vandenhoeck & Ruprecht.
Schaefer, Ernst. 1912. *Voluminum codicumque fragmenta Graeca cum amuleto christiano*. Leipzig: Teubner.
Schatkin, Margaret A. 1970. "The Influence of Origen upon St. Jerome's Commentary on Galatians." *VC* 24: 49–58.
Schliesser, Benjamin. 2017. "Faith in Early Christianity: An Encyclopedic and Bibliographical Outline." Pages 3–50 in *Glaube: Das Verständnis des Glaubens im frühen Christentum und in seiner jüdischen und hellenistischen-römischen Umwelt*. Edited by Jörg Frey, Benjamin Schliesser, and Nadine Ueberschaer with the help of Kathrin Hager. WUNT 373. Tübingen: Mohr Siebeck.
Schmidt, Karl, and Wilhelm Schubart. 1910. *Altchristliche Texte*. Berlin: Weidmann.
Schnabel, Eckhard J. 2014. "The Muratorian Fragment: The State of Research." *JETS* 57: 231–64.
Schoedel, William R. 1985. *Ignatius of Antioch*. Hermeneia. Philadelphia: Fortress.
Schöpflin, Karin. 2007. "The Interpreting Angel in Post-Exilic Prophetic Visions of the Old Testament." Pages 189–203 in *Angels: The Concept of Celestial Beings—Origins, Development and Reception*. Edited by Friedrich V. Reiterer, Tobias Nicklas, and Karin Schöpflin. Berlin: De Gruyter.
Schröter, Jens. 2015. "The Formation of the New Testament Canon and Early Christian Apocrypha." Pages 167–84 in *The Oxford Handbook of Early Christian Apocrypha*. Edited by Andrew F. Gregory and Christopher M. Tuckett. Oxford: Oxford University Press.

Schubart, Wilhelm. 1920. "Aus einer Apollon-Aretalogie." *Hermes* 55: 188–95.
Schüssler Fiorenza, Elisabeth. 1989. "The Phenomenon of Early Christian Apocalyptic: Some Reflections on Method." Pages 295–316 in *Apocalypticism in the Mediterranean World and the Near East*. Edited by David Hellholm. 2nd ed. Tübingen: Mohr Siebeck.
Schwartz, Jacques. 1965. "Survivances littéraires païennes dans le 'Pasteur' d'Hermas." *RevBib* 72: 240–7.
Seitz, Oscar J. F. 1944. "Relationship of the Shepherd of Hermas to the Epistle of James." *JBL* 63: 131–40.
Seitz, Oscar J. F. 1947. "Antecedents and Signification of the Term ΔΙΨΥΧΟΣ." *JBL* 66: 211–19.
Seitz, Oscar J. F. 1958. "Afterthoughts on the Term Dipsychos." *NTS* 4: 327–34.
Sheppard, G. T. 1987. "Canon." Pages 3.62–69 in *The Encyclopedia of Religion*. Edited by Mircea Eliade. 16 vols. New York: MacMillan.
Skeat, T. C. 1992. "Irenaeus and the Four-Gospel Canon." *NovT* 34: 194–9.
Small, Brian C. 2014. *The Characterization of Jesus in the Book of Hebrews*. BibInt 128. Leiden: Brill.
Snodgrass, Klyne. 2018. *Stories with Intent: A Comprehensive Guide to the Parables of Jesus*. 2nd ed. Grand Rapids: Eerdmans.
Snyder, Graydon F. 1992. "Hermas' The Shepherd." Page 148 in *The Anchor Bible Dictionary*. Edited by David Noel Freedman. Vol. 3. New York: Doubleday.
Soja, Edward. 1996. *Thirdspace: Journeys to Los Angeles and Other Real-and-Imagined Places*. Oxford. Blackwell.
Sorabji, Richard. 1988. *Matter, Space and Motion: Theories in Antiquity and Their Sequel*. London: Duckworth.
Soskice, Janet Martin. 1985. *Metaphor and Religious Language*. Oxford: Clarendon.
Soyars, Jonathan E. 2019. *The* Shepherd *of Hermas and the Pauline Legacy*. NovTSup 176. Leiden: Brill.
Spitta, Friedrich. 1896. *Zur Geschichte und Literatur des Urchristentums*. Vol. 2. Göttingen: Vandenhoeck & Ruprecht.
Staats, Reinhart. 1986. "Hermas." Pages 100–8 in *Theologische Realenzyklopädie*. Edited by Gerhard Müller. Vol. 15. Berlin: De Gruyter.
Steenberg, M. C. 2009. "Irenaeus on Scripture, *Graphe*, and the Status of *Hermas*." *SVTQ* 53: 29–66.
Stephens, Sarah A., and John J. Winkler. 1995. *Greek Novels, the Fragments: Introduction, Text, Translation, and Commentary*. Princeton: Princeton University Press.
Stewart-Sykes, Alistair. 1997. "The Christology of Hermas and the Interpretation of the Fifth Similitude." *Aug* 37: 273–84.
Stewart-Sykes, Alistair. 2011. *On the Two Ways: Life or Death, Light or Darkness: Foundational Texts in the Tradition*. PPS 41. Crestwood: St. Vladimir's Seminary Press.
Steyn, Gert J. 2011. *A Quest for the Assumed LXX Vorlage of the Explicit Quotations in Hebrews*. FRLANT 235. Göttingen: Vandenhoeck & Ruprecht.
Stock, St. George. 1903. "Hermas and Cebes—A Reply." *JP* 28: 87–93.
Stone, Lawrence. 1971. "Prosopography." *Daedalus* 100: 46–79.
Stone, Michael E. ([1976] 1991). "Lists of Revealed Things in the Apocalyptic Literature." Pages 414–54 in *Marginalia Dei: The Mighty Acts of God*. Edited by Werner E. Lemke, Patrick D. Miller, and Frank Moore Cross. New York: Doubleday. Reprinted in "Lists of Revealed Things in the Apocalyptic Literature." Pages 379–418 in *Selected Studies*

in *Pseudepigrapha and Apocrypha with Special Reference to the Armenian Tradition*. Edited by Michael E. Stone. SVTP 9. Leiden: Brill.
Stone, Michael E. 1990. *Fourth Ezra*. Hermeneia. Minneapolis: Fortress, 1990.
Strutwolf, Holger, and Marie-Luise Lakmann. 2016. "Tatians Seelenlehre im Kontext der zeitgenössischen Philosophie." Pages 225–46 in *Gegen falsche Götter und falsche Bildung: Tatian, Rede an die Griechen*. Edited by Heinz-Günther Nesselrath. SAPERE 28. Tübingen: Mohr Siebeck.
Stuckenbruck, Lorench T. 2013. "Ezra's Vision of the Lady: The Form and Function of a Turning Point." Pages 137–50 in *Fourth Ezra and Second Baruch: Reconstruction after the Fall*. Edited by Matthias Henze and Gabriele Boccaccini. JSJ Sup 164. Leiden: Brill.
Sulzbach, Carla. 2014. "The Fate of Jerusalem in 2 Baruch and 4 Ezra: From Earth to Heaven and Back?" Pages 138–52 in *4 Ezra and 2 Baruch: International Studies*. Edited by Gabriele Boccaccini and Jason M. Zurawski. LSTS 87. London: Bloomsbury T&T Clark.
Sundberg, Albert C. 1968. "Towards a Revised History of the NT Canon." Pages 452–61 in *Studia Evangelica IV*. Edited by Frank Leslie Cross. TU 102. Berlin: Akademie.
Sundberg, Albert C. 1973. "Canon Muratori: A Fourth Century List." *HTR* 66: 1–41.
Svigel, Michael J. 2016. *The Center and the Source: Second Century Incarnational Christology and Early Catholic Christianity*. GSECP 66. Piscataway: Gorgias.
Svigel, Michael J. 2019. "Trinitarianism in *Didache*, *Barnabas*, and the *Shepherd*: Sketchy, Scant, or Scandalous?" *Perichoresis* 17: 23–40.
Tagliabue, Aldo. 2017. "Learning from Allegorical Images in the *Book of Visions* of *The Shepherd of Hermas*." *Arethusa* 50: 221–55.
Tagliabue, Aldo. 2020. "Experiencing the Church in the *Book of Visions* of the Shepherd of Hermas." Pages 104–24 in *Experience, Narrative, and Criticism in Ancient Greece: Under the Spell of Stories*. Edited by Jonas Grethlein, Luuk Huitink, and Aldo Tagliabue. Cog Clas. Oxford: Oxford University Press.
Tarvainen, Olavi. 2016. *Faith and Love in Ignatius of Antioch*. Translated by Jonathon Lookadoo. Eugene: Pickwick. Translation of *Glaube und Liebe bei Ignatius von Antiochien*. SLAG 14. Helsinki: Luther-Agricola-Gesellschaft, 1967.
Taylor, Charles. 1892. *The Witness of Hermas to the Four Gospels*. Cambridge: Cambridge University Press.
Taylor, Charles. 1893. "The Two Ways in Hermas and Xenophon." *JP* 21: 243–58.
Taylor, Charles. 1901–3. "Hermas and Cebes." *JP* 27: 276–319; 28: 24–38.
Taylor, Charles. 1903. "Note on Hermas and Cebes—A Reply." *JP* 28: 94–8.
Tigchelaar, Eibert J. C. 1987. "L'ange qui parlait a Zacharie, est-il un Personnage Apocalyptique?" *EstBib* 45: 347–60.
Tilg, Stefan. 2014. *Apuleius' Metamorphoses: A Study in Roman Fiction*. Oxford: Oxford University Press.
Timotin, Andrei. 2016. "Gott und die Dämonen bei Tatian." Pages 267–86 in *Gegen falsche Götter und falsche Bildung: Tatian, Rede an die Griechen*. Edited by Heinz-Günther Nesselrath. SAPERE 28. Tübingen: Mohr Siebeck.
Toepel, Alexander. 2014. *Das Protevangelium des Jakobus: Ein Beitrag zur neueren Diskussion um Herkunft, Auslegung und theologische Einordnung*. Frankfurter Theologische Studien 71. Münster: Aschendorff.
Torrance, Thomas F. 1948. *The Doctrine of Grace in the Apostolic Fathers*. Edinburgh: Oliver & Boyd.
Trapp, Michael B. 1997. "On the *Tablet* of Cebes." Pages 159–80 in *Aristotle and After*. Edited by Richard Sorabji. BICS 68. London: Institute of Classical Studies.

Trebilco, Paul R. 1991. *Jewish Communities in Asia Minor.* SNTSMS 69. Cambridge: Cambridge University Press.

Trebilco, Paul R. 2013. "Studying 'Fractionation' in Earliest Christianity in Rome and Ephesus." Pages 293–333 in *Reflections on the Early Christian History of Religion: Erwägungen zur frühchristlichen Religionsgeschichte.* Edited by Cilliers Breytenbach and Jörg Frey. AGJU 81. Leiden: Brill.

Trebilco, Paul R. 2014. "Creativity at the Boundary: Features of the Linguistic and Conceptual Construction of Outsiders in the Pauline Corpus." *NTS* 60: 185–201.

Trebilco, Paul R. 2017. *Outsider Designations and Boundary Construction in the New Testament: Early Christian Communities and the Formation of Group Identity.* Cambridge: Cambridge University Press.

Trevett, Christine. 1983. "Prophecy or Anti-Episcopal Activity: A Third Error Combatted by Ignatius?" *JEH* 34: 1–18.

Trevett, Christine. 1996. *Montanism: Gender, Authority, and the New Prophecy.* Cambridge: Cambridge University Press.

Trigg, Joseph W. 1998. *Origen.* The Early Church Fathers. London: Routledge.

Tuckett, Christopher M. 2014. "What Is 'New Testament Study'? The New Testament and Early Christianity." *NTS* 60: 157–84.

Turner, C. H. 1913. "Is Hermas also among the Prophets?" *JTS* 14: 404–7.

Turner, C. H 1920. "The Shepherd of Hermas and the Problem of Its Text." *JTS* 21: 193–209.

van Henten, J. W. 1999. "Angel II. ἄγγελος." Pages 50–3 in *Dictionary of Deities and Demons in the Bible.* Edited by Karel van der Toorn, Bob Becking, and Pieter W. van der Horst. 2nd ed. Leiden: Brill.

van Nes, Jermo. 2015. "Under Construction: The Building of God's Temple according to Ephesians 2,19–22." Pages 631–44 in *Paul's Graeco-Roman Context.* Edited by Cilliers Breytenbach. BETL 277. Leuven: Peeters.

van Unnik, W. C. 1949. "De la règle Μήτε προσθεῖναι μήτε ἀφελεῖν dans l'histoire du canon." *VC* 3: 1–36.

van Unnik, W. C. 1952–3. "Zur Bedeutung von Ταπεινοῦν τὴν ψυχήν bei den Apostolischen Vätern." *ZNW* 44: 250–5.

Verano, Mike. 2018. "All the Rage: The Politics of Anger." *PsychCentral.* Available at https://psychcentral.com/blog/all-the-rage-the-politics-of-anger/.

Verhaak, P. F. M., J. H. Dekker, M. W. M. de Waal, H. W. J. van Marwijk, and H. C. Comijs. 2014. "Depression, Disability and Somatic Diseases among Elderly." *Journal of Affective Disorders* 167: 187–91.

Verheyden, Joseph. 2003. "The Canon Muratori: A Matter of Dispute." Pages 487–556 in *The Biblical Canons.* Edited by Jean-Marie Auwers and Henk Jan de Jonge. BETL 163. Leven: Leuven University Press.

Verheyden, Joseph. 2005. "The *Shepherd of Hermas* and the Writings that Later Formed the New Testament." Pages 293–329 in *The Reception of the New Testament in the Apostolic Fathers.* Edited by Andrew F. Gregory and Christopher M. Tuckett. Oxford: Oxford University Press.

Verheyden, Joseph. 2007. "The *Shepherd of Hermas.*" Pages 63–71 in *The Writings of the Apostolic Fathers.* Edited by Paul Foster. London: T&T Clark Continuum.

Verheyden, Joseph. 2015. "On 'Rotten Stones' and a Couple of Other Marginalia in the *Shepherd of Hermas.*" Pages 578–93 in *Studies on the Text of the New Testament and Early Christianity: Essays in Honor of Michael W. Holmes.* Edited by Daniel M. Gurtner, Juan Hernández Jr., and Paul Foster. NTTSD 50. Leiden: Brill.

Vermes, Geza. 2013. *Christian Beginnings: From Nazareth to Nicaea*. New Haven: Yale University Press.

Vielhauer, Philipp. 1975. *Geschichte der urchristlichen Literatur: Einleitung in das Neues Testament, die Apokryphen, und die apostolischen Väter*. 2 vols. Berlin: De Gruyter.

Vielhauer, Philipp. 1979. "Oikodome: Das Bild vom Bau in der christlichen Literatur vom Neuen Testament bis Clemens Alexandrinus." Pages 1–168 in *Oikodome: Aufsätze zum Neuen Testament*. Edited by Günter Klein. Volume 2. TB 65. Munich: Chr. Kaiser.

Villa, Massimo. 2015. "La versione etiopica del Pastore di Erma: Riedizione critica del testo (*Visioni e Precetti*)." *COMSB* 1: 115–18.

Villa, Massimo. 2016. "La versione etiopica del Pastore di Erma. Riedizione critica del testo (*Visioni e Precetti*)." PhD diss. University of Naples 'L'Orientale'.

Vokes, F. E. 1938. *The Riddle of the Didache: Fact or Fiction, Heresy or Catholicism?*. London: SPCK.

Vokes, F. E. 1993. "Life and Order in an Early Church: The Didache." *ANRW* 27.1: 209–33. Part 2, *Principat*, 27.1. Edited by Wolfgang Haase. Berlin: De Gruyter.

Von Staden, Heinrich. 2012. "The Physiology and Therapy of Anger: Galen on Medicine, the Soul, and Nature." Pages 63–87 in *Islamic Philosophy, Science, Culture, and Religion: Studies in Honor of Dimitri Gutas*. Edited by Felicitas Opwis and David Reisman. IPTS 83. Leiden: Brill.

Walde, Christine. 2008. "Sibyl." Columns 411–12 in *BNP*. Edited by Hubert Cancik, Helmuth Schneider, and Christine F. Salazar. Vol. 13 (Sas–Syl). Leiden: Brill.

Wallace-Hadrill, Andrew. 2003. "*Domus* and *Insulae* in Rome: Families and Housefuls." Pages 3–18 in *Early Christian Families in Context: An Interdisciplinary Dialogue*. Edited by David L. Balch and Carolyn Osiek. Grand Rapids: Eerdmans.

Walsh, Lora. 2017. "Ecclesia Reconsidered: Two Premodern Encounters with the Feminine Church." *JFSR* 33.2: 73–91.

Walsh, Lora. 2019a. "The Lady as Elder in the *Shepherd of Hermas*." *JECS* 27: 517–47.

Walsh, Lora. 2019b. "Lost in Revision: Gender Symbolism in *Vision* 3 and *Similitude* 9 of the *Shepherd of Hermas*." *HTR* 112: 467–90.

Walter, Johannes von. 1913. "Die Komposition von Hermas Sim. V und ihre dogmengeschichtlichen Konsequenzen." *ZNW* 14: 133–44.

Wayment, Thomas A. 2013. *The New Testament Apocrypha (100–400 CE)*. London: Bloomsbury T&T Clark.

Weiß, Alexander. 2009. "Hermas' 'Biography': Social Upward and Downward Mobility of an Independent Freedman." *Ancient Society* 39: 185–202.

Weiß, Alexander. 2010. "Keine Quästoren in Korinth: Zu Goodrichs (und Theißens) These über das Amt des Erastos (Röm 16.23)." *NTS* 56: 576–81.

Weiß, Alexander. 2015. *Soziale Elite und Christentum: Studien zu den ordo-Angehörigen unter den frühen Christen*. Millenium Studies 52. Berlin: De Gruyter.

Welborn, Laurence L. 1984. "On the Date of First Clement." *BR* 29: 34–54.

Westcott, Brooke Foss. 1875. *A General Survey of the History of the Canon of the New Testament*. 4th ed. London: MacMillan.

Wiles, Maurice. 1967. *The Making of Christian Doctrine: A Study in the Principles of Early Doctrinal Development*. Cambridge: Cambridge University Press.

Wilhite, Shawn J. 2019a. *The Didache: A Commentary*. AFCS. Eugene: Cascade.

Wilhite, Shawn J. 2019b. *"One of Life and One of Death:" Apocalypticism and the Didache's Two Ways*. GSECP 70. Piscataway: Gorgias.

Wilhite, Shawn J. 2019c. "Thirty-Five Years Later: A Summary of Didache Scholarship since 1983." *CurBibRes* 17: 266–305.

Willett, Tom W. 1989. *Eschatology in the Theodicies of 2 Baruch and 4 Ezra.* JSPSup 4. Sheffield: JSOT Press.

Williams, Rowan. 2005. *Why Study the Past? The Quest for the Historical Church.* London: Darton, Longman, & Todd.

Wilson, J. Christian. 1993. *Towards a Reassessment of the Shepherd of Hermas: Its Date and Its Pneumatology.* Lewiston: Edwin Mellen.

Wilson, J. Christian. 1995. *Five Problems in the Interpretation of the Shepherd of Hermas: Authorship, Genre, Canonicity, Apocalyptic, and the Absence of the Name "Jesus Christ."* MBPS 34. Lewiston: Edwin Mellen.

Wilson, William Jerome. 1927. "The Career of the Prophet Hermas." *HTR* 20: 21–62.

Windisch, Hans. 1928. "Die Sprüche vom Eingehen in das Reich Gottes." *ZNW* 27: 163–92.

Wolfsdorf, David Conan. 2017. "The Historical Socrates." Pages 30–49 in *The Cambridge Companion to Ancient Ethics.* Edited by Christopher Bobonich. Cambridge: Cambridge University Press.

Wright, Archie T. 2010. "Angels." Pages 328–31 in *The Eerdmans Dictionary of Early Judaism.* Edited by John J. Collins and Daniel C. Harlow. Grand Rapids: Eerdmans.

Wright, Brian J. 2017. *Communal Reading in the Time of Jesus: A Window into Early Christian Reading Practices.* Minneapolis: Fortress.

Wudel, Diane B. 2004. "The Seduction of Self-Control: Hermas and the Problem of Desire." *R&T* 11: 39–49.

Yarbro Collins, Adela. 1979. "The Early Christian Apocalypses." *Semeia* 14: 61–121.

Yarbro Collins, Adela. 1986. "Introduction." *Semeia* 36: 1–11.

Yarbro Collins, Adela. 2011. "Apocalypse Now: The State of Apocalyptic Studies near the End of the First Decade of the Twenty-First Century." *HTR* 104: 447–57.

Young, Steve. 1994. "Being a Man: The Pursuit of Manliness in *The Shepherd of Hermas.*" *JECS* 2: 237–55.

Zahn, Theodor. 1868. *Der Hirt des Hermas.* Gotha: Perthes.

Zahn, Theodor. 1873. *Ignatius von Antiochien.* Gotha: Perthes.

Zimmermann, Ruben. 2003. "Nuptial Imagery in the Revelation of John." *Bib* 84: 153–83.

INDEX OF AUTHORS

D'Abbadie, Antoine 28
Abramowski, Luise 150, 158
Adam, Karl 152, 163–4, 175
Adams, Edward 189
Aland, Kurt 46
Aldridge, Robert E. 143
Alexander, Loveday 136
Alikin, Valerity A. 172
Allison, Dale C. 105, 137
Anger, Rudolfus 31, 62, 217
Arbesmann, Rudolph 76
Armstrong, Jonathan J. 39
Attridge, Harold W. 156, 189
Aune, David E. 113

Bandini, Michele 20–2, 39, 66, 163, 212, 214
Barclay, John M. G. 59, 134, 172–3
Barnard, Leslie W. 65, 142
Barnes, Michele Rene 155, 164
Batchelor, Wayne B. 220
Batovici, Dan 21, 23–4, 26, 29, 37–8, 49–50, 58, 105, 150, 178–80, 182
Bauckham, Richard J. 55, 105, 135, 137–8, 140, 165, 169, 198
Bauer, Walter 83
Bautista, Ramon L. 162
Baynes, Leslie 96, 104
Beale, Gregory K. 189
Beasley-Murray, George R. 132
Beavis, Mary Ann 60, 77, 81, 83, 131, 152
Bebbington, David W. 177
Behr, John 36
Bennema, Cornelius 83
Berger, Klaus 122, 138
Bigg, Charles 134
Black, Max 188
Blenkinsopp, Joseph 120
Blidstein, Moshe 78, 87, 175–6, 180, 182, 191–2, 209–10, 212
Blischke, Mareike Verena 125

Blomkvist, Vemund 176, 191
Blumell, Lincoln H. 23
Bogdanos, Theodore 47
Bonner, Campbell 22, 24, 65, 78
Booth, Wayne C. 188
Bovon, François 51–2
Brakke, David 52
Bremmer, Jan N. 113, 177
Breytenbach, Cilliers 134
Briggman, Anthony 37, 148, 153–4
Brookins, Timothy A. 172
Brooks, David 221
Brooks, James A. 38, 49
Brouwer, Leendert 189
Brox, Norbert 1, 35, 39–40, 45, 49–50, 56, 61–3, 65–7, 69, 75–7, 79, 81, 83, 87–8, 92, 94, 99, 104–5, 112, 116, 121, 125, 130, 133, 136, 150–2, 156, 159–60, 168–70, 172, 175, 181, 190, 193, 196–7, 214, 216
Buch-Hansen, Gitte 153–4
Bucur, Bogdan 73, 84–5, 152, 156, 164
Burke, Trevor J. 189

Camelot, Pierre-Thomas 141
Cameron, Averil 91
Campenhausen, Hans Freiherr von 130
Cantalamessa, Raniero 153
Carlini, Antonio 21, 23, 62, 66, 134
Carmignac, Jean 57
Carroll, Scott T. 40
Cecconi, Paolo 21, 23, 26–8, 32, 62, 67
Cecil, David 111
Chadwick, Henry 25, 31, 68
Choat, Malcolm 24, 26, 50
Cirillo, Luigi 152
Coakley, Sarah 218–19
Cochran, Sam V. 220
Coleborne, William 64–5
Collins, John J. 56–8, 115, 138, 178
Collins, Paul M. 147

Comijs, Hannie C. 220
Coneybeare, F. C. 25
Corwin, Virginia 195
Cosaert, Carl P. 49
Cotterill, J. M. 116, 118
Cox Miller, Patricia 182

D'Alès, Athémar 39, 175
Daniélou, Jean 128, 157
Deissman, Adolf 172
Dekker, J. H. 220
Delage, Marie José 46
DeLaine, Janet 194
Delkurt, Holger 119
de Waal, Margot W. M. 220
Dibelius, Martin 61-3, 65-7, 78, 84, 88, 93, 104-6, 112-14, 118, 131, 133, 136, 150, 157, 168, 175-6, 180-1, 193, 197, 200, 210-11, 215-16
Diels, Hermann 23
Dindorff, Guilelmus 31, 33, 62, 217
Dobschütz, Ernst von 156
Docherty, Susan E. 136
Dorival, Gilles 41
Dostálová, Růžena 24
Downs, David J. 76, 171, 173, 178
Doyle, Arthur Conan 96
Drummond, James 129-32, 135
Dunderberg, Ismo 143, 153
Dunn, James D. G. 134
Dunn, Peter W. 78
Dyer, Bryan R. 59, 136

Ebner, Martin 194
Eck, Werner 91
Ehrman, Bart D. 1, 19, 22, 32, 38, 44, 48, 50, 52, 62, 82, 93, 134, 141, 143, 181, 191
Elliott J. K. 50
Engberg-Pedersen, Troels 208
Erho, Ted 28-9
d'Etaples, Jacques Le Fèvre 26, 31
Eynikel, Erik 126

Farrar, Thomas J. 209
Feldmeier, Reinhard 117, 197
Ferguson, Everett 39, 160, 197
Fincham, Frank D. 220
Fischer, Joseph A. 141

Fitzgerald, John T. 115
Fletcher-Louis, Crispin 57, 150
Flusser, David 143
Förster, Niclas 144
Foster, Paul 91, 130
Fowl, Stephen E. 205
Frey, Jörg 132, 135
Friesen, Steven J. 60, 172
Fuentes-Utrilla, Pablo 171

Gathercole, Simon 131
Gavaler, Chris 56
Gebhardt, Oscar von 20, 32, 217
Gerardo Americano, Sergio 33
Giaccone, Luigi 23, 66, 134
Gibbs, Raymond W. 188
Gieschen, Charles 150, 158, 164
Giet, Stanislas 64
Gil, Luis 171
Glancy, Jennifer A. 81, 92, 104, 131
Gleede, Benjamin 26, 40, 42, 116
Goff, Matthew 123
Gonzalez, Justo L. 69
Goodrich, John K. 172
Goodspeed, Edgar J. 42
Grant, Robert M. 33, 65
Greenfell, Bernard P. 25
Grillmeier, Aloys 150, 160
Gronewald, Michael 24-5
Gross, Sven 220
Grundeken Mark 63, 66-9, 105, 112-13, 128, 136, 150, 160, 171-3, 176, 197
Grünstäudl, Wolfgang 135
Guignard, Christophe 39
Gupta, Nijay K. 59, 189

Haas, C. 81, 155, 162
Hahneman, Geoffrey M. 39, 50
Hallaschka, Martin 119
Hammond Bammel, Caroline P. 45
Hannah, Darrel D. 150, 157-8
Hannick, Christian 46
Hanson, Paul D. 56
Harkins, Angela Kim 96, 195
Harnack, Adolf von 20, 23, 25, 32, 40-1, 134, 150, 217
Harris, J. Rendel 63, 190
Harrison, Stephen 113
Hartley, L. P. 111

Index of Authors

Hauck, Robert J. 86, 152, 155, 209, 211
Hauspie, Katrin 126
Havelaar, Henriette W. 39
Hawkins, Kirsten A. 220
von Hefele, Karl Josef 56, 178
Hegeman, Johanna M. 220
Heim, Erin 188–9
Heine, Ronald E. 45, 145
Hellholm, David 1, 57–8, 63, 69, 107
Hemmerdinger, Bertrand 36
Hengel, Martin 112, 150
Henne, Philippe 1, 39, 66–7, 73, 77, 97, 152, 155, 193, 197–8
Hilgenfeld, Adolf 26, 64, 67, 82
Hilhorst, Antonius 66, 75
Hill, Charles E. 49, 132
Hirsch-Luipold, Rainer 116, 118
van den Hoek, Annewies 38
Hogeterp, Albert L. 189
Holmes, Michael W. 1–2, 19, 22, 32–3, 38, 62, 82, 93, 128, 134, 141, 161, 175, 180–1
Hooper, Walter 215
Horrell, David G. 172, 194
Horsley, G. H. R. 23
Houghton, H. A. G. 46, 75
Howson, John S. 189
Huber, Lynn R. 47, 140
Hückstädt, Ernst 134
Humphrey, Edith McEwan 1, 121, 140
Humphries, Mark 44
Hunt, Arthur S. 25
Hurst, André 22
Hurtado, Larry W. 84, 113, 152
Hvalvik, Reidar 68–9, 119, 125, 156
Hwang, Alexander Y. 45

Ioannidou, Grace 24

Jachmann, Karl 56, 122
Jacobs, Alan 222
Jeffers, James S. 69, 105, 174
Jefford, Clayton N. 129, 133, 142–4, 213
Jensen, Robin M. 174
Johnson, Luke Timothy 156
Johnson, Mark 188
Joly, Robert 31, 38, 40, 56, 62, 64–6, 69, 77, 81, 83, 88, 105, 112, 116–19, 131, 141, 150, 175, 178, 181, 193, 208, 214

Jongkind, Dirk 21
Joyce, Paul 120
Junack Klaus 46

Kelly, J. N. D. 150, 157
Kieffer, René 188–9, 194
Kilpatrick, G. D. 25
Kirkland, Alastair 19
Knopf, Rudolf 194
Koch, Klaus 56
Koester, Craig R. 132, 140
Kok, Rob M. 220
Körtner, Ulrich H. J. 31, 33, 38, 60, 62–3, 65–6, 88, 92, 96, 105, 114, 123, 151, 168–9, 179, 190, 210, 215
Koschorke, Klaus 39
Köster, Helmut 119, 127, 129–30
Kraft, Heinrich 136, 168, 175
Kruger, Michael J. 49, 51
Kuluk, Alexander 120
Kuruvilla, Abraham 87

Lake, Kirsopp 20, 22, 32, 56, 88, 150, 178
Lakmann, Marie-Luise 208
Lakoff, George 188
Lambros, Spyr. P. 20
Lampe, Peter 116, 118, 171, 173–4, 194
van Lantschoot, Arnold 29
Lappa-Zizicas, Eurydice 22
Lawrence, Jean 220
Layton, Bentley 142
Lebram, Jürgen 123
Lefort, Louis-Théophile 29–30, 65
Legarth, Peter V. 142, 189, 194
Lehtipuu, Outi 88
Leiman, Sid Z. 105
Leipoldt, Johannes 29
Lenaerts, Jean 24
Leutzsch, Martin 31, 33, 38, 60, 62–3, 65–6, 88, 92, 96, 105, 108, 114, 123, 131, 151, 168–9, 171, 179, 190, 199, 210, 215
Levine, Baruch A. 105
Levison, John R. 85
Lietzmann, Hans 40
Lightfoot, J. B. 68, 141, 194
Lindemann, Andreas 82, 134, 141, 181
Link, Adolf 66
Lipsett, Diane B. 95, 100, 179–80, 182–4
Litwa, M. David 40, 146

Liu, Cuilian 220
Liu, Liang 220
Llewelyn, S. R. 23
Lona, Horacio E. 85
Longenecker, Bruce 172
Lookadoo, Jonathon 88, 98, 132, 139, 141, 144, 172, 189, 194
López-Rodriguez, Rosana 171
Lucchesi, Enzo 29-30
Lusini, Gianfrancesco 20, 31
Lust, Johan 126

MacDonald, Margaret Y. 104, 179
Maier, Harry O. 58, 65, 93, 133, 172, 183, 189, 195
Marjanen, Antti 145
Markschies, Christoph 21, 39, 60
Marshall, John W. 85
Martin, E. G. 105
Martín, Juan Pablo 160-1
Massaux, Édouard 129, 132
May, Ross W. 220
Mayo, José Eusebio Pérez 173-4, 199
Mazzini, Innocenzo 27
McDonald, Lee Martin 51
McFarland, Orrey 134
McGrath, Alister E. 215
Meggitt, Justin J. 172
Meier, Laurenz L. 220
Mercati, Silvo Giuseppe 23
Metzger, Bruce M. 123
Mews, Constant J. 47
Michaels, J. Ramsey 132
Mishra, Pankaj 220
Mohrmann, Christine 26, 75
Molendijk, Arie L. 177
Moo, Jonathan A. 123
Morgan-Wynne, John Eifion 162, 219
Moxnes, Halvor 101, 150, 158
Muddiman, John 132, 140, 176
Müller, F. W. K. 30
Müller, Ulrich B. 56
Muraoka, Takamitsu 126
Musurillo, Herbert 31

Nagel, Titus 132
Najman, Hindy 123
Newman, Barbara J. 47
Newsom Carol 57, 189

Nickelsburg, George W. E. 119, 138
Niederwimmer, Kurt 75, 132, 143
Noll, Mark A. 177

Oakes, Peter 172
O'Brien, D. P. 97, 106, 125, 148-9
Opitz, Hans-Georg 44
Osborn, Eric 153
Osiek, Carolyn 1, 35, 37, 39, 45, 57, 59-60, 62-3, 65-7, 69, 75-6, 78, 80-2, 87-8, 92, 95, 100, 102, 104-6, 108, 119, 121, 124, 130-1, 133, 135-6, 150, 152, 158-9, 161, 169, 171-2, 176-7, 179, 181-2, 190, 193, 197, 200, 214
Otranto, Rosa 25
Otterpohl, Nantje 220
Outtier, Bernard 30

Papandrea, James L. 150, 157
Parker, David C. 21, 46
Paulsen, Henning 82, 134, 141, 181
Peppard, Michael 189
Perrone, Lorenzo 218
Phan, Peter C. 147
Pintaudi, Rosario 24
Pleše, Zlatko 52
Poinsotte, Jean-Michele 42
Porter, Stanley E. 20, 136
Poschmann, Bernhard 175
Powell, J. Enoch 25
Pratscher, Wilhelm 148
Prinzivalli, Emanuela 22, 32-3, 38, 44, 62, 82, 93, 134, 141, 181
Prostmeier, Ferdinand R. 142-3
Puech, Aimé 56

Rabinowitz, Fredric E. 220
Rahner, Karl 175
Regev, Eyal 189, 197
Reiling, Jannes 37, 79, 88, 113-15, 123, 143, 168-9, 194, 213
Reiterer, Friedrich V. 125
Reverdin, Olivier 22
Reynolds, Benjamin E. 119
Rhodes, James N. 142
Richardson, I. A. 188
Ricoeur, Paul 188
Robinson, J. Armitage 142
Robinson, James M. 22

Rodrik, Dani 220
Rordorff, Willy 75, 142
Rothschild, Clare K. 39, 44, 87, 142, 205–7, 209, 220
Rowland, Christopher 56, 58
Rudhart, Jean 22
Rüpke, Jörg 58, 60–1, 63, 66, 92–3, 108, 118, 196
Ruwet, Jean 51

Sambursky, Samuel 153–4
Sanchez-Gonzalez, Marcos A. 220
Sanders, E. P. 57
Sanders James A. 51
Sanders, Georg 124
Sandnes, Karl Olav 197
Schaefer, Ernst 24
Schatkin, Margaret A. 45
Scheck, Thomas P. 41
Schliesser, Benjamin 134, 168
Schmidt, Karl 24
Schnabel, Eckhard J. 39
Schoedel, William R. 88, 195
Schöpflin, Karin 119, 121
Schröter, Jens 49
Schubart, Wilhelm 24, 114
Schüssler Fiorenza, Elisabeth 56
Schwartz, Jacques 116
Schwemer, Anna Maria 112
Schwinger, Malte 220
Seitz, Oscar J. F. 105, 136
Semmer, Norbert K. 220
Sheppard, G. T. 51
Simonetti, Manlio 22, 32–3, 38, 44, 62, 82, 93, 134, 141, 181
Singer, Peter 206–7
Skeat, T. C. 130
Small, Brian C. 156
Snodgrass, Klyne 11, 131
Snyder, Graydon F. 180
Soja, Edward 195
Sorabji, Richard 154
Soskice, Janet Martin 188
Soyars, Jonathan E. 36, 64, 83, 129, 133–4, 203, 211
Spector, Paul E. 220
Spitta, Friedrich 65, 118–19, 127
Staats, Reinhart 61, 66, 131
Stählin, Otto 38

Steenberg, M. C. 48–9
Stegmüller, Otto 23
Stephens, Sarah A. 114
Stewart-Sykes, Alistair 84, 143, 150, 152, 158, 218
Steyn, Gert J. 135
Stock, St. George 116
Stone, Lawrence 91
Stone, Michael E. 56, 121–2
Stranghoener, Daniela 220
Strutwolf, Holger 208
Sulzbach, Carla 121
Sundberg, Albert C. 39, 50–1
Svigel, Michael J. 78, 81–2, 84, 87, 151–2, 155, 157–8, 164, 198

Tabbernee, William 174
Tagliabue, Aldo 94, 96, 98, 184, 191
Tarvainen, Olavi 38
Taylor, Charles 116, 118, 125, 129–30
Thompson, Trevor W. 207
Tigchelaar, Eibert J. C. 119
Tilg, Stefan 113
Timotin, Andrei 208
Tischendorff, Constantine 46
Todd, Robert B. 154
Toepel, Alexander 52
Torrance, Thomas F. 134
Tornau, Christian 23, 26–8, 62, 67, 134
Trapp, Michael B. 117
Trebilco, Paul R. 92, 105, 126–7, 170
Treu, Kurt 24
Trevett, Christine 145–6
Trigg, Joseph W. 218
Tuckett, Christopher M. 50
Tuilier, Andre 75
Tulloch, Janet H. 104, 179
Turner, C. H. 26, 50

van Bekkum, Wout J. 177
van de Sandt, Huub 143
van der Mast, Roos C. 220
van Fenema, Esther M. 220
van Henten, J. W. 100
van Marwijk, H. W. J. 220
van Nes, Jermo 189
van Unnik, W. C. 51, 181
Verano, Mike 220
Verhaak, P. F. M. 220

Verheyden, Joseph 1, 39, 59, 63, 68, 92, 108, 129–30, 133, 159, 198
Vermes, Geza 158
Vezzoni, Anna 26–8
Vidman, Ladislav 24
Vielhauer, Phillip 56, 193
Vierhaus, Marc 220
Villa, Massimo 28–9
Von Staden, Heinrich 206, 220

Walde, Christine 115
Wallace-Hadrill, Andrew 195
Walsh, Lora 63, 97–8, 102, 107, 124, 163, 193, 197
von Walter, Johannes 152
Wayment, Thomas A. 23–4
Weinel, Heinrich 116
Weiß, Alexander 59–60, 92–3, 172
Wengst, Klaus 75
Westcott, B. F. 46
Whittaker, Molly 31
Wiles, Maurice 175

Wilhite, Shawn J. 75, 125, 142, 145
Willett, Tom W. 121
Williams, D. H. 174
Williams, Rowan 215
Wilson, J. Christian 56, 64, 66, 69, 84, 178
Wilson, William Jerome 65–6, 69, 83, 92
Windisch, Hans 160
Winkler, John J. 114
Wolfsdorf, David Conan 100, 117
Wright, Archie T. 119, 138
Wright, Brian J. 123
Wudel, Diane B. 180

Yarbro Collins, Adela 57–8, 178
Young, Steve 122, 183, 199, 201–2
Yuen-Collingridge, Rachel 24, 26, 50

Zahn, Theodor 32, 63, 105, 112, 121, 135, 141, 152, 175, 192–3, 217
Zhao, Xudong 220
Zimmerman, Ruben 140

INDEX OF REFERENCES

HEBREW BIBLE/OLD TESTAMENT

Genesis
1:1	43
22:16	151
29:1–30	83

Exodus
15:14	126
24:18	75
34:28	75

Numbers
14:33–4	41

Deuteronomy
6:4	148
7:1	126
30:15	125

Joshua
24:15	125

1 Kings (3 Kingdoms)
19:8	75

Job
6:28	44
8:17	44

Psalms
1:6	125
2:1	126
2:9	139
34:8 (33:8 LXX)	45
37:2 (36:2 LXX)	41
55:23 (54:23 LXX)	135
68:29 (67:29 LXX)	81
74:16 (73:16 LXX)	148
80:9–17 (79:9–17 LXX)	77
89:38 (88:38 LXX)	148
118:19–20 (117:19–20 LXX)	132
139:24 (138:24 LXX)	125

Proverbs
2:8–22	125
4:10–19	125
8	124
8:22	124
8:23–5	124
8:26–31	125
8:32	124
8:34	124

Ecclesiastes
12:12	123
12:13	216

Isaiah
5:1–7	76
45:23	151
54:1–10	96
54:1	121
58:1–14	76

Jeremiah
2:2–3	96
2:21	77
2:22	121
21:8	125
22:5	151
49:13	151

Ezekiel
1:6	129
8–11	119
8:2	119
9	120
9:2	120
16:3	121
34:2	40
40–8	119
40	120

Daniel

3:52–3	25
3:58–68	25
3:77–84	25
7–12	55
7:9–10	96
7:10	123
9:3	123
10:3	123
10:12	123

Hosea

1:1–3:5	96
2:19–20	121

Zephaniah

2:12	44

Zechariah

1:7–6:8	119
1:7–17	119
1:9	121
1:13	121
1:14	121
2:3	121
5:8	44, 48
14:9	148

NEW TESTAMENT

Matthew

4:1	75
5:35	130
7:13–14	143
7:17–20	46
13:20–1	130
13:24–30	81, 131
13:36–43	131
13:38	81
18:10	45
19:3–9	132
21:33–46	77, 81, 131
21:33	131
24:45–51	131
25:13	81
25:21–3	47
28:18	82, 131
28:19	147

Mark

1:12	75
4:18–19	130
10:18	148
12:1–12	81, 131
12:1–9	77
12:1	131
12:32	148
13:33–7	81

Luke

4:1	75
8:3	59
8:14	130
12:41–5	131
12:58–9	41
20:9–19	131
20:9–16	77, 81
20:9	131

John

3:5	132
10:1–18	132
10:1–5	132
10:7	132
10:8	132
10:9	132
10:10	159
10:18	131
12:49	131
13	83
13:4–17	83
13:14–16	83
14:6	132
14:31	131
15:1–6	77
15:20	83

Acts

4:25–6	139
12:15	45
13:33	139
17:24	81
24:5	180

Romans

3:21–4:25	134
3:21–6	134
5:6–8	134
6:1–11	133
7:7–8	180
8	218
8:15–16	218
8:26–7	218
8:26	218
11:36	81

15:5	133	2:8	134
16:14	41–2, 68–9	3:9	134
16:23	172	4:2	133
		4:3	69

1 Corinthians
1:23	134	Colossians	
3:16–17	194	1:16	148
6:13–20	194		
7	133	1 Thessalonians	
7:9	180	1:9	148
7:10	133	4:5	180
7:11	133	5:20–1	145
7:39–40	133	5:21–2	145
8:4	148		
8:6	81, 148	2 Timothy	
9:25	180	2:25	179
11:17–34	171		
11:30	171	Hebrews	
14	145	1:1	135
14:29	145	1:2	136
15:3–5	134	1:5	139
15:24–5	82	2:6–8	135–6
		5–7	156
2 Corinthians		6:13	151
5:21	134	8:7–12	136
7:10	134	9	156
8–9	59	11:3	43, 148
8:14	46	11:32–40	136
13:11	133		
13:13	147	James	
		1:1	137
Galatians		1:5–7	136
3:1	134	1:6	168
3:6–4:31	134	1:8	44, 136
3:20	148	1:14–15	180
5:23	180	2:1–4	59
5:24	180	2:19	148
		3:8	137
Ephesians		4:4	170
1:20–3	82	4:5	137
2:8–9	134	4:7	137
2:19–21	194	4:8	136–7
3:6	37	4:12	137
3:9	81, 148	5:17	168
4:4–6	159		
5:25	176	1 Peter	
		1:10–12	135
Philippians		2:4–5	197
2:2	133	2:4	197
2:5	133	2:5	197
2:6–11	83	2:11–12	135
2:7	83	5:7	135

2 Peter
1:4	180
1:6	180
3:2	135

1 John
2:16	180
4:1–3	145

Revelation
1:11	138
1:12	138
2–3	138
2:27	139
3:5	139
4–5	138
4:1	138
4:7	129
4:11	81, 148
5:6–9	138
6:1	138
10:2	138
10:4	138
10:8–11	138
12	139–40
12:1–6	139
12:1	139
12:3	139
12:7–12	139
12:13	139
12:14–17	139–40
13:8	139
13:13	139
13:14	139
14:13	138
15:1–2	138
15:1	139
15:5	138
16–18	140
16:14	139
17:1–18:24	60
17:8	139
18:1	138
19:6–10	140
19:9–10	138
19:9	138
19:20	139
20:11	96
20:12	139
20:15	139
21	140
21:2	140
21:27	139
22:8–9	138

APOCRYPHA

2 Maccabees
7:23	81
7:28	37

Sirach
7:10	168
15:11–17	126
18:1	81
24	124
24:2	124
24:8–12	124
24:9–12	124
24:9	124
24:10	124
24:23–7	124
24:30–1	124
33:14	216
50:27	123

Wisdom of Solomon
1:14	81
7:1–6	124
7:12–14	124
7:15–16	124
7:22	125
7:25	124–5
12:13	135
12:19	179
14:11	126
15:15	126

OLD TESTAMENT PSEUDEPIGRAPHA

Apocalypse of Abraham
10.1–17.21	100
10.3–4	120
10.4	119–20
17.1–18.14	123

2 Baruch
9.2	122
12.5	122
20.5–22.8	122
43.3	123
47.2	123

3 Baruch
1.3–17.1	120
4.7	120
11.4–9	120

1 Enoch
1–36	119
1.9	126
17.1–36.4	100, 120
20.1–7	120
46.1–2	96
47.3	96
48.8	139
54.3–5	126
63.1	126

2 Enoch
10.1–3	126
30.8	125
30.15	126

Epistle of Aristeas
132–8	148
139	126

4 Ezra
3.1–10.59	120
5.3	77
5.13	122
5.20	122
5.21–32	122
6.13–17	122
6.31–7.2	122
7.3–12	126
9.24–5	123
9.26–10.59	96, 121
9.38–10.4	121
10.7	121
10.25–7	121
10.33	122
10.40–54	121
13.57	62
14.47	123

Jubilees
31.29	148

3 Maccabees
2.3	81
6.9	126

Psalms of Solomon
9.9	126
17.24	139

Pseudo-Phocylides
63–4	209
65–7	216

Sibylline Oracles
3.11	148
4.168	179

Testament of Asher
1.3–5	126
1.3–4	216
1.8	126
2.1–6.8	126

Testament of Judah
20.1	216

Testament of Levi
3.2–3	126
9.10	126

DEAD SEA SCROLLS AND RELATED LITERATURE

1QM
XIII, 12	126

1QS
III, 13–IV, 26	125–6
III, 15	126
III, 18	126
III, 20–21	126
III, 25–6	126
IV, 2–6	126
IV, 6–8	126
IV, 9–11	126
IV, 11–14	126

4Q174
I, 18–19	139

CD
II, 6	126

PHILO

De agricultura
101	126

De migratione Abrahami
192   148

Legum allegoriae
3.203–8   151

Quaestiones et solutiones in Exodum
1.23   126

JOSEPHUS

Antiquitates judaicae
4.201   148

MISHNAH

Abot
2.1   126

APOSTOLIC FATHERS

1 Clement
23.3	137
28.1	180
30.1	180
35.2	180
48.2–4	132, 159

2 Clement
9.3	87–8, 194
11.2	137
12.1	81

Didache
1.1–6.2	45
1.1	143
1.4	180
1.5–6	143
3.7	143
3.8	143
4.4	168
8.1	75
10.3	148
11	145
11.7–12	145
11.12	145
12	145
12.1	145
12.2	145
12.3	145
13	145

Epistle of Barnabas
2.2	180
3.1–6	76
4.10	44
4.11	194
5.4	142
10.9	180
16.6	148
16.9	179
18.1–20.2	45
18.1–2	142
18.1	142
19.2	143
19.4	143
19.5	168
20.1	44, 142

Ignatius
Ephesians
9.1	38, 142, 194–5
10.1	141
14.1	38
15.3	194
19.2–3	88
19.3	88

Magnesians
5.1–2	143
6.1–7.2	194
7.1–2	133, 159
7.2	194
8.1–10.3	111
8.2	148
13.1–2	147

Trallians
11	142

Philadelphians
4	133, 159
6.1–9.2	111
7.2	87, 194
9.1	132, 142, 159

Smyrnaeans
6.1	38

Index of References

Martyrdom of Polycarp
14.3   147

Polycarp
Philippians
4.2   180
11.1-4   172

Shepherd of Hermas
Visions
1.1.1–*Sim*. 9.30.3 (1.1–107.3)   20
1.1.1–*Mand*. 4.3.6 (1.1–31.6)   21, 67
1–5 (1–25)   5
1–4 (1–24)   27, 30, 64–8
1–3 (1–21)   23
1 (1–4)   5
1.1–2 (1–2)   96, 183
1.1.1 (1.1)   62, 92, 104, 108, 183
1.1.2 (1.2)   6, 39, 62, 67, 93, 104, 111, 183
1.1.3 (1.3)   62–3, 74, 148–9, 161, 180
1.1.4–9 (1.4–9)   108
1.1.5–6 (1.5–6)   104
1.1.5 (1.5)   94
1.1.6–7 (1.6–7)   104
1.1.6 (1.6)   106, 149
1.1.8–9 (1.8–9)   23, 104, 174
1.1.8 (1.8)   60, 95. 183
1.1.9 (1.9)   79, 149, 183, 199–200
1.2.1–3 (2.1–3)   180
1.2.1 (2.1)   94
1.2.2–1.3.1 (2.2–3.1)   25
1.2.2–4 (2.2–4)   93
1.2.2 (2.2)   96–8, 115, 138
1.2.3 (2.3)   96, 104
1.2.4–1.3.2 (2.4–3.2)   96, 107
1.2.4 (2.4)   93, 95, 160, 174, 177, 183, 210
1.3.1–2 (3.1–2)   59, 79, 104, 108
1.3.1 (3.1)   6, 93, 104, 174, 199
1.3.2 (3.2)   139, 179
1.3.3–4 (3.3–4)   6, 139
1.3.4 (3.4)   106, 149

1.4.1 (4.1)   102
1.4.2 (4.2)   6, 98, 127
1.4.3 (4.3)   102, 122, 183

2 (5–8)   6, 123
2.1.1–3 (5.1–3)   120
2.1.1 (5.1)   62–3, 74, 161
2.1.2 (5.2)   122, 180
2.1.3–4 (5.3–4)   139
2.1.3 (5.3)   138–9, 149
2.1.3–2.3.4 (5.3–7.4)   123
2.1.3–4 (5.3–4)   6, 38
2.1.3 (5.3)   115
2.2.1–2.3.4 (6.1–7.4)   6, 139
2.2.1 (6.1)   74, 122
2.2.2–2.3.4 (6.2–7.4)   96, 151
2.2.2–4 (6.2–4)   137
2.2.2–3 (6.2–3)   174
2.2.2 (6.2)   59, 104, 108, 174, 199
2.2.3 (6.3)   104
2.2.4 (6.4)   137, 168–9
2.2.5 (6.5)   127, 149, 151
2.2.6–7 (6.6–7)   105
2.2.7 (6.7)   137, 169
2.2.8 (6.8)   151
2.3.1 (7.1)   133
2.3.2 (7.2)   177
2.3.4 (7.4)   60, 105, 129, 137
2.4.1 (8.1)   6, 62, 85, 96–8, 102, 106, 108, 115, 121, 158
2.4.2–3 (8.2–3)   60, 105, 149, 199
2.4.2 (8.2)   41, 60, 67–9, 105, 108, 123, 138
2.4.3 (8.3)   6, 11, 15–18, 47, 61, 65, 71, 98, 106, 117, 121, 134, 139, 161, 170, 184, 187–203

3 (9–21)

3.1.2–4 (9.2–4)   120, 190

Index of References

3.1.2 (9.2)	61, 74, 92, 94, 97, 122	3.5.4 (13.4)	94
3.1.3 (9.3)	94	3.5.5 (13.5)	94, 196
3.1.4 (9.4)	98, 118, 138	3.6.1–3.7.3 (14.1–15.3)	192
3.1.5–7 (9.5–7)	95	3.6.1–7 (14.1–7)	196
3.1.5–6 (9.5–6)	184	3.6.2 (14.2)	169
3.1.5 (9.5)	180	3.6.3 (14.3)	94
3.1.6–8 (9.6–8)	102	3.6.4 (14.4)	24
3.1.6 (9.6)	98, 199	3.6.5–7 (14.5–7)	170
3.1.7–9 (9.7–9)	97, 118	3.6.5–6 (14.5–6)	201
3.1.7 (9.7)	98	3.6.5 (14.5)	94–5, 130, 170
3.1.8 (9.8)	60, 105	3.6.6 (14.6)	24, 94, 150
3.1.9 (9.9)	149	3.6.7 (14.7)	184
3.2.1 (10.1)	94, 149	3.7.1–3 (15.1–3)	196
3.2.4–9 (10.4–9)	7	3.7.1 (15.1)	169
3.2.4 (10.4)	73, 98, 107, 189–90, 195	3.7.2–3 (15.2–3)	174
		3.7.3 (15.3)	73
3.2.5–9 (10.5–9)	189	3.7.5–6 (15.5–6)	179, 192, 196
3.2.5–6 (10.5–6)	197		
3.2.5 (10.5)	102	3.7.5 (15.5)	94
3.2.6–8 (10.6–8)	201	3.8.1–8 (16.1–8)	7, 47
3.2.6–7 (10.6–7)	192	3.8.2–8 (16.2–8)	102, 163
3.2.6 (10.6)	191	3.8.2 (16.2)	163
3.2.7–9 (10.7–9)	192	3.8.3–5 (16.3–5)	163
3.2.7 (10.7)	44	3.8.3 (16.3)	149
3.2.8 (10.8)	61	3.8.5 (16.5)	94, 117, 177–8
3.3 (11)	121		
3.3.1 (11.1)	94, 117, 121, 189	3.8.6 (16.6)	94
		3.8.7 (16.7)	93, 117–18, 177–8
3.3.2–3.8.11 (11.2–16.11)	190		
3.3.2–5 (11.2–5)	117	3.8.9 (16.9)	80, 94–5, 160, 192
3.3.2 (11.2)	95, 121		
3.3.3 (11.3)	121, 158, 190	3.9 (17)	7, 80, 107, 124, 139, 177, 190, 192
3.3.4 (11.4)	117, 121, 168		
3.3.5 (11.5)	7, 73, 94, 113, 117, 121, 149, 190, 197	3.9.1 (17.1)	98, 124, 134, 177, 210
		3.9.2 (17.2)	124, 149
3.4.1–2 (12.1–2)	102, 201	3.9.3 (17.3)	173
3.4.1 (12.1)	94, 149	3.9.4–6 (17.4–6)	173
3.4.2 (12.2)	94	3.9.4 (17.4)	173
3.4.3 (12.3)	37, 67, 94, 169, 184	3.9.7 (17.7)	173
		3.9.8 (17.8)	130
3.5–7 (13–15)	7, 198	3.9.10 (17.10)	124, 149
3.5.1–5 (13.1–5)	201	3.10–13 (18–21)	63, 96–9, 121, 176, 190, 220
3.5.1–4 (13.1–4)	192, 196		
3.5.1 (13.1)	105, 149, 198	3.10.1 (18.1)	98
		3.10.2 (18.2)	97–8
3.5.2–3.7.3 (13.2–15.3)	198	3.10.3–5 (18.3–5)	97
3.5.2 (13.2)	94, 197	3.10.3 (18.3)	97
3.5.3 (13.3)	158		

Index of References

3.10.4 (18.4)	97	5.1 (25.1)	38, 74, 99, 101, 111, 119–20, 149, 168
3.10.5 (18.5)	97–8		
3.10.6–7 (18.6–7)	75, 122		
3.10.7–3.13.4 (18.7–21.4)	102		
3.10.9 (18.9)	169		99, 101, 103, 105–6
3.11–13 (19–21)	7, 108	5.2 (25.2)	
3.11.1 (19.1)	176	5.3 (25.3)	99
3.11.2 (19.2)	160	5.4 (25.4)	99, 180, 212
3.11.2–3 (19.2–3)	60, 97	5.5–7 (25.5–7)	66, 107, 138
3.11.3–4 (19.3–4)	115	5.5–6 (25.5–6)	100
3.11.3 (19.3)	60, 135	5.5 (25.5)	11, 25, 37–8, 67, 99–100, 106, 158, 190
3.11.4 (19.4)	94, 97		
3.12.1–3 (20.1–3)	97		
3.12.1 (20.1)	115		
3.12.2 (20.2)	160	5.7 (25.7)	25, 100, 106, 179
3.12.3–3.13.4 (20.3–21.4)	25		
3.12.3 (20.3)	160, 176		
3.13.2 (21.2)	97, 160, 176	*Mandates*	
3.13.3 (21.3)	98, 118, 130	1–12 (26–49)	8, 107
3.13.4 (21.4)	38, 67, 176, 184	1–10 (26–42)	33
		1–2 (26–27)	100
4–5 (22–25)	67	1 (26)	8, 95
4 (22–24)	7, 99, 170	1.1 (26.1)	25, 36–7, 40–1, 43, 48, 67, 81, 106, 113, 148, 150, 159, 161, 165
4.1.1–2 (22.1–2)	74		
4.1.2 (22.2)	62, 120		
4.1.3 (22.3)	149, 157, 179		
4.1.4 (22.4)	7, 168–9		
4.1.5–10 (22.5–10)	103		
4.1.7–8 (22.7–8)	169	1.2 (26.2)	158, 214, 216
4.1.7 (22.7)	93, 168		
4.1.10 (22.10)	55	2–3 (27–28)	33
4.2.1–2 (23.1–2)	176	2 (27)	8, 95
4.2.1 (23.1)	98, 120	2.1 (27.1)	100, 177, 210
4.2.2 (23.2)	98		
4.2.3–4.3.6 (23.3–24.6)	99	2.2 (27.2)	44
4.2.4 (23.4)	7, 106, 135, 149, 157, 169	2.3 (27.3)	137
		2.4–7 (27.4–7)	143, 178
		2.4 (27.4)	178
4.2.5–6 (23.5–6)	135	2.6–3.1 (27.6–28.1)	24
4.2.5 (23.5)	38, 135, 149, 179	2.6–7 (27.6–7)	178
		2.7 (27.7)	79, 177, 200
4.2.6 (23.6)	168	3 (28)	8, 162–4
4.3.1–5 (24.1–5)	55	3.1–2 (28.1–2)	94, 100, 164
4.3.1 (24.1)	94	3.1 (28.1)	162
4.3.5 (24.5)	149	3.2 (28.2)	162
4.3.6 (24.6)	135	3.3–5 (28.3–5)	170, 180
4.3.7 (24.7)	98, 122	3.3 (28.3)	93–4, 100–1, 184
5–Sim. 10 (25–114)	22, 65, 67		
5–Sim. 8 (25–77)	67	3.4 (28.4)	163, 184
5 (25)	8, 67, 99–100, 214	3.5 (28.5)	184
		4 (29–32)	8–9, 101, 133
5.1–3 (25.1–3)	67		

280   Index of References

4.1 (29)	132	6.1 (35)	45
4.1.1–3 (29.1–3)	101	6.1.1–4 (35.1–4)	142
4.1 (29.1)	132	6.1.1 (35.1)	214, 216
4.1.4–6 (29.4–6)	132	6.1.2–5 (35.2–5)	216
4.1.4 (29.4)	94, 101	6.2 (36)	41, 45, 142,
4.1.6 (29.6)	94		162, 216
4.1.7–8 (29.7–8)	39, 67,	6.2.1 (36.1)	45, 142
	132, 175	6.2.3 (36.3)	142–3, 216
4.1.7 (29.7)	94	6.2.4 (36.4)	142
4.1.8 (29.8)	133	6.2.5 (36.5)	170, 173–4
4.1.9 (29.9)	40, 127	6.2.6 (36.6)	216
4.2.1 (30.1)	101, 180	7 (37)	9, 214, 216
4.2.2 (30.2)	95, 180–1	7.1–4 (37.1–4)	67
4.3.1–7 (31.1–7)	176–7	7.1 (37.1)	216
4.3.1 (31.1)	94, 101, 176	7.2 (37.2)	216
4.3.2–7 (31.2–7)	180	7.3 (37.3)	216
4.3.2 (31.2)	38, 176	7.4 (37.4)	149,
4.3.3–7 (31.3–7)	176		157, 216
4.3.4–5 (31.4–5)	179	8–10 (38–42)	27
4.3.5 (31.5)	177	8 (38)	9–10,
4.3.5–5.1.4 (31.5–33.4)	30		214, 216
4.4.1–2 (32.1–2)	133	8.1 (38.1)	149,
4.4.1 (32.1)	101		180, 216
4.4.4–5.1.4 (32.4–33.4)	23–4	8.2 (38.2)	180, 216
5–12 (33–49)	33	8.3–6 (38.3–6)	211
5–11 (33–43)	205–223	8.3 (38.3)	173–4
5 (33–34)	9, 162–4,	8.7–12 (38.7–12)	29
	174,	8.9–12 (38.9–12)	24
	205–223	8.10 (38.10)	172–3
5.1.1–2 (33.1–2)	87, 162	8.12 (38.12)	216
5.1.1 (33.1)	182, 209,	9–11 (39–43)	205–223
	219, 221	9 (39)	10, 95, 100,
5.1.2 (33.2)	209–10,		168, 209–12
	219, 221	9.1 (39.1)	136,
5.1.3–4 (33.3–4)	174		168, 211–12
5.1.3 (33.3)	162, 206,	9.2–5 (39.2–5)	23
	209–10, 219	9.2–3 (39.2–3)	170, 211
5.1.4 (33.4)	210	9.2 (39.2)	136
5.1.5 (33.5)	210	9.3 (39.3)	150
5.1.6 (33.6)	210	9.4 (39.4)	211
5.1.7 (33.7)	79, 94,	9.5 (39.5)	211
	103, 134,	9.6–7 (39.6–7)	136
	200, 210	9.6 (39.6)	211
5.2.2 (34.2)	209, 221	9.7–8 (39.7–8)	136
5.2.3–6.1.2 (34.3–35.2)	23	9.7 (39.7)	211
5.2.3 (34.3)	209	9.9 (39.9)	44, 118, 211
5.2.4 (34.4)	209	9.10–12 (39.10–12)	136
5.2.6 (34.6)	209	9.10 (39.10)	211
5.2.7 (34.7)	210	9.11–12 (39.11–12)	211
5.2.8 (34.8)	210, 221	9.11 (39.11)	162, 219
6–8 (35–38)	9,	10 (40–42)	10,
	214–15, 217		162–4, 174,
6 (35–36)	9, 214		209, 212–13

Index of References

10.1.1 (40.1)	169, 212	11.15 (43.15)	114–15, 144
10.1.2 (40.2)	162, 212	11.16 (43.16)	144
10.1.3 (40.3)	182	11.18–21 (43.18–21)	214, 219
10.1.4 (40.4)	127, 170	11.18 (43.18)	213
10.1.5 (40.5)	171,	11.19–21 (43.19–21)	24
	182, 212	11.19 (43.19)	213
10.1.6 (40.6)	95, 182	11.20 (43.20)	213–14
10.2.1–3 (41.1–3)	220	11.21 (43.21)	214
10.2.1 (41.1)	95, 212	12 (44–49)	10–11, 33
10.2.2–3 (41.2–3)	212	12.1.1–3 (44.1–3)	174
10.2.2 (41.2)	168, 174	12.1.1 (44.1)	25, 180, 212
10.2.3–4 (41.3–4)	162	12.1.2–3 (44.2–3)	24
10.2.3 (41.3)	174	12.1.2 (44.2)	181
10.2.4 (41.4)	212, 220	12.1.3 (44.3)	25
10.2.5–6 (41.5–6)	212	12.2.1 (45.1)	173–4
10.2.5 (41.5)	220	12.2.2 (45.2)	118
10.3.1 (42.1)	162,	12.2.5 (45.5)	180
	212, 222	12.3.1 (46.1)	94, 180
10.3.2–3 (42.2–3)	222	12.3.2 (46.2)	11
10.3.2 (42.2)	162,	12.3.4–12.4.5 (46.4–47.5)	29
	212, 219	12.3.4–6 (46.4–6)	101
10.3.3 (42.3)	94, 212–13	12.3.4 (46.4)	149, 157
10.3.4–5 (42.4–5)	222	12.3.5–12.4.1 (46.5–47.1)	80
10.3.4 (42.4)	212	12.3.6 (46.6)	79, 104, 200
11 (43)	10, 79, 113,	12.4.1 (47.1)	101
	123, 161–2,	12.4.2 (47.2)	101, 149,
	209, 212–14		158,
	60, 144		168, 184
11.1–6 (43.1–6)	143, 168	12.4.3 (47.3)	149
11.1–2 (43.1–2)	107, 213	12.4.7 (47.7)	100
11.1 (43.1)	114, 143,	12.5.2 (48.2)	137
11.2 (43.2)	161, 213	12.5.3 (48.3)	41
	115,	12.6.1 (49.1)	100
11.3 (43.3)	161, 213	12.6.3 (49.3)	137
	127, 143		
11.4 (43.4)	114, 143,	*Similitudes*	
11.5 (43.5)	161,	1–10 (50–114)	11
	213, 218	1 (50)	11–12, 33,
	143		100, 135
11.6 (43.6)	144,	1.1.1–3 (50.1–3)	112
11.8 (43.8)	213, 218	1.1 (50.1)	112
	25	1.3–4 (50.3–4)	60
11.9–10 (43.9–10)	146,	1.3 (50.3)	168
11.9	161, 213	1.4 (50.4)	42,
	161		112–13, 199
11.10 (43.10)	60, 144	1.5–6 (50.5–6)	112
11.11–15 (43.11–15)	143	1.6 (50.6)	112
11.11 (43.11)	113–14,	1.7–8 (50.7–8)	113
11.12 (43.12)	144, 213	1.7 (50.7)	158
	213	1.9 (50.9)	179
11.13–15 (43.13–15)	143	1.10 (50.10)	127
11.13–14 (43.13–14)	115, 213	2–5 (51–60)	61
11.13 (43.13)	115, 161		
11.14 (43.14)			

Index of References

2 (51)	12, 42, 46, 63, 116–17, 172, 174, 202	5.2.3–4 (55.3–4)	82
		5.2.4–6 (55.4–6)	23
		5.2.6 (55.6)	151
		5.2.7–8 (55.7–8)	131
2.1 (51.1)	2, 74, 101, 107	5.2.7 (55.7)	13
		5.2.8 (55.8)	151
2.2–4.8 (51.2–53.8)	41	5.2.9–11 (55.9–11)	76–7, 79
2.2 (51.2)	94, 171	5.2.9 (55.9)	82
2.3–3.3 (51.3–52.3)	29	5.2.11 (55.11)	76, 131, 151
2.3–4 (51.3–4)	171	5.3.1–9 (56.1–9)	33, 74, 77, 88, 120
2.4–10 (51.4–10)	23, 60		
2.4 (51.4)	46, 94, 171	5.3.1–6 (56.1–6)	77
2.5–7 (51.5–7)	76, 79, 173	5.3.1–3 (56.1–3)	77
2.5 (51.5)	94, 171	5.3.1 (56.1)	79
2.6–7 (51.6–7)	27–8, 171	5.3.2–9 (56.2–9)	107
2.7–10 (51.7–10)	23	5.3.2 (56.2)	77
2.8–9.5.1 (51.8–82.1)	22	5.3.3 (56.3)	13, 22, 78
2.8–10 (51.8–10)	22	5.3.4–9 (56.4–9)	77
2.9 (51.9)	171, 174	5.3.4–5 (56.4–5)	121
3–4 (52–53)	41, 130–1	5.3.4 (56.4)	77, 79
3 (52)	11–12	5.3.5–7 (56.5–7)	76
3.1 (52.1)	74, 138	5.3.5–6 (56.5–6)	78, 82
3.2 (52.2)	94	5.3.6 (56.6)	78
4 (53)	12	5.3.7–5.4.1 (56.7–57.1)	29
4.1 (53.1)	74	5.3.7 (56.7)	77–8, 174
4.2–5 (53.2–5)	23	5.3.8–9 (56.8–9)	79
4.2 (53.2)	130	5.3.9 (56.9)	89, 104
4.4 (53.4)	55, 127, 149	5.4.1–5.6.8 (57.1–59.8)	85
4.5 (53.5)	170	5.4.1–5.6.4 (57.1–59.4)	74, 79–83
4.6–5.1.5 (53.6–54.5)	24	5.4.1–5.5.1 (57.1–58.1)	74, 87, 101
4.6 (53.6)	179	5.4.1 (57.1)	79, 94, 151
4.8–5.2.2 (53.8–55.2)	29	5.4.2–5 (57.2–5)	181
5 (54–60)	13, 71, 73–89, 117, 147, 150–5, 202, 223	5.4.2 (57.2)	79, 95
		5.4.3 (57.3)	80, 94–5
		5.4.4 (57.4)	80, 149
		5.4.5 (57.5)	80
5.1–3 (54–56)	74–9	5.5.1 (58.1)	80
5.1.1–5 (54.1–5)	74	5.5.2–5.6.8 (58.2–59.8)	73, 86
5.1.1–2 (54.1–2)	75, 101	5.5.2–5.6.7 (58.2–59.7)	150
5.1.1 (54.1)	74–5, 120, 122	5.5.2–5.6.4 (58.2–59.4)	74, 82–6, 151–3, 155–6
5.1.2 (54.2)	75		
5.1.3–5 (54.3–5)	78	5.5.2–3 (58.2–3)	80, 82, 85–6, 152
5.1.3 (54.3)	75		
5.1.4 (54.4)	76	5.5.2 (58.2)	81–4, 148–9, 151–2, 160–1
5.1.5–5.2.2 (54.5–55.2)	23		
5.1.5 (54.5)	13		
5.2.1–11 (55.1–11)	73–4, 77, 86, 131		
		5.5.3 (58.3)	81, 102, 152
5.2.1 (55.1)	76, 131	5.5.4–5 (58.4–5)	81
5.2.2–8 (55.2–8)	76–8, 80	5.5.4 (58.4)	181
5.2.2–3 (55.2–3)	102	5.5.5 (58.5)	81
5.2.3 (55.3)	82	5.6.1–8 (59.1–8)	33

Index of References

5.6.1–2 (59.1–2)	131	6.3.6 (63.6)	178
5.6.1 (59.1)	81, 151	6.4.1 (64.1)	14
5.6.2 (59.2)	82, 134, 149, 151–2, 156, 167	6.4.4 (64.4)	41, 67, 171
		6.5.2 (65.2)	95
		6.5.3–4 (65.3–4)	171
5.6.3 (59.3)	82, 131, 134, 152, 156	6.5.3 (65.3)	23
		6.5.5–8.2.5 (65.4–68.5)	21, 67
		6.5.5–7 (65.5–7)	14
5.6.4–5.6.8 (59.4–8)	13, 74, 83–8, 152–5	6.5.5 (65.5)	23
		7 (66)	14, 22, 106
5.6.4–7 (59.4–7)	86, 154	7.1–3 (66.1–3)	149
5.6.4 (59.4)	82–3, 85–6, 131, 149, 152–3, 157	7.1 (66.1)	74, 99, 103, 106
		7.2–3 (66.2–3)	93
5.6.5–7 (59.5–7)	164	7.3 (66.3)	199
5.6.5 (59.5)	83–6, 161, 164–5	7.4–5 (66.4–5)	22
		7.4 (66.4)	148–9
5.6.6 (59.6)	86, 154	7.5–6 (66.5–6)	106
5.6.7 (59.7)	85–7, 149, 152, 154–5, 162	7.5 (66.5)	103
		8–9 (67–110)	18, 101, 134, 157–8
5.6.8 (59.8)	87		15–16, 61, 65, 116–17, 135, 151, 155–7, 202
5.7 (60)	74, 87–8, 153	8 (67–77)	
5.7.1 (60.1)	13, 87–8, 155		
		8.1.1–12 (67.1–12)	24
5.7.2 (60.2)	88	8.1.1–2 (67.1–2)	158
5.7.3–6.1.5 (60.3–61.5)	24	8.1.1 (67.1)	116, 155–6
5.7.3 (60.3)	88, 113	8.1.2–8.2.5 (67.2–68.5)	103
5.7.4 (60.4)	88–9	8.1.2–5 (67.2–5)	103
6 (61–65)	13–14, 22, 103, 118	8.1.2 (67.2)	149, 156
		8.1.6–18 (67.6–18)	15
6.1.1–4 (61.1–4)	14	8.2.5 (68.5)	103, 192
6.1.1–2 (61.1–2)	168, 184	8.3.1 (69.1)	15, 94
6.1.1 (61.1)	74, 120, 149, 199	8.3.2–3 (69.2–3)	158
		8.3.2 (69.2)	155–6
6.1.2 (61.2)	168	8.3.3 (69.3)	103, 149, 156–7
6.1.4–6.2.7 (61.4–62.7)	29		
6.1.5–6.5.7 (61.5–65.7)	142	8.3.4 (69.4)	156
6.1.5 (61.5)	107, 120	8.4.1–8.5.2 (70.1–71.2)	23
6.2.1–6.5.7 (62.1–65.7)	45, 162	8.4.1 (70.1)	15
6.2.1–2 (62.1–2)	118	8.4.4–8.5.6 (70.4–71.6)	15
6.2.1 (62.1)	14, 45, 142	8.5.6–8.6.4 (71.6–72.4)	29
6.2.2–3 (62.2–3)	174	8.6.1–2 (72.1–2)	15
6.2.3 (62.3)	149	8.6.1 (72.1)	157
6.2.6–7 (62.6–7)	142	8.6.2 (72.2)	179
6.3.1–7.1.2 (63.1–66.2)	23	8.6.4–8.8.3 (72.4–74.3)	23
6.3.1 (63.1)	14	8.6.4–8.10.4 (72.4–76.4)	15
6.3.2–3 (63.2–3)	41, 67	8.6.4 (72.4)	149
6.3.2 (63.2)	45, 178	8.6.6. (72.6)	192
6.3.3–5 (63.3–5)	178	8.7.1–3 (73.1–3)	169
6.3.3 (63.3)	142	8.7.1–2 (73.1–2)	15
6.3.4 (63.4)	94	8.7.2 (73.2)	141, 179

284　Index of References

8.7.3 (73.3)	192	9.3.3–4 (80.3–4)	201
8.8.1–2 (74.1–2)	16	9.3.4 (80.4)	190–1
8.8.1 (74.1)	170	9.3.5 (80.5)	191
8.8.2 (74.2)	170	9.4.1 (81.1)	102, 191
8.8.3 (74.3)	169, 179, 192	9.4.2 (81.2)	190
		9.4.3–4 (81.3–4)	160
8.8.5 (74.5)	169	9.4.3 (81.3)	130, 190
8.9.1–3 (75.1–3)	170	9.4.5–8 (81.5–8)	190
8.9.1 (75.1)	127	9.4.6–8 (81.6–8)	191
8.9.3 (75.3)	127	9.4.5 (81.5)	191
8.10.1 (76.1)	95	9.4.8 (81.8)	192
8.10.2 (75.2)	141	9.5.1–7 (82.1–7)	190
8.10.3–8.11.5 (76.3–77.5)	29	9.5.3–5 (82.3–5)	160
8.10.3 (76.3)	149, 172, 199	9.5.3 (82.3)	94
		9.5.5 (82.5)	95
8.11.1 (77.1)	16, 155, 179	9.6.1–8 (83.1–8)	196
9 (78–110)	11, 16–18, 47, 61, 65, 67, 71, 73, 106, 117, 132, 140, 142, 151, 157–60, 164, 183, 187–203	9.6.1 (83.1)	16, 40
		9.6.4–5 (83.4–5)	191
		9.6.6–9.7.6 (83.6–84.6)	30
		9.7.1 (84.1)	103, 149
		9.7.2 (84.2)	192
		9.7.4–7 (84.4–7)	201
		9.7.4 (84.4)	17, 138, 192
		9.7.5 (84.5)	192
		9.8.1–9.9.7 (85.1–86.7)	196
9.1.1–3 (78.1–3)	65–6	9.8.2–3 (85.2–3)	196
9.1.1 (78.1)	85, 100, 158–60, 161	9.9.2–4 (86.2–4)	201
		9.9.5–9.10.6 (86.5–87.6)	30
9.1.2 (78.2)	107, 161, 201	9.9.5 (86.5)	96
		9.9.7 (86.7)	191, 197
9.1.3 (78.3)	16, 103, 149	9.10–11 (87–8)	67
9.1.4 (78.4)	61, 63, 116, 120, 190	9.10.4–9.11.9 (87.4–88.9)	140
		9.10.4–9.11.8 (87.4–88.8)	190
9.1.5–9.5.5 (78.5–82.5)	30	9.10.5 (87.5)	183
9.1.8 (78.8)	149	9.10.6–9.11.9 (87.6–88.9)	103
9.2.1–5 (79.1–5)	25	9.10.6 (87.6)	183
9.2.1–2 (79.1–2)	159, 190, 197	9.10.7 (87.7)	183
		9.11.1–3 (88.1–3)	108
9.2.1 (79.1)	196	9.11.3 (88.3)	183
9.2.2 (79.2)	132, 197	9.11.4–5 (88.4–5)	183
9.2.3–4 (79.3–4)	47, 102	9.11.5 (88.5)	184
9.2.3 (79.3)	149, 158, 163	9.11.7–9 (88.7–9)	17, 29
		9.11.7 (88.7)	183
9.2.5–7 (79.5–7)	94	9.11.8 (88.8)	183
9.2.5 (79.5)	31, 158	9.11.8–9.12.5 (88.8–89.5)	30
9.2.6–7 (79.6–7)	16, 95	9.11.9–9.33.3 (89.9–110.3)	190
9.2.6 (79.6)	95, 181	9.11.9–9.12.3 (88.9–89.3)	117
9.2.7–9.6.1 (79.7–83.1)	29	9.11.9 (88.9)	94, 117
9.3.1 (80.1)	149, 190, 196–7	9.12.1–9.33.3 (89.1–110.3)	94
		9.12.1–3 (89.1–3)	94, 132, 197
9.3.2 (80.2)	102	9.12.1–2 (89.1–2)	85, 117, 197
9.3.3–9.4.3 (80.3–81.3)	16	9.12.1 (89.1)	17, 118, 159
9.3.3–5 (80.3–5)	160	9.12.2–5 (89.2–5)	25

Index of References

9.12.1 (89.1)	197	9.16.2 (93.2)	197
9.12.2 (89.2)	29, 149, 159, 165	9.16.3 (93.3)	160
		9.16.4 (93.4)	132
9.12.3 (89.3)	159, 197	9.16.5–7 (93.5–7)	38, 67, 160
9.12.4–5 (89.4–5)	132, 159	9.16.5 (93.5)	94
9.12.5 (89.5)	94	9.16.6 (93.6)	38
9.12.6–8 (89.6–8)	149, 159	9.17.1–9.29.4 (94.1–106.4)	17
9.12.6–7 (89.6–7)	157	9.17.1–4 (94.1–4)	25
9.12.6 (89.6)	132, 157	9.17.1–2 (94.1–2)	73
9.12.7 (89.7)	157	9.17.1 (94.1)	94, 137, 160, 198
9.12.8 (89.8)	40, 157		
9.13.1–9.14.5 (90.1–91.5)	41	9.17.2 (94.2)	127, 198
9.13.1 (90.1)	94	9.17.3–4 (94.3–4)	201
9.13.2–3 (90.2–3)	149	9.17.3 (94.3)	94
9.13.2 (90.2)	94, 140, 159– 60, 162–3	9.17.4 (94.4)	127, 133, 149, 160, 163, 198
9.13.3 (90.3)	94, 159	9.18.1 (95.1)	94, 150
9.13.5–9 (90.5–9)	29	9.18.3 (95.3)	169
9.13.5 (90.5)	133, 159, 163	9.18.4 (95.4)	133, 160, 163
9.13.6–9 (90.6–9)	196	9.18.5 (95.5)	94, 127, 149, 157
9.13.6 (90.6)	94		
9.13.7 (90.7)	133, 159	9.19.1–9.29.3 (96.1–106.3)	73, 198
9.13.8 (90.8)	140	9.19.1 (96.1)	44
9.13.9–9.14.2 (90.9–91.2)	201	9.19.2–9.24.2 (96.2–101.2)	30
9.13.9–9.14.1 (90.9–91.1)	199–200	9.19.3 (96.3)	94
9.13.9 (90.9)	200	9.20.1–2 (97.1–2)	130
9.14.1–2 (91.1–2)	196	9.20.1 (97.1)	170
9.14.1 (91.1)	94, 200	9.20.3–4 (97.3–4)	23
9.14.2 (91.2)	200	9.21.1–4 (98.1–4)	137
9.14.3 (91.3)	100, 176, 179	9.21.1–3 (98.1–3)	169
		9.21.3 (98.3)	169
9.14.4–9.18.5 (91.4–95.5)	21, 67	9.21.4 (98.4)	169
9.14.4 (91.4)	95, 158	9.22.1 (99.1)	23, 182
9.14.5 (91.5)	159, 165	9.22.2 (99.2)	182
9.14.6 (91.6)	159	9.22.3–4 (99.3–4)	182
9.15.1–3 (92.1–3)	103, 163	9.23.3–5 (100.3–5)	22
9.15.1–2 (92.1–2)	17, 47, 140	9.23.4 (100.4)	113, 149
9.15.1 (92.1)	94	9.23.5 (100.5)	100
9.15.2 (92.2)	95, 159, 163, 177–8, 181	9.24.2 (101.2)	163, 177, 210
		9.24.4 (101.4)	100, 160, 163
9.15.3 (92.3)	140, 174	9.25.1 (102.1)	149
9.15.4–6 (92.4–6)	160, 201	9.25.2 (102.2)	163–4
9.15.4 (92.4)	94, 105, 130, 136, 160, 197	9.26.2 (103.2)	105, 172
		9.27.1–2 (104.1–2)	199
9.15.5–6 (92.5–6)	136	9.27.2–3 (104.2–3)	149
9.15.5 (92.5)	94	9.27.2 (104.2)	105, 172
9.16.1–4 (93.1–4)	133	9.28.2–3 (105.2–3)	160
9.16.1–2 (93.1–2)	163	9.28.3 (105.3)	94, 96
9.16.1 (93.1)	94, 160	9.28.8 (105.8)	127

9.29.1–3 (106.1–3)	61	Acts of Thomas	
9.29.2 (106.2)	133	20	78
9.29.4 (106.4)	94		
9.30.1–4 (107.1–4)	25	Constitutiones apostolicae	
9.30.3–10.4.5 (107.3–114.5)	19	5.1	78
9.31.1–9.32.5 (108.1–109.5)	33	7.1.1–19	143
9.31.3 (108.3)	100		
9.31.4 (108.4)	163		
9.31.4–9.33.3 (108.4–110.3)	22	Didascalia apostolorum	
9.31.5–6 (108.5–6)	40	19.1	78
9.31.6 (108.6)	40	21	75
9.32.1–5 (109.1–5)	107		
9.32.1 (109.1)	192	Gospel of Thomas	
9.32.2 (109.2)	163	57	131
9.32.3–5 (109.3–5)	163	65	131
9.33.1–3 (110.1–3)	22		
9.33.1 (110.1)	100	Kerygma Petri	
9.33.2–3 (110.2–3)	192	1a	156
10	(111–14)	1b	156
	18, 65, 67, 103, 199	2	148
10.1.1–2 (111.1–2)	67	Pseudo-Clementine Homilies	
10.1.1 (111.1)	103, 106	3.18.3	159
10.1.2 (111.2)	108, 199		
10.2.2–4 (112.2–4)	108	Protoevangelium of James	
10.2.2 (112.2)	18	1.4	75
10.3.1 (113.1)	67, 202	4.2	75
10.3.2–5 (113.2–5)	23		
10.3.2 (113.2)	108, 202		
10.4.1 (114.1)	122, 183, 202	CLASSICAL AND ANCIENT CHRISTIAN AUTHORS	
10.4.2–4 (114.2–4)	174		
10.4.2–3 (114.2–3)	108	Alexander of Aphrodisias	
10.4.3–4 (114.3–4)	23	*De mixtione*	
10.4.3 (114.3)	222	2, 214.18–215.8	153
10.4.4 (114.4)	106, 202	3, 216.14–17	154
10.4.5 (114.5)	101, 202	3, 216.25–28	153
		4, 217.31–32	153
		4, 217.32–218.1	154

NAG HAMMADI CODICES

NHC VII, 3 (Coptic Apocalypse of Peter)

78.18–19	39	Ambrose	
		Hexaemeron libri sex	
		3.12.50	42

NEW TESTAMENT APOCRYPHA
AND PSEUDEPIGRAPHA

		Apuleius	
		Metamorphoses	
Acts of Paul		2.11	115
3.5	87, 194	2.12–14	113
3.25	78	2.12–13	114
		2.12	113–14
		2.13	114
		2.14	114–15
		3.24	113

Index of References

Aristides
Apologia
15.7–8 — 78

Athanasius
De decritis
4.2 — 44
4.3 — 44
18.3 — 43

De incarnatione
3.1 — 43

Epistula ad Afros episcopos
5 — 43

Epistulae festales
11.2 — 43
11.4 — 43
39 — 21
39.5 — 43
39.7 — 43, 52

Antiochus the Monk
Pandectes
7 — 33
15 — 33
25 — 33
29 — 33
61 — 33
66 — 33
74 — 33
77 — 33
79 — 33
85 — 33
94 — 33
98 — 33
102 — 33
110 — 33
122 — 33
127 — 33

Aristotle
De generatione et corruptione
328a 23–31 — 154

Arius Didymus
Fragments
28 — 153–4

Athenagoras
Legatio pro Christianis
10.1 — 148

Caesarius of Arles
Sermones
27 — 46
27.1 — 46
27.2 — 46
27.3 — 47

Catullus
Poems
62.48–57 — 42, 116

Cicero
De finibus
3.72 — 154, 207

De natura deorum
2.7.19 — 208
2.66.167 — 208

Clement of Alexandria
Excerpta ex Theodoto
26 — 159

Stromateis
1.1.1 (1) — 37–8
1.108.1 (21) — 96, 115
1.181.1 (29) — 37–8
1.182.3 (29) — 156
2.3–5 (1) — 37
2.3.5 (1) — 37–8
2.43.5–44.3 (9) — 38
2.43.5 (9) — 38
2.55.3 (12) — 37–8
2.55.4 (12) — 38
2.55.4–5 (12) — 37
2.55.6 (12) — 37–8
2.56.1 (13) — 38
2.68.2 (15) — 156
4.74.4 (9) — 38
5.5.31 (5) — 143
5.113.2–5.114.1 (14) — 133
6.39.2–3 (5) — 148
6.46 (6) — 38
6.131.2 (15) — 37–8
7.16.5 (3) — 156

Columella
De arboribus
16   63

Commodian
Instructiones
30   42
30.16   42, 116
65   42
65.4   42

Didymus the Blind
Commentrii in Zachariam
86   52
86.24–7   44
234.19–22   44
355.20–4   44, 142–3

Dio Chrysostom
Venator (Oration 7)
34   212

Diogenes Laertius
Lives 5.5 (Demetrius)
76   210

Lives 7.1 (Zeno)
134   154
156   208

Dionysius of Halicarnassus
Antiquitates romanae
4.62   115

Epiphanius
Panarion
33.5.13   75

Eusebius
Historia ecclesiastica
2.25.6   145
3.3.6   42–3
3.15.1   69
3.16.1   69
3.24.1–3.25.7   21
3.25.1–7   43
3.25.4   43, 52
3.25.6   52
4.11.6–7   68
4.23.11   69
5.8.7   36, 42

6.20.3   145
6.25   51

Galen
Artium studere exhortatio
3   207

De adolore
207
4–5   207
19–30   207

De pulsibus libellus ad Tyrones
471   206
473–4   206

De simplicium medicamentorum facultatibus
5.9   208

Si quis optimus medicus est, eundum esse philosophum
60   207
61   207

Hesiod
Opera et dies
287–92   125

Hildegard of Bingen
Scivias
3.9   47
3.9.1–6   47
3.9.7   47
3.9.8   47
3.9.10   47
3.9.14   47

Hippolytus
Refutatio omnium haeresium
5.8.20–1   159
5.9.21   159
5.17.9   159
8.19.1   146
9.13.2–3   40
10.25.1   146

Homer
Ilias
18.478–608   117

Irenaeus
Adversus Haereses
1.13.1–7	144
1.13.1	144
1.13.2	144
1.13.3	144
1.14.1–1.15.6	144
1.15.5	36
1.22.1	37
2.1.2	148
2.1.5	148
2.2.2	37
2.6.2	37
2.10.2	37
2.30.9	36
3.11.8–9	130
4.20.1	36, 148
4.20.2	36, 42, 48

Epideixis
3	147
4	36

Jerome
De uiris illustribus
10	45

John Cassian
Conferences
8.17	45
13.12	45

Justin
Dialogus cum Tryphone
11.2	156
15.1–11	76
43.1	156
63.5	133
127.2	148
134.1–5	83

Lactantius
Institutiones
6.3	143

Lucian
De morte Peregrini
11	113
12	113
13	113

Philopseudes
27	151

Muratorian Fragment
67	210
74	39, 50, 68
75–77	56, 64
77–80	40

Origen
Commentarium in evangelium Joannis
6.36	69

Commentarium in evangelium Matthaei
12.29	83
53	41
59	41

Comentarii in Romanos
10.31	41–2, 68–9

Contra Celsum
6.24	113
6.41	113

De oratione
2.1	218
2.3	218
8.1	218
10.5	218
14.5	218

De principiis
1. Praef. 4	40
1.3.3	40–1
2.1.5	40
3.4.2	41
4.2.4	41

Homiliae in Ezechielem
13.3	41

Homiliae in Leviticum
10.2	78

Homiliae in Lucam
35.3	41

Homiliae in Numeros
8	41

Homiliae in Psalmos
37.1.1   41

In Jesu Nave homiliae
10.1   41

Ovid
Amores
2.16.41   42, 116

Metamorphoses
14.101–53   115
14.129–53   96, 115
14.661–8   42, 116

Pliny the Elder
Naturalis historia
17.35   63
31.73–92   61
36.170   196

Pliny the Younger
Epistulae
2.20.5   151

Plutarch
De defectu oraculorum
413b   114

Pseudo-Cyprian
De aleatoribus
2   40
4   40

Pseudo-Tertullian
Carmen adversus Marcionitas
3.293–95   40

Rufinus
Commentarius in symbolum apostolorum
37   43
38   43

Tabula Cebetis
4.2   117
5.1–6.3   117
7.1–3   117
18.2   117

Tatian
Oratio ad Graecos
12.1   208
12.3   208
12.5   208

Tertullian
Ad uxorem
2.4   75

Adversus Praxean
27   153

De anima
5   208

De jejunio adversus psychicos
10   75, 78

De oratione
16   38–9
19   75

De praescriptione haereticorum
39.4   116

De pudicitia
10.12   39
20.2   39, 175

Theophilus of Antioch
Ad Autolycum
1.5   148
2.3   148
2.22   148
3.15   180

Vergil
Aeneid
5.721–42   115
6.10   115
6.42–901   115
8.625–731   117
9.299–302   151

Eclogae
2.70   116
3.64–5   116
10.31–77   116
10.40   116

Georgica		Vitruvius	
1.2–3	116	*De architectura*	
2.434–5	116	2.7.5	196
Xenophon			
Memorabilia	125		

INDEX OF SUBJECTS

adoptionist Christology 64, 83–4, 147, 150, 152, 155
allegory 61, 74, 80, 82–4, 97, 101, 117, 121, 190–1
angel of the Lord 15, 103, 156
angelomorphic Christology 85, 147, 150, 157–8
angels 102–3
anger 9–10, 93, 165, 174, 206–8, 212, 217, 219–22
apocalyptic (genre) 55–9, 77, 119–24, 138, 178
apostles 17–18, 21, 40, 50, 136, 145, 160, 195–8
Arcadia 16, 61, 63, 116, 120, 190, 195
Athanasius 21, 35, 43–4, 48–52, 84, 152
Athos, Mount 20–2
audience 59–61
authority (among characters) 106–9
authority (scriptural) 21, 48–52
authorship of the *Shepherd* 63–9

banquet 76, 173
Barfield, Owen 215
bishop 105, 172, 198
book 96, 104–5, 123–4, 138–9
branch 15–16, 95, 103, 127, 134, 156, 179
business practices 10, 12, 15–17, 60, 92, 170, 182, 184–5

Celsus 113
cheerfulness 10, 17, 93, 162, 212, 214, 217–18, 221–2
children, Hermas's 6, 59, 79, 93, 104, 108, 124, 174, 199–200
chronological snobbery 215
Clement (character in the *Shepherd*) 6, 41, 68–9, 104–5, 107, 123
Clement of Alexandria 35, 37–8, 49–50, 67, 96, 115, 133, 143, 148

composition history 63–9
Coptic translation 29–30

date of the *Shepherd* 63–9
deacon 105, 172, 192
depression 217, 219–20
desire 8, 10–14, 18, 78, 93–5, 104, 118, 126, 144, 170–1, 174, 180–1, 183, 185, 196, 213
distress 10, 108, 162–3, 168–9, 174, 182, 207–10, 212, 214–15, 217, 219–22
double-mindedness 10–13, 15, 37, 44, 59–60, 86, 107, 114–15, 135–7, 141, 143, 167–70, 174, 177–8, 182–5, 206, 210–15, 217, 219, 222
dream 56, 64, 119, 123

Eldad and Modat, Book of 105, 129, 137
elder 41, 60, 105–6, 123
Eleutherus 145
elm 12, 42, 46–7, 60, 63, 79, 109, 116–17, 171–2
Ethiopic translation 28–9
Eusebius 21, 36, 42–3, 48–52, 84, 145, 152

faith 7, 9–11, 17–18, 37–8, 95, 126, 133–5, 163, 167–9, 177–8, 198, 210–11, 213–18
fasting 13, 73–9, 82, 89, 107, 120–3, 174
feasting 13, 138
flesh 83–7, 151–5
Florilegium Patristicum 21–2
food 10–11, 13, 76–8, 80, 82, 88, 170–4

Gaius 145
gender 122, 183–4, 218, 220
genre 55–9
Gentiles 6, 126–7, 170, 193–4
Georgian translation 30
glorious angel(s) 16–17, 83, 103, 106, 157–8

Grapte 6, 41, 104–5, 107–8, 123
Greek witnesses 20–5
grief 134, 163, 174, 185, 207, 209, 213, 219–21

hierarchy 106–7
Holmes, Sherlock 96
house(hold), Hermas's 18, 79, 89, 99, 103, 108, 187–9, 199–203

interpreting angel 77, 119–21, 138
irascibility 9–10, 169–70, 174, 185, 206, 208–10, 212, 214–15, 217, 219–21
Irenaeus 36–9, 68, 129–30, 144, 154, 218

Latin translation 26–8
law 15, 82, 113, 126, 131, 134, 152, 155–8
Lewis, C. S. 215
location of *Shepherd's* writing 61–3

Marcus 36, 144–5
Maximus 6, 105
mediation 56–9, 119, 152, 160, 178–9, 181–2, 190, 193, 198–201
metaphor 11, 42, 47, 71, 73, 81, 184, 187–9, 193–4, 202–3, 211–12
Michael 15, 103, 139, 156–8
Middle Persian translation 30
mixture 153–5
mountain 16–18, 30, 44, 61, 73, 96, 137, 143, 156, 160, 163–4, 170, 181–2, 190, 198
multisemy 73–4, 84, 97, 155–6

narrative 1, 3–18, 57–8, 70, 80, 98–9, 106–7, 152, 183–4
New Prophecy 145–6

Origen 25, 40–2, 44–5, 49–51, 67–9, 218

patience 9–10, 163, 182, 209–10, 214, 218–19, 221–2
polymorphy 98–9, 190
polysemy 73, 84
poor, the 12, 27–8, 42, 46, 59–60, 76–7, 79, 88, 101, 108, 116, 171–4, 194–5
Proclus 145
prophecy 10, 79, 107, 113–15, 118, 121, 124, 143–6, 161–2, 168, 213–14, 217–19

prophets, the 17, 21, 40, 50, 135–6, 197
prosopography 91–2, 106–9

reception history 33, 35–53, 66
repentance 9, 14–15, 41, 58–9, 71–2, 93, 95, 98, 100, 107, 126, 133–4, 136, 141, 167–8, 175–85, 192–3, 196, 200–1, 223
restraint 180, 221
Rhoda 5–6, 39, 61–2, 67, 92–4, 96, 104, 108, 111, 148–9, 174, 183, 185, 199–20
rich, the 10–12, 17–18, 27–8, 42, 46, 59–60, 76, 79, 101, 116, 145, 171–4, 194–5
Rome 6, 56, 59–63, 82, 92, 104–5, 108, 111–13, 115–16, 121, 123, 133, 143, 145, 170–4, 194–6, 207, 222

salt mining 61, 93, 196
self-control 7–9, 17, 93, 95, 126, 163, 178, 180, 214–17
shepherd, the (interpreting angel) 8–18, 58–60, 65–7, 79–83, 99–103, 106–8, 113, 117, 119–20, 122, 130–2, 136–8, 148–9, 151–2, 155–60, 168, 173–4, 180–2, 189–99, 209, 216–17
shepherds (punishing angels) 13–14, 41, 118, 142, 174, 178
Simonides, Constantine 20
single-mindedness 7–8, 17, 93, 126, 163–4, 167, 174, 177–8, 182, 210, 222
spirit Christology 150, 158
stone 7, 16–18, 61, 63, 94–5, 102, 117–18, 132–3, 136, 157, 159–60, 169–70, 189–92, 195–8

temple 81, 141–2, 188, 193–5
Tertullian 38–40, 45, 49–50, 67–8, 75, 78, 116, 153, 175, 208, 218
textual criticism 20
textual issues in *Shepherd* 27–8, 62–3, 78, 92–3, 133 150, 157, 170, 181
Thegri 7, 106
Tiber River 6, 62, 111, 183
Tischendorff, Constantine 20, 46
tree 12, 15–16, 46, 116–17, 130, 134, 155–8, 167, 171
Trinitarian theology 84–5, 147–8, 164–5, 217–19
tower 6–7, 15–18, 30, 44, 47, 63, 92, 94–5, 97, 102–3, 106–8, 117–18, 133–4,

Index of Subjects

136–7, 139–40, 157–9, 161, 163, 181–2, 187–203

unity of the *Shepherd* 63–9

vice list 9–10, 44, 117–18, 126, 217
vine 12, 42, 46–7, 60, 63, 79, 101, 116–17, 171–2
vineyard 13, 76–8, 80–4, 89, 117, 122, 131, 134, 151, 167, 212
virgins 16–18, 102–3, 106, 108, 136, 159, 163–4, 183–5, 190–2, 200–2, 223
virtue list 9–10, 44, 93, 117–18, 126, 217
virtues, personified 102, 140, 163, 201

wife, Hermas's 6, 59, 93, 104, 174
willow 15, 95, 103, 116–17, 127, 134, 155–8, 167, 169
wisdom 47, 118, 123–5, 128, 136–7, 139–40, 149, 192, 216
woman, the 5–7, 58–60, 62, 65, 67, 96–9, 102, 106–8, 115, 117, 120–5, 138–40, 158, 161, 173, 176, 189–99, 218
women in the tower 102, 163

young men 6–7, 60, 92, 96–8, 102, 108, 121, 125, 190

Zephyrinus 145

www.ingramcontent.com/pod-product-compliance
Lightning Source LLC
Chambersburg PA
CBHW052152300426
44115CB00011B/1633